FIGHTING THE GOOD FIGHT

DELLA S. LOREDO

I have fought the good fight,
I have finished the race,
I have kept the faith.
Now there is in store for me the crown of righteousness.
2 Timothy 4:7, 8, NKJV

TEACH Services, Inc.
PUBLISHING
www.TEACHServices.com • (800) 367-1844

Copyright © 2015 TEACH Services, Inc.
ISBN-13: 978-1-4796-0606-1 (Paperback)
ISBN-13: 978-1-4796-0607-8 (ePub)
ISBN-13: 978-1-4796-0608-5 (Mobi)
Library of Congress Control Number: 2015916323

Published by

TEACH Services, Inc.
PUBLISHING
www.TEACHServices.com • (800) 367-1844

DEDICATION

To Marjorie Chapman Santala,
my favorite mom;
And in memory of Franz W. "Finn" Santala,
my favorite dad.

Acknowledgments

Many thanks to my long-suffering husband, **José Loredo**, and children, **David** and **Ariel**.

A big hug to each of those who took the time to evaluate this book's early drafts: **Sonia Brock; Celia and Catalina Gil; Robert Lingle; Peggy Mishele Sneed;** and **Dennis Williams.** Your insights and suggestions were essential in helping me polish this story.

Thank you (again!) to **Youth With a Mission (YWAM)** in Creel, Mexico, and translators **Josué Pérez Moreno** and **Domingo González Garcia** for the Tarahumara translations.

Thank you to the members of the National City branch of the San Diego Christian Writers Guild who helped me polish this manuscript: **Felicia Alvarez, Candy Rizzardini, Marta Wingler,** and **James Wyatt.**

My very biggest thank you and deepest appreciation to our incredible God, whose unfathomable love found a way to rescue traitors on a rebellious planet. Without Him, Chris's story (and ours) would have ended as a tragedy; His sacrificial generosity turned it into a tale of victory.

CONTENTS

Author's Note

This novel is an allegory—a representation of truth, but not truth itself. Like any parable, it has limits beyond which it breaks down and is unable to characterize the real world. So, although parables are useful in helping us see ourselves with new perspective, we must have a clear understanding of where the line separating reality from parable lies.

In this book, all of the physical properties assigned to supernatural beings lie beyond this line. For example, to create a cohesive story within this allegorical world, I found it necessary to invent societal constructs for the angelic representatives and to portray the Holy Spirit as a woman. These ideas have no biblical basis; they're simply literary devices that allowed me to represent supernatural, even infinite, beings using finite characters. Similarly, this book does not portray the end of our world as I believe it will occur, rather, it portrays the final events of Chris's world. The two overlap in some regards, but not in all.

As always, please compare any questions or insights this tale may generate with the only sure word of truth—the Bible. To make this easier, I've included a list of scriptural references alluded to in the book, as well as links to some excellent Bible studies, on my website, **DellaLoredo.com**. Please drop by and check it out.

Although I've dared to commit this representation of last-day events to print, I believe we should study end-time prophecy humbly. We should always remember that the future is God's domain, not ours. What's more, even if we could predict the exact details surrounding the final confrontation between Christ and Satan, knowing those details will not save us. Rather, discovering the Author of the prophecies will—knowing His transforming grace, His guiding voice, and His unchangeable truth.

So my intent with this book is not to provide a guide to last-day events, but to challenge God's people to examine and strengthen their relationship with their heavenly Father. That is what will see us through the events ahead ... whatever form those events may take.

Through all our trials we have a never-failing Helper.
He does not leave us alone to struggle with temptation, to battle with evil,
and be finally crushed with burdens and sorrow.
Though now He is hidden from mortal sight,
the ear of faith can hear His voice saying, Fear not; I am with you...
Reader, He loves you.
Heaven itself can bestow nothing greater, nothing better.
Therefore trust.
~ Ellen G. White, The Desire of Ages, p. 483

Cast of Characters

Adlai Menod, MD, PhD (physiology), PhD (biochemistry): Moden Industries' best agent in both company and entity management

Andrew Strider, MA (military studies): colonel and second-in-command of the Outlander Division. Wife: **Riana**

Benjamin Strider Sr.: Chris's late father. Wife: **Rose**, deceased

Benjamin Strider Jr. (**Benny**): Chris's eldest brother; a gardener. Wife: **Marie**; three sons

Bethany Strider Lanáj, MD: Chris's daughter; a colonel and chief medical officer in the Outlander Division. Husband: **Stanley**; children: **Cherie** and **Melanie**

Camille L. Desmon, PhD (psychology), MBA: Stan's sister and "wife"; junior partner of Moden Industries and vice president of Desmoden. Children: **Stanley** (disinherited), **Saxon, Sheridan, Sadira**. [**Kamíl** (kah-MEEL) **Lanáj** (lah-NAZH) **Desmón** (days-MOAN); nickname: **Kami** (KAH-mee)]

Cherisse Sondem: Garrick's executive secretary, sister, and "wife"

Christian Strider, MD: pediatrician. Wife: **Susana**; children: **Stanley** Strider Lanáj (adopted), **Bethany, Andrew, Jorge** (adopted)

Debora Damour: Queen of Paradise Island [**Debora** (day-BORE-ah) **Deón** (day-OWN) **Damoúr** (dah-moe-OOR)]

Doug Damour: King of Paradise Island, president of Damour Enterprises, world's richest man [**Doúg** (doe-OOG) **Deón** (day-OWN) **Damoúr** (dah-moe-OOR)]

Efraím Suarez, MD: pediatrician; Chris's medical partner

Errol Sondem, PhD (military studies): general in command of the Presidential Guard; brother to **Garrick** and **Cherisse**

Gabriel [ga-BREE-el] **Lanáj** [lah-NAZH]: general in command of the Paradisian Royal Army. Siblings: **Stan** (exiled), **Jané, Felíp, Rubén, Camille** (exiled)

Garrick Sondem, MD, PhD (physics), MS (pharmacology), MA (psychology), MBA: Stan's closest friend; director of security for Moden Industries and minister of defense for Desmoden. "Wife": Cherisse; children: three sons, including **Conner**. [**Garike** (gah-REE-kay) **Lok** (loke) **Sondem** (SONE-dame)]

Iona: Camille's executive secretary

Jané [zhah-NAY] **Lanáj** [lah-NAZH]: colonel in the Royal Guard

Jorge Strider, BA (military studies): captain in the Special Operations Forces of the Outlander Division

Joshua Damour: Crown Prince of Paradise Island; commander-in-chief of the Paradisian Royal Army [**Joshua** (joe-SHOO-ah) **Deón** (day-OWN) **Damoúr** (dah-moe-OOR)]

Juan Misi: Chris's great-grandfather; responsible for the scar on Stan's cheek

Lanse [LAN-say] **Meshon** [MAY-shone]: lieutenant general in command of the Paradisian army's Division of Protectors

Madelyn: Stan's executive secretary

Maurice Pim, MD, PhD (physiology): company physician for Moden Industries. Children include **Austin** Pim, MD

Mike Strider: Chris's second oldest brother; a gardener. Wife: **Michelle** and four sons

Patric: Camille's first assistant

Riana Strider, BA (military science): lieutenant in the Outlander Division. Husband: **Andy**

Rose Strider Moore: Chris's twin sister. Husband: **Ivan**; three sons: **Thomas, Evan**, and **Wilson**

Sadira L. Moden, PhD (chemistry), PhD (sociology), MBA: Stan and Camille's youngest child and only daughter; president of Moden Industries.

Saxon L. Moden, PhD (psychology), MBA: Stan and Camille's second son; executive vice president of Moden Industries

Sheridan L. Moden, PhD (military studies): Stan and Camille's third son; commander of Desmoden's army

Stanley L. Moden Sr., JD, PhD (sociology), DSc (biochemistry), MBA: Camille's brother and "husband"; senior partner of Moden Industries, president of Desmoden, and America's richest man. Children: Stanley (disinherited), Saxon, Sheridan, Sadira. [**Lustanli** (loo-STAN-lee) **Lanáj** (lah-NAZH) **Modén** (moe-DANE); nickname: **Lusu** (LOO-soo)]

Stanley Strider Lanáj, PhD (military studies): Stan and Camille's eldest son, adopted by Chris and Susana after he defected to Doug; major general and commander of the Paradisian army's Outlander Division. Wife: **Bethany**; children: **Cherie** and **Melanie.**

Steve Strider: Chris's third oldest brother; a gardener. Wife: **Jeannie**; three sons

Susana López Strider, DPT: Chris's wife; pediatric physical therapist

Taylor Menod: accountant and entity management agent with Moden Industries. Brother: **Adlai**

Wilson "Willy" Moore: Chris's nephew (Rosie's youngest son); junior pre-law student at UCLA

Timeline for the Race Trilogy

0 M.E.*   Doug creates Stan and his siblings (Gabriel, Jané, Felíp, Rubén, Camille)

The Making of a Demon (e-book coming soon)

ca. **2000**   Stan leads a rebellion against the *Deón;* he and his supporters are exiled from Paradise Island

3275   Camille is kidnapped by Uri during attempted coup d'état

The Race: An Allegory (Review and Herald Publishing, 2012)

8006   Christian Strider and Susana López run Doug Damour's 6,000-mile footrace

8008   Christian Strider and Susana López marry

Keeping the Faith: Still Running (TEACH Services, 2015)

8008   Christian Strider establishes the Kids' Klub
           Stanley L. Moden and Camille L. Desmon "marry"
           Stan establishes the counterfeit New-RABs and introduces the New-RAB transmitters

8009   Stanley L. Moden Jr. born to Stan and Camille's surrogate (changes name to Stanley Strider Lanáj in 8027 M.E.)

8012   Bethany Rose Strider born to Chris and Susana
           Saxon L. Moden born to Stan and Camille's surrogate

8014   Sheridan L. Moden born to Stan and Camille's surrogate

8015   Andrew Benjamin Strider born to Chris and Susana

8018   Peter Jeremy Strider born dead to Chris and Susana
           Doug issues lifetime hands-off order for Susana López Strider

8020   Stanley Moden Jr. defects to Doug Damour
           Chris and Susana disappear into Mexico and adopt Stanley

8021   Jorge born to Juan and María Corona; adopted by Chris and Susana
           Sadira L. Moden born to Stan and Camille's surrogate

---

*   The dating system used throughout the Race trilogy is that established by Stanley L. Moden Sr. Naming the system after himself, he called it *Modén Eshí* (M.E.)—"Moden Years"—and designated the year 0 as the year of his birth.

8022   Chris and family return to California after Doug issues lifetime hands-off orders on them; Chris and Susana resume their medical and physical therapy practices, respectively

Running into the Next Generation (e-book of short stories coming soon...ish)

8022–8043 Outlander Division of Paradisian Army established
Stanley: General (commander)
Bethany: Colonel (chief medical officer)
Andy: Colonel (second in command)
Jorge: Captain (special operations forces)
Stanley and Bethany marry
Andy marries Riana Jones
Adlai Menod remains undercover in Chris's medical office as his office manager
Stan sets up his own country, Desmoden (several states around globe)
Shifts in roles at Desmoden and Moden Industries:
Stan Moden Sr.: president of Desmoden
Camille Desmon: vice president of Desmoden
Sadira Moden: president of Moden Industries
Saxon Moden: vice president of Moden Industries
Garrick Sondem: minister of defense, Desmoden; director of security, Moden Industries
Sheridan Moden: commander of army
Errol Sondem: commander of Presidential Guard

PART I

WHO SHALL BE ABLE TO STAND?

"The great day of his wrath is come; and who shall be able to stand?"
Revelation 6:17, KJV.

General Gabriel Lanáj, commander of the Paradisian army, opened the tall glass door of the army's headquarters and automatically noted the large red digits circling the kiosk above the reception desk. *Still counting forward,* he noted regretfully.

He'd wished for one last delay. He'd lost many loved ones to the rebellion headed by his twin brother, but he clung to the hope that his niece and nephews would yet accept the clemency offered by his king, Doúg Deón Damoúr of Paradise Island. Still, His Majesty had already granted the outlander rebels several merciful postponements. Even his unfathomable mercy must reach an end. Peace required it. Justice demanded it.

Gabriel proceeded to the conference room, where Lieutenant General Lanse Meshon was calling a meeting to order. Lanse commanded the Division of Protectors, a unit comprised of two arms: the Royal Guard, tasked with the safety of individual outlanders loyal to His Majesty; and the Planetary Defenders, whose four regiments assured the stability of the planet itself. These regimental commanders had assembled for what they believed to be a routine council meeting.

Gabriel listened as the generals reported their increasing struggles to stabilize tectonic plates, preserve ozone layers, and maintain habitable global temperatures. He listened, and he marveled. For six long millennia this team had cushioned the damage to an increasingly *kanuf*-riddled planet—problems set in motion by his twin's ambitious pride. (Paradisian: sin)

Finally Lanse turned to him. "You see why I asked you to sit in on our meeting, Gabriel. Our troops are truly stretched to their limits. Each regiment needs at least one more battalion of soldiers."

As Gabriel gazed into the generals' hopeful faces, he felt anew the burden of his announcement. It must be done, but, oh, what vulnerabilities would result! And dear brother Stan, who was responsible for unleashing the monster of *kanuf* in the first place, would have no qualms about exploiting those vulnerabilities. Instead, he would latch onto each like a ravenous piranha. As long as his goals were served, Stan cared nothing for the suffering that would follow. But Gabriel did.

Soberly leaning forward, Gabriel said, "My friends, please accept my congratulations for the admirable work you and your troops have done over the last 6,000 years. In restraining the winds of *kanuf,* you have protected outlanders from destructive forces beyond their imagination."

Lanse cocked his head. "If I didn't know better, I'd say you were gearing up to fire someone."

A sad smile crossed Gabriel's face. "Have you noticed the time?"

All heads turned toward the timer above the doorway. Just then its red digits flipped to 23:59:00. Gasps filled the room.

"It's time," Lanse breathed solemnly. "The world's cup of *kanuf* is full."

"I'm afraid so," Gabriel said. "In his mercy, His Majesty has long postponed this step. But because of your protective interventions, *kanuf* has remained somewhat disguised. Now it must be allowed free rein so all may see it clearly." He regarded the regimental commanders solemnly. "You, faithful Planetary Defenders, are relieved of your duties."

A heavy silence settled over them. No doubt, each general was recalling the ruin they'd witnessed ... and realizing that none would compare to the devastation ahead.

After several moments, Lanse said, "Gabriel, what's to become of these troops?"

"They will deploy with the Royal Guard. Once Stan realizes that the Planetary Defenders have withdrawn from their posts, he'll unleash unprecedented chaos on this planet. Protecting His Majesty's own will be more challenging than ever. The Guard will need the extra manpower."

Having delivered the bad news, Gabriel left the committee to work out the reassignment details. He was making his way to his office when his assistant called to report, "*Mikaél's* in the War Room." (Paradisian: commander-in-chief)

"On my way," Gabriel said and immediately altered his course. Reaching the War Room, he bowed before his prince. "*Modén.*" (Your Highness)

"Hello, my friend." Prince Joshua greeted him with a kiss on the cheek. "You've noted the time?"

"I have. Lanse is reassigning the troops even now."

"Good work. However, the sealing is not quite finished. We've decided to delay the Planetary Defenders' reassignment."

Gabriel spun to the clock above the doorway, where the red digits stood fixed at 23:59:15. Another of the Deón's generous delays! Relief swept through him as the faces of his deceived niece and nephews again came to mind. There was still a chance for them, at least! He turned back to Prince Joshua with a smile. "By your leave, sir, I'll advise the council."

"Please do. However, don't increase their manpower. Allowing the outlanders a clearer vision of the *kanuf* they've chosen should spur a few more to accept our rescue."

"May it be so," Gabriel breathed fervently.

If he had been human, or even one of the Paradisian exiles to whom image was so important, Gabriel might have returned to the conference room with an arrogant stride, affecting a haughty demeanor. But he was not bound to the artificial ideas of dignity that encumbered the rebels. Nor was he concerned with the spurious definitions of manhood that burdened humans. Dignity was his birthright as a loyal son of the Deón. And his manliness was measured only by how well he lived up to the motto that he and his siblings had themselves chosen:

lanáj—"to serve." And so, seeing nothing unseemly in the natural expression of joy, Gabriel bounded down the hallway and burst into the conference room like an excited child.

"Look!" he cried, pointing at the clock. "A reprieve!"

The room erupted in cheers and back-slapping until Lanse brought them back to their present duty. "Gabriel, about those extra battalions?"

"I'm afraid not," Gabriel said, and explained their prince's orders.

"But after living with *kanuf* for 6,000 years, can this short delay really illuminate the danger enough that some will respond to His Majesty's appeals?"

"Prince Joshua thinks so," Gabriel replied. "And if there's but a small chance, we must try. What is a short delay after all the prince has sacrificed? Besides, has *Mikaél* ever been wrong?"

CHAPTER 1

HELP!

"Oh, please help us against our enemies,
for all human help is useless."
Psalm 60:11, NLT.

Captain Jorge Strider hiked swiftly along the mountain trail, his night vision goggles granting him easy passage through the moonless night. His black body suit rendered him nearly invisible; his training as a special ops member of the Paradisian army's Outlander Division made him nearly soundless. Were he alone, he'd be virtually undetectable, even with the unconscious child he carried on his back.

But he wasn't alone, and the four prisoners he'd freed from the enemy's Peruvian detention facility had none of these advantages. The three ambulatory hostages—a twelve-year-old boy and his parents—followed Jorge closely but clumsily. To his trained ears, their progress was just plain noisy. Yet they couldn't slow down to go more quietly. With every passing minute, their well-trained, well-equipped pursuers were closing on them.

Their only hope was to reach the river over the next rise before their pursuers caught them. The boat he kept hidden there would carry them to safety. And it wasn't far; Jorge could sprint the distance in a matter of minutes. But after falling into the enemy's trap, the family he'd freed, though once accomplished runners, had been severely deconditioned by their imprisonment. Jorge had pushed them as hard as he dared, and the difficult escape had already tested the very limits of their endurance.

In truth, this long trail wasn't Jorge's preferred escape route. It was Plan D of four options. Although he ran the trail regularly to remain familiar with it, he'd never been forced to use it on a mission. The enemy foiling all three alternative routes was only part of the trouble he'd encountered during this operation, and the many mishaps gnawed at him. Rescuing prisoners from the tenacious Stan Moden, president of the Allied States of Desmoden, was never easy. Still, Jorge had rescued prisoners from that detention facility numerous times without incident. Why had this mission gone so wrong? Could there be a mole in the Outlander Division? Or had he gotten overconfident and lax in his procedures?

The labored breathing of the five-year-old girl strapped to his back drove home the latter possibility with excruciating force. When he'd attempted to implement Plan C, she'd been mauled by guard dogs in an area that had never been patrolled by dogs before. He'd cleaned and dressed her nasty leg wounds, but infection had still set in. Now, with her unconscious little body tied to his, he could feel her fever rising.

A curve in the trail revealed the graveyard that topped the mountain, and Jorge surged forward with new energy. Maybe, after three long days of hiding and trekking, they'd get out of this mess yet! Deliverance was just through that cemetery and down the hill.

The family also seemed to catch a second wind. Jorge sensed their relief as they followed him through an opening in the stone wall. Still following the trail, they quickly weaved between headstones to the far side of the cemetery. He heard their pursuers reach the first opening just as he approached the far gap in the wall that would be their deliverance.

But with his first glimpse of that opening, Jorge stopped abruptly. The boy grunted as he collided into his back. Reaching down to scoop up a stone, Jorge tossed it into the wire mesh stretched across the gap—a fence that had never been there before. A loud *ZAP!* testified to the electricity running through it.

They were trapped.

"There's no way out," a pursuer called triumphantly. "You've pestered us long enough, Phantom—now you're mine!"

Whispering instructions to the family, Jorge quickly unstrapped the makeshift harness and secured the unresponsive girl to her father's back. Then he transferred his night vision goggles and last remaining handgun to him as well. He had one final plan, although he recognized it as an act of desperation.

They could not all escape—this he knew. But if he could draw the soldiers to the back of the graveyard, the family might be able to circle back along the wall unseen and sneak out the front. They would still have to find a path around the cemetery and make their way down to the hidden boat. But they just might make it.

At his signal, the family crept away, dashing from the cover of one gravestone to the next. Jorge stayed near the fenced-off opening, darting in different directions and tossing rocks here and there to create the impression of several fugitives scattering to hiding places.

When he heard two enemy troops drawing near, he dove behind a tombstone to crouch in absolute silence. Only the heartbeat drumming loudly in his ears broke the stillness.

A faint glint drew his attention to his left, and he watched the muzzle of a rifle poke around the headstone.

Jorge held his breath. Maybe a desperate dive behind another tombstone?

Before he could move, another glint appeared on his right. Another muzzle.

An ugly grin twisted the face that appeared above him. "Gotcha!"

Jorge squeezed his eyes shut in defeat. He would have liked to watch the twenty-two years of his life pass before his eyes in that moment. But he could not be so optimistic. His death would not be a quick one. Even if Stan Moden knew the meaning of the word "mercy," he wouldn't grant any to Jorge. He had been a pest for too long. He knew too much. And, perhaps most important, he was the son of the hated Dr. Christian Strider, son of Juan Misi.

CHAPTER 2
THROUGH THE WATERS

"Fear not, for I have redeemed you …
When you pass through the waters, I will be with you."
Isaiah 43:2, NKJV.

D r. Christian Strider leaned his elbows onto the dinner table to edge a little closer, anxious to catch every word. The storyteller paused, his gaze chasing around the table. "They came right to where I was hiding. They knew exactly where I was."

"How?" Chris's six-year-old granddaughter, Cherie, asked breathlessly.

"Infrared satellite," Jorge whispered. "They could see the heat of our bodies. I didn't know it then, but they'd already cornered the family. We had nowhere to go, no way of escape."

"What did you do?" Cherie asked.

"I didn't know what to do," Jorge admitted. "But then—" He sat back, his face breaking into a huge grin.

"Then, what, *tío*?" Cherie cried. "What happened?" (Spanish: uncle)

"Doug … sang."

The first to catch on, Chris threw his head back and roared with relieved laughter. The other adults at the table—his wife, their four grown children, and their one daughter-in-law—soon joined in.

Chris's two granddaughters exchanged a puzzled glance. "Doug sang?" Cherie asked.

"*Doug* sang," Jorge repeated meaningfully. "See, our transmitters have several different modes."

"Mine too?" Cherie looked down at the small silver device hanging from her neck.

"Yes, yours too," he assured her. "I always keep mine on in privacy mode during an operation. The enemy can't hear Doug's voice on that frequency, but runners can, so I can receive Doug's instructions. But when the rifles poked around the tombstone, Doug said, 'Activate your transmitter.' That changes its frequency to one that everyone can hear, even his enemies."

"And Doug sang through your transmitter," Chris's wife, Susana, said in wonder. "I've never heard him sing."

"He's got a great voice—and you should have seen those soldiers!" Jorge said gleefully. "They bolted off like a bunch of scared rabbits." To Cherie, he added, "See, Doug's voice hurts his enemies' ears—so much that they can't stay within hearing distance."

Cherie and her two-and-a-half-year-old sister, Melanie, burst into squeals of delight. Then Melanie wanted to know what song Doug sang.

"A new song," Jorge answered. "The words are from the *Manual*, but I'd never heard them put to music before. It went like this:

Fear not when you pass through the waters; I am with you.
Though the rivers flood o'er your head, I am there.
Fear not when you walk through the fire; I am with you.
I am with you always; I am there.

Fear not! Fear not!
I have created and redeemed you.
I have saved you; you are mine.
Fear not! Fear not!
I am with you always.
For you—yes, you—are mine."

A hush fell over the group as Jorge sang, his clear tenor conveying all the hope and poignancy those words must have had for him that night.

"Beautiful," Susana said with a sniffle.

Cherie turned to her father, Chris's adopted son, Stanley. "*Papi*," she admonished with a hint of disapproval, "you shouldn't send my *tío* there. It's too dangerous."

"I'll keep that in mind next time," Stanley replied with a sad smile. As the commander of the Outlander Division of Doug's army, he made many decisions that placed his loved ones in danger. He sometimes confided to Chris how that responsibility weighed on him.

Gently, Chris explained, "*Tío* Jorge is the best, pumpkin. If he doesn't find Stan's prisoners and rescue them, Stan just keeps on hurting them."

"Besides," Jorge said brightly, "Doug gives me the power I need for every situation. Come, you want to learn the song he sang?"

"Yeah!" the two girls chorused. They hopped down to trail their uncle into the family room, where he reached for his guitar. The others followed. Soon everyone had learned the new song, and some were adding harmonies and a descant as well.

Still, as Chris listened to their voices raised in song, a troubling premonition settled over him. He rolled his shoulders, trying to shake off the feeling, but it lingered—the distinct impression that they would never again be together like this, with every family member present, until after the Awakening.

A natural thought after our recent scare, he told himself—for they'd believed the worst when Jorge dropped off the radar for three days. Yet when the family separated to their own homes, Chris found himself wondering with each hug if this was the last time he would see that individual. He chided himself for the thought; yet he couldn't banish it from his mind.

When the house emptied, he followed Susana to the kitchen for cleanup. She promptly took the dishrag from him and reached up to kiss him on the cheek. "Go ahead, *mi amor*. Go talk to Doug about whatever's eating at you."

He didn't bother arguing. After thirty-five years of marriage, she knew him too well. Instead, he wordlessly planted a kiss on her forehead and retreated to his study. Picking up his copy of *The Runner's Manual,* he sank into the over-stuffed chair in the corner and randomly paged through the book. As he perused the well-worn tome, he stopped to reflect on highlighted passages of hope and comfort. Soon Doug's voice came over his transmitter.

"*Áchimi tamí bichíima, towí ke akemi?*" (Rarámuri: Do you trust me, Runs-Barefoot?)

That question posed in that language held special meaning for Chris. He didn't need to ponder his answer, but responded firmly, "*Ayena abi, Onó.*" (Rarámuri: Yes, Dad)

"Difficult times are a-comin', son." The transmitter now translated Doug's native Paradisian into English with a gentle Texan accent. "Hard times. The end's right close. But before the dawn comes, the winds of strife that Stan's set in motion must blow as never before. The night's gonna get very dark. Especially for you." He sighed softly. "And me. Such terrible work to do. But it has to be done."

"Tell me how to help, Doug," Chris said. "I'm willing to do whatever you ask."

"Thank you, pardner. You've already done most of it. You've raised four strong runners, all right fine leaders in the Outlander Division, and you helped Stanley establish it. What's more, you've influenced countless others through y'all's work in the Kids' Klub. You've run well, son. Yet tonight you'll have to bear the hardest thing I've ever asked of you. I'd like to spare you, but it has to be, and there are still two more young runners who could use your help."

So this uneasiness wasn't just his imagination. But what could Doug mean? Chris had been through some pretty hard times. He'd been a fugitive on the run from Doug's powerful archenemy, Stan Moden. He'd lived in uncomfortable, primitive circumstances for months. He'd even been tortured by Stan's men.

Yet something worse was ahead. Tonight.

He was indeed willing to do anything Doug asked. His love for and loyalty to his sponsor had only grown stronger with time. But he was sixty now—a healthy sixty, but not as resilient as he'd been in his youth. Was he up to whatever trouble lay ahead?

"Read with me, son," Doug urged. "Start with the fortieth section of Isaiah's story and read on for a spell."

The longtime runner obeyed, recognizing this exercise as Doug's way of fortifying him for the coming storm. He thoughtfully read aloud, sucking every morsel of meaning from the rich passage. After a while, Doug directed him to Paul's letter to his friends in Philippi, where one particular sentence gripped him: "I've learned the secret of being content in any situation: I can do anything through him who gives me strength."

Chris laid his head back and savored the familiar words, allowing them to ease his restlessness. As he did, Doug's peace overcame his anxiety. Doug's strength replaced his inadequacy. Doug's assurance erased his doubts.

"Now why don't you go spend some time with your wife," Doug said at last.

Chris found Susana in the family room, smiling softly as she flipped through old photo albums. The homey aroma of baking bread and soothing strains of praise music filled the air. Still unnoticed, he watched her from the doorway, enjoying the expressions that flitted across her face. An overflowing sense of gratitude and love surged through him. His wife was a beautiful creature in every way, and he was the luckiest man alive to walk through life with her at his side.

When she turned a page and laughed, he asked, "What's so funny?"

She started slightly, but when she registered his presence, a light came into her eyes that made his heart turn somersaults. She still looked at him like he was the most important person on earth.

"These old pictures," she answered as he joined her on the sofa. Pointing to a picture of Jorge as a baby, shortly after they had adopted him, she said, "Andy always made such a mess when he gave Jorge his bottle."

Chris smiled. "Remember that time we found the kids heating his bottle in the middle of the night? What was it Stanley said?"

" 'I'm used to mixing chemicals in a lab,' " Susana mimicked with a giggle. "I think I can heat a baby bottle.' "

They both laughed, something they did a lot of over the next hour as they relived memories. When they came to one of their daughter's baby pictures, Susana said wistfully, "Bethany was a beautiful baby."

"That's because she takes after you."

She grinned up at him. "You're such a smooth talker. I knew I kept you around for some reason."

Gazing into her velvety brown eyes, he said, "Whatever the reason, I'm glad you did. You have truly been *mi tesoro precioso*." (Spanish: my precious treasure)

Her expression conveyed all the accumulated love of their lifetime together. He gazed at her, fixing the image in his mind to cherish forever. Then, finding words inadequate to express his feelings, he demonstrated them with a kiss.

He took his time with that kiss. They were still kissing when a man cleared his throat. They looked up to see six brawny special ops men bearing the insignia of Stan Moden's army.

Chris shot to his feet, but two of the soldiers immediately subdued him, securing his arms behind him. A haughty four-star general sauntered toward him. About the same height as Chris, the man was probably a hundred pounds heavier—all muscle. Except for his boxer's nose and deep blue eyes, he looked very much like Stanley.

"So this is the great Dr. Christian Strider, son of Juan Misi," the general drawled in a voice that also sounded like Stanley's.

One of Stanley's biological brothers, Chris realized. *Stan Moden's son.*

Chris's initial reaction was pity. For twenty-four years, ever since they had adopted Stanley and learned of the brutal, loveless home he'd been born into, Chris had hoped to rescue the younger siblings too. He'd often begged Doug for the chance to help them learn of the pardon he offered.

Yet as he looked into the eyes of the man before him, Chris saw no remnant of a pliable child, no hint of one who might rethink his course. He saw only the unrestrained, ruthless cruelty of one fully abandoned to evil.

"He doesn't look so intimidating now, does he?" the general asked his soldiers. "In fact, from this perspective, he looks almost human. Could a mere human have set all of Moden Industries on its head, organized the infamous Kids' Klub, and raised an Outlander Division for the enemy's army? What do you think, men—have we got the wrong guy?"

The other soldiers snickered.

The general stepped closer. "My father asked me to bring you a special gift, Strider."

"What 'gift'?" Chris asked warily.

A sneer spread over the man's face. "You, Dr. Strider, are to have the privilege of watching your wife … die … quickly."

Chris felt the blood drain from his face.

A wolfish grin replaced the sneer as the man turned to Susana, now on her feet with a revolver pointed at her head. Circling her, he leered at her in a way that made Chris's blood sizzle in his veins. Then he brazenly ran his fingers down her sweet face and added, "Although Father did say that we should feel free to enjoy her company first." Susana jerked her face away, her eyes widening in horror.

Fury, like a raging inferno, sprang up within Chris. He lunged against his attackers, but his struggles were futile. Even one of Stan's soldiers was easily twice as strong as he could ever be.

The general turned back to Chris, again sneering. "Yes, Father thought you'd like that. You'll be happy to know he wanted me to keep you relatively unharmed." He chortled. "For now. You, it seems, are to be a present for my mother. And believe me, she won't be quick about your death."

The general stepped back and looked around at his men. "So, whose turn is it to go first with the lady?"

"That'd be me," said a smirking captain who passed directly in front of Chris.

A soldier was still holding Chris's arms firmly behind him, but he managed to land a decent kick to the captain's knees, causing him to stumble. A sergeant fired his rifle at Chris, but the general pushed it up as he did. The shot landed in the ceiling, raining bits of plaster down on Chris's head.

"Idiot!" the general spat. "My father wants him alive."

Suddenly a pair of gunshots rang out from the backyard, shattering the sliding glass door. The two soldiers behind Chris fell to the floor, freeing him. When he lunged toward Susana, the sergeant fired again. A searing pain exploded in his left shoulder and knocked him backward.

"Chris!" Susana screamed and threw herself toward him.

The general caught her by the upper arm and raised his pistol to her head. Then he glanced at Chris with murder in his cold eyes.

"No!" Chris yelled. But his protest was lost in the noise of the gunshot. Susana crumpled to the floor like a rag doll. The general stood over her, laughing.

Chris struggled up and ran to her. Lifting her bloody head, he cradled it in his lap.

Beside him, the general began shouting. There was more gunfire, scuffling, and yelling, but Chris was not a part of it. For him, time had stopped. He knelt on the floor holding his most precious *tesoro*, her blood warming his lap.

Tears streamed down his face unchecked as he pleaded, "Please, Doug, not this ... anything but this ... please no."

He was still cradling Susana and weeping when he felt Jorge's arm around his shoulders. Slowly he became aware of his son on the carpet beside him. Three other members of Doug's army stood guard over them. The room was deathly still.

Then police swarmed into Chris's home. They ran up the stairs, checked rooms, barked orders, and asked questions. Jorge provided explanations while Chris remained frozen in the pool of blood, hugging Susana to himself.

The soldiers eventually tore Chris away from her and led him to the sofa. He was no longer weeping. He had gone numb.

Jorge discovered the hole amid the blood on Chris's shirt and asked, "Dad, are you hurt?"

Chris didn't respond, still aware of little more than Susana's body lying on the floor. Nothing else seemed important. Nothing seemed real.

As his son tore open the shirt and dressed the wound, pieces of the evening came back to Chris, phrases that repeated themselves over and over, renewing him in that inexplicable way that the words from the *Manual* always did.

> *When you pass through the waters, I am with you.*
> *Fear not; you are mine.*
> *Fear not; she is mine.*

Jorge's urgent voice intruded on Chris's trance. "Come on, Dad. We need to get you to a hospital. You're still bleeding quite a bit."

Chris searched his son's face. "Is this real, *muchachón*?"

Tears sprang to Jorge's deep brown eyes. "Yeah, Dad," he whispered. "It's real."

Although Jorge said no more, the father in Chris recognized the bewilderment in his son's eyes and understood the danger: confusion could foster doubt. Suddenly his responsibility became clear. His own reaction to this catastrophe might very well influence his children's relationship with Doug. Latching onto the strength of the inspired words still echoing in his mind, he determined not to allow his grief to overwrite Susana's lifetime of faithful service. Instead, he would honor her—and Doug—by finding some way to buttress his son's faith.

Looking back to Susana's still form, he said, "Doug warned me something was up. I'm glad he did. It gave us a chance to remember the good times. She was happy, son. She died happy."

"Doug warned me too, Dad. I only wish he'd called earlier." A hint of anger tinged Jorge's voice. "Maybe, if we'd gotten here sooner—"

"No." Chris shook his head emphatically. "No. Doug's timing is always right. And he allows nothing to happen to us that he can't use for good. You have to believe that. This had to be. I don't know why, but he does. As a wise old runner once told me, 'When we get to Paradise and can see it all, we'll realize we wouldn't have changed a thing if we could.' "

He reached out to rub Jorge's wiry black hair. "Have faith. When we pass through the waters, he is right here with us. He was with you in Peru, and he's with us now. Choose faith, son. Choose faith."

CHAPTER 3
MERCY

"Lord, have mercy on me. See how my enemies torment me."
Psalm 9:13, NLT.

Major General Stanley Strider Lanáj lined up with the other pallbearers to hoist Susana's coffin off the hearse. As they carried it toward the gravesite, he mused that his adoptive mom was perhaps the noblest woman he'd known. She had even risked her own children's safety to welcome him, her enemy's son, into her home.

Oh, why had his biological parents gone after *her*? Why hadn't they attacked him instead? *He* was the son who had betrayed them, defecting to Doug and handing over mountains of sensitive information to be used against them!

He scoffed at his own question. He knew very well why. They'd often told him: If you really want to hurt someone, don't kill *him*, but those who matter the most to him. That's why they'd targeted Susana—to hurt Stanley. And Chris. They hated his adoptive dad almost as much as they hated him.

They placed the coffin on the platform above the grave, and Stanley laid his hand on the casket, silently bidding her farewell. He tried to repress the feeling that this parting was his fault. Yet he knew it was. If he had not joined this family, his birth parents would not have targeted Susana. Or if he had protected her better, everyone within her influence would still be enjoying her cheerful optimism and genuine kindness. He'd read the signs; he knew the war between Stan and Doug was coming to a head. He'd even guessed that Stan might make a move like this one. He'd simply expected that *he* would be the one in their crosshairs.

Foolish mistake. So very, very foolish.

Absorbed in his reflections, Stanley automatically took a seat beside Bethany, his spinning mind recognizing too late where his legs had led him. He loved his wife more than life itself. She was friend and confidante, lover and link-mate. And that link was a wonderful gift in many ways. In fact, it had probably saved his sanity when he first defected. Still, sometimes he preferred not to have his soul bared to his wife. That's why he'd been evading her since Susana's death. Once she touched him, she would read his emotions as easily as a billboard and surmise everything he'd been keeping from her.

As her delicate hand moved to grasp his, Stanley glanced around, desperately seeking a task to occupy him. He caught his youngest daughter's eye, and held his hands out to her. She very obligingly hopped off Chris's lap and onto his. And, with Melanie being the wiggle-worm she was, he'd be safe for the duration of the ceremony.

Secure from discovery, he focused on the service. Susana had been loved by many, and the graveside ceremony in Ventura was crowded and beautiful—as far as such things can be beautiful. Aedan McElroy, a longtime friend of the family and leader of the RAB (Runners' Assemblies Building) they had attended for most of their lives, presented an inspiring homily. His personal knowledge of the family allowed him to review the highlights of Susana's life in a way she would have appreciated, a way that emphasized the blessings Doug had bestowed on her. He also reminded them of the temporary nature of death and of their future inheritance on Paradise Island. Far from encouraging tears and wailing, the service promoted an atmosphere of hope and thanksgiving.

Afterward, most of the attendees joined the reception at Aunt Rosie's home. Stanley busied himself by mingling with the guests, trying to relieve his dad of as much responsibility as he could, for Chris couldn't stand such gatherings. By sunset, the group had thinned to only relatives, and Stanley went looking for Dad to let him know it was safe to come out of hiding. He found him and Aunt Rosie in her sewing room involved in another intense conversation about running. Being twins, Chris and Rosie had always been close. Yet she had never committed to Doug's race, and her reticence weighed heavily on Dad's heart.

It bothered Stanley, too, and with an urgency Dad couldn't comprehend since he didn't yet understand the significance of Mom's murder. But Stanley understood it fully. Susana's murder would trigger the Final Battle; his biological parents had intended it to. So, although Aunt Rosie always claimed she intended to join Doug's runners, she would lose the opportunity forever if she didn't do it soon. Yet something always stood in her way: she was waiting to run it with her husband … her grandchildren needed her just now … she had too many social responsibilities at present …

Having been raised on the other side of the war, Stanley recognized these rationalizations for what they were—the workmanship of one of his birth parents' agents. They often tricked people into rejecting Doug's clemency simply by repeatedly postponing the decision to accept it. Stanley had tried to warn Aunt Rosie of this, but she never slowed down enough to actually hear him.

What's more, he strongly suspected there was more to the story. The descendants of Juan Misi, Chris's great-grandfather, were prime merchandise to Stan. And Aunt Rosie and Uncle Ivan lived much better than they should. This home alone, which they had renovated and enlarged several times over, represented more money than two blue-collar workers could possibly earn. It didn't take Stanley's genius to add up the facts: his birth parents were somehow buying off Aunt Rosie. He was so sure of it that he sometimes withheld information from Chris—for what could his birth parents want from Rosie but information? Oh, she wouldn't purposely betray her brother; the transactions would be more subtle than that. But Stanley was always conscious that whatever he conveyed to Chris might find its way back to Moden Industries through the twin sister Dad loved so well.

As Stanley entered the sewing room, he heard Aunt Rosie say, "Now just isn't a good time, Chris. But I will. I promise."

Seeing him, she said, "Hi, Stanley. How are things going? Do we need more refreshments?"

"No. Everything's fine, Aunt Rosie. Everyone's left now except for the family."

"Finally!" Dad exclaimed, and Aunt Rosie laughingly hurled a pillow at him.

When the remaining family prepared to leave, Dad's oldest brother pulled Stanley aside. "I want you to watch over your dad for me. He's liable to do stupid stuff like forgetting to eat when he's mourning. Promise me you'll take care of him."

"I promise, Uncle Benny."

His uncle clapped him on the shoulder. "You done real good with takin' care of all these arrangements. You're a good son, Stanley. He's lucky to have you."

You wouldn't say that if you knew the truth.

Absorbed in his ruminations, he wasn't paying much attention while he waved goodbye to his relatives. That's when Bethany struck, sneaking up behind him to slip her hand into his. The action was so natural that he didn't immediately register the danger. But when she gasped, he recognized his oversight and winced. Just that quickly, she'd learned everything he didn't want her to know.

"Can I talk to you for a minute?" she murmured.

"Um, not right now. I need to—" he looked around for inspiration.

Chris grinned. "A word of advice, son? When your wife wants to talk to you, you might as well get it over with. Delay only makes it worse."

"Listen to Dad," Beth said, and tugged him toward the room where they would be staying for the night. Closing the door behind them, she put both hands on her hips. "This is not your fault, Stanley."

"I know," he said without thinking it through first. Her linked abilities included a lie detector.

She lifted her eyebrows in a do-you-really-want-to-play-this-game expression.

Rubbing his face, he said wearily, "You don't know everything I do, Beth."

Her beautiful brown eyes twinkled. "There you go again," she teased, "throwing that off-the-charts IQ of yours around."

He turned away from her. Picking up a picture on the dresser, he distractedly ran his fingers around the frame. "I saw things when I was there. Heard things. I should have put them together. I should have anticipated that they would do this. I should have protected her. She was the perfect target—a quick strike that would do maximum damage. I should have seen it coming."

"Okay, just for the sake of argument, let's say that's true. At worst, that makes you a fallible human—"

He swiveled to quirk an eyebrow at her, and she giggled. "Excuse me—a fallible Paradisian. But you still didn't murder her."

"No." He swallowed hard before whispering, "My kid brother did."

He didn't need his link-sense to interpret her wide-eyed stare for the horrified surprise it represented. When she finally found her tongue, she asked softly, "Is that who did it, then?"

He nodded. "I haven't told Dad, but based on his description, it had to be Sheridan."

Taking the picture from him, she replaced it on the dresser and gathered his hands in hers. "When did you last talk to Doug?"

"This morning—"

He stopped, frowning. No, he'd rushed out before talking to Doug this morning. Did he even talk to him yesterday? The day before? He must have been subconsciously avoiding Doug along with Bethany.

"That long, huh?" she said. "Honey, Doug would remind you that you're not responsible for the actions of your birth family."

"But I should have prevented it!" he roared, all his rage and guilt erupting together. "I should have protected her!"

"When?"

He gaped at her, uncomprehending.

"When did the danger begin, General? You must suspect the possibility of danger in order to protect against it, right? And we've lived here under Doug's direct protection since we were kids. At what point, precisely, did the danger begin? When during the last twenty years should you have implemented this protection you speak of so glibly?"

He couldn't answer the question. It would be impossible to pinpoint, even in retrospect.

"Has Stan ever violated a hands-off order before, even once during the six thousand years of this war?"

"Never. He didn't want to pay the consequences."

"So how exactly were you supposed to know when that changed? How could you possibly protect Mom from a danger you didn't know existed?"

Unable to argue with his wife's logic, Stanley sank onto a nearby chair and buried his face in his hands.

"I'll be takin' that guilt off your hands now," Doug said through Bethany's transmitter. "If you're through with it, that is."

Stanley wagged his head. "How many times have we gone through this, Doug? How do you put up with me?"

"That's like askin' how you put up with that wiggly daughter of yours," Doug replied tenderly.

Stanley surrendered. "It's yours, *Ada*. Please take it." (Paradisian: Dad)

"You better lie down first, buddy, or you just might fall over. I think that guilt's 'bout the only thing holdin' you up."

"But I need to get some work done before you issue the Declaration."

"I am the architect of time, son. I think I can arrange to give you enough for the work I've assigned you."

A wry smile came to Stanley's lips. "Of course you can, Doug. Sorry about that."

He lay down and soon felt a gentle buzzing sensation under the transmitter as Doug drained away the recriminations that had poisoned his days and haunted his nights. Bethany's kiss on his forehead was the last thing he remembered before falling into a deep, restful sleep.

CHAPTER 4
DECEIVED

*"Be careful. Don't let your heart be deceived so that you turn away
from the Lord and serve and worship other gods."*
Deuteronomy 11:16, NLT.

Wilson Moore laughed at the super-full cooler his mother handed him. "Thanks, Mom. That should last an hour or two." Kissing her cheek, he headed out to his car.

He was all of two steps out the front door when she came running after him. "Here, Willy, you can take the rest of this meatloaf too!"

"Mom, I was kidding! There's enough here for the whole New-RAB." Accepting the container she urged on him, he added, "Really, you can stop worrying. I've never starved at Uncle Chris's before. I don't think I'll starve now."

"Well, I don't know who you think will cook for you. I'm not sure your uncle knows which end of a knife to use."

Did she really think he needed someone to cook for him? He was a junior pre-law political science major at UCLA—an honor student, no less. He could probably figure out how to feed himself, wouldn't you think? But his mom still didn't consider him grown up.

Aloud, he just said, "Well, I'm sure that between Uncle Chris, Jorge, and me we can figure out how to order a pizza."

"That's what I'm afraid of. You can't live on pizza!"

"Okay, Mom." He kissed her cheek again. "But I really need to go or I'll be late, and this is an important meeting. With one of the higher-ups in Doug Damour's government," he added on impulse, even though his work was supposed to be secretive.

"Well that's nice," she said, obviously not catching the significance. "You drive careful, now."

"I will, Mom." What did she think—that he was going to purposely crash the car he'd slaved to buy?

"And study hard. Don't party too much."

"I don't party, Mom." *Not anymore.*

She followed him to his new Mustang convertible and blew a kiss as he pulled away. Willy appreciated his mom's thoughtfulness, but it frustrated him that she still saw him as a child. He'd worked hard to earn some respect. It wasn't like he was a rich kid who got everything handed to him. He covered tuition with scholarships won by good grades, and he worked maintenance to cover his other needs. Besides that, his reliable community service had merited him a good reputation with the New-RAB. No sir, Willy Moore was no slacker. He intended to leave his mark on the world. His family may not appreciate him yet, but they would someday.

Maybe all family "babies" had the same problem, but he figured he had it worse than most. Besides being the youngest son of Ivan and Rosie Moore, he was the youngest cousin in the whole Strider clan. Everyone jokingly called him the "accident," since his next brother was twelve years older. Willy laughed along good-naturedly, but he honestly didn't think it was very funny. To make matters worse, he was only 5'9"—an okay height in other families, but a midget among the Striders. His 6'4" Uncle Steve still enjoyed asking him how the weather was "down there"—like that joke hadn't gone stale years ago.

Willy's drive from Ventura to LA was unremarkable. He arrived at the designated meeting place early—another posh restaurant. Taylor Menod, special assistant to General Gabriel Lanáj, really knew how to live. She always stayed in the Biltmore, met him at the best restaurants, and dressed in designer everything from hairpins to shoes.

She arrived precisely on time, and he stood when she approached the table. Not that he usually stood in the presence of women, but something about her elicited old-fashioned respect. In his most distinguished tone, he said, "Good day, Ms. Menod. I trust your flight was pleasant."

Trust your flight was pleasant? When did he start talking like a dweeb? But that's what this woman did to him.

"Quite pleasant," she responded regally. "I thank you. And how are you, Mr. Moore? I believe you said you were to attend a funeral this morning? No one dear to you, I hope."

"Actually, she was my aunt, the wife of the uncle I'm staying with while attending UCLA. She was a wonderful person. We'll all miss her."

"I am sorry for your loss, Mr. Moore, but perhaps it will be of some little comfort to know that you recently prevented the deaths of numerous other individuals. At least their families need not suffer as yours is now."

The tense muscles at the base of Willy's neck relaxed a little. Ms. Menod paid him well for the work he did for General Lanáj, but the money alone wouldn't induce him to spy on his own family. Yet he'd tried talking to them, and they just didn't listen. So it was moments like this—learning that he'd helped undo some of the damage that Uncle Chris's conspiracy theories caused—that made everything worthwhile. And when his conscience bothered him, he reminded himself that it would bother him more if he'd done nothing to protect these innocent lives.

"So there was something useful in that last batch of shredding?" he asked.

"Indeed there was. We learned that the fanatics were planning to bomb a certain embassy in Peru."

When Willy caught his breath, she added, "Not to worry. The information allowed us to find the explosive device and disarm it before anyone was harmed. You may have saved as many as a hundred lives."

"That is good news," he said. "But—well, you really believe my cousins are capable of perpetrating these atrocities?"

"I'm afraid there's no question that these incidents stem from within the Outlander Division. However, we believe most of its members to be ignorant of the radical faction's activities. Even those involved may be deluded as to the true purpose of their efforts." She glanced down at the table. "However, we do have solid evidence that their so-called general, Stanley Strider 'Lanáj,' as he has the audacity to call himself, is directly involved. In truth, we believe him to be the mastermind behind the terrorist activities. He's a brilliant man."

When Willy winced involuntarily, she added, "Of course, he is not, strictly speaking, your cousin, having been adopted by your uncle when he was almost eleven years old. A child's character is already well-established by that age. Even the greatest psychologists may be unable to correct ingrained tendencies in an older child."

Willy nodded gratefully at her generosity toward his family.

"We are not sure which other members are knowingly involved," she continued. "Perhaps the materials you provide will supply more information on that score. We are particularly anxious to discover the identity of the individual whom our soldiers have dubbed The Phantom. This incident in Peru was but one of his crimes."

"I'm sorry; I've heard nothing about him." Nodding at the briefcase on the floor between them, Willy added, "Maybe there will be something more about him in this batch of shredded papers."

"Perhaps so. In any case, thank you for your cooperation, Mr. Moore. You truly have been most helpful. In fact, you have merited General Lanáj's personal notice. He asked me only yesterday what he could do to demonstrate his gratitude. Would you perhaps be interested in attending Harvard Law?"

Willy struggled to maintain some element of composure. Was she kidding? Even Uncle Chris hadn't attended Harvard! Not bad for the youngest, almost-shortest cousin!

Clearing his throat, he managed, "Um, yes, I certainly would."

She inclined her head in a stately nod. "Very well. Then you may count on General Lanáj's reference. As a highly regarded alumnus, his recommendation carries considerable weight. I cannot recall the institution ever refusing an applicant whom he has endorsed.

"Wow. Thank you. And please thank General Lanáj for me. This is much more than I expected."

"We are both happy to be of service. We truly are most concerned about these fanatics."

"I can see why. They call themselves part of the Paradisian army."

"Precisely, and their actions not only reflect poorly upon us as Paradisians but also hinder His Majesty's vision for world peace. His goal is quite attainable, you know, if only he could persuade his athletes to unite—RABs and New-RABs cooperating together to better our world. Nevertheless, these rebels, with their fanatical interpretation of the outdated version of *The Runner's Manual,* continually hamper his efforts. He will gladly and richly reward those who assist in neutralizing the damage they cause."

She smiled a beatific smile that lit up her crystalline blue eyes. "That includes you, Mr. Moore. I assure you, he will not forget your cooperation."

✽ ✽ ✽ ✽ ✽

Jorge was eating lunch in the Paradisian Embassy's cafeteria when he received a call from Stanley's secretary. "Captain Strider, Major General Lanáj would like to see you in his office."

Jorge's stomach tightened at her choice of address, which informed him that this wasn't a casual request from his big brother. It was a summons from his commander. What's more, he knew what it was about.

Having lost his appetite, he carried his unfinished meal to the trash and made his way to the wing occupied by the Outlander Division. When he entered his brother's office, the tightness in his stomach twisted into an outright knot, for Stanley looked up with that unreadable expression that drove his troops nuts. They loved and respected their commander—a wise administrator, a fair disciplinarian, and a devoted servant-leader who would move mountains to come to their aid. But he could also be quite intimidating. At six-foot-three, he carried 280 pounds of muscle, possessed the superhuman strength of all Paradisians, and projected a natural air of authority, thanks to his childhood training as Stan Moden's successor. What's more, he knew every detail of the Outlander Division, right down to when they emptied the trash. Between that knowledge and his quick mind, there was no room for fudging around Major General Stanley Strider Lanáj. He could see through the slightest exaggeration or cover-up. Yet his facial expression gave away nothing unless he wanted it to. The total effect could be quite daunting.

"Please be seated, Captain," Stanley said formally. When Jorge did, Stanley continued, "I have completed my review of your latest operation in Peru. Additionally, I have asked three colonels to review the information and to submit their evaluations."

Jorge ran a dry tongue over his lips. "May I ask what their conclusions were?"

"All in due time. I would first like to hear your own evaluation, now that you've had more time to ponder the events."

Jorge bowed his head. "General, I have reviewed every moment of those three days in my mind. I've gone over every move, every choice, again and again. I honestly don't know what I did wrong. As far as I can see, I followed the appropriate procedures. And I'd used all but the last of those escape routes before, successfully and without difficulty."

He looked up to meet his brother's eye. "Sir, if the problems I experienced on this mission were the result of some mistake on my part, I can't figure out what it was."

Stanley searched his face for a long moment, his expression still wholly inscrutable. Finally he said simply, "Neither can I."

Jorge's stomach relaxed. He hadn't messed up!

"The reviewers each came to the same conclusion. However, that conclusion is far more disturbing than simple human error." Stanley solemnly leaned forward. "The enemy had foreknowledge of your operation, Captain."

"So we have a mole in the Outlander Division—a fellow runner turning on us?" Jorge shook his head. "I'd rather believe I made a mistake."

"Yet we can't allow emotion to blind us. What's more, certain other operations have experienced similar irregularities over the last year, although none as seriously as this one."

"You mean Greenland?"

"Greenland. Togo. New Zealand. Ukraine."

Jorge frowned as he called up the specifics of each mission. "But they don't have anything in common. Different facilities, different teams, even different continents."

"They do have one thing in common."

"What's that?"

Stanley held his gaze. "You."

Jorge knew his brother too well to take offense. Stanley's logical mind was simply following the evidence. "That's true," he mused aloud. "I help plan and oversee all the complicated missions, even when I'm not on the operation itself. You're thinking it's someone who has access to my records—a clerk or something?"

"Possibly. But it's also curious that each of these missions required a significant measure of your particular brand of creativity. A mole close to you is one scenario. Another is someone on the outside who occasionally has access to your records."

"I never carry records beyond these doors, and I don't discuss the specifics of an operation with anyone outside the division."

"Including Dad?"

Jorge eyed his brother incredulously. "Dad? Do you honestly think he would betray us—betray Doug?"

When Stanley didn't answer, Jorge's disbelief grew into anger. Addressing his brother rather than his commander, he stood up to lean over Stanley's desk. "Dad helped you build this division from the ground up. He raised both of us like his own flesh and blood. He risked everything, even suffering torture, to save your life—from your own biological father, no less. He even lost Mom to Stan. How could you possibly suspect *him* of siding with the enemy?"

His brother's impassive expression never changed. "Be seated, Captain."

Jorge's anger was not appeased, but he complied with the order. He would never believe this, not of Dad. But there was something behind Stanley's question, and Jorge was determined to discover it, if only to prove him wrong. "I'm listening," he ground out.

Stanley circled the desk to sit on the front of it. "No," he said, almost gently, "I don't think Dad would betray us—not knowingly. And perhaps I should have mentioned this to you sooner. Andy is aware of my concerns."

In referring to their other brother by first name instead of as "Colonel Strider," Stanley was advising him that what he was about to say was off the books, brother to brother. Jorge sat back to listen.

"Jorge, I know how my birth parents work. I know what to look for. They can be very deceptive, and they often pair their trickery with monetary rewards to give their target greater incentives to believe their lies. So when I see someone living well above their means, I get suspicious."

"But Dad doesn't live extravagantly. In fact, he lives below his means so he can support worthy ministries. You know that."

"Yes," Stanley agreed. "But Aunt Rosie lives quite well. Too well."

"Ah," Jorge said, finally understanding. "And Dad talks to Aunt Rosie. You're afraid he might inadvertently say something that she sells to Stan."

Stanley nodded.

"Still, I follow our protocols to the letter—I know how important it is. Beforehand, I only discuss a mission with its operatives. Afterward, I don't mention specific details to anyone outside the division. Even if he—or, for that matter, your daughters—were to retell the stories to Aunt Rosie, it wouldn't provide the enemy with the kind of specific knowledge they'd need to trap me like they did in Peru."

"All right," Stanley said. "Then let's look elsewhere. I want you to review your entire process for potential vulnerabilities. Where do you get your inspiration? Is it perhaps while talking to someone in particular? Do the ideas come while researching books you've checked out of a library? Or consider where you are when you're perfecting your strategies. Do you scratch routes down on napkins in a coffee shop and toss the napkins into the trash? Do you doodle on the paper placemats in the cafeteria? Garrick could—"

"Garrick?"

"Dr. Sondem—Stan's minister of defense. He could be buying your trash from the janitor in your favorite fast food joint. He could buy stray pieces of paper left in your uniform from the dry cleaner. He could hack into the library computer to see what books you've read recently. He's quite resourceful."

"I see what you mean," Jorge said and paused for a moment to consider. "I usually get my ideas while reviewing the plans and blueprints of the facilities we're penetrating, but those always come from our computers, which are supposed to be safe."

"I make sure of it," Stanley affirmed. "And if we'd had a breach, the irregularities wouldn't be limited to missions involving you."

"Right. Well, I sometimes doodle out ideas at home, rarely anywhere else. But I'm careful to shred the paper if I do."

Stanley's eyebrow lifted. "Here, shredding is only a temporary measure. We incinerate anything we shred."

"We do?" Jorge said. "I didn't know that."

"Yes, we do. Garrick would happily employ battalions of jigsaw puzzle enthusiasts to reconstruct our shreds if I gave him the chance."

An uncomfortable hot sensation crept around Jorge's neck. "I recreated the map of all my escape routes for this mission several times at home. I hadn't been in that facility for a couple of months. I wanted to make sure I knew them cold."

Stanley glanced down.

Hoarsely, Jorge asked, "Sondem is buying my trash from the garbage collector?"

"Possibly," Stanley said.

Jorge buried his face in both hands. "Then it *was* my fault. That poor little girl. That poor family!"

When Stanley fell silent, Jorge knew he'd made him uneasy. His oldest brother was easily the smartest guy he'd ever met. He'd graduated from high school at eleven and finished a PhD at nineteen—while commanding the newly organized Outlander Division, no less. But this brainy guy wasn't so great at handling emotions.

Clearing his throat, Stanley said clumsily, "You mean, that 'poor family' that you—what, rescued from torture and death? That 'poor girl' who's alive to enjoy the clown's antics on the children's ward today?" He grabbed Jorge's shoulder roughly. "Come on, *hermanito*. You made a mistake. It happens. But the outcome was good, thanks to Doug's intervention. And you learned something that will make you a wiser operative in the future." (Spanish: little brother)

Jorge managed to push his self-recrimination aside, more for his brother's sake than because he truly felt better. "Thanks, Stanley. I deserve disciplinary action, and I'll gladly accept whatever you determine necessary. But you're right, I have learned something. I hope it does make me a better special ops man."

Then, in a bid to change the subject, he noted, "You said Sondem could 'possibly' be buying my trash from the garbage collector."

Stanley nodded. "More likely from Willy."

"Willy? You really think he could be involved? He's such a zealot for the New-RAB."

"Yes, he's very sincerely deceived. But deception is a powerful weapon, and one that Stan is very proficient at wielding."

"So proficient that he could convince him to betray his own relatives? I mean, come on! Willy's not a bad sort."

"He doesn't have to be bad. They are good at tricking someone into doing bad things from good motives. They've probably told him that he's helping to right some terrible wrong or that extreme measures are needed to prevent injury to innocent people. It's all done in stages, little by little, manipulating the Subject's vulnerabilities, stroking his ego, and fostering doubt about other people's motives. Once you maneuver him into doing some 'small' thing, you can hold that over him, if need be, to induce him to do something worse."

Jorge shook his head. "I don't know—"

"That's because you don't understand how protected you are as a runner, how protected you've been all your life because you were raised a runner. Debora's counsel, the Royal Guard's shield, the safeguard of Doug's Law—these all shelter you. As the world crumbles from the effects of *kanuf*, you're still secure on Doug's foundation. Willy doesn't have that. His life, his worldview, has no bedrock. He's much more vulnerable to every new philosophy and every swing in public opinion. His world is constantly shifting—it's both more dangerous and more confusing than yours."

An image came to Jorge's mind, a vision of a certain spark that would light Willy's eye, just for a second, whenever the subject of Doug's faithfulness came up. When someone talked about how secure they felt in his care, Jorge would sense a deep yearning within his cousin. But almost immediately something would sneak up behind and sucker-punch the yearning. Fear maybe, or guilt. Whatever it was, it inevitably scored a knockout.

"Okay, I see what you mean," he conceded. "But even without Doug's protection, he still has common sense and family loyalty."

"A good agent can get almost anybody to do almost anything by introducing the right elements of deceit and change—whether promises or threats—into a person's environment at the right time. They simply need to know how to push that Subject's buttons. Getting Willy to collect your trash for Stan? Even I, with my rudimentary training in manipulation, could manage that."

Still unconvinced, Jorge demanded, "How? How, specifically, would you do that?"

"First, I'd capitalize on the word 'trash.' Most people don't feel any particular need to protect what someone has already thrown away. But mostly I'd use his vulnerabilities. Willy's most useful liability is his drive to be important. He's always wanted to show up his cousins and especially his brothers. As an agent, I'd fan that discontent from the time I gained his ear through the New-RAB transmitter. I'd commiserate with him about how everybody belittles him, how no one appreciates him or takes him seriously."

"Yeah, I could see that. Not that it's true, but that's how he sees things."

"Exactly. So then, when I had him primed—he thinks I'm his friend, that I 'get' him, that he can trust me—I start planting ideas that cut down these relatives he's so jealous of. I might insinuate that someone's taking advantage of them, tricking them into doing something bad—whatever I sense will work for him. In this case, I'd spin some lies about the Outlander Division. I'd invent some story he couldn't disprove that explains things he doesn't understand—all the secrecy surrounding your job, for instance—and casts it in a bad light. Stan's been impersonating Gabriel for decades on the New-RAB films. I could use that claim that 'Gabriel' is distraught about the 'damage' you're wrecking. In Willy's case, I'd do this until he asks what he can do about the problem—I'd let him be the one to offer the help. At first I'd say he couldn't help, that it would be too dangerous."

"And that only makes him want to do it more."

"Right—because of his drive to be 'special.' Eventually I relent. I'll tell him that it would really help Gabriel if he could get some information from your computer, your cell phone—or even 'just' your trash. Exactly how long this process takes depends on a number of factors such as what I want the Subject to do, how risky or difficult the task is, how out of character it is for him, and so forth. You can often speed things up by offering rewards like money, fame, or status. And if need be, you can add threats or blackmail. Deceit and threats, flattery and rewards—these are the agents' most useful tools, and they're very adept at using them. I honestly don't think there's a person alive who could withstand them on their own."

Jorge didn't respond. He couldn't deny Stanley's knowledge; after all, Stan himself had trained him in these techniques. Yet it hurt to think that his own cousin could betray him.

CHAPTER 5

RAISED FIST

"Anyone who harms you harms my most precious possession. I will raise my fist to crush them."
Zechariah 2:8, 9, NLT.

Chris paused after passing under the archway that separated the Outlander Division's headquarters from the rest of the Paradisian Embassy in Los Angeles. He was going to an urgent meeting of the Executive Committee, but he could never just barrel through this foyer with its memorial wall. It seemed disrespectful to try, especially now.

He had a process he followed in this room. First, he reflected on the circular seal in the middle of the marble floor, where Josh's military insignia, a lamb, was bordered by the pledge that each soldier in the Outlander Division made: *Because I am covered by his blood, I will daily seek his fellowship and unreservedly obey his call.* He remembered the day Susana had crafted that pledge. Chris had declared they'd never raise an army of individuals willing to make such a sweeping promise. But a twelve-year-old Stanley had insisted that was the army Doug deserved, so that was the army the Outlander Division would be. He'd been right. Last Chris heard, there were 144,000 such individuals.

Next, he looked to the left wall, where the division's motto was inscribed: *We can do all things through him who strengthens us.* He meditated on how Doug had fulfilled that promise time and again throughout his life, even when the goal seemed truly impossible.

He then studied the right wall and the division's mission statement: *To rescue the deceived and restore them to communion with their creator.* Chris was not in the Outlander Division, but he considered himself part of this mission. And there was so much more to do. His own twin sister remained blind to her need, as did all three of her sons. And Willy, currently living with Chris, seemed to be moving deeper and deeper into the dark cavern of deception.

Finally, Chris walked respectfully around the central seal to the Wall of Victors straight ahead of him. Across the top of this wall were inscribed the words: *Be faithful, even to the point of death; I will give you life as your victor's crown.* Below this were rows and rows of pictures of fallen soldiers. He solemnly gazed at each face and read the accompanying plaques, lingering over those he'd known personally, like Lorenzo and Monica Wells. He'd known Lorenzo as a child, and he'd coached both him and his young wife, who grew to be close friends of Stanley and Bethany. But today he was able to mourn them with new sympathy—and with new determination that their deaths would not be in vain.

"Thought I'd find you here." Stanley's hand fell on Chris's shoulder.

"We're ready to start."

Chris nodded. "Did I ever tell you about Josh's prophecy when Bethany was born?"

"No," Stanley said with obvious interest.

"He said, 'She and her husband will do a work unprecedented in both type and importance.' " Chris swept the foyer with his arm before meeting the younger man's gaze. "Doug has done amazing work through you, son. Your commitment to him and your reliance upon him have allowed him to finish what needed to be done before the Awakening."

Stanley seemed to swallow hard. "Thanks, Dad," he said hoarsely.

They proceeded down the hallway to a conference room. As the committee members greeted Chris warmly, he realized that Susana had helped almost every one of these young leaders reach their fullest potential.

Stanley leaned over to whisper, "Are you all right, Dad? You look a little overawed."

"I was just realizing how important your mom's influence was. She lived well, son."

"My beloved biological father doesn't waste his resources on those who don't," Stanley returned dryly.

Showing Chris to a chair beside Andy, Stanley rounded the table to call the meeting to order. As Chris watched him efficiently dispatch several problems, he mused that he was truly proud to call this man both son and son-in-law ... even though some might consider it a rather unconventional arrangement.

When Chris's daughter, Bethany, the chief medical officer for the Outlander Division, swept through the door, she was still in surgical scrubs. "I'm so sorry, General. I came as quickly as I could."

"It's all right, Colonel." Stanley's eyes softened as he pulled out a chair for her, now four months pregnant with their third child. "We got the message that you were still in surgery on the young girl that Jorge rescued. The skin graft went well?"

"Yes. I think she'll heal fine. Oh—and Jorge will be right along. He was speaking with her family."

Jorge came through the door as she finished, and Stanley lifted a hand to announce lightheartedly, "Behold, the lost is found!"

Jorge made several elaborate bows to the applause (and chuckles) of the other officers, all of whom had worried over his recent disappearance. Physically Jorge was much smaller than the rest of the family—five-foot-six and very lean. But what he lacked in size, he made up for in personality. He seemed to consider it his calling to entertain.

When Jorge tired of the limelight, Stanley said, "I've called this meeting at Doug's behest. He directed that my dad, whom you all know, join us, as well as my sister-in-law, Lieutenant Riana Strider. Since everyone's now here, I'll connect to our king without further delay."

Placing the red phone in the center of the table on speakerphone, he said, "Your Majesty, the Executive Council of the Outlander Division is assembled per your request. All members are present plus the two guests you specified."

"Howdy, y'all," Doug answered. "Thank you for coming. I've called this meetin' because I have an important announcement. As y'all know, Stan Moden and I have been at war for over 6,000 years, but it's been more of a cold war since the Battle of Grace Hill. What most of y'all don't know is that this uneasy cease-fire has been secured only within the bounds of certain rules."

Stanley nodded as if he understood exactly what Doug meant—something he knew from his training as Stan's heir, no doubt. Although that training sometimes made it difficult for him to relate to normal people, it had provided him with invaluable information that helped him direct the Outlander Division.

"A week ago Stan ordered an attack on Chris and Susana Strider, a clear violation of a hands-off order that has been in place for over twenty years," Doug continued. "According to the terms Stan himself agreed to, this violation voids the ceasefire agreement between us. That means it's time to bring this war to its conclusion, time to fight the battle that will forever end all war."

Everyone seemed to lean forward in their seats. The room fell absolutely still.

"In other words," Doug said, "I'm callin' the Final Battle."

Chris nearly jumped up and cheered. The Final Battle meant the Awakening was near! He'd see Susana again, be reunited with Josh, and meet Doug on Paradise Island!

Most of those around the table accepted the news matter-of-factly, as if they'd been expecting it. Stanley had likely anticipated the move and prepared his ranking officers for it. Only Riana gasped in surprise. Andy, seated between her and Chris, grasped his wife's hand. "It's okay," he whispered. "We're ready."

" 'Do not tremble, do not be afraid.' " Doug's voice was tender as he quoted from *The Runner's Manual*. " 'Did I not proclaim this and foretell it long ago?' *Kanuf's* effects are now so pervasive that the earth itself is being destroyed, little fawn. I need to bring Stan's little experiment to an end. It may seem sudden to you, but this date's been on my calendar from the beginning. All's well."

"Thank you, Doug," Riana said.

"What do you need us to do?" Stanley asked.

"For your marching orders, I'm turning you over to your *Mikaél*."

"Good evening, ladies and gentlemen," came Josh's familiar baritone.

"Good evening, sir," Stanley said. "The Executive Council is assembled and awaiting your orders."

"Thank you, General. Your orders are as follows. First you, Stanley, must personally deliver the Declaration of Battle to President Stan Moden. Jorge, you are to assist in this mission."

Bethany locked eyes with her husband, her face losing some of its color. But Stanley responded without hesitation. "Understood, sir. And thank you."

Chris empathized with his daughter's concern for Stanley's safety; after all, Josh had just ordered Stanley—the number one man on Stan's hit list—to walk right into his birth parents' lair. However, he also understood the yearning behind Stanley's gratitude. His adopted son still had three siblings locked within the lies of Moden Industries. For two decades, he had masterminded numerous operations to rescue others from Stan's grasp. Yet his own biological brothers and sister still lay beyond his reach. Though knowing the danger, he had begged his commander-in-chief for an opportunity to personally invite them to accept Doug's rescue. Now, by insisting that the declaration be delivered in person, Doug was giving Stanley that chance.

"Second," Josh continued, "You, Andy, are to deploy the troops according to the plans already in place. Stanley will not return to the LA headquarters. You will assume command in his absence."

"Understood, sir." Andy, Chris's second son, didn't seem at all flustered by the order. But then, he was the division's second-in-command and had been at Stanley's side from the beginning. Stanley had probably prepared him for it.

"Third, several of you will leave your homes in two days and will not return. Stanley, Bethany, Jorge, and Chris, I'm speaking to you. Say your good-byes and pack light. Chris, bring along Juan Misi's necklace. You won't have another chance to retrieve it before you return it to him."

"Glad to!" Chris exclaimed. For almost four decades, he'd been the guardian of his great-grandfather's trophy, the reminder of all the lessons his ancestor had learned on Doug's racecourse. The assurance that he would soon be returning it to Juan Misi was another indication that the Awakening was near.

Josh continued: "And make the necessary arrangements to turn your medical practice over to your partner."

Chris frowned. "Um, am I hearing you right? You want me to legally transfer my share of the practice to Efraím—in two days?"

"Yes, *boní*. My dad's prepared your partner and your lawyer for this. It won't be as hard as it sounds." (Rarámuri: younger brother)

Although he didn't understand the whys and wherefores of the order, Chris had too much experience with Josh to question it further. With a shrug he said, "Okay, Josh, if you say so."

Andy elbowed him and whispered, "He's speaking as our commander-in-chief, not your coach."

"Oh—then I mean, Yes, sir!" Chris saluted but couldn't keep the silly grin off his face.

Josh chuckled. "Thank you for maintaining order, Colonel Strider."

Sitting forward, Jorge said, "Sir, although I have the greatest confidence in my brother's abilities, I don't think even he can just saunter into Desmon Tower. I know Doug's put a hands-off order on him, but if they violated Mom's, they'll certainly have no qualms about violating Stanley's."

"Correct on every point, Captain," Josh said. "We will work out that problem in committee immediately following this meeting."

"How do I obtain the Declaration of Battle?" Stanley asked.

"Your uncle, General Gabriel Lanáj, will meet you in New York with the documents," Josh said. "Any other questions?"

When no one raised a hand, Stanley said, "Not at this time, sir."

"Very well," Josh said. "Then I'm returning control of this meeting to my father. I'll stand by to meet with the subcommittee he designates."

"All right, group," Doug said. "This is the event we've been workin' toward for six millennia. The days ahead won't be easy. But the end is certain." His voice grew tender. "I'm itchin' to hug each of you myself, and it won't be long now."

Expectant smiles lit each face, and Chris's own excitement mounted.

Continuing, Doug said, "Now I'm gonna ask y'all to split into two groups. Josh will meet with Stanley, Bethany, Jorge, Chris, and Riana in this room. Andy will chair the meeting between me and the rest of y'all in the other conference room."

When their committee reconvened, Josh expressed their objective concisely. "Okay, group, our assignment is to figure out how to get Stanley in and out of Desmon Tower—alive."

A long and sometimes impassioned discussion ensued. Ultimately it centered around Riana's area of expertise: explosives.

✵ ✵ ✵ ✵ ✵

As Willy entered the house, he passed the open door to his uncle's study and then backtracked to listen in on a bizarre phone conversation.

"Yeah, Efraím," Uncle Chris was saying. "Two days. Josh wants me to legally turn the practice over to you before then."

He's selling his practice in two days? Why haven't I heard about this?

"Doug didn't say where he's sending me, only that I won't be back."

Wait a minute—he's leaving? Permanently? Then what am I supposed to do?

"Okay, I'll get things squared away with the lawyer. And Efraím, thanks. You've been a great friend and partner through the years."

He's really saying goodbye to his longtime buddy from medical school. This is serious!

When his uncle hung up, Willy entered the study. "Uncle Chris, I couldn't help overhearing. Are you leaving?"

His uncle looked up. "Willy—good. I need to talk to you. Have a seat."

As they settled into the overstuffed chairs by the window, Willy asked, "What's going on?"

"Son, you know that Stan Moden had Susana killed. What you don't know is that it was an act of war, one that violated the longstanding ceasefire between Stan and Doug. Essentially, it will precipitate the Final Battle."

"Really?" Willy's tone betrayed his skepticism. Uncle Chris was always talking about a war between those two super-moguls, but Willy hadn't seen any evidence of it. And when he asked Ms. Menod about it, she'd said the only "war" was the one the fanatics in the Outlander Division wanted to start. Yes, Aunt Susana had been murdered, but for all he knew it had been a burglar, not some mythical boogie man.

Uncle Chris released a soft sigh. "Look, I know we don't always see eye to eye on things where Doug's concerned. I only wish I could help you understand before it's too late."

Willy was in no mood for another of *those* lectures. Quickly he said, "I've got to run right now. I just came home to grab something. And I don't mean to sound ungrateful. I really do appreciate all your help. But if I need to find a new place to stay within two days, I need to get working on it."

Uncle Chris gazed at him with a sad expression that was *so* irritating. Mom's brother was a nice guy—he really was. He'd welcomed Willy into his house and made him feel at home, just as he had the other cousins that had attended college in LA. But the free room and board came with a different kind of price tag: listening to his extremist ideas. He was such a fanatic about running. And he had such strict views of right and wrong. Willy had tried to introduce him to more tolerant ideas, to help him see that what was right for one person wasn't necessarily right for everyone else and that people from different cultures might relate to Doug in different ways. But Uncle Chris seemed to believe that he had the only correct perspective where Doug was concerned, and his close-mindedness could really be exasperating.

Worse, such arrogant intolerance hindered King Doug's plans for global unification and peace. People needed to drop their petty emphasis on the trivialities that separated them and focus on the more important things that united them.

"No, Willy," Uncle Chris said at last. "You don't have to leave. You can stay as long as you like—at least until the world ends."

Willy managed to avoid rolling his eyes. But really, was all the melodrama necessary?

"Jorge and I will be leaving in two days," his uncle continued. "We won't be back. I hope we can talk again before then."

"Sure, Uncle Chris. And thanks. You can count on me to take good care of the place."

Willy ran up the stairs to his room. But when he opened the door, he stopped short. The briefcase that Ms. Menod had given him for transporting the household's shredded documents was lying open on his bed, and he sure hadn't left it there. He muttered a curse, which he repeated with increasing fervor as he drew nearer the case. It was empty.

Who had done this? And where were the two bags of shreds that had been in that briefcase?

"I burned them," came Jorge's voice from the shadows behind Willy.

The unexpected voice startled him, and he jumped before spinning to the intruder. "Burned what?"

"I know what you've been doing, cuz. Stanley figured it out."

"I don't know what you're talking about."

"How much did Stan pay you to betray us? Is that where your new Mustang came from—blood money?"

"Stan? You think I sold you out to Stan?"

"I didn't want to believe it. Then I remembered seeing that briefcase in here. Funny thing, you having such a fine case that you never carry."

Having been caught red-handed, Willy gave up the know-nothing act. But he wasn't about to let Jorge make him into the traitor. He wasn't the one involved in a radical terrorist organization. "I didn't sell you out to Stan. I didn't sell you out at all. The guy you say you're working for, General Gabriel Lanáj, wanted the stuff. He asked me to help him undo the damage you've been causing without his authority."

Jorge's surprised expression was priceless.

Wagging his head, Willy pressed his advantage. "You think you're so righteous. You claim to be working for Doug, but you're really working against him. I hope you didn't know this, but a terrorist called The Phantom used your information to bomb an embassy in Peru. The stuff I gave General Lanáj allowed his men to find the device before it exploded. We saved as many as a hundred lives."

Jorge stared at him, obviously dumbstruck. Finally he said quietly, "Willy, your intel is a little off. Someone's been feeding you lies. I know The Phantom—quite well, actually. He's never bombed or intended to bomb anything. He used that last batch of information to free a family that Stan had taken captive, including a five-year-old girl. Because of the information you handed over, they were intercepted by Stan's men and almost killed. The little girl was badly hurt. I visited her in the hospital this afternoon."

Willy faltered momentarily before yelling, "You're the one getting suckered! I meet regularly with General Lanáj's own special assistant!"

"I meet regularly with General Lanáj himself," Jorge countered. "And he's fully aware of all our operations. What's more, I talk to King Doug every day."

"I don't believe you!"

Jorge shook his head with that same sad expression that Uncle Chris had worn. And if it was irritating on his uncle's face, it was downright maddening on his cousin's.

"Willy, honestly, I'm telling you the truth. I know The Phantom well. I've met the family he rescued on that mission. I saw the horrible wounds on the little girl's legs from the dogs Stan's men sicked on her. If you would just talk to Doug directly with a real transmitter, he could help you see that you're being used by the wrong side. They're lying to you."

Willy had had enough of this crazy emphasis on trifling details. What did it matter which model of transmitter he used? What difference did it make which RAB he chose to attend? For that matter, why was it such a big deal that he preferred swimming to running? These legalistic radicals had no appreciation of personal liberty, no room in their little brains for opposing views.

Disgusted, he said, "I have to go. I'm late as it is. Snatching his backpack from his desk, he added, "But, please, feel free to make yourself comfortable in my 'private' room."

As he drove back to campus, Jorge's claims played themselves over in Willy's mind. As he argued aloud with his absent cousin, he pressed home all of King Doug's good intentions and frustrated goals that he'd heard from Ms. Menod. And he became more and more certain of his own honorable position and more and more angry at Jorge for accusing him unjustly. By the time he arrived at campus, he was again fully convinced of the necessity of his actions and the justice of the cause he'd espoused.

Sitting in his car, he activated the transmitter around his neck and waited only a minute or two before the voice of his agent, Cherisse, came over the line. He always enjoyed talking to her. She got how unappreciated he was. She didn't consider him too young or immature to do important work. She was the one who first confided to him that the Outlander Division was causing most of Doug's trouble. And she had introduced him to Ms. Menod so he could help. He didn't relish the thought of admitting to her that his cousin had discovered his activities. But then, maybe he didn't have to. He'd just report that Chris and Jorge were moving. That way, Cherisse would still trust him with future assignments.

CHAPTER 6

DECLARATION

"Declare what is to be, present it–let them take counsel together.
Who foretold this long ago, who declared it from the distant past?
Was it not I, the Lord?"
Isaiah 45:21, NIV.

Protected by the diplomatic ribbon on his chest, Stanley strode down the familiar hallway of Desmon Tower's top floor with a confident step. Undisguised glares followed him. To these Paradisian exiles, he was the crown prince who had betrayed them twenty-four years before. Every individual, from the highest executive to the lowliest janitor, despised him. The very air was electrified by their rage.

Yet he was glad to be here. Since he'd defected to Doug's ranks, hundreds of other Paradisian offspring had followed his example. Yet none of his three siblings had. He had long yearned for the opportunity to personally invite them to accept Doug's rescue. He didn't know how he'd manage that in his parents' presence. But it was a chance, the only chance he'd ever have.

Arriving at the desk of Stan's executive secretary, he formally introduced himself. "Good afternoon, Madelyn. I am Major General Stanley Strider Lanáj, commander of the Outlander Division of the *Ekanu Mejad Paladisi* and emissary of Doúg Deón Damoúr, King of Paradise Island." (Paradisian: Paradisian Royal Army)

Madelyn's almond eyes grew round. "Stanley! *You're* the emissary we're expecting?"

"I am. My father is available, I presume?" He framed it as a question but voiced it as a command, exactly as Father had trained him.

"He's waiting for—" Her eyes rested on his diplomatic ribbon, and she nervously twirled the white streak in her long black hair. "—well, apparently for you."

"Excellent. I'm sure you'll notify my mother of my arrival. Please notify my brothers and sister as well."

He didn't await her response; that would imply that she could refuse it. Instead, he stepped to Stan's office door and quirked an eyebrow at her as if impatient. She buzzed him through.

The senior Stan did not look up from his desk when his long lost son entered—a deliberate move to make Doug's emissary, whomever it might be, feel unimportant. Taking advantage of this, Stanley examined his father closely. The renowned mogul looked no older than when he had fled from him. In fact, though over 8,000 years old, his father appeared as young and robust as Stanley himself.

Glancing around the plush office, Stanley noted that little had changed there either. The cello and nine-foot Steinway, the bookshelves of collector's volumes, the paintings and sculptures, the case of Yankees memorabilia—all were as they'd been twenty-four years before.

With that thought, time seemed to warp backward, and he was again a fearful ten-year-old, daunted by his father's greatness and despairing of ever living up to his expectations. The adult Stanley recognized that Stan cultivated that sense of intimidation very purposefully. Yet the knowledge did nothing to blunt its effectiveness. Simply being in the same room with the man rekindled intense feelings of inadequacy.

Determinedly, he squared his shoulders. Enough! Yes, his father was more powerful, more intelligent, and more experienced than him—and he should remember that. Still, he dare not let his insecurities spoil the opportunity he'd sought for so long. What's more, he had no real reason to fear. King Doúg had chosen him for this meeting. Prince Joshua had thoroughly prepped him for it. And after rescuing him from Father as a child, they would certainly not abandon him to his virulent hatred now.

Reaching up, he rubbed his transmitter, a silent plea for help. With the device in privacy mode, only he could hear Doug's immediate response: "I'm here, son. I'll be with you every moment. My grace is all you need for any eventuality."

His tense jaw relaxed. He was ready, not because he was more powerful than Father, but because Doug was.

Striding across the massive office to the desk, he drew himself up to his full height and said, clearly and unapologetically, "Father."

Stan looked up and nearly dropped his pen. Jumping to his feet, his surprise melted into a smirk. "Well, the prodigal son returns."

Camille entered as he spoke, followed by two young men and a younger woman.

"Mother." Stanley nodded politely to her. Addressing the other three, he said, "Saxon, Sheridan, Sadira—I am your brother, Stanley Strider Lanáj."

Each one nodded an impassive greeting and assumed a position behind the desk. On Stan's immediate left, Camille hadn't changed at all since Stanley last saw her. She was as elegant, and as coolly formidable, as ever. Beside her stood thirty-one-year-old Saxon, the company's executive vice president, in an expensive custom-made suit. At 6'2" and 220 pounds, he was less herculean than his brothers, but his prowess in the martial arts reportedly compensated for his relative lack of muscle.

At Father's right stood Sadira, president of America's largest business at only twenty-two. Stanley had never understood why his parents chose the youngest child for that position, but he had assumed their favoritism would cause some friction and rivalry between the siblings. Yet he saw no evidence of that. In fact, he actually felt a twinge of jealousy as he surveyed them. Something had changed since he'd been part of this family. They conveyed a certain cohesiveness, as though they shared a common purpose, did things together, and maybe even dined together. The picture tugged at his heartstrings, toying with the remnants of his childhood need for his parents' approval and affection.

Near the front of Stan's desk, wearing a richly medaled military uniform, stood twenty-eight-year-old Sheridan. Roughly Stanley's size, Sheridan radiated smug self-confidence. And his arrogance was not unfounded. He'd become commander of Stan's army only after crushing several talented rivals.

Stanley still wrestled with his feelings toward this brother. Emotionally, the rawness of his loss cried out for vengeance against Susana's murderer. Yet, considered rationally, Susana's death was merely part of a mission, a direct order from Sheridan's commander-in-chief. As a soldier himself, Stanley understood the duty to carry out orders. Besides, he wanted to view his brother's action with some element of charity.

But as he took his measure, a contemptuous glint came into Sheridan's eye, as if he knew Stanley's thoughts and was mocking his pain. It was not the expression of a soldier who had dispassionately carried out an order, but of a hit man who exulted in his work. Sheridan was actually proud of having murdered the selfless woman whom Stanley had called Mom.

That expression ignited a smoldering fury deep within Stanley. He'd been able to rationalize his brother's deed before looking him in the eye. But he could never do so now. He saw nothing redeemable in this man and nothing defensible in his actions. He could never—he *would* never—forgive him.

Drawing Stanley's focus, Camille said, "You have some gall coming here."

"Gall perhaps," Stan said with a snort. "But not much in the way of brains."

"Oh, yes. Thank you for reminding me." Unbuttoning his uniform jacket, Stanley continued, "You didn't think I'd trust your assurance of safe conduct, did you, Father? You taught me better than that." Holding Stan's cold green eyes, he opened his jacket to reveal the bomb he wore.

Except for the slightest twitch of Sheridan's left eyebrow, Moden Industries' well-trained first family remained impassive. Stan's chuckle broke the momentary silence. "Well, perhaps you did learn something from me after all. I suppose that device would explode if any pressure's applied to it—including, perhaps, your falling to the floor dead?"

"Of course," Stanley said. "Isn't that what you'd do?"

"A handheld trigger as well, should you feel threatened. And there appears to be enough explosive there to take out the entire family, thereby exterminating our top leaders in one blow."

"Actually, there's enough explosive here to blow Desmon Tower off the map."

"Tsk, tsk. Damour doesn't like lying. A bomb that size couldn't possibly do such damage."

"You mean you never perfected X-49?" Though truly surprised, Stanley welcomed the discovery. When Stan didn't answer, Stanley shrugged. "I did. And I'm sure you'll be gratified to learn that it's every bit the stable, highly compact explosive you'd hoped for."

Stan's color rose. "Impossible. I hadn't trained you in explosives yet. You never even saw that compound."

"True. But I did see the file in the Priority Computer before I left, including not only its formula, but your very thorough and helpful notes on the problems you were experiencing with it. Perfecting it was a simple matter with all that information."

Stan's eyes narrowed. "I see." Undoubtedly, the combination of Stanley's photographic memory and his unrestricted access to Moden Industries' Priority Computer had caused his father numerous sleepless nights.

Stan glanced at Camille, who shook her head slightly, before reseating himself. "Well, since your mother and I agree that you seem an unlikely suicide bomber, I suppose we can all relax."

"Yes, I have no desire to die today. In fact, my wife and I have a dinner engagement tonight. She'd be upset if I stood her up." Seizing the tiny opening this tangent might create, he continued without pause, "I don't believe you've met my wife, the daughter of Dr. Christian Strider, son of Juan Misi. What an incredible man he turned out to be—the strongest man I've ever met."

Though not a typical segue into the topic of Doug's rescue, this description would rouse his siblings' interest, for they'd been raised to value strength above all else. Indeed, although outwardly Sheridan scoffed and Saxon raised a dubious brow, their eyes betrayed curiosity.

"Ridiculous," Camille said scornfully, while Stan exclaimed, "Strong? He's only a human!"

"Yes," Stanley agreed. "Yet Doug's so fortified him that I'm sure Sheridan saw no fear in him whatever, even when threatened with torture and death. If Doug can work out such strength in a human, what could he do with a Paradisian?"

"Make him into quite the slobbering puppy, it seems," Camille said.

"So you've taken his name, have you?" Stan said.

"Yes, I've taken the name of the man who was a true father to me. I've also chosen to perpetuate the motto of my parents' *yushún*." (Paradisian: family) His siblings' expressions registered subtle traces of surprise while their parents' glares sharpened. Not yet registering the cause, Stanley finished his thought. "I couldn't keep that presumptuous name of yours, now could I, Father? Even Mother won't use that."

"That's quite enough," Stan warned.

But Stanley had realized what had triggered his parents' alarm—the embarrassing secret he'd alluded to—and it just might help weaken his siblings' bond to them. "Quite enough what, Father? Do you mean my mention of you and Mother coming from the same *yushún*? You don't want my siblings to know about your incestuous marriage? I have to admit, I was certainly shocked when I learned you were biologically brother and sister."

Stan sprang up to round the desk, the pinkish scar on his left cheek turning beet red. Stanley lifted the trigger, reminding him that an attack would be unwise. Stan's eyes flicked to the trigger, to the bomb, and back to his son's face. Stanley stood firm under the glower, keeping his facial muscles relaxed in the blank expression Mother had taught him.

Camille quickly slipped her hand into Stan's—a pragmatic move. Skin contact allowed her to transfer some of her seemingly limitless self-control to her fiery-tempered linkmate.

Stanley employed the brief pause to deposit more taboo information into his siblings' data banks. "After being told repeatedly that all our relatives had died in the war, I was also surprised to learn that we have family still living on the island—an aunt and three uncles, including Father's identical twin brother, who commands Doug's army."

Saxon's and Sadira's pupils dilated, although Sheridan remained unaffected.

"Yes," Stanley said, "I suppose Sheridan would need the information about Uncle Gabriel, wouldn't he? They withheld the information from the rest of us to contribute to our sense of isolation—so we'd feel trapped, with no support outside this building. In reality we have more family outside this organization than within it. And Doug reestablishes all who accept his clemency in families of their own."

"I should warn you about working with family," Stan said sharply. "They sometimes betray you."

"Yes," Stanley said meaningfully. "Uncle Gabriel has mentioned that too."

Again stepping toward him, Stan ground out, "I believe I can wring your neck just fine without applying any pressure to that bomb."

Stanley held up the trigger. "Please try. I don't *want* to die today. Frankly, my wife is worrying over that possibility right now. But from a tactical perspective, my death would be a small price to pay for ending the war right here, right now."

Camille grabbed for Stan's hand and then winced as he squeezed it. But her intervention worked once more. Stan stalked away to stare out the floor-to-ceiling window, back turned, arms crossed.

Meanwhile, Camille echoed Stanley's words thoughtfully, an odd expression in her eye. "She's worrying '*right* now'?" She studied Stanley intently. "Is it really possible that you two are linked?"

Stan spun from the window. "What? Is this true?"

Stanley held his silence but mentally excoriated himself. He sometimes forgot how odd it was that he should know his wife's exact emotional state. But Camille, an astute psychologist who was herself linked, would certainly not miss such a reference. And his parents would see the gift as a great vulnerability to be used against him.

At his silence, his parents exchanged a satisfied glance before Camille said, "Enough chatter. You were granted safe passage for a reason, young man. Under what pretext do you trespass upon our headquarters?"

Stanley extracted a light blue envelope with Doug's royal seal from his jacket pocket. "I bring a message from my king—a Declaration of Battle."

Stan strode forward to snatch the letter while Stanley summarized its contents: "He's honoring the request for battle presupposed by your attempt on my adoptive parents, thereby violating their hands-off orders."

"Attempt?" Stan snapped. "General Moden, did you misinform me, boy? Wasn't that attempt fifty percent successful?"

With a sneer trained on Stanley, Sheridan answered, "I personally assured a fifty percent success rate, Father."

Seeing another potential opening, Stanley said, "Then there must have been a substantive change to Clause 11.4 of the Protocol for the Termination of Runners. Because when I left, it read: 'A strategic mission will be considered successful only if its completion results in a favorable change in the attitudes of surviving runners or in the prevention of imminent defection of non-runners.' Under that definition, I can assure you, your *attempt* was completely unsuccessful, for you failed to consider the power of Doug's grace to sustain his runners through any difficulty."

"You've certainly developed an annoying propensity to preach, haven't you?" Camille snapped.

"I do seem to remember a childhood tendency toward inane babbling," Saxon said innocently. Stanley's neck warmed as he remembered how his rambling had annoyed his father.

To distract them all from his embarrassment, Stanley motioned to the pages of light blue parchment that his father was now scanning. "Due to the scattered nature of your states, King Doúg has granted you a four-month preparatory period. The Final Battle will commence on February 12."

"Good," Stan said. He handed the document to Sheridan. "We're looking forward to it." Leveling a stony glare at his eldest son, he added, "I'll enjoy personally carving your heart from your chest."

"Your errand is now complete," Camille said. "You have no further reason to impose your presence upon us. Please see yourself out."

Stanley searched for some way to extend the interaction. He'd been able to interject so little of how important Doug was to him! And his siblings' subtle responses had shown only the slightest hint of interest. Wasn't there something more he could say?

As if listening in on his thoughts, Doug said, "You've done all that can be done, son."

"Well," Stanley said aloud, "if we've exhausted all the celebration your firstborn's homecoming can generate, I suppose I'll be off."

Shaking Saxon's hand, he said, "It's good to see you again. I do wish we weren't on opposite sides of this war; I've missed you."

Refusing to offer his hand to Sheridan, he said merely, "I'll see you on the battlefield. I believe we have a score to settle."

Continuing to Sadira, he extended his hand. "Unfortunately, it seems our only acquaintance will be as adversaries. I would have liked the opportunity to know you."

She didn't reply, but as he withdrew his hand, he realized she'd transferred a piece of paper to his palm. He carefully hid it and his reaction to it as he left the office, but he was impatient to read it. Could it be that his pleas actually had an effect on his sister?

✳ ✳ ✳ ✳ ✳

Back at the offices of the Outlander Division, housed within the Paradisian Embassy in New York, Stanley whistled his way down the hallway to the lounge at the far end. He was itching to tell Chris the exciting news Bethany had just reported. Plus he really needed his wise mentor's advice. As he approached the lounge, Chris yanked open the door from the inside. "Stanley! I'm so glad to see you intact!"

"Yes. Mission accomplished."

"So, what's the scoop?"

"Oh," Stanley replied nonchalantly, "we're naming our son after you." Not the news Dad had asked about, but Stanley couldn't wait to share it.

Dad's face lit up with his ready smile. "The ultrasound today—it's a boy?"

"So they say."

"Congratulations!" Chris pumped his hand. "And you're really naming him after me?"

"Yes, with the hope that he'll grow to be half the man his namesake is."

"Thank you, son," Chris said, obviously affected. "That means a lot." He drew him into a hug and then waved him to the sofa while reseating himself in the corduroy easy chair. They exchanged a few more words about the baby before Chris returned to his original question. "Now tell me—how did things go at Desmon Tower?"

"Well, I have good news, bad news, and puzzling news."

"Let me guess—the good news is that you're alive to tell me about the bad news and the puzzling news?"

Stanley chuckled. "Yes, that's about it."

"Then hit me. What's the bad news?"

Stanley sobered. "Dad, I—" He rubbed a hand over his face. "They know about our link. I made some comment without even realizing it could point to it. But my mother doesn't miss anything."

"And this is a problem because … they'll use it against you?"

"I couldn't have handed them a more powerful weapon." Stanley's agitation forced him to his feet, and he began pacing. "And once they realize she's pregnant, grabbing her will become one of their very highest priorities."

Chris didn't respond, but the concern etched in his brow said it all.

Dropping onto the sofa to capture Chris's eye, he said earnestly, "Dad, I promise I'll protect her. I've already told her we can't go anywhere public, including tonight's dinner. I'll do whatever it takes to keep her safe."

"I know you will, son. It's not her safety that concerns me. It's what this could do to you."

"To me?"

"Just look at you—I can't remember when I last saw you pace."

Stanley buried his face in his hands. "I don't think I've ever been this worried, Dad."

"That's my point. Stan's linked—he knows the strength of the attachment. He knows he doesn't necessarily have to touch Beth to affect you. The threat alone could serve his purpose of reducing your effectiveness."

Stanley nodded thoughtfully. "All he really has to do is distract me."

"Take reasonable steps to protect her, yes. But don't let the problem absorb you and sap your mental energies. Commit it to Doug and follow his direction, then let him bear the weight of the burden."

Stanley stared at the ground for a moment before looking up with a crooked grin. "Well, since I seem to have a free evening, I guess I've got plenty of time to talk to Doug about it, don't I?"

Chris chuckled. "You mentioned some puzzling news?"

Stanley pulled Sadira's note from his pocket. "My sister slipped me this."

Chris read aloud: "Please help me. I want to serve Damour." He studied Stanley's face. "I know you were hoping to influence your siblings toward Doug. You don't think this is a response to your words?"

"I'd like to think so, but it can't be. I didn't see her write it, so she must have done that earlier."

"H'mm." Chris silently reread the note. "So, a trap?"

"That's what I'm afraid of."

"Would Stan risk her safety after expending so much time grooming her to manage the company? She'd be awfully hard to replace."

"That's what he'd want me to think—to judge her as too valuable for him to endanger as a spy. But the corporation is only his means of financing the war. With the war's end in sight, he'll probably be shutting it down. That would make her much less valuable to him, and we all know how 'attached' they are to their kids."

"Yes, I see what you mean."

"So ..." Stanley expelled a harsh sigh. "I don't know what to think. What would you do, Dad?"

Chris's face crinkled into a pensive frown. "Remember the story of the wheat and the tares in the *Manual*?"

Stanley nodded. "You think Doug would sooner have tares grow among the wheat temporarily than risk losing one of his true runners?"

"That's my guess. But see what he says."

They lapsed into a companionable silence as Stanley's mind wandered to the changes he'd seen in his birth family. They'd actually looked like a family. What would it be like to do things with his parents? What would it feel like to have Father call him "boy" with a hint of fondness, as he had Sheridan today?

He felt a bit guilty wondering about such things. After all, his adoptive parents had been great to him, freely lavishing on him the love he'd never received from his birth parents. Chris and Susana had risked their lives, and even their children's lives, to give him a true home and make him a part of a real family. He wouldn't trade what he'd enjoyed with them, or the chance to live his life as Doug's follower, for whatever small bit of family spirit the Modens had managed to cobble together. And he certainly wouldn't want to offend Chris by letting him see that he still craved his birth parents' love.

"If a swan is raised by ducks," Chris said, interrupting his thoughts, "does he cease to see the beauty of the other swans?"

"I suppose not," Stanley said.

"Nor are the ducks insulted when he does."

Stanley smiled. How Chris figured out things like this was still a mystery, but he felt liberated by the validation of his feelings. Sitting forward, he rested his elbows on his knees. "They looked like a real family today. Like they belonged together, maybe even enjoyed being together."

"I'm sure things changed after you left. They realized they needed some kind of connection with their children—"

"Offspring."

"Pardon?"

"We were never children, only offspring."

"I see," Chris said. "Well, they probably figured out that even 'offspring' need to feel some identification with their 'parental units' in order to absorb the principles they wanted to impart."

Stanley's gaze wandered to the rug. "I know he's a terrible man, the very personification of evil. I know of the wanton pain he causes, his ruthlessness, his unchecked drive for power. And yet, seeing him today somehow renewed all my childhood thirst for his affection, even though I know that's an impossible dream."

"It's normal for children to seek a relationship with their birth parents," Chris said. "But when parents are unwilling, even unable, to fulfill that yearning, it doesn't mean the child is undeserving."

Stanley looked up, intending to say something, but the words caught in his throat. Looking down again, he managed to whisper, "Thanks, Dad."

He waited until he had more control of his voice before starting again. "There are some things I've always meant to say to you. When I was looking Stan in the eye today, fingering the trigger of that bomb, I realized that I never had."

He paused, ordering his thoughts. "When you first adopted me, I only told you part of the reason why I knew so much about you. It was true that I knew all the runners, especially the high-risk Subjects. But the truth is, I used to sit and stare at your picture every day. I wanted so badly for Father to look at me, even once, with the same tenderness in his eyes that I saw in yours. Sometimes I'd pretend you were my father and that your expression was directed at me. That's why I learned Rarámuri, as part of that fantasy. I still remember the first time you looked at me like that, down at the hacienda in Chihuahua. I felt like I finally had a real home, a real family. A real father."

His eyes watered as he met Chris's gaze. "Thanks for that, Dad. Thanks for everything."

CHAPTER 7

SHUDDER

"Tremble, you complacent women; shudder,
you daughters who feel secure!"
Isaiah 32:11, NIV.

13 October 8043 M.E.

Camille Desmon finished the day's work and headed down the hallway to her brother's office. When she found Sadira pondering a chemical formula at her worktable there, she greeted her. "Good evening. How are you feeling about tomorrow?" Sadira would defend her dissertation for her PhD in chemistry the following day.

Sadira flashed a self-assured smile. "I'm calm and confident, Mother."

"Excellent." Yes indeed, they had certainly chosen the right offspring as president of Moden Industries. Sadira was intelligent, capable, and possessed all the necessary leadership qualities. She even projected Stan's self-confidence, almost as if she truly were his daughter.

"I shall wish you good luck, although I'm certain you won't need it." Camille nodded to the flowers on the worktable. "Who sent these?"

"Austin Pim. But the real question is, Who sent these?" Sadira's blue-green eyes twinkled as she held up a box of chocolate truffles. "Would you like one? They just arrived from 'A Secret Admirer.' "

Camille inspected the proffered card and scoffed. "Any man who won't identify himself isn't worth the trouble, child." Selecting a piece, she added, "Although there's no harm in enjoying the chocolate, is there?"

"My thoughts, exactly, Mother."

A good child, this one.

Camille didn't love the offspring she'd raised; she didn't even like them all. In fact, she barely tolerated Sheridan and thoroughly despised Stanley. But she did like Sadira, who was sharp and perceptive as well as creative and obliging. All this despite her one fundamental flaw: she was merely human.

Sadira didn't know this, of course. The "Paradisian" offspring all believed themselves to be the child of two Paradisian parents. But Paradisians didn't reproduce. The offspring the exiles had raised were actually the genetically altered *in vitro* products of human parents. This was what Stan and Camille had feared Stanley would reveal. They'd been greatly relieved to learn that he was apparently still ignorant of the full truth.

However, the part he did reveal could still be troublesome, so she and Stan had devised a solution that she wished to implement without delay.

"Sadira, you may ask me about Stanley's accusations concerning your father and me if you wish."

The girl hesitated. "I did wonder, Mother. But I'm certain there's an explanation for his misinformation."

"He's not misinformed, child. Your father and I are brother and sister."

Sadira's pupils dilated, but she held her tongue.

"It was his implication of perversion that angered us. The truth is that every married couple in this building—Garrick and Cherisse, Patric and Elaine, Adlai and Taylor—all are married to siblings. All Paradisian couples are brother and sister. It has never been otherwise." This was actually true. Since marriage didn't exist on Paradise Island, the only "married" Paradisians were among the exiles—and those relationships were merely legal states undertaken for the purpose of projecting a certain image.

"You've never mentioned this before," Sadira said carefully.

"We're over eighty centuries old, child. We've been married for seventy-nine of those centuries. We scarcely think of ourselves as siblings any longer." How easily the lies rolled off her tongue.

"What of the risk of birth defects?"

"Non-existent in Paradisians. Males produce an enzyme, *mij dinósh*, which reverses all mutations." They'd used that enzyme to engineer the stronger, smarter, longer-lived humans who believed themselves to be Paradisian offspring.

"According to traditional Paradisian mores," Camille continued, "the perversion is in what Stanley has done, marrying and reproducing with a non-relative." She scoffed as she added, "One of a different species, no less. But Damour has obviously allowed him to violate his rules in this matter. He's always been rather inequitable." Stan's idea of using the problem to paint Doúg as an arbitrary tyrant was a particularly nice touch.

"I see." Sadira glanced at the flowers on her worktable. "Then am I to marry one of my brothers?"

"You are far too young to marry at all. Paradisians rarely marry before their 100th birthday. However, you may marry whomever you wish—or no one at all. We left Damour to free ourselves of tiresome restrictions; we will not burden you with them."

"Thank you, Mother."

"Of course, child. Now, do you know where your father is?" As soon as her lips formed the question, she sensed Stan's presence down the private hallway. "Oh, let me guess: he's in the lab, trying to determine where he went wrong with that explosive Stanley mentioned."

Sadira laughed. "Yes, ma'am." Indicating the papers on her worktable, she added, "I found the formula and notes from the time Stanley left. Father's backtracking to find his error."

Camille traversed the hall to Stan's lab, where he stood rubbing one shoulder while watching Adlai alter molecular structures on the doodle board. She enjoyed seeing the two together again. Adlai had been undercover in California for decades, posing as Strider's office manager. The work had been vital, but Stan had nonetheless missed his most trusted research assistant.

Slipping up behind them, Camille massaged Stan's sore shoulder, more for her enjoyment than his benefit. Unlike some men's muscles, which felt as healthy as a double chin, Stan's were meaty and firm, so well toned that they almost massaged back. She enjoyed holding the power of these muscles in her hands. She coveted it.

"You seem to be making progress," she noted.

"Yes, Adlai is most helpful," Stan said. "It's good to have him back."

Adlai removed a pair of reading glasses as he turned around. "Very good to be back."

Stan dismissed Adlai for the evening and then gravely verbalized what Camille had been thinking. "The glasses are new since he left for California."

"Yes," she agreed. "He's also gone completely gray, and his face is now etched with lines."

"He hasn't said anything, but he doesn't move as freely, either. Certain motions—bending and squatting, for instance—seem to be difficult for him."

The two fell silent, privately considering the implications of Adlai's plight. Adlai Menod and his sister, Taylor, were the youngest of the exiles, having been only about 500 years old when they were expelled from their homeland and cut off from the live-sustaining fruit of the *Viv Zabé*. (Paradisian: Life-Tree) Because they had the least exposure to Viv fruit before their exile, its effects were wearing off for them first. The other exiles followed the progressing condition, which they had dubbed *lakviv*, closely. If they did not regain access to Viv fruit soon, they were all doomed to the same fate. Already varying degrees of the symptoms plagued some.

Finally Stan broke the pensive mood. "I haven't talked to Sadira yet."

"No need. I spoke with both her and Saxon. I'll leave Sheridan to you."

Stan grunted. "You know, you can't honestly pin the failure of the Strider operation on him."

"Perhaps not, but I am disappointed. I was looking forward to finally having some fun with Strider."

Stan grasped her shoulders and surprised her with a kiss on the forehead—the most intimate of kisses to a Paradisian. "I'm making you a promise, Kami. You will have your day with Strider. I'll see to it."

She smiled. Stan could be utterly charming when they were on good terms. "Thank you, *zuulu.*" (Paradisian endearment: elder brother) She embraced him, enjoying the companionship she so missed when they were at odds. But, although she gratefully accepted these occasional moments, she never expected the rekindled coal of brotherly affection to burn for long. Something about leopards and their spots.

"What do you think of Sadira's suitors?" she asked, releasing him. "Flowers from one and chocolates from another?"

"As long as they don't interfere with her work, I don't care."

"She allows nothing to interfere with her work. You did an excellent job with her—she idolizes you. She'd never do anything to compromise your good opinion."

"Yes, she's a useful child," he agreed with a hint of fondness.

✵ ✵ ✵ ✵ ✵

Camille had just finished dressing the next morning when a knock sounded at her bedroom door. "Enter," she called from her vanity.

Sadira came in and sank gracefully onto the love seat. "Has Father left?"

"I assume so. He usually goes to the gym at four. Did you check his room?"

"He's not there."

Camille lowered her mascara to watch the girl's reflection in the mirror. She appeared calm, but she had swiped one thumbnail with the other thumb once before catching herself and folding her hands primly in her lap. "Is there a problem? You may call his cell phone."

"No, ma'am, no problem. We're working on a delicate venture, but I'm sure it will succeed. It's simply that I'd like to take the day off after my defense. I have no meetings, and Austin wishes to take me out to celebrate the completion of this doctorate."

Ah—that explained it. Asking a favor of Stan made even Camille nervous. "Your father can spare you for one day. You may go."

"Thank you, ma'am," the girl said with a relieved smile. "And I'll likely spend the night with Austin. We've been dating for several months now."

"Very well." Camille picked up her lipstick, and Sadira rose to leave. At the doorway, she turned back. "Would you tell Father—" She pursed her lips. "Will you tell him that I won't be in, then?"

"Yes, I'll tell him."

"Thank you, Mother."

CHAPTER 8

SENT

"So is my word that goes out from my mouth: It will not return to me empty, but will accomplish what I desire and achieve the purpose for which I sent it."
Isaiah 55:11, NIV.

The military radio implanted behind Stanley's right ear pinged, and Jorge said, "Subject and her date just entered the building, General."

"Roger that, Captain." The vinyl seat of the dark-windowed sedan creaked as Stanley shifted restlessly. Although he'd been part of innumerable such operations, he'd never before rescued a Moden; that is, he'd never matched wits directly with his biological father. He didn't like the man, but he knew better than to underestimate him, especially when sitting just outside his penthouse apartment.

Doug had said to err on the side of generosity—to assume that Sadira's request was genuine—but to exercise due vigilance in case it was not. Stanley had certainly been vigilant—obsessive, even. After all, the security of his entire division was at stake.

"Subject's date is exiting the building alone," Jorge reported.

"Roger that." Stanley once again scanned the area for suspicious persons. The Moden offspring were monitored very closely. However, he saw no evidence of a tail on Sadira tonight; apparently she'd played her part well.

And there she was—striding out the back door with the Moden gait, the one that said, "The world's mine, and I dare anyone to question it."

"Subject in view," Stanley said. "Watch my tail." A moment later, Jorge's SUV circled the block.

Sadira approached the car and sat stiffly in the passenger seat. "Good evening."

"Hi," he said in a neutral tone. "I need to scan you for bugs and tracking devices."

She nodded in that imperial manner that grants a favor rather than acquiesces to a demand. Stanley took out his old nanny's "favorite pen," the one she had used to scan his parents' home for bugs right under their noses. It was one of the few mementos he had of the woman who had sacrificed her life to save him.

After completing the scan, he started the car and pulled onto the street. "Did you have any trouble?"

"None. Austin believes I've returned to the penthouse. My parents—don't expect me until morning."

Her hesitation was barely noticeable, but Stanley noticed nonetheless. "Are you having second thoughts? There will be no going back, you know."

"I'm certain of my decision. I know what kind of people they are, and I don't believe in their mission. I certainly can't lead the business that supports their war effort."

"Then why are you fidgeting?" Despite her resolute expression, she had twice stroked one perfectly manicured thumbnail with the other thumb.

Her head swiveled elegantly toward him. "They're all I've ever had."

Her haughty tone certainly betrayed no insecurity, but then it wouldn't; she was a Moden. Still, the simple statement recalled all of the feelings Stanley had experienced in the same situation—how alone he felt, how confused the world seemed, and yes, how terrified he was. But these were "weak" emotions according to the Moden worldview, and, even at age ten, the protective façade their parents had demanded of them was so deep-seated that he could express none of them. Only Chris and Susana's sympathetic care and the link with Bethany had allowed him to struggle through the storm of emotions blowing through him—and, eventually, to heal.

He wanted to offer his sister such support, to communicate that it was okay to feel lonely and afraid, that it was healthy to ask for help. But how? Having no insight into such matters himself, he wondered what Chris would do. And then he remembered: Chris had simply admitted his own feelings.

Even that was risky. With her training, Sadira would consider any admission of weak emotions repulsive. Yet, if she chose to accept it as such, his honesty would grant her permission to accept the support she needed. And so, he took the risk.

"I was almost eleven when Doug rescued me from our parents. I fled with our nanny, Mrs. Jenkins, but she died during the escape. I've never felt so completely alone as I did that night, although I couldn't admit it then. Now I can even admit that I was frankly"—the Moden in him still made him hesitate—"well, scared."

Now stopped at a red light, he met her gaze with the last word and watched her reaction. He saw no contempt, no hauteur, no disapproval—only puzzlement. Then the rigid set of her shoulders relaxed slightly. "I didn't know the details of your defection. It must have been difficult."

Yes! Although she had admitted nothing of her own feelings, she hadn't disdained his. It was a step in the right direction. Still, he kept his tone subdued. Like an injured animal, she might yet be scared off. "It was difficult. But then I met Uncle Gabriel and was embraced by a family that actually loved me. I soon realized that, as one of Doug's runners, I was part of a very big family."

She said nothing, but her eyes softened. He thought he saw yearning.

The light changed, and he returned his attention to the road. "If things work out tonight, my wife and I will ask Doug if you can stay with us. Maybe we aren't well acquainted yet, but you're still my little sister."

"I'd like that. Thank you."

The relief in her tone told him his message had been received and decoded. Time to dispense with such uncomfortable talk. "I must ask—when did you write that note you slipped me? I was watching you all closely, and I never saw you write it."

"Yes, I imagine you were watching us closely," she said with a hint of humor. "But you missed nothing. I determined that I wished to defect several weeks ago. However, I had no idea how to accomplish it. I am watched rather closely."

"I hadn't noticed," he said wryly.

She smiled outright. "When Madelyn called me to Father's office, she informed me that you were the previously unnamed ambassador we were expecting. It occurred to me that, if our parents had raised you as they raised us, you could receive an unexpected note without appearing startled. I scribbled the note then, before leaving my office. During the meeting I observed you to see if my assumption was well-founded. When you maintained an impassive demeanor in that difficult situation, I took the risk. You did not disappoint me. No one suspected a thing."

She was relaxing some and had allowed a trace of sorrow in her voice at the end.

"I have to admit, I envy you—the fact that you can regret leaving our parents. You must have had an actual relationship with them. To me, they were just people who visited the penthouse when it was convenient. I mostly tried to stay out of their way."

"From Saxon's accounts, things changed considerably after you left. They're home more often. We do things as a family. We receive some praise." She paused. "It's rather curious. They separated from Damour because of his rules, yet your departure made them realize they must adopt many of His Majesty's principles in childrearing if they were to raise offspring who followed their ideals. Their lives are now full of such contradictions."

"My dad—I mean, the man who adopted me—he's fond of saying that Doug's Laws aren't arbitrary restrictions but the outgrowth of laws of behavior that are as real as the laws of physics. It sounds as though even our parents have had to recognize that."

"Yes, I believe so," she agreed.

Scanning the streets, she asked suddenly, "Where are we going?"

"We've rented a hotel suite for you to meet with Doug via transmitter."

"We're staying in the city?"

"For now." Glancing at her, Stanley knew what she was thinking. With their parents' resources, no hiding place in the city would be safe.

"Look, Sadira, I'll be frank. I've spent my life rescuing people from Father's grasp. I've dreamed of seeing you and our brothers free of him. So I truly hope you're on the level. But I also know Father would love to infiltrate our camp, and, with the safety of so many at stake, I must take precautions against that possibility."

She nodded with no apparent offense, and Stanley found that, for once, he was glad of their parents' training, which emphasized the subjugation of emotion to logic. "Yes, I see your dilemma, and I applaud your vigilance. You can't be too cautious when dealing with Father. However, he *will* initiate a exhaustive search once he discovers my absence in the morning."

"Yes, but I expect to have a definitive answer regarding your true allegiance by then."

She lifted one eyebrow in challenge. "Do you now? You must know I'm thoroughly trained in withstanding torture and confounding lie detectors."

"I'm sorry to hear it," Stanley said softly, for he could easily imagine the methods his parents had used to train her in such matters. "But the Paradisian army never employs torture, and I doubt you've ever encountered a lie detector like the one you'll meet tonight."

They arrived at the hotel, where they entered through a back door and stepped into the service elevator. "I need to warn you that Father's twin will be here," Stanley said. "You can tell them apart because Uncle Gabriel doesn't have any of Father's scars. And his accent is normally British, even when he isn't angry." He punched the proper button and turned to her with a slight frown. "Come to think of it, he rarely gets angry. In over twenty years, I've only seen him mad once, and all he did then was clench his jaw."

"Hard to imagine that of Father," Sadira noted.

When they entered the suite, Stanley watched Sadira's trained gaze travel automatically around the room, clocking every exit and evaluating the occupants, who included several brawny Royal Guards, for potential threat. The uninitiated might interpret this as an enemy scouting out a location. Stanley saw it as a habit, one ingrained in them since childhood.

When he introduced their uncle, Sadira shook his hand and said cordially, though stiffly, "How do you do, sir? I must admit, I am surprised to learn that I have an uncle, although Stanley did apprise me of the fact."

"Very thoughtful of him," their uncle replied. With a wink at Lanse, he added, "General Meshon can testify to some bite wounds inflicted by a certain nephew who hadn't been forewarned."

Sadira cast Stanley a questioning look, and he shrugged. "What would you think if this mirror image of Father showed up while you were fleeing him?"

"I see your point," she conceded with a smile.

Turning to Chris, Stanley began, "And this is my real dad—"

"Dr. Christian Strider, son of Juan Misi," Sadira said. "I didn't realize I'd have the honor of meeting you."

Chuckling, Chris extended his hand. "Let me guess: your mother quizzed you on the high-risk Subjects?"

"Yes, and Father speaks very contemptuously of you, which is as close as he comes to complimenting an outlander. I'm happy to meet you, sir."

"It's a pleasure to meet you," Chris said with a warm smile, and Sadira seemed to relax instantly. Stanley had always admired Mom and Dad's ability to put people at ease. He was sometimes a little jealous of Bethany for inheriting that talent; he certainly hadn't picked it up.

"And this," Stanley said as he grasped Bethany's hand, "is my wife—Dad's daughter, Bethany."

"I'm glad to meet you." In a conspiratorial whisper Bethany added, "I thought I'd tag along so you don't feel so alone with all these big, burly men hanging around."

Sadira laughed naturally for the first time. "After growing up around my father's men, I'm not easily intimidated, but I do appreciate your thoughtfulness."

"Well, now that the introductions are done, let's get down to business." Stanley led Sadira to a conference room and seated her at the table. Gabriel,

Lanse, Chris, and Bethany joined them, while the other guards maintained their positions around and outside the suite.

"Okay," Stanley said, "here's the plan. We're going to call Doug, who will interview you to determine where your loyalties lie."

Although her demeanor didn't change, Stanley saw wariness spark in Sadira's eye and realized she had misinterpreted his remark. "I should clarify that Doug's definition of 'interview' is different than our parents' definition. He will simply talk with you. The rest of us will be here to participate in the discussion."

"I see," she said. "It sounds less painful than our interview techniques."

Chris caught her eye and winked. Tapping the scar on his left cheekbone, he said, "Having experienced Garrick's interview techniques, I can attest to that."

She broke into an uncertain smile that reminded Stanley of his own first talk with Doug. He'd been petrified. Even though Mrs. Jenkins had first counteracted many of his parents' lies, he was convinced Doug would somehow reach through the line to grab him. "I understand you've never spoken to Doug before. Do you have any questions before we place the call?"

She hesitated only an instant before replying bravely, "No."

Stanley cautiously offered her a tiny smile of reassurance, hoping thereby to will her a measure of the courage Mrs. Jenkins had shared with him. But he avoided demonstrating any obvious support, for that would humiliate her; she would see it as exposing her vulnerability. In any case, the tiny smile seemed to be enough. The distrust in her eyes dimmed, and she added, "I'm ready."

Stanley nodded matter-of-factly and called Doug. "We're meeting with Sadira per your directions, Doug. Everyone you designated is here."

"Well, howdy all, and a special howdy-do to you, Sadira. It's nice to meet you."

Stanley had observed that Doug's voice inevitably affected new listeners although he couldn't always predict the result. Sometimes it rocketed them into action; sometimes they were overcome with terror; sometimes they were so calmed that they fell asleep. Sadira immediately relaxed. The tension in her jaw slackened, and her rigid shoulders eased. "Hello, Your Majesty."

"Oh, you can call me Doúg, child. All my friends do."

"You honor me, Doúg," she responded effortlessly. "Thank you."

Stanley glanced at Chris, who returned his smile. Sadira's ability to pronounce Doúg's name, which triggered a cough in his enemies, was a strong point in her favor.

A guard interrupted them, calling Chris into the living room. Meanwhile Doug said, "Tell me why you're interested in changin' horses, child. What got you interested in joinin' my rodeo?"

"Well, sir, I think it started when I realized how many contradictions there are in my parents' lives. For instance, they both insist that love makes you vulnerable, yet they love each other."

"Really?" Stanley interrupted. "Are you sure?"

Sadira nodded. "Oh, yes. They claim they don't, but they do things that can have no other explanation. They're linked, you know."

"Yes, but a link is just a physiological phenomenon. It doesn't require love."

"Perhaps not, but if you're linked, you understand the strength of the connection. Either love or hatred must result when joined by such a bond. Mother and Father seem to volley back and forth between the two, yet they always come together in the end. I think they must in order to accomplish their goals."

"You're an astute observer," Doug commented. "What else have you seen?"

"Another troubling contradiction—my parents say they revolted against you because of your rules. They say intelligent beings like Paradisians don't require rules. Yet they've enacted numerous rules for Desmon Tower; they're just my father's rules rather than yours. What's more, your rules are much more reasonable and humane."

"That's certainly true," Stanley agreed.

"I also came to love the *Manual* and the world it describes," she continued. "My brothers and I are required to study it to learn your strategies and to use it against runners. But I found myself wishing for such a world, where love isn't a shameful weakness, and where real weakness is treated mercifully. Still, I saw it as the fairy tale my parents claim it is until just recently."

"What happened to change your perspective?" Doug asked.

"A few months ago I was reading over Father's shoulder and happened to notice the scar on his head."

"I remember a number of scars," Stanley said. "But I never saw one on his head."

"Well, I suppose you were a bit shorter then," she teased.

"A little," Stanley conceded with a chuckle.

"He keeps it well hidden under his hair and claims it doesn't exist. But it's definitely there—the scar of the prophecy."

Stanley nodded thoughtfully. " 'He will strike your head, and you will strike his heel.' "

"Yes!" she exclaimed, suddenly animated. "All my life I thought Father was telling me the truth and the *Manual* was lying. When I spotted the scar, I suddenly realized I had it exactly backwards—the *Manual* was speaking the truth and Father was lying. It was a huge, earth-moving paradigm shift. I realized the *Manual's* world wasn't some fairy tale but the real world!" Growing somber, she continued, "And I understood that the world I occupied, the life I was living, was the false world, one that Mother and Father had created."

"Yes," Stanley said, having had exactly the same experience. "Everything—the whole universe—was precisely backwards to everything you thought you knew. Good was bad. Truth was falsehood. Friends were enemies."

"Exactly. I couldn't see anything the same way again. I couldn't trust anything I thought I knew. I constantly had the surreal feeling that I was living in a novel or a movie—that nothing was *real*. Worse still, I wasn't just living this lie, I was helping to perpetuate it."

She hesitated, brushing her thumbnail once. "Furthermore, I've obstructed those who believed the truth. Doúg, sir, I am truly sorry for the ways I've harmed your runners. I stand ready to accept my punishment for these actions." Lifting her chin, she added, "Including the Wells. That was my assignment."

Stanley's anger instantly flared. Lorenzo and Monica Wells had been good friends and colleagues in Doug's work. Two years before, they had disappeared while boating. The authorities had declared it an accident, but Stanley had suspected Moden Industries' involvement. Now he knew the truth: not only was Moden Industries responsible, but his baby sister had completed the assignment.

Bethany reached for his hand, and he felt the tingling of an energy transfer. He readily accepted the calmness she offered him. When his fury cooled to a more manageable level, he recognized that he, too, had hurt plenty of runners while working for his parents. Nevertheless, Doug had forgiven him, fully and freely.

The motion of Bethany's hand caught Sadira's attention, and she apparently recognized the energy transfer. As Bethany removed her hand, Sadira lifted her eyes to Stanley's. "You knew them, didn't you?"

Stanley nodded woodenly.

"I'm truly sorry," she said.

He recognized her sorrow as genuine. Yet he didn't trust himself to speak, still struggling as he was with his own emotions. Thankfully Bethany spoke the words he wished he could say.

"Losing Lorenzo and Monica was painful," she said quietly. "But we don't hold it against you, Sadira. Neither of us. Because Doug has forgiven us freely, we can forgive you, too."

"Thank you, *mi corazón*," Stanley whispered. (Spanish: my heart)

"I forgive you, too, child," Doug said gently.

Clearly confused, Sadira said, "Just like that? No penance?"

"Just like that," Doug affirmed. "The 'penance,' the price of forgiveness, has already been paid."

Sadira bowed her head. "Thank you."

"You're mighty welcome," Doug said.

During the silence that followed, Stanley realized that Dad was still gone and went to check on him. Passing into the living room, he asked a guard about Chris's whereabouts. The guard pointed toward a darkened room where Stanley saw the profile of two men weeping together.

"Who's he with?" Stanley asked.

"Prince Joshua," the guard answered.

Stanley nodded. He wouldn't put it past Josh to come all this way just to comfort Dad in his loss. He might interview Sadira while here, but that was probably more for the sake of those listening. Doug likely knew her true motivations already.

Stanley thanked the guard and returned to the others. As he entered, Doug was saying, "How do you feel about giving up the power that goes with being president of America's largest business?"

"I don't enjoy the power," Sadira said flatly. "Oh, it's nice to say, 'I want a chocolate milkshake,' and have it appear. Still, I see the fear in people's eyes when they're called to Father's office, or even mine. Father revels in that power, but I've never grown accustomed to it. I like your approach, sir. You lead by discerning what's best for your subjects, by helping them."

Chris returned to the room then, accompanied by Josh. As the mighty crown prince of Paradise Island entered, Sadira's guarded expression returned. Again, Stanley recognized this reaction from his experience. By now, she'd become used to Doug's voice and decided that he either couldn't or wouldn't attack her over the phone. But she still didn't truly trust any of the powerful Deón.

How could she? She'd heard such spine-tingling stories. And now one of them just waltzes in unannounced, placing her entirely within his control.

Stanley and the other soldiers came to attention, and Sadira sprang up to sink into a deep curtsy. Approaching her, Josh solemnly ordered, "Rise, Sadira." When she cautiously lifted her head, he offered his hand. "Josh Damour, at your service."

"Prince Joshua, sir." She hesitantly rose and took his hand, no doubt believing she would be struck dead on contact. As she gazed into his eyes, probably the first time she had looked into eyes that truly loved her, the effect was visible. Layer after protective layer dropped away until she stood frozen before him, too humbled to speak. If anyone present had questioned her sincerity, there could be no doubt now. Whatever she was when she entered this room, she would leave it changed by this single encounter with unconditional love.

Josh leaned forward to kiss her gently on the cheek. "I'm so very pleased to meet you, dear one."

She blinked several times before managing to speak. "You are too magnanimous, sir. Considering what I've done to thwart your purposes, I certainly didn't expect such generosity."

Josh smiled warmly. "We do things a bit differently than you're used to. Welcome to our world, Sadira."

In a suspiciously husky voice, she said, "I like your world, sir."

Giving Sadira a chance to compose herself, Josh made his way around the room with cheek-kisses and hugs. Then he took his place at the table. "Shall we get back to work?"

Josh's interview was surprisingly brief. Then he fished a transmitter from his shirt pocket. "Sadira, this is yours," he said, and applause broke out.

Reverentially accepting the device, she asked, "My own? So I can talk to Doúg anytime?"

That's right," Josh said. "Only you can remove it."

"Thank you, sir." She opened the clasp and fastened it around her neck. When the chain shortened and the clasp disappeared, she breathed, "Oh, it's really real!"

Josh handed her a copy of *The Runner's Manual.* "I realize you're familiar with this, but you must continue to study it. New runners face some tough challenges just now. You must still learn our principles and disciplines, but you don't have the advantage of the racecourse. Nevertheless, we welcome you and look forward to the time you'll join us on Paradise Island with all the other runners."

"Thank you, Prince Joshua. Thank you ever so much." With a laugh, she added, "How ironic. Mother and Father have been fighting to regain entrance to the island for over six millennia, when all the time it was so much easier than that."

"Easy for some perhaps," Josh said. "But for most, self-surrender is very difficult indeed. Unfortunately, it's no longer possible for some, including your parents."

Turning, he clapped Stanley on the back. "Will you accept Sadira into your family?"

"Absolutely," he replied with a smile.

"And Chris," Josh said, "will you act as her coach and teach her to run?"

"I'd love to," Chris said. "Is this 'one'?"

Josh chuckled. "Yes, *boní.* This is 'one.'" Turning to Sadira, he swept his hand around the table. "Allow me to introduce you to your new family."

A smile spread across her face. "Thank you. It's funny, but, despite the danger, I've never experienced such peace and security as I do right now."

"I understand exactly what you mean," Stanley said. "I felt the same when I escaped Father's control."

His own words had the effect of driving home the wonderful truth: His sister was Doug's runner! How he had yearned for this moment! Sensing the reins of his emotions slipping from his grasp, he abruptly changed the subject. "But we must get you to safety. Dad, I'm keeping Jorge here in New York and Andy in LA. I'm hoping you'll disappear with us."

"I'm already packed," Chris said.

"Sadira, I'll call your parents in the morning," Doug said. "When will they expect you?"

"Seven o'clock. But they'll think you kidnapped me. I apologize if I've overstepped myself, but I left some information for them. I'm so tired of lies, and I didn't want them to believe a lie about my defection, so I left two proofs that I acted voluntarily."

"Good thinking, child. I despise falsehood myself. What proofs did you leave? I'll tell them where to look."

After she relayed the specifics, Doug asked if she'd like him to tell them anything else.

"Yes, sir. Could you tell them—?" She glanced down. "Um, would you tell Father—?" Suddenly the confident and eloquent young woman seemed unable to express herself. "Never mind, sir," she said at last.

Josh squatted down beside her chair. "Sadira, look at me." He gazed into her eyes for a moment. "Tell them she loves them, Dad."

She blinked back tears. "I'm sorry. You must think I'm terrible to care for people like them."

"No, we don't," Josh said gently. "We love them too."

As the group prepared for departure, Sadira asked, "Prince Joshua, sir, are you leaving?"

"Yes, I need to return to the battle preparations—if my mission's been accomplished?" He looked to Chris, eyebrows raised in question.

Chris nodded. "Yeah, Josh. Thanks a million." With a grin, he glanced at Stanley. "Or should I say" —he snapped to attention and saluted—"Yes, sir, *Mikaél!*"

With a laugh, Josh moved to Chris's side. Laying an arm across his shoulders, the commander-in-chief of the world's most powerful army said, "For you, I'll always be just plain Josh, *boní.*" (Rarámuri: little brother)

"Thank you, *bachí,*" Chris murmured. (Rarámuri: big brother) "As always, I don't deserve your generosity."

Sadira whispered to Stanley, "What did he say? And what language?"

"Rarámuri, also called Tarahumara," Stanley whispered back. "Josh called Dad his little brother."

"Wow."

"Not something you'd see Father do, is it?"

"Hardly."

Stanley returned his attention to Chris's conversation as his dad asked, "You knew, didn't you? The last time you visited Susana and me, after Andy was born. I teased you about not walking in on a kiss when you visited again. You laughed, but your eyes were sad. You knew she'd be—well, resting next time I saw you."

Josh nodded. "Yes, *boní*, I knew. Knowing the future isn't always fun."

"I never forgot what you said—'Treasure every moment.' Thank you."

With a nod, Josh turned toward the door. "Well, I'm off." But then he stopped and returned to Sadira. "Was there something else?"

"Well, if it's not too forward of me to ask, sir, I was wondering about the scar of the prophecy."

"Would you like to see it?"

She sucked in a breath. "May I?"

"Yes, you may. That's what it's for." Sitting on a chair, Josh took off his shoes. The Paradisians grew very solemn, and Stanley found himself holding his breath. He'd never seen these scars before either.

As Josh pulled his socks off, Stanley suppressed a horrified gasp. Angry, red scars, each almost an inch across, glared up at them from near the heel of each foot. Stan had actually driven large square nails between the bones of Josh's feet! Stanley's feet ached with the vision, and an involuntary shudder went through him.

"The Battle of Grace Hill," Sadira breathed, as if she'd just unlocked a riddle. "Father claims he won that battle."

"He thought he did at first," Josh said. "He walked away, and I didn't. Only later did he realize how blatantly he'd revealed his true character. That's the day he lost the war."

Sinking to her knees, Sadira peered up at him. "Does *he* know that?"

"Yes," Josh said. "He knows he's already defeated."

Stanley watched helplessly as the obvious corollary dawned on her. When tears sprang to her eyes and she clapped a hand over her mouth, he knew she'd surmised the whole truth: Their parents, in full comprehension of their hopeless situation, had consciously, purposely plunged their own children into the same bleak predicament they had chosen for themselves, merely to prolong a war they'd already lost.

He wished he could help her process this awful revelation. But this was horror beyond comprehension. The most he could do was give her a moment to pull herself together. So he drew the room's attention away from her by asking Josh, "Can't the leaves of the *Viv Zabé* heal your scars?"

"Yes, but my dad has decreed that these scars should remain, a perpetual reminder for all generations of the malignity of evil."

"Did it hurt a lot?" Sadira had now discarded all attempts at hiding her emotions. Pain and sorrow shone clearly in her face.

"Yes, it did, actually," Josh said. "But the physical pain was nothing compared to watching your parents and their followers turn away from us."

Sadira reached forward and touched one wounded foot. She was apparently too absorbed in the insight dawning upon her to realize what she was doing, for she suddenly jerked her hands away, blushing.

"It's okay," Josh said. "You can touch it if you want."

"This is what Doúg meant, isn't it?" she asked breathlessly. "The penance, the price of my forgiveness?"

Josh nodded.

Her eyes overflowed as she whispered, "Thank you."

Josh cradled her face in his hands and kissed her forehead. "You're welcome, dear one. You are very, very welcome."

CHAPTER 9

REBUKE

"You thought I was someone like yourself;
But I shall rebuke you and indict you to your face."
Psalm 50:21, REB.

15 October 8043 M.E.

"Dr. Desmon," Madelyn called over the intercom. "Dr. Moden needs you urgently in his office. It's Mr. Damour, ma'am."

"On my way," Camille said with a scowl. The Final Battle had already been called, the date set. What possible excuse could Doúg have fabricated to call and annoy them?

When she arrived in Stan's office, he stood a few paces behind his desk, arms crossed, silently glaring at the phone. She sensed his trepidation—none of them liked speaking with Doúg.

"She's here," Stan said.

"Good morning, Kamíl," Doúg said. "Have you noticed that you're short one child today?"

Camille cast a puzzled frown at Stan, who motioned to the empty seat at Sadira's worktable. "What's that to you, Damour?" he asked.

"I thought you'd like to know she's safe. She's requested political asylum. I've granted it."

Camille's shock was mirrored on Stan's face. A heartbeat later, her brother bellowed, "You kidnapped her!"

"No, Stan," Doúg said. "You've been lying about me for so long, you've become confused. Kidnapping is your tactic, not mine. Nevertheless, Sadira did anticipate your response. She left two proofs of her intent."

"Did she indeed?" Camille said caustically. She didn't believe the child had left voluntarily any more than Stan did. "And what might those be?"

"First, Austin Pim can tell you that they had no plans to spend the night together. That was her invention to allow herself time to escape."

Camille stepped to the door and ordered Madelyn to summon Austin.

"And what's the other so-called proof?" Stan demanded.

"After Sadira slipped a note to Stanley requesting his help, he sent her a disposable cell phone in a box of candy. The box is in the drawer of her worktable. She said you would find something under the tray of candy."

Camille's skin crawled when, opening the drawer, she found the very box of chocolates from which she'd eaten. The card reading "From a Secret Admirer" fluttered to the ground as she opened the box. She removed the tray of candy and discovered a space underneath that hid a disposable cell phone and two notes.

Only one number had been dialed on the phone, one identified as belonging to "SSL"—as in Stanley Strider Lanáj.

Camille handed the phone to Stan and picked up a note written in a strangely familiar hand.

> Moden Security monitors you closely. Use the burner phone under the tray of chocolates to reach me. Check for cameras and listening devices before placing the call.
>
> - SSL

Camille reread the note, trying unsuccessfully to interpret it in a way that did not involve Sadira's willing defection. Finally Stan snatched the paper from her hand.

She withdrew the other note, written in Sadira's handwriting.

> Dear Father and Mother,
>
> I pen this with a heavy heart, knowing you will be disappointed and angry at my choice. But, as you yourselves have taught me, I cannot allow emotion to interfere with needful action. So I must inform you that I am defecting to Doug Damour. I do this of my own free will.
>
> Sadira

A vivid image burst into Camille's mind: She saw herself standing over a dog with newborn pups, a bleeding wound on her hand and an expression of shock on her face. That her beloved pet should attack her, even to protect her pups, had simply astounded her. Sadira's letter evoked those same feelings: shock … disillusionment … betrayal. Anger.

"Well?" Stan demanded, and Camille robotically handed him the note.

She followed his eyes as he read it once, twice, three times. She sensed the same sense of loss in him as the truth sank in. Indeed, when he looked up, his gaze traveled beyond her to a painting on the wall. She didn't have to look to know that the picture absorbing his attention was of a fine black stallion galloping through a meadow. Stan had painted that masterpiece himself, beautifully depicting the animal he had tamed right after their exile, a horse he called Roku, "beloved stallion." The animal had became a substitute of sorts for the beloved twin brother who betrayed him during the war. He was inconsolable when the animal died.

Then Stan's sorrow transformed suddenly into rage. Grabbing the first thing his hand found, he heaved a clock from his desk at Roku's painting. The clock crashed into the wall underneath the picture with a loud, confused chiming and tumbled to the floor, shattered.

"How dare you, Damour!" he raged. "First you steal my eldest son, and now my only daughter!"

"You've confused us again, Stan," Doúg replied softly. "I'm not the one who chose the road of rebellion. If you remember, I warned you that it would destroy even your closest relationships."

"You'll get nothing useful out of her! She's not been briefed on our battle plans!"

"Again, you misjudge me. My interest in humans has never been in what they can do for me, but in what I can do for them."

"Enough of this drivel!" Stan reached for the phone to disconnect the call.

"Stan," Doúg said quickly, "Sadira asked me to give you a message."

"What is it?" Stan asked warily.

"She asked me to tell you, to tell you both—" Doúg's voice dropped to a low but clear murmur. "—that she loves you."

With a mighty roar, Stan yanked the phone from the wall and hurled it at the same spot underneath the painting. Turning to the window, he glared straight ahead, arms crossed. Camille felt waves of fury emanate from him.

Sinking into a chair, Camille tried to collect her own thoughts. Why were they so outraged at Sadira's defection? It must involve more than losing a valuable resource, for they had not felt such outrage at Stanley's defection. What's more, Stanley had possessed considerable information of tactical importance, which Sadira did not. No, there must be something else behind their outrage.

I warned you that it would destroy even your closest relationships.

Yes, that was it. The underlying answer lay in their attachment to Sadira. Camille could not admit to loving Sadira, but she had grown quite fond of her, as had Stan. Why shouldn't they? The girl had been highly useful—an amiable, quick learner who had lightened their workloads considerably.

Nevertheless, the attachment was uncomfortably close to love. Close enough to remind her of her inability to eradicate the yearning for love that had plagued her for centuries. She had come to believe that Doúg purposely burdened all rational beings, from the time of their very creation, with the need for love. Before the rebellion, fulfilling that yearning had brought her great joy and satisfaction. But now love was simply too costly, requiring sacrifice and vulnerability. That's why she had tried—oh, so hard!—to free herself of the burden. Yet every so often, something reminded her of her failure. Those reminders sometimes generated melancholy. They always generated rage.

Suddenly Camille remembered the first of Sadira's "proofs." Perhaps Austin could provide information useful in recovering the traitor. She strode to the door and, with exaggerated calmness, asked Madelyn, "Where is Dr. Pim?"

"Right here, ma'am." Austin moved within view.

"I buzzed in when he arrived," Madelyn offered apologetically.

"Dr. Moden's telephone is not working properly," Camille said. "You'll see to that, of course." Motioning to Austin, she said, "Won't you join us?"

Austin followed her in, and they seated themselves before Stan's desk. The great man himself remained at the window, back turned, and showed no indication of moving. Apparently she was to conduct this interview.

"Austin," she said, "you've been dating Sadira for several months now, have you not?"

"Well, no, ma'am. We've only gone out twice so far." Austin glanced nervously toward Stan. "We have another date Saturday night."

"So you intend to see her again?"

The boy's brow furrowed. "Not if you and Dr. Moden disapprove, ma'am."

"No, Austin, that's not the problem. We both think highly of you, I assure you." Actually, this was true. For a human, he was remarkably intelligent and competent.

He seemed to relax somewhat. "Then, may I ask, what *is* the problem, ma'am?"

"Did you and Sadira spend the night together last night?"

"No!" Austin's face paled and his gaze flew to Stan. "Sir, I wouldn't take advantage of *your* daughter, of all people. I don't have a death wish. It was only our second date."

"Calm yourself," Camille said. "You are not in trouble, nor are you in danger of being so. However, we do have an urgent need of the truth in this matter. Did the two of you talk about, even mention, sleeping together last night?"

"No, ma'am. Not at all. I'm no idiot."

"I see." Camille scowled at this confirmation, even though she'd already accepted Damour's version of events. "Tell me, exactly where and at what time did you last see Sadira?"

"I walked her inside your building around 10:15, ma'am. I wanted to see her to the door, but she insisted that I return to the car."

"Did you notice anyone following you or loitering about?"

Concern crinkled his forehead. "No, ma'am."

Of course not. He had studied medicine, not subterfuge. He would be of little help in finding her.

"Ma'am, has something happened to Sadira?"

Camille considered the boy. The news would spread soon enough. She might as well tell him. "Sadira never came home last night, Austin. She told us she would be spending the night with you, so we weren't concerned. But that, apparently, was a ruse implemented to allow her the opportunity to defect."

"What? No! She's never— I mean, she seemed so—" He shook his head. "I don't believe it."

"It's come as quite a shock to us all." Looking to Stan, she asked, "Dr. Moden, do you have any questions for the young man?"

Stan grunted.

"Then you are dismissed, Austin." She walked him to the door and summoned Madelyn into the office. As the secretary connected a new telephone, Camille said, "We need you to issue an immediate memo to all employees. Sadira Moden has joined the list of traitorous offspring."

Madelyn gasped. "Sadira?" She looked to Stan, who was still standing at the window. "Dr. Moden, is this true?"

In a deceptively calm voice, he asked, "Are you questioning my sister's competence, Madelyn?"

"No, sir," she said quickly. "I'm—I'm just so shocked. She seemed so committed, so enthusiastic, so—"

"Yes," Camille interrupted, having heard quite enough of Sadira's virtues. "It seems she duped us all. As I was saying, include in the memo that she's not yet been trained in the more sensitive areas of the organization. She has no important information to share with the enemy."

"Yes, ma'am. Shall I notify Dr. Sondem to implement the usual protocol for tracking defectors?"

"Yes." *For all the good it will do.*

After Madelyn left, Stan said, "Camille, you should know—it's not true." He had still not moved from his position at the window.

"What's not true?"

"That she had no important information."

The air she was breathing seemed suddenly deficient in oxygen. It was bad enough losing this child, who so perfectly fit their needs. But she had never suspected that Stan had also violated the rule they'd adopted after Stanley's defection. No offspring was to be allowed access to sensitive information until they reached twenty-five years of age and demonstrated unwavering loyalty.

Anticipating her criticism, Stan grumbled, "It wasn't intentional. I don't even know if she realized what she overheard. But she's smart. She probably figured it out."

"How did it happen? What did she hear?"

"Sheridan and I had just finished working out. We were standing in the hallway outside my gym finalizing the details of the BW-683 attack. I had left the door between the hall and the office open, as I usually do when I'm elsewhere in the suite. When I went to shower, Sheridan passed through here on his way to his own office. He discovered that Sadira had arrived early and was working in here. She probably heard our entire discussion."

Camille stepped to the window beside him. "I suppose you had no reason to consider it a problem then."

"Precisely."

They stood in silence for several moments, each chasing their own thoughts. Finally Camille said, "How badly will this affect us?"

He shrugged. "The manpower issue's not inconsequential. I'll have to pick up the duties as president of the company again."

Camille winced. Sadira's competence as an executive had saved Stan untold hours. "And what of the BW-683 plans? That attack is critical in rallying the world against Damour, isn't it?"

"Yes, and it's too late to alter the virus itself," he said reflectively. "But I've been thinking—she has little specific information about it. Even if she overheard the entire conversation, I doubt she'd have enough to help them actually repel the attack."

"So her information won't be pivotal in the war?"

His brow furrowed as he considered the assessment. "No, I guess it won't."

"And, at this point in our history, the optimal management of the business isn't critical. Perhaps this loss isn't as significant as we first believed."

Stan's focus wandered behind her to Roku's painting. "No. I suppose not."

CHAPTER 10

CONCEALED

*"People who conceal their sins will not prosper, but if they confess
and turn from them, they will receive mercy."*
Proverbs 28:13, NLT.

"No, we don't obey Doug's Laws to earn anything from him." Chris flipped the pages of his *Manual* to the history recorded by John. "See here? Obedience flows naturally from our love for him because of what Josh has already done."

"Whatever we discuss, it seems to come back to that," Sadira said. "Josh paying the price for us."

"Spot on!" Gabriel exclaimed.

Chris broke into a broad grin. "You're a quick study, Sadira."

A huge yawn snuck up on him, and she chuckled. "I've kept you up all night with my questions. I should let you take a nap."

"A nap would be nice," Chris agreed and laid his weary head back against the van's headrest. They had split into two groups. Chris and Sadira were traveling with Gabriel and half the guards; Stanley and Bethany rode with Lanse and the others. Through the night, they had driven, flown, and then driven some more, still en route to their hideaway in Alaska.

Chris was nodding off when Doug called Sadira through her receiver, and she jumped. "How did he do that?" she whispered. "My transmitter's not on."

It didn't surprise Chris that she could already hear Doug's untranslated voice through the receiver. She had somehow managed to nurture a heart tuned to Doug's principles in the most hostile of circumstances. "I'll explain the various components of the device later," he said. "For now, just activate the transmitter to answer him."

She did and answered, "Yes, sir?"

"I just talked to your folks, child," Doug said. "I gave them your messages."

"How did they take it?"

"Oh, 'bout how you'd expect—they hung up on me. But not before I'd communicated everything."

"Thank you, sir."

"You're welcome, *ve nela*. Your father said something I wanted to ask you about. He said you didn't have anything useful to tell me." (Paradisian: my daughter)

"He wouldn't have said that unless it weren't true," Gabriel offered.

"Exactly my thoughts," Doug agreed.

"I'm not supposed to know anything useful to you," Sadira said. "But I overheard something. I intended to mention it last night. I'm afraid I forgot."

"You had other things on your mind," Gabriel said.

"Yes," Sadira said. "Anyway, last week I overheard Sheridan and Father discussing an upcoming biological attack. Sheridan probably realized later that I could have heard them and told Father."

"Well, that would explain his comment," Doug said. "If y'all don't mind, I'd 'preciate knowing what you heard."

Confusion crept over Sadira's features. Covering the transmitter, she whispered, "Why doesn't he just order me to tell him?"

"That's not his way," Chris answered. "Doug always gives us the option of refusing him."

"If he didn't," Gabriel added, "your parents never could have rebelled in the first place."

"Oh, I guess that's true." Uncovering the transmitter, Sadira said, "I'm happy to tell you what I know. It isn't much, but maybe it will help. Before the war, they're planning to release an agent designated BW-683 into the food supply around the various Allied States of Desmoden. Then they'll blame you for the consequences, saying you were targeting them. They've already got the press releases ready."

"And what do you know of BW-683?" Doug asked.

"Unfortunately, very little. The files are well protected; I couldn't hack into them without setting off the notification system, thereby announcing that I had tried. Consequently, I only have general information. I can say that BW stands for Biological Warfare, and that Father's been spending a lot of time with his virologists. In the virology lab, the 600 series are herpetic viruses."

"Any idea how he intends to disseminate it?"

"No, but it must involve meat. Father just issued a mandate ordering all Moden employees and associates to become ovo-lacto vegetarians. Because of the timing, I think it's meant to protect his troops from the virus."

"A reasonable deduction," Doug agreed.

"Oh!" Sadira exclaimed. "I just remembered: Sheridan was specifically laughing about Thanksgiving turkeys, so they're apparently expecting to have it ready before the holidays."

"All right, *ve nela*," Doug said. "Thank you for your help. If you think of anything else, you know how to reach me."

After Doug signed off, the movement of the car quickly lulled Chris to sleep. The next thing he knew, they were pulling up in front of a large, solitary cabin.

"Where are we?" he asked with a yawn.

"Your new home," Gabriel said. "The nearest city's about forty miles away."

"It's great," Chris said. He'd never been to Alaska, but his inner nature lover was immediately smitten with the wild beauty of the pristine woods and meadows surrounding the log cabin. He searched in vain for the high snow banks he'd envisioned, but some bizarre heat waves had recently swept through areas of the far north. Only scattered areas of snow remained.

The group settled into the large, eight-bedroom lodge and quickly developed a daily routine. Stanley and Bethany primarily worked via the Internet and telephone to organize troops and refine strategies from afar, while Chris taught Sadira to run. This required another major shift in ideals for her. Stan had demanded that his children be physically fit, but his emphasis had been on strength rather than endurance. Although she found the shift in perspective difficult, Sadira maintained a rigorous schedule and wasted no time. Even during her breaks, she diligently studied *The Runner's Manual.* Chris never once found it necessary to prod her forward. Indeed, she probably knew better than he did what challenges lay ahead. She seemed determined to prepare for them.

✲ ✲ ✲ ✲ ✲

Willy was having a really hectic day. No one person could possibly finish everything on his agenda. The professor he worked for had dumped a stack of essays on him to grade. He had to help with a class at the New-RAB that evening. Plus he had to finish a paper due tomorrow and study for a test. Just reviewing the list made him tired. And, caught in traffic, he was already running late for his tutoring gig.

Finally reaching the library, Willy found that the new student he'd been assigned wasn't where he should be. Willy had to go looking for him and finally found him hunched over a video game. The tutoring session was also tough—the kid wasn't very bright and needed everything repeated about a hundred times. But maybe it wasn't the kid's fault. Teaching wasn't Willy's strong suit. Still, he couldn't evade the responsibility, so he tried to do it right. He really did want to help the kids assigned to him. And, anyway, it would look good on his applications to law school.

By the time he finished the tutoring session, he was a half hour late for the stop-smoking class. The New-RAB's pacesetter, Quinn, frowned as Willy blew in—he'd had to fill in until he arrived.

"Sorry," Willy whispered as the speaker continued the meeting. "I was tutoring. Got here as quick as I could."

Quinn nodded without smiling. "I need to talk to you afterward."

"Sure," Willy said agreeably, but winced internally. Another delay!

He busied himself with the behind-the-scenes stuff that kept the program running smoothly. He usually enjoyed doing these organizational tasks, especially since it helped people. But tonight he was really feeling squeezed.

When the meeting ended, he stowed the materials, locked up the sound booth, and put things in order. He had just slung his backpack onto his shoulder when Quinn reappeared. "If you're ready, we can talk in my office."

"Oh." Willy glanced at his watch. Truth was, he'd forgotten. "I'm kind of pressed for time tonight. Could we do it another time?"

"I need an answer urgently. It won't take long."

Willy reluctantly followed Quinn to his office. Respecting Willy's need to keep things short, the pacesetter got right to the point: "A vacancy's opened up in New-RAB administration. It would be a great opportunity for you, and you've got the managerial skills it requires in spades."

"What position are we talking about?"

"Assistant Regional Overseer."

Willy was momentarily speechless. To be considered for that position, especially in a large region like LA, was huge! Not only would it look great on his applications, but it would put him in elbow-rubbing proximity to bigwigs in both the financial and political worlds. However—and this was a big however—it wasn't a paying job, and it would require a lot of time. Like he wasn't already too busy.

"Quinn, I'm really honored, and I'd like to say yes. But I'm honestly not sure I have the time to do it right."

The pacesetter's gaze shifted to his pen, which he was tapping on his blotter. Willy got the impression that he wanted to tell him he was an idiot for not jumping at the chance, to forget he'd mentioned it, that he'd offer the position to someone who'd appreciate it. But when he looked up, he merely said, "Think about it. Let me know by Sunday."

When Willy finally got home and sat down to do the term paper, he discovered an e-mail from Cherisse asking him to call her. He again thanked his lucky stars that he wasn't a member of the traditional RABs. Uncle Chris was always answering direct calls over his transmitter. He talked about it like some kind of privilege, but it seemed like a colossal pain to Willy. He wouldn't want someone interrupting his day like that. E-mail requests were much better, putting him in control; he answered Cherisse when and where he wanted.

But he didn't want to irritate anyone associated with General Lanáj, not before he got certain things straightened out, so he always answered her right back. He activated his transmitter and sorted through the rest of his e-mail until she answered a few minutes later.

"Hello, Willy," she greeted cheerily. "I have some good news. The lawyer informed me this afternoon that the DA has agreed to seal your juvenile record. He's satisfied with your community service hours and is ending your probation."

The knot in Willy's stomach relaxed. That knot had been twisting his guts around and around for over two years, so long that Willy had almost forgotten it didn't belong there. Although Cherisse had assured him that General Lanáj could arrange this, he hadn't actually believed her until this moment.

"Thank you," he breathed. "Thank you so much—for using your influence with the judge, for helping me work out the restitution, for keeping it all quiet. Honestly, I don't know what I would have done without your help."

"We're very happy to be of service. One mistake shouldn't ruin the rest of your life. And you've earned this, Willy. You've proven yourself to be a caring and responsible young adult. We have every confidence that you'll honor your commitment to repay the restitution we disbursed on your behalf with legal services once you've passed the bar."

"You can count on it. And anything I can do before that, you just let me know."

"As a matter of fact, there is something."

"Just name it."

"General Lanáj feels that you would be perfect for a position that has opened up there in Los Angeles—Assistant Regional Overseer."

Willy's ears grew hot. He glanced at the time of Cherisse's e-mail: sent about a half-hour after he'd talked to Quinn. Had his pacesetter reported to the New-RAB world headquarters that Willy was reluctant to accept the post? Was it coincidence that Cherisse had heard from the lawyer today, just when Willy had all but refused Quinn's request?

He squirmed in his seat as another thought came to him: Could she have been holding on to that news, waiting for a time when she needed it to maximize his sense of obligation—to make him do what she wanted?

He shook his head. He was letting Uncle Chris's conspiracy theories get to him. Enough of those stupid, suspicious notions. He had no reason—and no right—to doubt Cherisse. The fact was, she had really helped him, mobilizing people to assist in ways he never could have imagined. What's more, they'd done it all on the down low. To this day, no one in his family knew about the accident, and that meant more to him than anything.

Clearing his throat, he said carefully, "As a matter of fact, Quinn mentioned that to me this evening."

"Did he? And what did you say?"

"I wasn't sure I could swing it time-wise. But if I don't have to do any more community service, that won't be such a problem. So I'd be happy to accept the position. Actually, I'm really honored that General Lanáj would think of me."

"Excellent. Then I'll pass your answer along to the appropriate people."

After ending the call, Willy turned his attention to that term paper, but soon found himself rubbing at the knot in his stomach. Though better, it wasn't truly gone. But maybe a total cure was too much to hope for. After all, somewhere a little girl, now seven years old, was limping around on a deformed leg. Because of him. She would never outlive the events of that one night. Maybe it was only fair that he should never outlive the guilt.

Chapter 11
WHIRLWIND

"They sow the wind and reap the whirlwind."
Hosea 8:7 NIV.

26 October 8043 M.E.

Camille positioned her aching right shoulder under the shower's pulsating spray, allowing herself a few precious moments of relaxation. She had expected this last push before the Final Battle to be stressful, but the hardships were rendered doubly tiresome by the unrelentingly sour mood that Stan had adopted since Sadira's defection. Further, Camille's doubts about Sheridan were mounting, and her insistence that they should replace him as commander of the army put her in direct opposition to her brother.

She sighed. Would that she had let Stan kill the boy as a newborn! But no—instead, she had suggested that a *polín's* talents would be useful. Actually, his creativity was valuable. And his military strategies were brilliant, rivaling even Stan's. Talented, loyal, and ruthless, he was a charismatic leader who easily won his soldiers' loyalty. He seemed born for the job.

Yet one question haunted her: Was he *reliable*? Creativity often partnered with impulsivity, and Sheridan had amply demonstrated that trait as well. Garrick considered unpredictability an asset in a commander; he preferred to keep the enemy guessing. Well, Sheridan certainly kept everyone guessing. But Camille simply couldn't bring herself to trust him. Preferring more consistency in a commander, she had long preferred Garrick's son, Conner Sondem, for the position.

She rolled her head from side to side, loosening up her perpetually stiff shoulder. She'd sustained that injury over forty-seven centuries ago when Uri kidnapped her during an attempted coup d'état. The mere memory quickened her pulse, and she had to remind herself that a recurrence was unlikely. Garrick's myriad security measures had thwarted all subsequent attacks.

Finishing her shower, she dried herself off and donned her blue silk robe. However, as she entered her walk-in closet, the pungently sweet odor of ether tickled her nostrils. Immediately clamping down on her breathing, she jumped back in an attempt to retreat. In some pathological compulsive part of her brain, a clock began ticking. Paradisians could hold their breath for up to twenty minutes at rest or seven minutes while active. She hoped she would not need to challenge either statistic.

As she sprang backward, a powerful individual grabbed her from behind, pinning her arms to her sides, and shoved an ether-soaked cloth in her face. Recognizing her attacker's superior strength, she knew he must be either Paradisian or one of the genetically modified humans they had raised. In other words, a member of their own camp.

A kidnapping—part of a coup d'état!

The thought rallied her defenses as nothing else could. She did *not* intend to play the role of hostage again! She simultaneously stomped the hard heel of her slipper onto the attacker's instep and smashed the back of her head into his nose.

He pushed the cloth harder against her face, causing her eyes to burn intensely. Nevertheless, his hold on one arm loosened slightly.

Yanking that arm free, she jammed the elbow into his gut.

He grunted, and his grip slackened further.

She threw a fist backward into his face, which allowed her to break free and spin around. As her knee crashed into his groin, she registered the attacker's identity: Sheridan!

Sheridan? But he was a fine warrior with excellent skills. Why wasn't he fighting back?

She dared not hesitate to consider the question now. Although the errant general faltered, trying to catch his breath, he wasn't immobilized.

She thrust the heel of her palm sharply upward. A satisfying crunch testified that she had broken his nose. When he stumbled back, she hooked a foot behind his leg to trip him. Then she bound his hands and feet with belts. The entire skirmish took less than sixty seconds.

Once he was secured, she demanded, "Why didn't you retaliate?"

He mumbled something under the hand he held to his profusely bleeding nose.

"What?"

"I ... diden ... wan ... do urd ... oo."

"You didn't want to hurt me?" she repeated incredulously. Why would a traitor be so concerned about her comfort?

And then she understood. This was no uprising—merely one of his absurd games! He had an annoying tendency to kidnap individuals simply to showcase his abilities for Stan.

Supremely insulted, she hissed, "How dare you target me."

"I eeded ... de beth."

"You needed to conquer the best?"

When he nodded, she spat in his face. How dare he treat her as an object, as a mere tool to ingratiate himself to Stan!

Camille summoned their driver, who arrived with his gun at the ready. Sheridan tried to justify himself during the drive to the office, but Camille soon tired of his prattle. When she finally ordered his silence at gunpoint, he muttered, "Father will understand."

Camille sincerely doubted that. Perhaps Sheridan thought the current rift between his parents made her fair game, but Stan would interpret this prank as she did—as a human stepping out of his place to challenge their authority.

Nevertheless, this incident may provide the answer she had sought. Stan would undoubtedly demote the boy as a result.

When they arrived at Desmon Tower, she snagged four Presidential Guards to escort Sheridan to Stan's waiting area. She wasn't certain that the regular army would support her over their general, for many of the offspring were fiercely loyal to Sheridan. But Stan had handpicked the Paradisian-only Presidential Guard for their loyalty. They were organized as an independent unit under Garrick's brother, General Errol Sondem.

Camille went ahead to notify Stan of the morning's happenings. When she approached Madelyn's desk, the secretary jumped up. "Dr. Desmon! Dr. Moden's so upset! You didn't answer your phone!"

Marvelous. On top of everything, I'll have to handle Stan's moods.

"What's he's angry about?" Camille asked irritably.

Madelyn's brow crinkled. "He's not angry, ma'am. He's worried—about you."

Oh, of course—the link.

Madelyn babbled on. "He's called Patric and Iona so many times, he has them worried too. I've only seen him like this once, when you were kidnapped. He was sure you were in danger but didn't know where. He called the penthouse, but your housekeeper was ranting hysterically about people waving guns around, so that only made things worse. When you didn't answer your cell phone, he sent Errol out looking for you. Patric has your whole staff out searching too."

Just then, the guards escorted Sheridan off the elevator at gunpoint, and Madelyn gasped. "It was General Moden? A coup d'état?"

"Certainly not. Just one of his pranks, although a particularly ill-considered one." Camille was relieved to see Madelyn relax. They surely didn't need any rumors of insurrection getting started. "You may call off the searches. Everything is under control. But I do thank you for your diligence, Madelyn."

Camille opened Stan's door to find him pacing restlessly. When she entered, he rushed to her and held her in relieved silence. "Kami, Kami, Kami," he breathed at last. "Are you all right? What's happened?"

"Sheridan attacked me."

Stan pulled away, flushing crimson. "He *what*?" he roared, his British accent reappearing. "Are you injured?"

"No, I'm fine. It was merely one of his stunts—which you have only encouraged, I might add."

This magnified Stan's anger, as she knew it would. "I never encouraged anything involving you! How dare he! Where is the boy?"

"In your waiting area."

In a flurry, Stan rushed at the door and yanked it open. "Sheridan! Here! Straightaway!" He pointed emphatically to the space in front of him. "Madelyn, summon Garrick and Conner."

The guards escorted Sheridan into the office, where Stan flew at him and slammed him against the wall, hands at his throat. When Sheridan tried to fight back, the guards pinned his arms and legs. Stan continued to strangle him until the boy turned blue and passed out.

"Stan," Camille intoned, and he abruptly released Sheridan and let him drop to the floor, where he began to cough and breathe again. Stan reared back and kicked him in the gut before ordering him up. The guards lifted him to his feet, still coughing and gasping for air.

"How dare you!" Stan roared. "Play your pranks on your brother—I couldn't care less. But how in your little human brain could you think I'd allow you to touch my sister—wife?"

Sheridan, though not fully recovered, shakily drew himself up to his full height, his expression both defiant and confused. "You taught me to challenge all restrictions. I wanted you to know I'd learned my lessons and could take on the best."

"Learned your lessons?" Stan glowered at him with frank loathing. "You pathetic donkey! You've learned nothing at all!" He stepped up to him, inches from his bleeding nose, and growled between clenched teeth, "Nobody—nobody!—touches *my* wife."

"Father—"

"Don't call me that. You are no longer our son."

Sheridan's jaw dropped. "What?"

Stan ripped the general's insignia off the boy's uniform jacket. Turning to Conner, he slapped the insignia into his hand. "Lieutenant General Sondem, I hereby promote you to full general and place my army under your command."

Sheridan objected, "Father, you can't mean—"

Stan wheeled around and clouted him on the jaw. "I am not your father," he seethed.

Camille watched with satisfaction as something like humility, or at least tempered arrogance, came into Sheridan's eyes.

"Understand this," Stan continued, enunciating clearly. "You are no longer a Moden. You are no longer a Desmon. You no longer live in my home. You are no longer a member of my armed forces. You are hereby reassigned to housekeeping. *Per-ma-nent-ly*. Your new name is Sheridan Lakwadín."

Glaring directly into his eyes, Stan growled, "Is this quite clear?"

Sheridan's face lost what remained of its color. "Yes, sir."

"You will also undergo correction per Dr. Desmon's direction, which shall be …?" He turned to Camille.

She stepped toward Sheridan and cocked her head. "Dr. Moden, I believe the source of this poor boy's trouble is an excess of testosterone, a malady that drives him to inappropriate forms of aggression—"

A brilliant idea came to her then. Sheridan was rather a loose cannon whom she was delighted to see replaced. However, he was also admired by an army of well-trained, well-equipped soldiers. Humiliating such a leader without thoroughly despoiling his reputation might very well rile those excellent soldiers against them.

"—including the attempted rape of his own mother," she finished.

Conner's and the guards' eyes popped. Even in Desmon Tower, such a crime was unthinkable.

Sheridan squeezed his eyes shut in thorough defeat. He obviously understood the isolating effect her accusation would have.

"Therapeutic castration it is," Stan said with a chuckle.

Sheridan's eyes snapped open. "No!"

"Without anesthesia," Camille added.

"But Mother—"

Stan cuffed him. "Don't you disrespect my wife any further. She is not your mother."

Sheridan finally seemed to understand. He slumped against the wall and would have fallen to the floor if not for the guards holding him. "My apologies, ma'am," he whispered. He offered no resistance as the guards removed him from the office.

Relief washed over Camille as the door closed behind him. She had never liked that boy. Stan had insisted that he had him under control, but she had never fully believed it.

When the others cleared the office, Garrick held back to ask, "Camille, are you well?"

"I'm very well, thank you. He underestimated my abilities."

He nodded and dropped his voice to a whisper. "Just to be clear, the rape charge is false, isn't it?"

"Yes."

Garrick chuckled. "Nice touch. Thank you for averting that potential revolution."

When Garrick left, Stan turned to search Camille's eyes. Then he drew her into an embrace. "Yes, you're fine. That's my little sister."

She buried her face into his broad shoulder. "Oh, yes, I'm just fine. Our plans are crumbling at our feet, but I'm fine."

Stan didn't respond, but she sensed the anger and frustration that swept through him. First Stanley, then Sadira, and now Sheridan. Thankfully, raising human offspring had been Stan's idea rather than hers, because it surely wasn't working out as planned.

"Stan, are we wise in keeping Sheridan alive? He knows our habits and schedules intimately. He may retaliate against us or Saxon. He's also privy to sensitive information that he could sell to Damour."

"I think it's safe to assume Damour wouldn't buy his information. His ethics are too scrupulous. Your other point is valid, but I believe we can monitor him adequately. I'd rather not kill the insect. I want him worse than dead. I want him debased and humiliated. And there's no suffering in death, is there?"

"Yes, that's true. I must admit, the idea of him cleaning toilets is immensely satisfying."

"I was concerned about an uprising among the troops, but you effectively thwarted that possibility. Even his most faithful supporters will fall away when they learn what he's accused of. And Garrick knows how to monitor troublemakers. We can always kill the boy if necessary."

CHAPTER 12
UNDONE

*"Woe is me! for I am undone; because I am a man of unclean lips ...
for mine eyes have seen the King, the L*ORD *of hosts."*
Isaiah 6:5, KJV.

Pouring coffee on the floor Sheridan had just mopped, Tony Fiden mocked, "You missed a spot, Dr. Lakwadín." Snickers rippled through the lunchroom.

Ordinarily, Sheridan would never tolerate disrespect from the likes of Tony, a worm of a man who had let himself get fat and flabby since his own falling out with Father. But Sheridan was no fool. Thanks to Mother's slanderous accusation, the entire Paradisian community considered him fair game. And he, weak after the previous day's surgery, was in no condition to take on the entire group of scoffing maintenance workers. Instead, he contented himself with slopping sudsy water on Tony's pants as he mopped up the mess.

Being ridiculed by the nobodies who had scurried out of his way only two days before was maddening. Transitioning from powerful general to emasculated housekeeper was humiliating. Being disowned by America's richest man was disorienting, even though he was already a multimillionaire in his own right. But the worst of it all—and he knew this was Father's intention—was the name he'd saddled him with. One moment he was *Modén*, "exalted one"; the next he was *Lakwadín*, "disgraced one." He would bear his dishonor in his very name for the rest of his life. And, unlike others who had fallen out of favor, he would never be able to redeem himself in his father's eyes.

You are hereby reassigned to housekeeping. Per-ma-nent-ly.

Yes, Father had made that quite clear.

He walked his mop and pail toward the men's locker room, but almost ran into Uri—The Zombie, they'd called him as kids. He was a strange, sad man with no thumbs and no big toes—the marks of a traitor—whom Father had permanently assigned to cleaning septic tanks. His eyes especially creeped Sheridan out—a dead man had more life in his eyes. And his wrists were scarred from multiple suicide attempts because the wounds of those exposed to Viv fruit healed too fast to allow them to die; still, Uri kept trying.

Sheridan stepped back to give him a wide berth, but The Zombie latched onto his arm. With freakish intensity, he hissed, "Now you'll understand." Then he shambled away with his distinctive, slump-shouldered gait, leaving Sheridan to stare after him. Understand what?

As he rolled his pail into the locker room, Father's words again rang through his mind: *How in your little human brain could you think I'd allow you to touch my wife?*

Sheridan's attack was meant to prove, hopefully once and for all, that he was worthy of the Moden name too. This had always been harder for him than for Saxon or Sadira, whom his parents claimed were more intelligent. It didn't matter that he'd excelled at things his siblings didn't, like his military acumen, his ability to withstand pain, and his ability to rally his troops. Unlike his siblings, he'd never been guaranteed a top position in Father's work, so proving his worth had become an ongoing struggle.

But Father had always appreciated his practical jokes. In fact, for many years, the only time he'd enjoyed Father's approval was when he'd pulled off a successful stunt. He smiled wistfully as he remembered his first such prank.

"Sheridan, are you the one who kidnapped Savana's prize guard dog and locked him in my vault?" Father had asked.

"Yes, sir, Father."

"Why?"

"To show you I could."

Father had chuckled. "Well done, boy. That took some ingenuity."

Father had even smiled the next time, when Sheridan kidnapped their neighbor's pampered poodle, although he didn't congratulate him as warmly. It all worked out because the neighbor was a woman, and Father could charm anything female, but that time Father tempered his praise with a warning. "Your plan and execution were excellent, but don't kidnap any more outlander property without my permission."

He had turned to leave Sheridan's room then, but turned back around with an arched brow. "And don't kidnap any outlanders without my permission, either."

Sheridan interpreted that as both permission to kidnap people and a challenge to do so. Shortly thereafter, he left Tony Fiden tied up in a maintenance closet. When Tony's supervisor stormed into Father's office to report the incident, Father threw his head back and laughed. That time he actually gave Sheridan a fond tousling of his hair. "You're doing just fine, boy," he said. "Just fine. Next time, try to accomplish it without letting the Subject know who you are."

And so it had continued, Sheridan's escapades getting more daring, and Father's confidence in him rising. In time, Sheridan held the organization's records as the youngest offspring to be given a mission of his own, to kill an outlander, and to be given his own command. He'd had less need of extracurricular pranks since then because his assignments provided sufficient opportunity to secure Father's approval.

But the Strider mission had not gone as planned. He'd never understood why Father needed to deliver Strider to Mother—some old debt, apparently. But their failure to capture the old man severely disappointed her, and in her anger, Mother had urged Father to turn the command of Desmoden's army over to Conner and demote Sheridan to a lowly desk jockey.

That's why he'd devised the risky prank in the first place. Mother was universally acclaimed as a great warrior. Getting the better of her would prove, even to her, that he could conquer the fiercest combatants, that he recognized no artificial limitations or rules, that he was more daring and ruthless than Conner, and that he could be relied on to accomplish things Conner would never dream of doing.

So why had it backfired so catastrophically? Apparently he'd crossed some kind of line, but what? Past escapades had sometimes involved Saxon, and Father had never been angry. And it wasn't the failure that made the difference, for Father never even mentioned that. Rather, it seemed to be the prank itself. Why?

Sheridan picked up some stray clothing as he prepared to mop the floor. *How in your little human brain …?*

He sighed in frustration. After a sleepless night, his mind was a cauldron of boiling emotions and fragmented thoughts. But of the many things he didn't understand, amid all the anger and pain, disappointment and confusion, why did that particular insult keep popping back to the surface like a rotten potato?

He mopped the floor methodically, slapping the mop from side to side in the rhythm of that phrase. *How*—swish—*in your little*—swish—*human brain*—swish. *How*—swish—*in your little*—swish—*human brain*—swish. *Human brain*—swish. *Human brain*—swish.

"*Human* brain?" he exclaimed, suddenly processing the word for the first time. After all, it had been an insult, and you don't actually pay attention to insults. But Father had hurled slurs at him plenty of times before and never called him human. In fact, he couldn't remember him ever using that term on a countryman, no matter how angry he'd been. So why had Father lobbed such outrageous abuse at him?

He shook his head and went back to work. As his mop crisscrossed the floor, his brain again started the chant. But somewhere along the line, it changed of its own accord: *I am not*—swish—*your father*—swish. *I am not …*

That recalled another of Father's pronouncements: *She is not*—swish—*your mother*—swish. The combination pulled another phrase from deep in his subconscious: *egg donor.*

Sheridan had what Garrick jokingly called a phonographic memory—he remembered everything he heard. However, those bits of auditory information sometimes got confused, jumbling together in his head, so that he had trouble making anything of the mess. Yet if his brain had isolated this phrase, it was probably connected. So he concentrated, sorting through his mental files until he found the one that had produced it. Once he did, he recalled the whole conversation as clearly as if it had just happened.

One evening when a five-year-old Sheridan had pretended to be asleep, he had snuck into the dimly lit living room and listened as his parents chatted over a cup of tea. When they mentioned an egg donor, his ignorant young mind interpreted it as an egg donut. He remembered being very disappointed the next morning when no donuts materialized. He had never thought of the conversation again. But now it came flooding back, word for word, unclouded by the limitations of a five-year-old's knowledge.

"I have a special gift for you, Lusu," Mother was saying when Sheridan snuck to the doorway.

"I like gifts," Father said enthusiastically. "What is it?"

"We'll be able to get the same egg donor after all."

"That's excellent news. When?"

"Her appointment is for tomorrow."

"Good." Father chuckled as he added, "For a human, she's been remarkably helpful. That will make number four a full sibling to the boys, won't it?"

"Yes. Yes, it will."

Sheridan leaned back against the lockers with a sick feeling. Could it be? Were his parents really not his parents at all? Worse, could he actually be *human*?

He wanted to marshal logic against such an unthinkable conclusion, but the only facts he could muster supported rather than undermined it. Like the fact that the exiles hadn't generated offspring until recently, when they suddenly produced an explosion of them. Or the time he discovered some research involving *mij dinósh*, an enzyme that corrected genetic mutations in mice; Father had swiftly redirected his attention and then wiped the information from the hard drive. Or the fact that no Paradisian couple even shared a room, let alone a bed. And then there was his parents' overreaction to Stanley's revelation of their sibling relationship, a reaction that suggested they feared he would reveal something even more damaging.

But *human*? He collapsed onto the bench and dropped his head into his hands. Here he thought being *lakwadín* was bad!

No, certainly it couldn't be true. Father could have been talking about some other boys, some other family—not them. Their strength alone far surpassed that of any human. Never mind their intelligence.

Unless ... was that why Father had prevented him from seeing the *mij dinósh* research? Surely they'd studied its effects on other species—maybe even humans? Maybe they'd canceled out the damage that had accrued through centuries of genetic mutations, returning humans to their original state—stronger, smarter, and longer-lived. Such humans would be so similar to Paradisians that they could pass for their children.

Rebelling at the thought, Sheridan's other side demanded, *But that doesn't make sense. Most Paradisians don't even like kids. Why would they want to raise humans as their own?*

He immediately came up with one very good reason: labor. Father and Mother were anxious to the point of desperation about the Final Battle. They needed more manpower. That's probably why they produced only one generation of offspring; they needed them to complete this particular project.

That was it: the offspring were bred for labor. Slaves from birth.

Sheridan chuckled, and the chuckle grew into bitter, self-deprecating laughter. He'd certainly conjured up quite a theory. Father always said he had an active imagination. And now look at what he'd done—he would forever doubt his very parentage, yet he could never either confirm or refute the ridiculous notion.

"Good work, Sheridan," he murmured. "You've concocted a harrowing tale that will haunt your Subject for the rest of his life. Father would be proud."

He rose to his feet. "But enough nonsense. Get back to work."

"Lakwadín!" The maintenance supervisor's voice preceded him down the hallway.

Sheridan stepped to the doorway. "Here."

"Some clumsy oaf spilled soda on an electrical floor box in the recovery room." The supervisor tossed him some keys and sauntered off again.

Sheridan started to object—he was housekeeping, not maintenance. But then he reconsidered. An electrical floor box meant a computer might be connected. And of all the computers that might contain evidence about his cock-amamie theory, those storing medical records were the least protected. In the Moden mentality, the super-secret battle plans, business strategies, and political secrets stored in the Priority Computer network were infinitely more important than someone's list of medications.

He tossed the keys into the air and snatched them with a smile. "Yes, sir! Be happy to take care of that."

The supervisor frowned at him over his shoulder. "You're a strange one, Lakwadín."

Yeah, that seemed to be the prevailing opinion.

Sheridan made his way to the infirmary and found the affected floor box. Being in the workroom where medical personnel did their charting, it not only involved a computer, but was relatively private. The only spectators he'd have would be sitting in a booth somewhere, watching the spyware that he himself had commissioned. And he knew how to circumvent that.

As he was evaluating what work would be required, he overheard Austin Pim, the physician on duty, shouting at a student nurse. "What are you doing? Never give that much potassium to a Paradisian of the parent generation!"

The student nurse objected, "But that's what the standing orders call for. See here?"

"No, no, no! You're using the wrong protocol! Those orders are for the Paradisian *offspring*. Be careful, would you? That's a very dangerous mistake. Where's your supervisor, anyway?"

"Right here," called a nurse entering the room. "What's the problem?"

"She's using the standing orders for offspring on a parent," Austin raged. "Watch your students more closely, or I'll report you to my father."

"I'm very sorry, sir," the male nurse replied. "It won't happen again. I'll make sure of it."

Apparently satisfied, Austin stepped away, and the nurse turned a furious eye on his student. "Another mistake like that, and I'll make sure you flunk out of the program. You shouldn't be handling any meds without me at your side, and you're certainly not qualified to decide which standing orders to use."

"I'm sorry," she pleaded. "I thought I was helping."

"Helping? We're lucky he was the one who noticed your mistake. If that had been his father, we'd both be downstairs undergoing correction as we speak. And—oh, yeah—the patient would be coding."

"Coding? The difference between the generations can cause cardiac arrest?"

"It has to do with the Viv fruit. It alters physiology, including sensitivity to medications. The parent generation generally requires lower dosages. In fact, in many respects, the offspring physiology is more similar to humans than to the Paradisian parents."

Sheridan's brow knit together. What an interesting bit of information. Funny thing, though—it sounded remarkably like Father's favorite technique for constructing lies. Following this reasoning, Viv fruit exposure could explain any difference between the parent and offspring generations, and the explanation could never be tested—at least not until they overthrew Paradise Island. And by then, who cared?

He smiled to himself. *You are good, Father.*

Finishing his evaluation, Sheridan brushed off his coveralls and moved toward Austin. "Whoever the idiot with the slippery cup was, he did a great job of frying things in there. What do you want repaired first?"

"Oh, um …" Austin glanced around. "Here, let me look."

Sheridan followed him into the workroom thinking it odd that he would have to "look" to know which equipment he needed most urgently. But then, Austin had always struck him as a squirrelly sort. Whatever had Sadira seen in him?

Austin shut the door behind them and, without "looking" at all, named a couple of monitors. Then he turned to Sheridan with an intense gaze. "What do you know about Sadira? Is she okay?"

Sheridan rolled his eyes at the doctor's stupidity. Quickly removing the cover of the overhead light, he located the telltale blue dot on the neck of the light bulb and gave it a good, solid whack with his hammer. Glass shattered all over the room.

Covering his head with his arms, Austin yelled, "What are you doing? Are you nuts?"

Sheridan grabbed his arm hard and snarled, "Shut up! I just saved your sorry hide, but this room isn't soundproof." Gesturing outside the room, he added, "The next bug may pick up yelling."

Austin paled. "A bug? In here?"

"Of course. Most all of the light bulbs are bugged. But this one's monitored randomly and there's a thirty-second delay in transmission, so we're okay. No one will hear you expressing concern about a traitor."

Austin passed a hand over his eyes. "Thanks. I had no idea."

"I didn't do it for you. I'm not exactly Employee of the Month, you know." Raising an eyebrow, he continued, "On the other hand, turning in someone who's expressed treasonous concerns just may help my case."

Austin's eyes widened, and Sheridan watched in amusement as the implications registered. As if Sheridan could ever redeem himself! But Austin didn't know that, and after the stress of yesterday, Sheridan needed some fun.

The doctor backed away, hands raised defensively. "I-I didn't mean anything, honest. I was just, you know, wondering. Curious. I—" He broke off when he bumped into a chair.

What *did* Sadira see in this guy?

With Austin trapped against the chair, Sheridan stepped forward and just stood there towering over him for a long moment. The doctor's Adam's apple bobbed as he swallowed hard. Sheridan could almost hear his thoughts: *What was I thinking? Nobody can see what's happening in here, and I've heard stories about this guy. He kills for the sheer pleasure of it.*

When Austin's right hand began inching toward the pocket of his lab coat, Sheridan asked, "Whatcha got in that pocket, doc? A scalpel? That's a good idea. You never know when you may need to defend yourself. There's just one problem."

The Adam's apple bobbed and then bobbed again. "Wh-what?"

"Before you even get to that knife, I could kill you in about a dozen different ways. With my bare hands."

He held Austin's eyes captive for a few tense seconds and then abruptly stepped back out of the doctor's personal space. Flashing the trademark grin that made the girls swoon, he added lightly, "If I had a reason to."

Austin's sigh of relief was a total body experience. He collapsed into the chair and wiped the beads of sweat off his lip.

Sheridan laughed without restraint and then sobered. Quietly, he said, "No. I haven't heard anything about Sadira. But that's good. If we'd caught her, my parents would be parading her mangled body all over the building. Truth is, we've never caught any of the offspring defectors. Not one."

"Thank you." Austin paused, studying his shoes, and then looked up to search Sheridan's eyes. "Do—do you miss her?"

Sheridan squinted at him. "You really do think I'm some kind of monster, don't you?"

"No! No, I don't. Just the opposite—you're incredible, a true hero of Moden Industries."

Sheridan snorted. "Isn't that the same thing?" Turning to his toolbox, he said, "I need to get to work."

When Austin left the workroom, Sheridan quickly swept up the broken glass and restored the two monitors the doctor needed. Then he fixed the computer. It took a while, but with other computer terminals available, nobody disturbed him. When he finished, he poked his head out the door and called, "Austin, those monitors are up. I'll be working on the computer next, but it will take some time."

"Thanks, Sheridan." Austin returned to collect some information from the monitors and closed the door behind him.

"Thank *you*, doctor," Sheridan murmured. He couldn't have arranged this opportunity better if he'd tried. He easily skirted a series of firewalls to open some protected files that had remained untouched for decades. Then, with a few more keystrokes, he sat staring at the prenatal record for his own birth—to Camille Desmon.

A wave of relief swept over him. If his mother had carried him, he wasn't human! That settled the question.

But as he moved to exit the file, an entry jumped out at him: *Height: 65 inches.* He wanted to chalk it up to a simple typo, but it couldn't be. Camille Desmon was 71 inches tall. A typo might make her 72, or even 61. But 65?

He checked the records for his siblings' births and discovered that, for Stanley, Camille Desmon had been 66 inches tall. For Saxon, 69 inches. For Sadira, 64. And in that conversation about the egg donor, Father had said they were all full siblings. So the only way they could be full siblings with different sized mothers was if they were born to surrogates.

Still, that didn't prove anything. Maybe Mother had a fertility issue that precluded her carrying a pregnancy. Or maybe she had hired someone to carry her children just to avoid the inconveniences of pregnancy; that would be just like her. No, what he needed was something definitive—a chromosome test.

It took him a few minutes to figure out the medical abbreviations, but once he did, he realized that karyotypes had been done on many of the embryos, including him. His chart documented a nice, normal 52,XY.

He smiled in relief. He was Paradisian. How silly of him to entertain any other idea.

But then he got curious. How amazing would it be to see his very own chromosomes? So he searched out the karyogram—the photograph of the chromosomes—and automatically started counting the sequentially ordered pairs. When he tallied twenty-three, he frowned at the page. Twenty-three? He must have counted wrong.

He recounted, this time adding up each individual chromosome, and still arrived at only forty-six. Where were the three pairs of missing chromosomes?

Suddenly he had trouble breathing. A 46,XY karyotype? That was human! He desperately began opening other prenatal records randomly to count the chromosomes. But every single karyogram pictured forty-six chromosomes, even though the prenatal records reported either 52,XX or 52,XY.

Despite the cover-up in these records, he could no longer avoid the unmistakable conclusion. The so-called Paradisian offspring were really humans carried by surrogate human mothers. *He* was human. Genetically modified to optimize his faculties for the work assigned him, but human all the same.

And now he understood his father's fury. As a Paradisian, and especially as Father's biological sister, Mother's status loomed way above that of any human, including his own. On the other hand, Saxon, being only human, was fair game for his brother's pranks.

Father's challenge returned to him: *How dare you!*

How dare he, indeed! How dare any measly human consider himself worthy of challenging a Paradisian of Mother's caliber? Sheridan might as well have challenged Father himself. This placed the incident in an entirely different light. Even Sheridan would never have dared confront Mother if he'd known the truth—if he'd known who he really was.

Sheridan completed the cleanup in a wretched daze. It was lunchtime when he finished. He mechanically bought some cafeteria food and took it up to the tenth floor, where a large balcony overlooked the street. The place usually sat abandoned, as it did now, making it a good place to think.

And he certainly needed to think. Discovering oneself to be adopted could be disorienting enough. But to learn that he belonged to a different species, and one he'd been taught to despise? His entire personal history—his *whole* life—was founded on lies.

Where did the lies stop? How could he know? Was everything he thought he knew based on lies? What about the really big issues that transcended his personal existence, like the war with Damour? Was the purpose of Moden Industries truly one of liberating the world from Doúg's tyrannical rule?

Leaning on the railing, Sheridan rubbed his face with both hands. Where could he find the answers to such overarching questions? His parents excelled at everything they did, including lying. He had no way of telling where the lies stopped and the truth began. He needed an objective source of truth. Where could he find such a thing? Did it even exist?

I speak the truth; I declare what is right.

He searched his memory for the source of that random quote and finally placed it in *The Runner's Manual.* And that solved his dilemma. For, although accusing Doúg of lying was one of his parents' favorite ploys for discrediting him, they had repeatedly assured Sheridan that the dictator was actually *incapable* of falsehood. This was why Sheridan could use the *Manual* to inform his battle plans. And, because his parents had largely relied on him to design their battle strategy, he was quite certain they would not provide him with faulty information on which to base it. So this meant that, not only did Doúg proclaim his honesty, but his parents did too—perhaps the only thing on which they both agreed.

Realizing the irony, Sheridan laughed aloud. He had to go to his enemy to discover truth! But if that's what it took, so be it. The problem would be accessing a copy of *The Runner's Manual,* which was banned for most offspring. However, Sheridan had needed it as the army's commander. Maybe he could still get his hands on that copy.

Taking out his cell phone, he dialed his father's executive secretary. "Madelyn, this is Sheridan. There are some personal items in my old office I'd like to get—shirts, razor, stuff like that. My par—" He sighed. "I mean, Drs. Moden and Desmon sent my things from the penthouse to my hotel yesterday, so I don't think they'd mind if I collect my stuff from the office."

"Hold, please." She put him on hold and returned a moment later. "Dr. Moden says you may collect your personal belongings, but I'm to accompany you."

Shortly thereafter, Sheridan stood in his old suite on the top floor. While Madelyn hovered, he collected some things from the office and loaded them into a box. Then he went into the adjacent bedroom and grabbed the two books on the bedside table, including a copy of *The Runner's Manual.* He was so relieved Madelyn didn't notice it that he almost forgot the clothes hanging in the closet. He stepped back to snatch them up at the last minute.

"I think that's it," he said.

"Fine," she said coolly. "Dr. Moden says you should have no reason to return to this floor in the future unless summoned."

"I understand."

He stopped at the doorway to say goodbye to his old life. He'd worked hard to earn the rights to this prestigious office. Now it belonged to his archrival. What's more, he'd been banished from the only home he'd ever known. He had no parents. No siblings. Not even any friends, if they valued their lives. His entire existence had been wiped out.

Sheridan Moden was dead.

* * * * *

Sheridan Lakwadín lay on the bed in his hotel suite, fingers laced behind his head, staring up at the corner where mauve walls met a white ceiling. He'd spent every spare minute of the last two days reading through *The Runner's Manual* and trying to answer the question that now absorbed every waking moment: What is truth?

He'd found the answer. It had hidden right under his nose all this time. But it wasn't good news. In fact, it was horrible news. It had forced him to see himself honestly—as a liar, thief, torturer, rapist, and murderer. For the first time, he understood those things were wrong.

No, that wasn't true. He'd known all along. Of course, he'd known. There had always been a voice in the back of his head, the one put there "so that men are without excuse." He had ignored that voice, regarding it as a weakness that would keep him from winning Father's good opinion. He had tried to silence it through progressively more sinister acts. But the voice had always been there. And now he knew it had been right all along.

He wanted the truth? Then this was it: He, Sheridan Modén Lakwadín, was a bad man—a truly bad man.

Actually, that awful name Father gave him fit perfectly. He really was *lakwadín*. He'd been disgracing himself since he could talk and blaspheme Doug. He'd been disgracing himself since he could help carry out his parents' plans against Doug's runners. The more he'd tried to silence that voice, the more he'd disgraced himself. He'd done it over and over again, earning the name more and more every day.

Even more sickening, he would be *lakwadín* for another nine centuries or so, with no hope of ever being anything better. Because no matter what he did in the future, he could never undo the *kanuf* he'd already committed. He could never return the lives of those he'd killed. He could never restore the peaceful sleep of those he'd terrorized.

No, only Damour's grace could ever make him into something more than *lakwadín*. But not only had he irrevocably lost Father's approval, he had also, in trying to gain it, done everything possible to alienate Damour. And his parents had been both truthful and correct about one thing: there were only two sides. This left Sheridan nowhere to turn and no hope of ever improving his situation. Worse yet, that was exactly how it should be. He deserved nothing better.

This, then, was truth.

He went to the bathroom mirror and looked into the eyes of the desperately wicked man he now knew himself to be. He automatically adjusted the neckline of his polo shirt to cover the red birthmark just below his left collarbone. But when his gaze met the bruises where Father had nearly strangled him, he heard himself mumble, "He should have finished the job."

It was a strange idea. Sheridan wasn't prone to depression, nor had he ever before considered that his life might be worthless. Even now, with his spirits as low as they had ever been, he didn't ponder the notion out of emotion but of logic. By contributing to the Moden community, he was supporting his parents' mission. Even as a janitor, the work he performed freed someone else to commit the atrocities he had once perpetrated. So staying at Moden Industries meant both supporting evil and living a horrible, lonely life as the castoff son of Moden Industries' leaders. Yes, he could escape, but to what purpose? To spend the rest of his life looking over his shoulder? To be tortured and killed on his father's terms when he finally caught up with him?

Father had purposely put him in a position where he would be endlessly humiliated, and he would never give him another chance. He knew his father well enough to recognize that's the only reason he hadn't killed him—he wanted him to be miserable. Like The Zombie.

Now you'll understand. As Uri's words returned to him, his reflection's blue eyes widened. That's what Uri meant: Sheridan would now understand the hopelessness of a life without purpose and without the possibility of improvement. He would now understand the reason for the dead look in Uri's eyes. He would become another zombie. Could there be a more horrifying fate?

These were not the pessimistic musings of a depressed man but an honest, objective evaluation. Like Uri, Sheridan Lakwadín could never hope for anything more than a miserable and useless life. However, he differed from Uri in one key respect: he had never been exposed to Viv fruit. Uri's repeated suicide attempts had failed because his body healed too well. Sheridan would not have that problem. For him, suicide was an option.

He continued to mull over these ideas through the next day. By the time he got off work, he'd made his decision. He found a sturdy rope in one of the maintenance closets and, carefully hiding it from the man who'd been tailing him, took it back to the hotel suite. There he dressed up, took the elevator to the elegant dining room on the hotel's top floor, and enjoyed an excellent meal.

Then he returned to his suite to hang himself.

CHAPTER 13

FAITHFUL SERVANTS

"Well done, good and faithful servant."
Matthew 25:21, NKJV.

A hook protruded from the living room ceiling where a light fixture must have once hung. Sheridan had wondered if it would support his weight, but it held when he tested it. He fashioned a hangman's noose in the rope and placed it around his neck. Then he stood on a chair to secure the rope to the hook.

He had never been one to hesitate when something needed doing, and he didn't falter now. As his hands formed the knot that would take his life, they moved quickly, never wavering. Likewise, his thoughts never vacillated. He had weighed the pros and cons of living, and the cons came out way ahead. His conclusion was well-reasoned; his decision firm.

As he adjusted his position to kick the chair out from under him, his eyes lit on *The Runners' Manual* lying on the coffee table, and a passage popped into his head: *Whoever believes in him is not condemned.*

"Except me," he muttered.

Whoever *believes in him is not condemned.* ***Whoever*** *comes to me I will* ***never*** *drive away.*

"Really?" Sheridan squinted at the book doubtfully. "Even me?"

It was another strange idea. Father insisted they were beyond Damour's forgiveness, exempt from his grace. Was that another lie? Damour had accepted all the defecting offspring, including Sadira, who had personally killed two runners. Father said he was only using them, that he wouldn't actually allow them access to the island or to the Viv fruit. Could that be a lie too?

Suddenly the memory of standing face-to-face with his oldest brother in Father's office came to his mind. One curious thing had struck him then: Stanley's obvious sense of peace, despite the unlikely circumstance. Sheridan had never known such serenity. Oh, he'd known fleeting satisfaction when on Father's good side, when Father had publicly praised him, rewarded him with rich gifts, and lavished honors on him. Yet even then, the threat of earning Father's disapproval hung over him like the sword of Damocles, leaving him with a relentless sense of uncertainty.

Actually, Damocles was lucky; he had the option of a simpler life that offered some measure of tranquility. Sheridan never had that choice. A Moden had only two alternatives: obedience and luxury, or disobedience and torture. A simple, serene life was never in the cards.

But now—was peace really possible, even for him? Of course, it would cost plenty after all he'd done. A million bucks? Maybe more. Probably some retaliatory torture, too. In the *Manual,* no one ever recorded what they'd paid for their acceptance, but it wasn't the sort of thing he'd expect them to talk about. Certainly Father's minions wouldn't dare make the details of their corrections public.

Look at you, his mind argued. *You've got a noose around your neck! What have you got to lose?*

He chuckled. "Good point." The truth was, he had plenty of money, he knew how to endure pain, and experiencing such peace would be worth just about anything. Besides, he liked the idea of turning his military intelligence over to Damour. He could never atone for all the evil he'd committed, but helping Damour with what he knew would at least be a step in the right direction—*and* it would drive his parents nuts!

Sheridan chuckled again as he removed the noose. Stepping down from the chair, he laid on the sofa to reread the *Manual.* His objective was to answer one question: Could Damour's "whoever" include him?

✻ ✻ ✻ ✻ ✻

Chris had always felt most at home in nature, so he loved coaching Sadira on Alaska's trails. His busy schedule provided a welcome distraction, allowing him little time to dwell on how sorely he missed Susana. But his favorite time of day was after dinner, when outlanders and guards gathered around the fireplace to pop popcorn or roast marshmallows ... and, of course, to tell stories. Each evening, Chris let his granddaughters choose a story for him to recite. They took this responsibility very seriously, laboring long over whether to pick a story represented by one of the figurines in Juan Misi's necklace or by one of the stones in either Chris's or Susana's wedding rings, for Chris wore Susana's ring on the unbreakable *tsuma* chain of his transmitter. Per family tradition, he told the stories in Rarámuri, although he repeated them in English for Sadira and some of the guards.

Just as they finished story time one evening, Doug called Chris over his receiver. "Son, I'll have need of your medical expertise tomorrow. Do y'all mind a trip back to DC?"

"No, of course not. I'm yours to command, Doug."

"Thank you, pardner. No need to bother the others—you'll be back in a jiffy. I'll send a jet for you in the mornin'."

"I'll be ready."

✻ ✻ ✻ ✻ ✻

Sheridan again lay on his bed, fingers laced behind his head. He'd just finished reading *The Runners' Manual* through again and was considering a man named Paul, who had called himself the worst of sinners. Like Sheridan, he had tortured and killed runners. Yet Damour had forgiven him. It perturbed Sheridan that Paul never said what he'd paid for it. He preferred to know the specifics of the deal up front. Some references called Damour's grace a "free gift," but that must just be the sanitized party line. Still, if Damour's offer to accept "whoever comes" applied to someone like Paul, it apparently was all-inclusive.

So how did one go about applying for Damour's grace? In one place Paul said, "All who believe are justified." But in another he said, "Everyone who calls on his name will be saved." That worried Sheridan because, like every Paradisian he'd ever known, he couldn't say Damour's first name.

Just to prove the point, he cleared his throat and tried now. "Doúg," he said without coughing.

The shock propelled him to his feet. "Doúg Deón Damoúr—I *can* call on his name!"

Wildly encouraged, he pulled out his cell phone and began to dial General Gabriel Lanáj's number. Then he abruptly stopped. He couldn't call that number; Father would know at once. If the Presidential Guards were tailing him—and they were—they were monitoring his calls and e-mails too.

He considered the dilemma and decided he needed to acquire a burner phone that Father's men didn't know about. So he went for a stroll and shoplifted a phone. This created an unexpected problem that, frankly, Sheridan found annoying: he actually felt guilty about stealing! He managed this difficulty by slipping some bills into the store owner's pocket to cover the phone's cost.

He strolled back to his hotel and rescanned his rooms for surveillance devices, which he did each time he returned to the suite. So far, he had apparently kept a low enough profile that Garrick hadn't felt it necessary to bug his quarters. Then he called General Lanáj, who answered by identifying himself.

Sheridan hesitated, perhaps for the first time in his life. Until now, he'd always seen himself as *modén* and, therefore, as better than anyone else. Now he understood he truly was *lakwadín,* and it seemed terribly audacious of a *lakwadín* to request help from someone as important as the commander of Damour's army.

"*Arijíb Gabriel Lanáj,*" the general repeated. (Paradisian: I am Gabriel Lanáj.)

What do you have to lose?

Speaking in Paradisian, Sheridan said, "This is—well, you would know me as General Sheridan Moden." Quickly, he added, "Please don't hang up."

General Lanáj switched to English, his tone wary but not hostile. "I shan't."

"I can say his name: Doúg Damoúr. Does that mean even I can call on his name and be saved?"

"Yes," the general responded firmly.

A wave of inexpressible relief washed over Sheridan. "Would—? Look, I know I have no right to request this, and you have no reason to grant it, but I don't know who else to ask."

"What can I do for you, son?"

Sheridan stared at the phone. Son? Even Father had never called him that. It took him a moment to find his voice again. "Would you help me call on His Majesty's name?"

"I'd love to," General Lanáj said. "How can we meet?"

✲ ✲ ✲ ✲ ✲

Lieutenant Riana Jones Strider was tossing the last of her toiletries into her duffle bag when a knock sounded at the door. She opened it to find Colonel Jané Lanáj—General Gabriel Lanáj's sister and assistant—standing there.

"My brother would like to see you if you have a moment," the colonel said.

"Your brother, the general?" Riana said incredulously. "He wants to see *me*?"

"If it's not too inconvenient."

The tall Paradisian led her through the hallways to a modestly furnished office. General Lanáj smiled and motioned Riana to a chair while he finished a phone call. Then, rounding the desk, he took a seat beside her and clasped her hand between his.

Riana had never met this great man before, and she certainly wasn't in the habit of allowing strange men to hold her hand. Yet his bearing was so open, so truly loving and wholly non-sensual, that the action seemed perfectly normal, even soothing. In fact, it reminded her of her late grandfather.

"My child," he said warmly. "I've wanted to meet you for some time. You are greatly loved on Paradise Island."

Joy bloomed within Riana's chest. She would never want anything more! If she was loved by the Damours, her life was complete.

His voice grew somber. "I must ask you to postpone your return to Los Angeles until tomorrow. I have a difficult assignment for you, although the primary challenge comes from within your family. Some will not look kindly on your participation. You see, the operation involves the rescue of General Sheridan Moden, Susana's murderer."

When her jaw slackened, he patted her hand. "I will not order you to participate. Doug hopes that you will lead the rescue team, but he is leaving the choice with you."

A sharp pang wrenched at Riana's heart. How she had loved her mother-in-law! What's more, she had only married into the Strider family six months before. To say that some would not look kindly on her participation was like calling a tornado a little breeze. Some family members would consider it an outright betrayal. And how could she let them down after they had accepted her, a poor, inner city girl from Detroit, so wholeheartedly?

Still, how could she refuse anything Doug asked? No, she wouldn't turn down the assignment. She would have some explaining to do, but Andy would understand. He would never refuse Doug's requests himself. They had a joint motto: *Whatever Doug commands, we will do.* As for the other family members— well, as long as she was following Doug's instructions, he would give her the wisdom and strength to handle the fallout.

"I'm honored that Doug trusts me with this mission," she said sincerely. "And participating in any rescue is a privilege. I will be happy to accept the assignment, General."

He kissed her tenderly on the cheek. "Your reputation as Doug's willing servant is well earned, child."

The general briefed her on the specifics of the mission and assigned two privates and Sergeant Kyle Sharp to accompany her. She gathered her team and laid out the plan without divulging the name of the individual to be rescued. Their disguise was simple—a medical examiner's jacket over street clothes—and Colonel Lanáj had already arranged to borrow one of the ME's vans. Having worked in an ME's office during college, Riana felt comfortable assuming the behavior and lingo they'd need to carry off the operation. Within a half hour, all was ready.

She was following her team to the underground garage when Jorge suddenly appeared at her elbow. Her chest tightened as he fell into step beside her.

"Off on a rescue operation?" he asked amiably.

Nobody outside the team knew about this mission, but it didn't surprise her that Jorge did. He had the uncanny talent of having ears everywhere while being seen nowhere. What's more, most any mission involving a high-level defector would ordinarily be his, or at least under his supervision, for he was unquestionably the best special ops man they had. Yet it didn't surprise her that General Lanáj had excluded him. She loved her brother-in-law; he was a generous and caring man. But he was also a man of strong emotions. His face had come to mind first when the general mentioned unhappy family members.

Keeping her tone light, she answered, "Nothing fancy. I guess they didn't want to waste your time on something so straightforward."

"Well, good. I hope it stays simple for you."

She smiled, the tightness in her chest relaxing. "Thank you, Jorge."

He walked with her in silence for a moment. "So who's the lucky fellow?"

Her chest tightened again, but she flashed a teasing grin. "Are you testing me, Captain? You know I can't tell you that."

He chuckled. "Good for you, Lieutenant." He sobered as he opened the door to the parking garage for her. "Be careful out there."

The team proceeded to an upscale hotel, the kind that didn't like having an ME's van parked out front. This worked in their favor, for the staff fell over themselves trying to be helpful and get them away quickly. The manager herself ushered them upstairs to a fancy suite. She slipped her key into the door, opened it, and stepped inside, only to be immediately overcome. Losing all color, she stumbled a little, her wide eyes fixed on something straight ahead. Riana quickly reached for the manager's arm and turned her around. Escorting her back into the hallway, she fanned her with her clipboard until a little color returned to the woman's cheeks.

"These things are even hard for us," she soothed. "You never get used to them. But there's really no need for you to stay. We can call you if we need anything."

"Thank you." The manager's trembling fingers unbuttoned her collar. "I'll be in my office."

Afraid that the distraught woman might faint on the way, Riana assigned one of the privates to see her back downstairs. Then she turned back to knock at the door, which had closed behind her other two men. Kyle opened the door and reported, "All's clear, ma'am."

"Thank you." Riana passed into the room and looked toward the window. Although the drapes were closed, enough light filtered in to clearly see the man hanging suspended from the ceiling, and she gasped at two simultaneous impressions. First, the man, at least in profile, looked so much like her husband—same ears, straight brown hair, and high cheekbones—that she actually thought it was Andy on first glance.

Second, this was supposed to be a staged suicide. The person's face should be normal in color because a hidden rope around his chest should be supporting his weight. However, this man appeared truly dead: his neck swollen around the rope; his tongue protruding from his mouth; purple spots dotting his face where the capillaries had broken.

We're too late—something went horribly wrong!

Maybe he had rigged the rope incorrectly and actually hanged himself by mistake. Maybe he had slipped before the setup was ready for his weight. Or—the most likely possibility—maybe the enemy had intercepted the mission and put this high-profile defector to death before the rescue team reached him. Whatever it was, something clearly went awry.

"Lieutenant?" Kyle touched her arm.

"I think we're too late," she whispered. "He looks—"

"Dead?" The corpse's head popped up with a big grin. "Gotcha!"

Riana stared at the prankster, momentarily caught between relief and outrage. Then she laughed. "Yes," she agreed. "You definitely got me."

He roared with laughter and explained that he had wanted to be a convincing corpse. She agreed that he had put his knowledge of special effects to good use. Then, still dangling from the ceiling, he commanded, "Private Barnes, snap to. Position that chair under me." It was an order—there was no other word for it—issued by one accustomed to giving orders and having them obeyed.

The private did as commanded, but questioned suspiciously, "Who are you, and how do you know my name?"

"You'd know me as General Sheridan Moden," the recovered corpse answered nonchalantly.

The private visibly stiffened and glanced wide-eyed at Riana.

The general continued, "And I know you—and Sergeant Sharp and Lieutenant Strider—the same way I know every soldier in the Outlander Division. By surveillance pictures."

"Okay, that's creepy," Kyle murmured to Riana.

The man, now balancing on the chair and unbuttoning his shirt to free himself of the rope, said casually, "It's meant to be. Creepy is one of the few weapons we have that you don't."

Riana approached him carefully. Despite what she knew of this man, she had determined not to dislike him right off. People changed, often dramatically, when they left Stan's ranks for Doug's, so she tried not to judge the new person on the behavior of the old. But she wasn't a fool, either. This fellow was an odd one, with a strange sense of humor that easily made light of life-and-death situations. But rescued individuals generally wanted to shed all ties to their old way of life. Was this dangerous man's continued identification with the enemy merely a function of his quirky personality? Or was he still part of them; had her team been drawn into a trap?

Keeping her eye on him, she asked Kyle, "You checked for listening devices as well as for enemy presence, Sergeant?"

"Yes, ma'am," Kyle answered.

"They did—I'll vouch for them," the general agreed cheerfully. "Good idea, by the way. This would be a great way to set you up for an ambush."

Riana's neck prickled at this echo of her thoughts. "Is that what this is?"

When the hands of her two fellows moved to their concealed guns, the general cast an amused expression at them. Riana understood at once what he found amusing. Still shirtless after freeing himself of the rope, he stood towering over them on the chair. She knew at a glance that, even armed, the three of them were no match for this well-muscled Paradisian super-soldier.

"At ease, men," she said, and consciously relaxed her own posture. "Guns would do us little good against a soldier as skilled as General Moden. Even as a group, we're outmatched and would be immobilized before we got off a decent shot. However, this mission has gone directly through Doug, who knows our relative vulnerability. We can trust him."

The general's gaze returned to her, his amusement replaced by wonder. "It was exactly that kind of confidence, that peace, that drew me to your side," he said earnestly, and Riana believed he meant it. "I have to say, I find it completely incomprehensible."

It was Riana's turn to grin. "It's meant to be. Peace is one of the many weapons we have that you don't."

"Touché," he said, laughing.

"But I promise you," she added, "you will understand it soon."

He immediately sobered. "I hope so."

The general descended from the chair, shrugged into his shirt, and climbed into the body bag on the stretcher as if it were a cozy sleeping bag. As they zipped it up, he chuckled and wondered aloud how many people lived to tell what the inside of one looked like. Riana didn't particularly appreciate his sense of humor, but, considering that he'd been raised as an assassin, maybe the miracle was that he had one at all.

They were wheeling the stretcher to the door when he hissed, "Psst!"

Signaling a halt, Riana asked, "Yes, General?"

His muffled voice responded, "No one would notice if I took something small with me in here."

She unzipped the bag to expose his face. "What did you have in mind—your wallet? Laptop, maybe?"

"Nah, I can replace those. What I really want is my *Runner's Manual*."

This clear evidence of the transformation already occurring brought a lump to her throat. Finding speech impossible, she simply motioned for Kyle to retrieve the book. Then she looked into the face of a man whom she had hoped never to meet—a man who would have scared her into blithering idiocy only a week before—and smiled.

CHAPTER 14

MORNING MIST

"I have swept away your offenses like a cloud, your sins like the morning mist. Return to me, for I have redeemed you."
Isaiah 44:22, NIV.

Sheridan walked into the enemy's division headquarters with nothing but the clothes on his back and the *Manual* he clutched in one hand. Accustomed to packing all manner of hidden weapons, even when not on enemy territory, he suddenly felt very naked, very vulnerable. Being in a position of superior strength, he'd been able to have a little fun with Lieutenant Strider's team. Her assessment of his skills was accurate—he could have easily taken them all out if necessary. But he couldn't stand against the entire Paradisian Embassy.

But then, I'm not here as a combatant, am I?

It was another in a series of strange ideas, yet he truly had no reason to fight these people. Whatever they did to him, he still wanted them to crush his parents. Even if King Doúg ordered him executed, he wouldn't resist; he'd intended to do that himself.

He was relaxing some with this realization when Lieutenant Strider led him into a central sitting room ... where sat General Gabriel Lanáj himself. Commander of the world's most powerful army. One of history's most formidable warriors.

Sheridan's entire perspective automatically shifted—he couldn't help it. His deeply ingrained process of evaluating his environment for threats reflexively kicked in, reported that he was now in a position of both inferior strength and inferior status, and put all his defenses on high alert.

Not here to fight, Sheridan reminded himself.

The man who rose from the sofa looked exactly like Father. Yet his face radiated such peace that Sheridan thought he could never confuse them. Again, the desire welled up in him to know such serenity. He hoped the lieutenant was right—that he could experience that peace. If he did, maybe he could someday relinquish this compulsion to evaluate everyone he met for their comparative rank and strength.

How freeing that would be! Could such a world really exist?

Smiling broadly, General Lanáj offered his hand. "I'm very pleased to meet you, nephew."

Sheridan accepted the hand, only to find himself drawn into a hug that ended with a kiss on his cheek. Although he'd been thoroughly educated in Paradisian culture and knew this cheek-kissing thing to be the typical Paradisian greeting, it still felt strange, especially coming from a lifelong enemy. He had expected what he deserved—a cool, suspicious reception followed by a painful initiation and a long period of apologizing for his evil past. He would have understood that. He didn't understand this warm welcome at all.

A short man in a captain's uniform entered the room, apparently just passing through. But he came to an abrupt halt when he saw Sheridan. He shot a quick, outraged expression at Lieutenant Strider before settling a fierce expression on him.

Sheridan decided to meet the problem head-on. "Captain Jorge Strider, I can only express my deepest regret for how I've hurt you and your family." He shook his head. "I was so very wrong."

Captain Strider's glare remained fastened on him as if monitoring a poisonous serpent, but he didn't address him. "General Lanáj, Lieutenant Strider— do you know who this man is?"

"Yes, we do," General Lanáj answered as Lieutenant Strider said softly, "Yes, Jorge."

"He murdered my mother."

"We know," General Lanáj said.

"And meant to rape her."

"We know."

The captain transferred his angry gaze to General Lanáj. "Don't expect my help." With that, he executed a sharp about-face and stalked out of the room.

Sheridan actually felt relieved—someone was finally treating him as he deserved. But he couldn't understand why the renowned general tolerated such impudence.

General Lanáj nodded at Lieutenant Strider, and she followed the captain, leaving Sheridan alone with the great general.

"I am sorry," the general said.

"Don't be. I deserve that—that and much more. But I am surprised that you allow such disrespect from a subordinate."

"Jorge has been through a difficult time. And we do things rather differently in Doúg's service. There are no 'subordinates' here. Our ranking system merely preserves the chain of command."

"H'mm," Sheridan said, which meant it made no sense to him. Still, the comment so closely echoed his wish for a world blind to rank and power that it fanned his hope of knowing such a place.

"Well, please come, sit down." General Lanáj motioned him down a hall.

"Actually, I'd prefer to stand, if you don't mind."

"As you wish." The general ushered him into a conference room as he explained, "We cannot compromise the location of a safe house until Doúg has decided your case. However, we should have plenty of time before your parents discover what's really transpired."

"I understand. And I'll do whatever you think best, but I believe I can be of more use to you than to hide. I assure you, my intelligence is complete. I know my father's entire battle plan, contingencies, everything."

"I appreciate your willingness, but Prince Joshua won't wish to take advantage of your military intelligence or prowess—which I know is exceptional—until your needs have first been cared for and you've begun some instruction in running. Doúg will decide your readiness for participating in the battle preparations."

"I see," Sheridan said, although he didn't truthfully see at all. Father would use a person's knowledge and abilities without concern for their willingness, never mind their well-being. The idea that he needed to be "cared for" before his knowledge could be tapped seemed truly bizarre.

"Have you any questions before we begin?"

Actually, he had a million questions. He was already so disoriented he might as well have landed on Neptune. But where he came from, asking questions was tantamount to admitting stupidity. "No, sir. No questions."

"Very well. We're awaiting someone before beginning the interview."

Sheridan stiffened reflexively before remembering himself. When he did, he agreed, "Yes, I certainly deserve that much."

Puzzlement briefly crossed General Lanáj's face. "Oh, I do beg your pardon. I sometimes forget how Stan has perverted language. But I meant a genuine interview, involving only conversation."

"Oh." Embarrassed at his confusion, Sheridan glanced away.

"Not to worry. The fault lies not with you, but with your parents."

Unsure how to respond to such deference, Sheridan said simply, "As you say, General Lanáj."

The general lifted his right eyebrow in an expression that recreated Father's questioning look exactly, except that Father raised his left eyebrow. "Your brother and sister call me Uncle Gabriel."

"Maybe they don't know our true heritage."

"Ah. And you do, I suppose?"

"Not everything. But I know I'm only human."

"*Only* human, is it?" General Lanáj asked with a hint of amusement. "The Deón think a great deal of humans. And Prince Joshua sacrificed much to redeem them. I daresay he would object to your belittling them. For my part, I am honored that some members of your biological family consider me family."

"You know who my real parents are?"

"Yes. You see, Paradisians actually have no capacity for procreation, so I was rather confused when your brother married and sired children. That's when Joshua briefed me on the reprehensible genetic experiments that my siblings had conducted."

When Sheridan opened his mouth, General Lanáj held up a hand. "However, Doúg has not authorized me to inform you of your parents' identities. He's also reserved the right to inform your siblings, who know nothing of their true heritage, in his own way and in his own time. I trust you will not usurp his right to do so."

"I understand." Sheridan wondered if he'd ever see his siblings again anyway. Or if he'd be in any condition to tell them anything if he did. Although he'd never been a sappy sort of guy, the thought brought a wave of something like homesickness.

General Lanáj studied him with that all-seeing expression Father got, and it gave him the same eerie feeling, as if the man could very nearly read his mind. Immediately he banished any mushy thoughts about wanting—needing—a family and sense of belonging. Though it was perhaps the only thing he'd ever really wanted, he was now less likely than ever to attain it.

"I hope you won't consider me overly sentimental," General Lanáj said, "but I rather relish being called 'uncle.' "

Was that an invitation? "Even if it comes from the likes of me?"

"Especially so, for your use of it would be entirely voluntary, wouldn't it?"

A bit bewildered, Sheridan couldn't answer.

"Furthermore, I suspect we're related in a way that your siblings and I are not. May I presume to ask a personal question?"

"Of course." Sheridan figured he had no right to refuse anything.

"Did your parents treat you differently, perhaps with more suspicion than your siblings? Perhaps they questioned your intelligence?"

Sheridan stiffened at the dead-on evaluation—too close, too personal, to come from ordinary military intelligence.

"Pardon me," the general said quickly. "I don't mean to touch a sensitive spot. But if I'm right, I believe I know the reason." He undid the top buttons of his uniform. "I'll show you what I mean, shall I?" He pulled his shirt back to expose a red, oval birthmark resembling a crown just underneath his left collarbone. Sheridan unconsciously reached up to finger his matching birthmark. Father had one too, but on the right side.

"Before the rebellion, most people could tell Stan and me apart only by the location of this birthmark. I expect the placement of yours reminded your parents of me. They've always considered my fealty to Doúg as a betrayal of them. I shouldn't be surprised if they unleashed their anger at me upon you, treating you as my whipping boy, so to speak."

Musing aloud, Sheridan said, "They said I wasn't as smart as the others. They said—they said so many things. I was unworthy. I didn't work hard enough. As a child, I worked ten times harder than Saxon or Sadira to prove my worth. And then they'd question it again at the first hint of a mistake."

"I expected as much. I'm certain your road was very difficult."

"But it doesn't make sense. They know we're not really related. The birthmark's just a fluke."

"A fluke?" the general exclaimed. "Oh, no. The *poli* carries great meaning."

"Really? They never mentioned any particular meaning."

"No, I don't suppose they would. You see, the *poli* is how Doúg marks those he's particularly gifted as administrators. *Polini* become the community leaders. We're singled out from birth and educated for this type of service. Upon spying the *poli*, someone new to a community knows he's found one who can help him settle there, arrange appointments with government officials, or gather whatever information he may require."

Sheridan tapped his birthmark. "So you're saying that when my parents saw this ..."

"They interpreted it as Doúg's having set you apart for a special work in his government. Undoubtedly that merely intensified their resolve to have you solidly in their camp—to defy his claim."

"Which explains why they were always questioning my loyalty. I spent my entire childhood being tested. But in recent years, I was treated well, praised, honored—respected, I think. I've been Father's go-to man for tough problems. We've worked closely and well. So if the *poli* is His Majesty's mark, why would Father rely on me and trust me enough to put me in command of his army?"

"Heading the army is the most important job he has to fill just now, and that *poli* indicates that you possess exactly the superb administrative potential that the position requires. He merely had to become convinced of your loyalty first. Furthermore, by giving you such a key position in *his* organization, he was thumbing his nose at His Majesty in a very personal way."

"H'mm. Suddenly a lot of things make sense."

"Yes, although I disagree with my elder brother's methods, he rarely acts capriciously. His highly complex plans sometimes span centuries. Underestimate his cunning and intelligence, and you will likely find yourself entangled in his web."

An attractive woman with curly brown hair and dancing brown eyes entered the room, and General Lanáj sprang up to bow before her. "How wonderful to see you, Your Majesty. This is my nephew. And Sheridan, this is—"

"Her Majesty, Queen Debora." Sheridan bowed low. His knees actually felt weak.

"Rise, Sheridan." She stepped forward to kiss him on the cheek. "I'm delighted to meet you. Doúg, Joshua, and I have longed for this day."

The Moden in him heard, *so we can torture you for all you've done to our runners*, but nothing in her manner suggested that's what she meant. She seemed truly delighted to meet him.

"You're very kind, ma'am," Sheridan said warily. His parents had no respect for what they called the Deón's tyrannical rule, but they certainly respected their power. They had inculcated appropriate caution in their children by regaling them with vivid tales of Deón might. This woman appeared Paradisian, or even human, but she was neither, and Sheridan was suitably wary of the raw power at her disposal.

The three gathered around one end of the oak conference table, Sheridan standing while Queen Debora and General Lanáj sat. Neither objected to this although it would put them at a disadvantage if he were to attack them. He found this inattention to security puzzling, but decided it must reflect Her Majesty's great strength. In any case, he was grateful that he didn't have to reveal the humiliating circumstances that rendered sitting so uncomfortable.

They spoke with King Doúg by phone for some time. Sheridan told of his demotion to *lakwadín,* of reading the *Manual* through twice, and of almost committing suicide. He recounted how Paul's story had given him hope. He expressed his genuine sorrow for the evil he'd committed and concluded, "I understand if you can't give me asylum, Your Majesty. I've spent my life opposing you. I've done terrible things that I can in no wise justify. I know this now. I should have known it long ago. I stand ready to accept your judgment and to pay whatever restitution you decree, whether monetary or physical."

"Sheridan," King Doúg said slowly, "the price of your forgiveness far exceeds your ability to pay it—in any manner."

The words hit Sheridan like a kick in the gut. He hadn't realized how desperately he yearned for forgiveness and for the peace he'd seen in Stanley. But he shouldn't have hoped for something so outrageous. And he surely couldn't blame King Doúg for refusing him.

He made a full bow, the better to hide his disappointment. "I understand, Your Majesty. Thank you for considering my case."

"No, Sheridan, I don't think you do understand," King Doúg said. "Many people and many complex systems have been affected by the *kanuf* you've set in motion. Cutting short the life of only one person means that the children they might have had, the good they might have done, the evil they might have buffered, the light they might have shed, the lives they might have mentored—all this and so much more is left wanting. Every sinful act produces consequences, and these consequences have consequences. Are you able even to calculate all the effects of your *kanuf*?

"No, sir," Sheridan said weakly, overcome by a sense of hopelessness beyond any he'd ever known.

"And if you cannot calculate the effects, you certainly cannot pay restitution for it."

"No. I cannot," Sheridan agreed, now realizing the sheer stupidity of his offer to pay recompense. How could he ever make up for even one of the lives he had stolen?

"And so, the price is too high for *you* to pay. Such restitution can only be made by Deón abilities." Doúg paused. "By Deón blood."

Sheridan frowned, confused. When he didn't respond, His Majesty continued, "Joshua has already paid the price for your forgiveness. All of it. You can do nothing to add to it."

"I—I—" Sheridan drew in a breath and tried to order his chaotic thoughts. "Are you saying you're accepting me as your subject—solely on the basis of what Joshua did?"

"Oh, Sheridan," His Majesty said gently. "I'd like you to be so much more than a subject. I love you. I should like to be your *adu*." (Paradisian: Daddy)

Sheridan caught his breath, thoroughly dumbfounded. As a young boy, he had once tried calling Father *Adu* and had been backhanded for using such a familiar term. Now King Doúg's tender words, his unqualified acceptance, his *love*—something Sheridan had craved but never known—all hit him so forcefully that it simply blew away his defenses. He could have withstood any reprimand or punishment; he had spent his life constructing defenses against these. But he was wholly defenseless against love.

When his chin began to quiver uncontrollably, he bowed his head to hide his emotion. But warm drops fell from his eyes and splashed onto his crossed arms. He'd never cried before, and he certainly didn't want to now, not in front of Queen Debora. Yet he was simply too overwhelmed to control himself.

His present company seemed to find no shame in weeping. Instead, Queen Debora wrapped her arms around him. He had no experience with such tenderness—his own mother had never comforted him—so this served only to release more tears. Yet as he rested in her embrace, those tears took on new meaning. He could see everything—his old way of life, all the atrocities he'd committed, all the hatred and lies—being washed away with them. When he lifted his head, he saw himself rising to an entirely new life, a life as—and the wonder of it astounded him—the son of his father's archenemy.

Sheridan at last composed himself. Drawing away from Her Majesty, he thanked her. Then he did something that he never would have believed. He said, quite honestly, "I would consider it the highest honor to call you *Adu*, sir."

"Then you shall," King Doúg said with obvious joy. "From this moment on, you are my son as surely as is Joshua. I cannot give you my name, for there is more to it than you know or are able to bear. But two of my other children, your brother and sister, have accepted the name of Lanáj."

Sheridan's eyes flew to General Lanáj, searching for any disapproval. He perceived only pleasure. "I'd be honored to accept the name as my motto if my … uncle doesn't object."

The general burst into jolly laughter and clapped him on the shoulder. "I shall be honored."

After ending the call, Queen Debora gave Sheridan a transmitter and a Paradisian passport imprinted with his new name—and only his new name—Sheridan Lanáj. Contrary to the Paradisian custom of retaining previous surnames as a middle name, this document evidenced no recognition of his former names. The arrogance of *Modén,* the shame of *Lakwadín*—these were forever expunged by this legal record. He was officially a new man.

A commotion in the hallway drew his attention and reminded him that, however generous the Deón may be, others would not so easily forget his past.

"Believe me," came Captain Strider's raised voice, "you don't want to go in there! You don't understand how that man's hurt us!"

"I don't have to, *mi hijo*," came a gentle but firm voice that Sheridan immediately recognized. "Doug asked me to take care of him. And as Doug's representative, it's my privilege to 'be kind to everyone, not resentful.' "

The door opened and Dr. Christian Strider, son of Juan Misi, walked into the conference room, still wearing a sling from the bullet that Sheridan's man had put in his shoulder. Determined not to retaliate when the doctor clouted him, Sheridan grasped his arms behind his back and awaited the punch.

But no blow came. Instead, he watched the doctor's face like a TV screen as several emotions crossed it in rapid succession. The light of recognition quickly gave way to the dark shadow of inexpressible pain, and then to the flame of intense anger. But, inexplicably, the anger softened into forgiveness, to which was added the miracle of compassion.

The whole process took only seconds, but it changed forever Sheridan's view of strength and weakness. He'd always believed that compassion was a weakness, yet he saw no trace of that in the doctor's face. Instead, he saw a strength beyond any he possessed.

Dr. Strider nodded a greeting to Queen Debora and General Lanáj, swiped a strand of straight, salt-and-pepper hair away from his face, and stepped forward to extend his hand to Sheridan. "Chris Strider. I'm afraid I didn't catch your name when we first met."

The former General Sheridan Moden—that great leader of men, that orator who could rally and energize his troops with a few words—was struck dumb.

Uncle Gabriel came to his aid. "Allow me to introduce my nephew, Chris. When you first met, he was General Sheridan Moden, my brother's youngest son and commander of his army. Doug has just adopted him and renamed him Sheridan Lanáj."

The doctor was still standing there with his hand extended, and Sheridan finally brought himself to accept it. "I—" He cleared his throat. "I am so *very* sorry for what I did to you—" His voice cracked. "And your wife."

The doctor looked down briefly. When he looked up again, he was blinking back tears from his deep, black eyes—eyes whose transparency told Sheridan that their owner could never tell a convincing lie. In an equally sincere voice, Dr. Strider said, "Then it's forgiven and forgotten, and nothing else needs to be said about it. You're now Doug's runner—my brother."

"I don't deserve your forgiveness," Sheridan whispered, his voice too unreliable to trust.

Dr. Strider smiled. "If it's earned, it isn't real forgiveness, is it? Doug's never bartered with me for his pardon. How can I do any less for you?"

Sheridan nodded, feeling more unworthy, yet more loved, than he ever had. After a lifetime of trying vainly to earn love, this new system both confused and amazed him. He didn't understand how King Doúg could accept him so fully. But seeing his forgiveness modeled through this man—a man from whom he had taken so much, a man who had every reason to hate him—helped him accept His Majesty's regard as genuine, even though he didn't understand it.

Dr. Strider turned to Queen Debora. "Is this two?"

Although Sheridan didn't understand what he meant, she obviously did. "If you will accept the assignment, it is."

"I will," Dr. Strider said. "And I thank you for the opportunity."

Her Majesty cradled his face in her hands. "You have suffered so much, *keni raná*, and have honored Doug by growing stronger through it all." She kissed him on the cheek. "I love you." (Rarámuri: my child)

"Thank you," the doctor murmured, clearly moved.

She turned to Sheridan. "You are to join your sister in hiding, where Chris will teach you both to run. This is a difficult time to learn, and you will have much to absorb in a short period, but we joyfully welcome you to the family."

"Thank you, Your Majesty," Sheridan said. "I'll do whatever you think best."

Debora took his hand between both of hers. "You may call me *Ami*, Sheridan." (Paradisian: Mommy)

Sheridan brought her hand to his lips and kissed it. "Thank you ... *Ami.*" He reverently enunciated the name that his mother had never allowed him to use.

Dr. Strider motioned for Sheridan to follow him. "Let's take care of your medical needs. And then I believe we're to be off. Is that the plan, Gabriel?"

The general opened the door for them. "Yes. Although you should perhaps chat with Jorge before we leave. And Riana will doubtless appreciate an encouraging word."

Dr. Strider—Chris, as he insisted on being called—led Sheridan to an exam room and asked why he needed a doctor. Sheridan explained about his punishment and how the surgical site was feeling worse rather than better. He expected Chris to react with vengeful satisfaction, but he was surprised yet again when the doctor winced in genuine sympathy.

Chris examined him and discovered an infection in the wound. Opening a supply cabinet, he drew a bottle of antibiotics from it, and then paused. As he pulled out a box of testosterone patches, a smile spread over his face. He handed them to Sheridan and said, "These will help with the symptoms of hormone deficiency. But I have to tell you that when my daughter said Doug had specifically directed her to stock these in this facility, we both had a good laugh. We both just 'knew' there would never be a use for them here. As usual, Doug will have the last laugh over this."

"Are you saying Doug knew about this ahead of time?"

"So it seems."

"But how?"

Chris shook his head. "I don't know. I asked Josh about his foreknowledge once and he just said it was 'beyond outlander comprehension.' After thirty-plus years of running, I've seen it so often, I don't even wonder about it anymore. All I know is, the Damours can foresee the future."

"Does that mean they already know the outcome of the Final Battle?"

"Yes. They win."

A foreign feeling, a heaviness, fell in Sheridan's chest. "I can't help but feel—well, sad for my parents and the others."

"I can understand that. But Doug did warn them about the effects of evil before they ever left the island."

Sheridan nodded.

Laying a hand on his shoulder, Chris said, "You may not realize it, but you're already a different man than you were when—when we first met."

"Am I?"

"Yes. What you're feeling is compassion. The man I met that night wasn't capable of such an emotion."

His new mentor's assessment was probably meant as a complement. But as Sheridan looked into the eyes of this generous man, the words rang in his ears like a death knell.

"Chris, my parents can smell weak emotions like compassion better than a shark smells blood, and they love to use them to their advantage. If I am developing such a thing, it can only be a liability for everyone around me." He paused before adding reluctantly, "Especially for you."

"Then prepare to be amazed," Chris answered without hesitation. "Because Doug has a way of turning weakness into strength."

CHAPTER 15

CRACKED CISTERNS

"My people have committed two sins: they have rejected me,
a source of living water, and they have hewn out for themselves
cisterns, cracked cisterns which hold no water."
Jeremiah 2:13, REB.

2 November 8043 M.E.

Iona's voice over Camille's intercom said, "I'm sorry to interrupt your meeting, ma'am, but Madelyn sent Dr. Sondem over. He needs to speak to you and Dr. Moden urgently."

Camille exchanged an uneasy glance with Stan across her desk. Anything that disturbed Garrick's equanimity deserved their immediate attention. "Send him in."

Garrick's concern was palpable as he burst through the door. "We have a major problem."

"What's wrong?" Stan demanded.

"Sheridan's body is missing."

"What?" Camille exclaimed. "Who would want his body? We don't want it, and we're his parents."

Garrick turned a stony countenance on her. "The real question is whether there was a body in the first place."

"Explain yourself," Stan ordered.

"The Medical Examiner's office has no record of receiving it. In fact"— Garrick's voice dropped almost to a whisper—"they have no record of being called to pick it up."

Camille bolted upright in her chair while Stan groaned. "You don't think—?"

"That's exactly what I think," Garrick replied. "There's no indication he contacted Damour. His e-mails, phone calls—everything's clean. But Sheridan would know how to evade our surveillance. And the *Manual* checked out to him was never returned, nor can we find it in his old office."

"Madelyn," Stan growled. "How could she overlook that?"

"But surely Damour wouldn't accept Sheridan," Camille objected. "Not after all he's done."

"We didn't think he'd accept any of the offspring," Stan countered. "Especially Sadira—she killed two of his runners. I think he's doing it just to spite us."

"But he called to let us know he had Stanley and Sadira. We've received no message this time."

"Maybe he thought we wouldn't figure it out," Garrick suggested. "Or that we wouldn't care. You did disown him."

"Wouldn't care?" Stan snarled, his accent turning British. "Wouldn't care that he has the one man who knows our every battle plan, every contingency, the location of every regiment and every stash of weapons, who knows every—everything?" Stan was on his feet now, pacing in front of Camille's desk. She flashed Garrick a dirty look, and he mouthed, "Sorry."

"We have to redo it all." Stan spun to Garrick. "Get Errol and Conner and come to my office. No one leaves until we rework the whole plan."

When he yanked open the door, Camille called, "Stan, wait!"

He swiveled to her, eyes narrowed.

"Apologies," she said quickly. "I meant no disrespect. However, we don't actually know the boy's defected. He may have simply left on his own."

"She's got a point," Garrick said. "If any lone individual could successfully elude us, Sheridan has both the know-how and the money to do it."

Stan stepped back toward the desk. "Ring Damour, Camille."

She felt the blood drain from her face. "Me?"

"Have you gone deaf?" he bellowed.

"Gabriel would know," Garrick interjected. When Stan turned a hard gaze on him, he added, "Come on, Stan. None of us like to talk to Doú—" Garrick coughed. "To *him*. Including you. If Sheridan's defected, Gabriel would know it—in fact, he probably even arranged it."

Stan grunted, which was close enough to a concession for Camille. She reached for the phone. When Gabriel answered, disbelief rang clearly in his voice. "Kami? Is that really you?"

"It is," she said curtly. "Do you have our son?"

"Which one?"

"Sheridan."

"Your son? We were given to believe you'd disowned him."

"Don't be impertinent, Gabriel. Is he under your protection or not?"

"He is."

"I see. Then you should know you're harboring a criminal, a man who would rape even his own mother."

"I'm sorry for you, if that's true, although I'm hardly surprised after learning how you raised him. The laws of behavior will function whether you deny them or not. I should think you'd have learned that by now."

"Don't presume to lecture me, Gabriel. I'm the psychologist."

"Yes, but it never ceases to amaze me how one's prejudices can affect the interpretation of scientific information."

"The issue at hand is Sheridan's criminal activity."

"Whatever my nephew has done, it is entirely between him and Doúg. I have nothing to do with judgment. Sheridan called on His Majesty's name. His Majesty answered, forgave, and adopted him. That's good enough for me." He paused before adding meaningfully, "We both know he's earned the right to conduct such a transaction."

"Then we have nothing to discuss." She slammed the phone down.

"So they have him," Stan said.

"They do," Camille affirmed.

"Garrick, my office. Straightaway." Stan stormed through the door, scattering clusters of secretaries and assistants.

"Garrick, how long do you think this meeting will take?" Camille asked.

Garrick shut the office door and pulled a chair near hers. Once seated, he leaned in toward her conspiratorially to speak in a voice so low that she also had to lean in to hear him.

"Once again, that's the wrong question. The real question is whether it will do any good."

"Why?"

"I've never understood your attitude toward Sheridan. You seem to think he's not as sharp as your other offspring, even though he's a *polín*."

"He's not Paradisian," she hissed. "Therefore, he cannot be a *polín*."

"Believe that if it makes you feel better. But I've never seen a better military mind, not in the entire history of this planet." He paused, his steady gaze hinting at accusation. "And now he's on Damour's side."

A sense of dread washed over her as she gazed into Garrick's black eyes. They were strong, intelligent eyes, and the man behind them was a brave warrior and an astute tactician. Although she had immediately recognized the danger of the situation, seeing Garrick so affected magnified her discomfort ten times over.

"Sheridan is a true military genius," Garrick murmured gravely. "Add to that his knowledge of how we think, and he'll likely deduce our entire plan from our first move. He'll devise a counterstrategy within hours. On top of that, he'll be working with Stanley. From what I've seen of his work, he's almost as bright in these matters as Sheridan. Attach Gabriel to the team, and—" He shrugged.

"We should have killed Sheridan when he overstepped his bounds," she said ruefully.

"Why didn't you? Please tell me it wasn't love."

Camille shrieked in laughter. "Certainly not! Stan wanted him to suffer, to be humiliated. We both did. Death would have been too easy."

Garrick frowned. "Well, I suppose I'd have done the same."

Camille sighed. In retrospect, perhaps it was ill-considered. As carefully as they'd avoided the emotional vulnerability of love, they'd nevertheless fallen into the trap of letting other emotions, like anger and hatred, affect their judgment.

Aloud she mused, "First, Stanley and all the information he had about both company and entity management. Now, Sheridan and all his military information." She paused, searching Garrick's face. Although she wanted to see some encouragement there, she found none. "Have we any hope at all, Garrick?"

He passed a hand over his face. "I don't know. Frankly, I doubt it. But I, for one, am going down fighting."

Stan burst through the door at that moment and stopped short. "Garrick, I ordered you to my office."

He sounded calm, but Camille sensed fury. She didn't understand its cause until she realized how their secretive posture would appear to her brother.

Trying to alert Garrick to the danger, she laid a cautionary hand on his knee. But her warning went unheeded. Garrick casually rose and strolled toward the door. "Oh, come on, old friend. We're going to be shut up in there for days. What difference does five minutes make?"

In one quick motion, Stan grabbed Garrick by the arm and, yanking it up behind him, shoved him against the built-in bookcase next to the open door. "The difference is what you do in those five minutes, *old friend*. And don't you ever talk to me like that again."

"Yes, sir," Garrick said, though his tone betrayed confusion.

Stan released him and stepped back, ready for a retaliatory strike.

Garrick eyed Stan as he smoothed back his straight, black hair and touched his fingers to a gash near his right eye. Glancing at the blood on his hand, he surveyed Stan thoughtfully. "I honestly don't know what you're referring to, Stan. But I apologize if either my words or actions seemed disrespectful. If I may be dismissed, I'll await you in your office."

Stan grunted, and Garrick ducked through the door. He growled, "What are you looking at?" to a few of the staff who had gathered for the show. They quickly cleared out of his way.

Stan slammed the door behind him and strode to Camille's desk. She backed away. "Stan, Garrick and I are not plotting against you. He always speaks softly when conveying information that could discourage the employees. I had to lean in to hear him. You do the same."

After studying her for a moment, he turned on his heel and left without a word. But her link-sense informed her that he remained unconvinced, and that infuriated her. She and Stan had had their differences through the centuries, but she had supported him faithfully through every difficulty. Not only was there no rational basis for his suspicion, but any rift in their solidarity would serve only to injure their cause at this most critical juncture. They simply could not afford to entertain petty arguments. Not now.

CHAPTER 16

FORGIVING

*"Be kind and compassionate to one another, forgiving each other,
just as Christ God forgave you."*
Ephesians 4:32, NIV.

As Chris led Sheridan toward the lodge's front door, Sadira threw it open from the inside. "I can't believe it! You defected too?"

"Look who's talking!" Sheridan shot back. "Father's little darling herself."

"Am not," she replied indignantly.

"Well, not now, that's for sure!" he agreed with a hearty laugh.

"Children, children!" Chris gestured for a timeout. "How about greeting each other with a big hug instead?"

They exchanged a puzzled expression before turning it on him. "Hug?" they asked in unison.

"Oh, sorry," Chris said with a chuckle. "Forgot what family I was talking to. You've probably never hugged in your life."

Cherie and Melanie burst through the backdoor as Chris ushered Sheridan into the living room. "*Aparochi! Aparochi!* We missed you!" (Rarámuri: maternal grandfather)

Chris dropped to his knees and caught the girls in his arms. "I missed you too, pumpkins." Snuggling each against a shoulder, he planted a kiss atop each precious head. It felt so good to be home. It had been an emotionally exhausting trip.

As he stood, Chris informed Sheridan and Sadira, "In case you were wondering, that's a hug."

Cherie pulled on his pants leg and, holding a hand over her mouth, whispered, "*Aparochi,* who's that man?"

"He's the surprise I brought you. Girls, this is your Uncle Sheridan. Sheridan, this is Cherie and Melanie—Stanley and Bethany's daughters."

Sheridan seemed to have no idea what to do with children. Stiffly holding out his hand, he boomed, "Pleased to meet you."

The two girls cowered behind Chris, who explained, "They'll have to get used to you."

Gabriel, who had lagged behind to unload some supplies, entered the living room and greeted everyone. As he did, Sheridan asked Chris, "What did they call you? Was that the language of your tribe?"

"Yes—Rarámuri, also called Tarahumara. *Aparochi* is the word for a maternal grandfather."

Throwing a log on the fire, Sadira added, "He uses it with the girls most of the time. I'm learning it too."

"Oh, good—a contest!" Sheridan exclaimed. "I'll bet I can learn it faster than—"

At that moment Stanley and Bethany walked into the room, and Stanley stopped short, shock apparent in his face. He roared something harsh-sounding at Sheridan in a language Chris assumed to be Yiddish since he understood the word "chutzpah."

But if Stanley meant to protect his daughters from his anger by speaking in tongues, he failed. Melanie, who had inherited Bethany's sensitive spirit, burst into tears. Chris picked her up to console her as Stanley turned to the two Royal Guards in the room and ordered in Paradisian, "You will keep this man under *armed* guard during his *short* stay."

The two guards cast bewildered glances at Gabriel, who said softly, "Belay that order."

When Stanley glowered at his uncle, Gabriel added, "Major General Lanáj, would you show me to the study?"

Stanley whirled around and stormed off in that direction. Bethany, obviously confused by her husband's anger, addressed Gabriel. "General Lanáj, sir, permission to join you?"

"Please do, Colonel." Turning to Chris, Gabriel added, "Perhaps you will as well."

On his way out of the room, Chris said to Sheridan, "I don't know what my son said, but please forgive him. It's been hard for us all."

"He only spoke the truth," Sheridan said. "Certainly nothing requiring forgiveness from the likes of me."

Chris stopped to study him. Under the strong, formidable exterior, he saw a lost little boy—confused, all alone in a very strange world, and maybe even scared. Melanie seemed to share the vision. Still in Chris's arms, she reached up to touch her uncle's face, and he flinched slightly. "I love you, Unc' Sher'dan," she declared.

He swallowed. "Um, I don't know the appropriate response to that. Thank you—I think."

Chris proceeded to the study, still carrying Melanie. As soon as he entered, Bethany's indignant words assaulted him. "Is it true, *Onó*? Is he the one that killed *Mami*?" (Rarámuri: Dad)

Melanie looked from her mother to her father and back to Chris, obviously confused that her three favorite people seemed to be at odds. Wriggling down from Chris's arms, she ran whimpering to her great-uncle Gabriel, who was sitting in the leather chair behind the desk. She buried her face in Gabriel's massive chest, and he wrapped his arms around her in a protective cocoon. "It's all right, *ve nela*," he cooed. "They're not angry with one another. Everyone will be fine." (Paradisian: my daughter/niece)

Chris was momentarily distracted by this interaction, thinking how different the twins—Gabriel and Stan—were, only because one chose to love Doug and the other to hate him.

"Well, is he the one?" Bethany demanded, bringing Chris back to the problem.

"Yes, sweet pea. He's the one."

"But— Why— How *can* you?"

Chris suddenly felt mortally exhausted. The strain of dealing with his own emotions during the long, sleepless night had taken its toll on him, leaving him little energy for the present strife. With a heavy sigh, he slumped into the over-stuffed chair in the corner and buried his face in his hands. He'd already been through this story once with Jorge, but it wasn't going to be any easier the second time around.

"Gabriel, would you excuse us?" he said at last.

Gabriel stepped out with Melanie, pausing only to lay a supportive hand on Chris's shoulder. As the door closed behind him, Chris took a few moments to study the injured faces of his two children. In them, he saw the same battle with forgiveness that he had often fought.

Sitting back in the chair, he answered his daughter's question. "I can forgive Sheridan for two reasons. One, because Doug has repeatedly forgiven me, even when I was responsible for his own son's death. He's also asked me, actually commanded me—and you—to forgive Sheridan."

Bethany protested, "Yeah, *Onó*, but—"

"The second reason is because I once killed your mother too, and she not only forgave me, but took me back."

When they frowned at him, he insisted, "That's right, I did. Except the death I caused her wasn't nearly as quick or painless as the one Sheridan brought about."

"Dad, you're tired." Stanley sat on the adjacent love seat. "You're not making any sense. Maybe you should get some sleep, and we'll talk about this later. Meanwhile we'll—" He looked to Bethany and sighed. "We'll be civil to Sheridan. If that's what you want."

Chris stared at his wedding ring for a moment before twisting it around to point out the largest gem, a blood-red ruby. "You know this story."

"Yes," Stanley said. "The story of how Josh died in your place."

Chris nodded. Slowly, he rose and stepped to the window. "What you don't know is why he had to."

"Yes, we do." Bethany objected. "Some woman falsely accused you of rape."

"That's only part of the story. I've never told you the rest because, to be honest, I didn't want you to know how low your father could be. But you're both adults now. I think you'll live through the revelation that your father isn't perfect."

The love seat creaked softly as Bethany eased down next to Stanley. Only the ticking of the mantel clock broke the silence while Chris gathered his nerve to tell his children the one story he wished he could erase from his memory. Finally he began, his voice scarcely more than a whisper.

"It was when we ran the race. Your mother and I had been dating for three months. I was pressuring her to sleep with me."

"You?" Stanley and Bethany exclaimed in unison.

"Yes, me." Their reaction didn't surprise him. The father they knew was very different from the man he'd once been. "Your mother refused. I got mad. I ran into a local woman who took a shine to me and—"

"Oh, don't say it," Bethany breathed.

Chris bowed his head. "I kissed her, right in front of your mother. On purpose. I *wanted* to hurt her." He paused and felt their stares boring into the back of his skull.

Finally he continued. "I almost slept with the woman—I intended to—but finally realized what an idiot I was being. Meanwhile, your mother returned to the campground thinking I was going home with the woman."

"But you didn't." Bethany's statement sounded more like a plea.

Chris turned around to face them. "I left right after your mother did. But I inadvertently left the woman with enough evidence—hair, fingerprints, a picture—for her to do a really good job of framing me for rape. After I left, I walked around, thinking and finally understanding what a jerk I was. When I got back to camp, your mom was—" He shook his head. "She was devastated. I've never seen her so hurt. Her upbeat, compassionate, optimistic—well, her brightness—it was gone. It was like the best part of her had died."

He rubbed his face, trying to wipe away the shame the memory still evoked. After all these years, he could still see the look in Susana's eyes and feel the pain he'd caused her. "We talked. I asked her to forgive me. She did, right then. I asked for another chance. That she refused." He sighed heavily. "I felt as though my world was ending. I truly thought I'd lost her forever. I really loved her—which, of course, only makes what I did all the more revolting."

Hesitantly Bethany began, "When—? How—?"

Chris retook his seat. "She watched me closely for a while." A rueful smile came to him. "The longest ten days of my life. She wanted to see if I'd really changed, although I didn't know that's what she was doing. After talking to Debora and Doug a lot, she offered me another chance. I couldn't believe it—I knew I didn't deserve it. But I'm awfully glad she did."

Leaning forward, he continued, "Kids, I think you both know I loved your mother. And I miss her—" He again bowed his head as tears sprang to his eyes. "I miss her more than I can say," he finished in a whisper, and then paused to regain control of his voice. "But I also know she would forgive this man, and she would urge us to do the same, simply because Doug asked us to. She would also remind us of the effects *on us* if we don't forgive him."

Stanley, who had remained silent during the story, now abruptly stood and faced the window, arms crossed, in a defiant stance that reminded Chris of Stan.

"He's not the same man who killed her," Chris continued. "I can say that not only because Doug's accepted him as a runner, but also because I've seen the difference for myself. I saw the hatred burning in his eyes that night. They were the eyes of a man who wouldn't know compassion if it knocked on his head. Yet last night I saw compassion in those same eyes. I heard the genuine remorse in his voice."

"Remorse won't bring her back," Bethany said bitterly.

"That's true. What he did was a terrible evil, and one that wounded us deeply. But something of the sort had to happen. Josh explained it to me. Doug allowed Stan to trigger the Final Battle so he couldn't claim that Doug hadn't given him enough time to prove his case. But that meant Stan had to kill someone on the hands-off list. His hatred for me—and for you, Stanley—led him to us."

" 'It is impossible that no offenses should come, but woe to him through whom they do come,' " Stanley angrily quoted from the *Manual*. His back was still turned.

"But the 'woe' is not ours to deliver, son. Besides, that passage continues, 'If your brother does wrong, reprove him; and if he repents, forgive him.' The real point is that each of us has committed evil too, evil that hurt the Damours and cost them a great deal. Yet Doug forgives us, over and over. We can't do any less for Sheridan and remain Doug's runners. Remember, the *Manual* says we'll be forgiven *if* we forgive others. In fact, not only does Doug expect us to forgive him, but to love him and take care of his needs."

Stanley turned from the window. "I can't possibly. If I pretend to, I'd be a hypocrite."

"Not necessarily. Think about when you train for a race, honing your body into better shape, into something that you aren't now, but that you hope to become—is that being hypocritical?"

"Of course not. I may not be a five-minute miler now, but I have the potential to become one with training."

"Exactly. And while you may not truly love your enemy now, you can come to love him through Doug's grace. It just requires some serious training. You begin to model the behavior in small ways, kind of like running faster fartleks. You train by spending time studying Josh's relationships in the *Manual*, admitting to Doug that you've got a problem, and surrendering to Debora's transforming work."

Stanley considered that for a moment before exploding, "But I can't! Not *him*!"

"You have to, and Debora will enable you to do it. If you don't, you'll be overcome by bitterness. The last thing your mom would want is for her death to result in us slipping away from Doug. And that's what bitterness ends in. I've told you how my father stopped running because of bitterness. I've told you how it almost killed me. Don't let those things happen to you.

"What's more, Stanley, you know how he was raised. You know how your father encouraged you boys to fight, how he encouraged Sheridan's escapades against you and Saxon. What do you think *you* would have become if not for Mrs. Jenkins?"

✸ ✸ ✸ ✸ ✸

Although Stanley had brushed Dad's words aside at the time, they stuck with him, elbowing him in the ribs every time he saw Sheridan. They apparently made an impression on Bethany, too, for she began talking to Sheridan. But then, she would. She had such a sweet disposition, and she preferred to think the best of everyone.

But Sheridan was getting off far too easily. He deserved to be punished severely. This conviction made Stanley testy, especially with his wife. So when he walked into the living room where Sheridan and Bethany were sitting on the sofa while speaking to Doug, Stanley's irritation flared. And when Sheridan stumbled over his words and Bethany reached out to touch his arm, Stanley's outrage blazed.

There was nothing flirtatious about her action. Stanley knew this, not only from what he saw, but from the emotions he sensed through the link.

Bethany was expressing her support, nothing more. Yet his anger flared as hotly as the most jealous of husbands.

Interrupting their conversation with Doug, he demanded, "Bethany, I need to speak to you. Now."

Bethany looked up, her obvious surprise followed immediately by pain. It didn't help that his link-sense informed him that the source of her pain was disappointment—with him. He hated that.

He led his wife to their room and did his best to play the part of the injured husband. Bethany let him rant for some time before he realized she had remained perfectly silent during his tirade.

Stopping, he crossed his arms to look down at her. "Well, aren't you going to say something?"

She met his gaze with eyes confident in their innocence. "Why?" she asked gently. "You don't believe any of those accusations."

If the argument were with anyone else, he would have soldiered on, pressing his point as though it were valid. But she knew him as no one did. She *knew* when he was fibbing, and she knew when he was inventing a reason to be angry. As soon as she called his bluff, all his bluster fizzled. Dropping to the edge of the bed, he plopped his head into his hands. "I hate what he's doing to me."

"He's not doing anything to you. This is Stan's doing. He raised you both to believe that mistakes should be punished to the fullest measure. It's his voice in your head that makes it so difficult to extend or receive grace, his voice that makes you so susceptible to guilt. With Debora's help, you've progressed a lot in that struggle. But it's harder with your brother."

Stanley bristled at the reference to their fraternal relationship, and then realized that the reaction merely supported her conclusion. It was precisely because Sheridan was his brother that the battle for forgiveness was harder. He saw himself in Sheridan; he expected more of him.

With this insight, he nodded in surrender. It disappointed him, for, until it had resurfaced after Susana's death, he'd thought he'd conquered this problem.

As if knowing his thoughts—and maybe she did—Bethany laid a hand on his head. "We'll always need Doug's grace. And frequently a problem raises its ugly head one last time before we can vanquish it altogether."

"I need to ask Doug to send Debora."

Bethany kissed his head.

"Tell me about Sher—about … my brother."

"He's wrestling with the same problem you are, but from the opposite angle. The slightest misstep sets him back into a vicious cycle of guilt and self-re-crimination. He's learning to give it up to Doug, but it's a daily—no, hourly—fight. Remember the strain you were under after Mom's death, the guilt you felt? Well, magnify that by about a million—that's what he's battling. Then add to it all the changes you experienced after leaving your parents' home, how strange everything was, how the whole world seemed upside down. I think the one thing that gets him up in the morning is running. That's when he feels at peace."

Stanley studied his wife with a touch of envy. She was so intuitive and could so easily empathize with others—to feel their deepest longings and understand their struggles. How many times had her support gotten him through difficult times? Yet this was something he *should* be able to help his brother with. And, suddenly, he actually wanted to. "What can I do?"

"I think it would help a lot if he could talk to you," she said gently. "You and Sadira are the only ones who really know what he's going through, and Sadira's still a very new runner herself."

"I'll need to talk to Debora first," he admitted.

She kissed him. "I do love you, Stanley Lanáj."

They spent a few minutes talking to Doug together and asked that he send Debora for some more in-depth therapy. While waiting for her, Stanley decided to do some work in the study. He passed through the formal dining room on the way, which Dad had commandeered as a classroom for Sadira and Sheridan. As he walked by the table, something caught his attention—the corner of a blue spiral notebook peeking out from under a *Runner's Manual*.

Having seen Sheridan writing in it, he knew it must be his running journal. Stanley had kept a similar journal when he first left his parents. He had started by recording the specifics of his daily workouts, but it became a place to jot down passages he liked, incidents he wanted to remember, and questions. Especially questions. He'd had plenty of those at first. Somehow that collection of ramblings had helped him work out the confusing differences between his parents' world and Doug's world.

Part of him knew that the journal teasing him now was private and none of his business. Yet he was strangely drawn to it. Almost without realizing it, he picked it up. He was hooked as soon as he opened it. Sheridan had many of the same questions Stanley had once recorded. But Sheridan's journal was particularly filled with memories of the atrocities he'd committed. They had apparently not become routine with practice, for he remembered every one—names, dates, places. The memories clearly haunted him. Often he would begin to repeat an event and then cut it off with this recital:

STOP! Prince Joshua paid the price for my pardon. Doug forgave me. Debora is changing me. I choose to accept their pardon.

IT IS FINISHED!

As Stanley flipped through the journal, Chris's words—*What do you think you would have become if not for Mrs. Jenkins?*—took on new meaning. He suddenly knew he was looking at a picture of that person, and the picture horrified him ... terrified him ... humbled him. He had wanted Sheridan to suffer for his evil? This journal proved his suffering. And Stanley's unforgiving attitude would have only added to his brother's burden.

As he leafed through the book, he came to an entry that particularly moved him. He relived the event in living color as he read it.

I woke up this morning dreaming about the day before Stanley defected. I was only five when he left, so I don't have a lot of distinct memories of him. But that last night has stayed with me clearly. Father decided to quiz us on the night sky, and I didn't do so well. Father got "annoyed." He delivered one of his ultimatums: I would learn all of the named constellations by the weekend, or I would be "in trouble." Not good.

After our parents went to bed that night, Stanley sneaked into my room and took me up to the roof. He taught me everything I'd need to know for my upcoming astronomy test and patiently quizzed me until he was convinced that I knew the material. Thanks to him, I passed Father's next quiz, so I suffered no discipline. Of course, Stanley was gone by that time.

In our home, his action was unusual. Unusual? No—exceptional! Our teachers and nannies had to teach us, of course, but Stanley certainly was under no such obligation. I realize now that he was already under Doug's influence, so he had started learning love and compassion. I was granted both that night.

As we returned to the penthouse, I thanked him for his help. He put an arm around my shoulders and said, "Sure. I have to protect my little shadow, don't I?" He didn't really like my stealthy antics—he only called me The Shadow because I kept jumping out of hiding spots to scare him. But his words warmed me somehow.

Ever since, whenever Father berated Stanley, which he did regularly, the memory of that night came back to me. I've always looked up to him and felt an odd yearning to connect with my oldest brother, especially odd since we were enemies. I hate that I've ruined any chance to realize such a connection. I don't blame him, certainly—the rift between us is of my construction. I just wish I could find a way to bridge it. But I'm afraid I blew my chance forever when I fired that gun.

Debora walked in then, and Stanley looked up at her. "I've been such a fool, *Ama*. I don't deserve Doug's grace any more than Sheridan does."

"You are not a fool, my son, merely plagued by the cruel mantras of your old master. Are you ready to learn some new ones?"

"Yes," Stanley said, nodding emphatically. "Yes, I am. I want my little brother back."

✻ ✻ ✻ ✻ ✻

Chris smiled to himself when he saw Debora arrive. He knew exactly what—or rather, whom—she was here for, and he was happier than usual to see her. Sheridan and Stanley were each tormented, and healing their relationship would go far toward assuaging the suffering of both.

That evening in front of the fireplace, a glimmer of the old camaraderie returned. Stanley related the first story he'd told since his brother's arrival, one about a young Sheridan throwing spit wads at his brothers. It drew raucous laughter from Sheridan, and when Stanley referred to him as The Shadow—apparently an old nickname—the younger brother's eyes took on a suspicious shine.

Sheridan reciprocated by telling a story about how he, wondering how long it would take their parents to miss one of their offspring, tied Saxon up and left him in a closet. Camille noticed his absence first—nearly twenty-four hours later. "And as you probably remember," Sheridan said to the already roaring Stanley, "Saxon is Mother's favorite!"

From that point onward, the evening storytelling was comfortable again. Sheridan and Sadira quickly picked up Rarámuri, each one claiming they'd learned it first. Their rapid success didn't surprise Chris, for he remembered how quickly Stanley had learned. During the day, Stanley increasingly requested Sheridan's help to work out matters related to the upcoming battle. The two brothers were soon working together seamlessly.

Cherie and Melanie easily welcomed their Uncle Sheridan into the family circle. And Chris was surprised by how attached Sheridan became to his nieces. One evening, he found him on hands and knees, playing "horsey" for them. Considering that Sheridan had never had anyone play horsey with him as a child, Chris saw this as an example of his willingness to change.

Meanwhile, Chris continued Sadira and Sheridan's running instruction, lessons made more difficult by the short time they had available, as well as their upbringing. Thankfully, Chris's experience with raising Stanley made the job easier. He knew from the outset which areas would be the most challenging and which approaches were most likely to bring the point home.

He still felt Susana's loss keenly, but he discovered that a good run helped when he felt especially lonely for her. This is why he sought the seclusion of the forest one particular afternoon. Running in contented solitude, the sun stroking his skin with its warmth, he fell into unhurried conversation with Doug. Soon a delicious, restful calm filled him.

On his way back to the lodge, he heard Stanley and Bethany laughing together in the meadow, and he paused in the trees to watch them. When they first came into view, Bethany was sneaking up behind Stanley to put a snowball down the back of his shirt. Then she ran off again, giggling.

Stanley, sputtering and laughing, yelled, "Bethany, I'm warning you! You know I can hurt you!"

She ran back to him, hiding another snowball behind her back. As she came to stand in front of him, she purred, "Yes, but I also know you never would." She pulled him down to her level by the jacket collar and kissed him, and then stuffed the other snowball down the front of his shirt.

He sputtered some more, shaking the ice out of his clothes. Then he sprinted to catch up with her, scooped her up as if she weighed nothing, and laid her on the ground where he began tickling her.

They both laughed until she cried, "Okay! Stop, stop! I'll behave."

"I doubt that," he said, but gave up the tickling. Stroking her long black hair away from her face, he said, "I love you, *mi corazón*."

The whole interaction was so familiar, so similar to something he and Susana might have done, that it resulted in a wave of deep loneliness sweeping over Chris. He bowed his head and pinched the bridge of his nose.

"I'm so sorry."

Chris jumped at the unexpected voice. He turned to find Sheridan standing behind him. Apparently his nickname, The Shadow, was well-earned.

"I honestly had no idea what I was stealing when I pulled that trigger," Sheridan continued as he stepped beyond Chris to lean against a tree facing the meadow.

Chris opened his mouth to tell him he didn't have to say these things, but he was still too overcome with emotion to find his voice.

"Truth is, though," Sheridan continued, "at the time, it would only have made the satisfaction all the sweeter." He shook his head. "How ignorant I was. I valued strength and power over everything else. I believed that love was weakness, and *lashani* the worst weakness of all. Now I see that it's the greatest strength."

He turned to Chris. "I'd never experienced love before, Chris. Not from my parents or my nannies. I certainly knew nothing of *that* sort of love." He nodded toward Stanley and Bethany. "I thought it only existed in fairy tales." He watched them for a moment and then, breaking into a grin, yelled, "Hey, this is a PG-13 meadow!"

Bethany whooped and Stanley laughed as they jumped up and headed for the cabin.

Sheridan turned back to Chris, still grinning. "I thought they may want to know they weren't alone."

Chris chuckled. Finding his voice at last, he said, "Sheridan, the *Manual* tells us to forget the former things and not to dwell on the past. You don't have to keep reminding yourself of the evil things you've done. Doug's forgiveness frees us from that."

Sheridan nodded thoughtfully. "I understand, and I am truly grateful for the provisions that make that possible. Still, I can't help but marvel at how wrong I've been, how little I've understood. In this last month, I've been so—well, loved, and by the very people who should hate me. It's a little overwhelming. I've come to realize that, despite my mother's 'professional assessment' that you have a dependent personality and my father's rants about your gullibility and despicable weakness—" He stopped to look intently into Chris's eyes. "You, Dr. Christian Strider, son of Juan Misi, are truly the strongest person I've ever known."

"If I am strong, it's only because Doug 'gives strength to the weary and increases the power of the weak,' son."

Sheridan's eyes softened. "See there? That's exactly what I mean. In all my twenty-eight years of life, the man I called father has never called me 'son.' You, who have such good reason to despise me, have been a better father to me in these few weeks than Stan ever was. Or ever could be. This *lashani* thing simply amazes me."

CHAPTER 17

FREE?

"Everyone who sins is a slave to sin ...
If the Son sets you free, you will be free indeed."
John 8:34-36, NIV.

Balancing boxes of pizzas in her hands, Riana swiveled and contorted until she managed to ring her in-laws' doorbell with her elbow. Then she giggled. Andy was already barging through the front door with the ice chest, making her hard-won ring less of a request for entrance than a warning of invasion.

"Wills," Andy called, "Pizza's here!"

"Be right there," Willy called. A moment later, he emerged from the kitchen with chips and a slow cooker of nacho cheese dip. Andy raised his eyebrows at the slow cooker. "Getting domestic, are we?"

Willy laughed. "Mom gave me a really simple recipe. It just doesn't seem like football without nachos."

"Well then," Andy said with mock gravity, "I'd better test it—make sure it's safe to eat before Tío Daniel gets here."

As the three chowed down, Riana tried to fade into the brown corduroy of the sofa. The big UCLA-USC game that occasioned today's get-together hadn't started yet, but they had come early so Andy could talk with Willy, and she didn't want to get in the way.

Willy held a special place in Andy's heart because he saw himself in his cousin. Or rather, he saw what he might have become if not for Doug's grace. Though raised by two enthusiastic runners, Andy had once been pretty down on the whole running scene. The very fact that everyone expected him to fall into line behind his parents made him want to do something else. He'd made some bad mistakes before turning back to Doug.

Willy seemed driven by a similar need to make his own mark on the world. When he came to live with the Striders as a college freshman, he had, like Andy before him, experimented with the party scene. But after a few months of "fun and freedom," Willy abruptly swore off all mind-altering agents, became unrecognizably studious, and joined the New-RAB with a newfound mission to "help people."

The sudden turnaround puzzled Andy. Something must have precipitated it, but Willy refused to discuss it. He just became increasingly devoted to the New-RAB, Stan's dangerous counterfeit of Doug's RAB. And Andy became increasingly concerned. After learning that Willy had gone so far as snitching on them to Stan, her dogged husband was determined to help Willy face his pain, whatever that pain may be.

As they ate, the two cousins chatted easily, each bringing the other up to speed with his life. When Willy mentioned his recent promotion in the New-RAB, she felt Andy stiffen beside her. Stan Moden's vendetta against Juan Misi's descendants made Willy a prize catch, and this promotion meant he was drawing Willy deeper into his trap.

Casually, Andy asked, "So what's this position entail?"

"Mostly it's resource management—getting donated goods to where they're needed."

"Sounds like important work," Andy said. "But I thought you were pretty stretched already."

"Yeah, I was." Willy shifted in his chair. "I dropped some other things I was doing."

"It's easy to overcommit," Andy said. "I've done that myself. And then I felt guilty that I couldn't do my best. Now I talk to Doug about any responsibilities people want me to take on. He's sincerely interested in helping me maintain balance, whereas everyone else just wants to advance their project, whether it overloads me or not."

When Willy began drawing circles in his nacho sauce with a tortilla chip, Riana knew he needed more privacy. Improvising a reason, she retreated to the kitchen. But she couldn't help herself—she had to listen behind the closed door.

"Who asked you to accept the position?" Andy pressed.

"My pacesetter." Willy answered. "And my agent."

"You tried telling them 'no,' didn't you?"

"It doesn't matter. I worked it out. I'll be able to help a lot of people in this position."

There it was again—that helping-people theme that absorbed him. Helping people was a good thing, of course. But Willy's concern seemed extreme, even desperate. Like maybe he was trying to make amends for something.

"And it'll look good on my applications to law school," he added.

"Not if your GPA drops," Andy said bluntly.

"It won't."

"It's just that I see you getting swept deeper into the New-RAB, an organization you don't know that much about, and that I know to be—"

Andy broke off to heave a sigh, probably in response to a don't-go-there expression from his cousin. "Wills, I honestly just want to help. I worry about you."

"*You* worry about *me*?" Willy shot back. "Oh, that's rich. What do you know about the so-called Outlander Division? Do you know it's involved in terrorist activities that kill innocent bystanders? Do you know that Stanley's gone rogue, that he's running it completely separate from Doug and General Lanáj?"

"No, he's not. In fact, I'm running it at the moment."

"You?" Willy exclaimed.

"Yeah, me. And because I'm currently overseeing all of the division's operations, I can assure you that both Doug and General Lanáj are very much involved. I talk to them regularly."

"*You* do?"

"Yeah. Several times a day."

Riana could almost hear Willy's thoughts, even from the kitchen. Stan's agent had constructed a giant tower of misinformation for Willy, and he'd been willing enough to put Stanley inside it. But he was having more difficulty fitting his favorite cousin into it, to believe that Andy might be working out some nefarious purpose.

When the couch creaked familiarly, she envisioned Andy leaning forward to press his point. "Wills, you know me. You know Riana. Do you honestly think we could play a part in killing innocent people?"

Willy's silence testified that the tower was wobbling. Yet something still held it up. What could that be? What was so compelling that he'd rather believe horrible lies about his relatives than allow the tower of lies to topple?

"What have they got on you, Wills?" Andy said softly. "Whatever it is, we can work it out with Doug's help."

"Nothing!" his cousin exploded. "They've given me a great opportunity!"

"Doug could give you better opportunities without overwhelming you. Let me introduce you to him. Right here, if you want. Or we could go down to the RAB and talk to the pacesetter if you'd rather—"

"You think I haven't been to the RAB?" Willy snapped. "I've seen how those hypocrites get off on watching people humiliate themselves."

Riana stifled a gasp, but Andy just asked calmly, "Humiliate themselves? What do you mean?"

"All that emphasis on confessing the mistakes you've made—that's just crazy."

"No, it's necessary. Confession's an important step on the *only* pathway that leads to true freedom."

She wished she could have looked into Willy's eyes at that moment. Yet she could guess what she'd see—what she'd seen there so often in the past. Whenever discussing freedom, Willy's eyes gleamed with yearning ... until he fought it back. Then he'd sometimes sermonize about being "free" to determine what was right for his own life; sometimes he'd abruptly change the subject; sometimes he'd laugh derisively and walk away.

What would he do today? Would he finally admit his need and accept help?

After a heavy silence, he said defiantly, "I'm doing good work there, Andy. That's all that's important. Maybe I don't have all the advantages you do. Maybe I don't have connections to as many bigwigs as you do. But I'm doing the best I can."

"Wills—"

"And I'm helping people." He picked up the remote, flipped on the TV, and turned the volume up. Riana could barely hear him repeat resolutely, "I'm helping people."

She slumped back against the wall. How terrible Willy's pain must be, that he actually preferred to believe the lies. Would he ever face it and admit that he needed help?

* * * * *

A few days later, Willy was pacing around the dining room as he scrolled through his contacts. Even after resigning from his required volunteer hours, his life had gotten more hectic since accepting the position of Assistant Regional

Overseer. But he didn't really mind. Busy was good. Less time for thinking about the stuff Andy had said—stuff he had no business thinking about anyway.

As Assistant Regional Overseer, his biggest responsibility was matching donated goods to the places where they were needed. He was the one who moved West LA's outgrown school clothes to the poor kids in East LA. He got supermarkets' overstocked canned goods delivered to the hungry winos on Skid Row. He coordinated the transfer of old medical equipment from state-of-the-art hospitals to just-getting-by free clinics.

He usually enjoyed the work, kind of like playing a complex, ever-changing video game. As long as the pieces of cheese on one side of the screen approximated the number of hungry mice on the other, it was truly satisfying. But when the mice grossly outstripped the amount of cheese available, the game quickly lost its appeal. Especially since it was no game. Actual lives depended on his decisions.

"Where is that stupid number?" he grumbled. "What's her name ...?"

To the rest of the country, the drought had become old news. With a seemingly endless pick of catastrophes to report on elsewhere, the national news didn't even carry updates about Southern California's drought anymore. Maybe this apathy was understandable. Over the last several months, natural disasters had become so frequent that they didn't rate a mention unless thousands of people died. And So-Cal's water problems weren't new. They'd been buying water from their neighbors for generations.

But things had grown much worse over the last three months. The shortages might not affect the really well-to-do in Bel Air yet, but the middle-class consumers of Los Angeles had certainly clocked the scarcity and rising prices of fresh meat and produce in their local supermarkets. And for the poor Angelinos, things were getting truly desperate. Willy had seen the hopelessness in far too many eyes already. Even the soup kitchens and shelters were serving only one meal a day—on a good day. And now, just when it seemed things couldn't get worse, the truckers had gone on strike. On the day before Thanksgiving.

"Ah, Skye!" Willy exclaimed triumphantly when he found the number. It was his last shot at solving an unsolvable problem. He dialed the number, and his counterpart in San Diego answered.

"Hey, Skye," he said, "I know you're probably as bad off as I am, but I've got to ask. My turkey supplier just pulled out, and I've got, among others, several women's shelters with bunches of hungry kids. Any way you can help us out up here?"

"Actually, I just got a call from Doug Damour's personal secretary, Adlai Menod. He'll be calling you shortly. He's sending us as many turkeys as we want."

"No way!"

"I'm serious. Just tell him how many you need, and he'll deliver them in time for Thanksgiving dinner tomorrow. Doug's using his own truckers, so transport's not a problem. Happy Thanksgiving to us all!"

Skye was right. Within minutes, Willy got the call, and his problem was solved. He executed an enthusiastic fist pump as he hung up. "Yes! Thank you, Doug!"

The next day, Willy went home to Ventura for Thanksgiving dinner. When his relatives asked him what he'd been up to, he shrugged and said, "Well, yesterday I made sure that all the poor in LA County got a turkey dinner today."

Everyone turned incredulous faces to him, and his oldest brother demanded, "You *what*?"

He returned their regard nonchalantly, as if curing the world's evils was on his daily to-do list. "Didn't I tell you? It's what I do. I'm the Assistant Regional Overseer for the New-RABs of Los Angeles County."

"Assistant Regional Overseer," his mom repeated reverentially.

Willy basked in the back-slapping and proud-of-yous that ensued. And he was treated with more respect during the rest of the get-together. Of course, the crucial thing was that he'd genuinely helped a mess of people. But having his family know that he did such important work was a great perk.

A couple of days later, he was back at Uncle Chris's place watching a football game when his phone rang. With a groan, he put the game on mute and picked up the call.

"Overseer Moore," said a frantic-sounding woman, "this is Mrs. Belton at the downtown women's shelter. I'm in desperate need of Pedialyte. We have several children with vomiting and diarrhea."

A similar call came an hour later. By then, Willy had figured out what Pedialyte was and where to get hold of the stuff, so he was able to resolve the need efficiently. But then came yet another call, and then another, and another. As the supplies of Pedialyte plummeted, Willy's free day spiraled into a nightmare.

The calls finally stopped around 3:00 a.m. He was dropping into bed when it hit him: the places experiencing illness today had all received Doug's turkeys on Thanksgiving.

He immediately called Cherisse. As soon as she picked up, before he even explained the problem, she wailed, "Oh, Willy, not you, too! I am so, *so* sorry this happened. I swear to you, I knew nothing about it. I can't believe His Majesty did this—deliberately!"

"What do you mean?"

"The turkeys—they were tainted!"

"The turkeys?" he echoed, only half comprehending. "Tainted how?"

"They were infected with some kind of pathogen."

"What an awful mishap!"

"But that's just it—it wasn't accidental. It was planned!"

"No way!"

"Yes! General Lanáj oversaw the whole operation personally. All this time he was berating the Outlander Division to me while secretly working with them to carry out His Majesty's awful scheme. For all I know, he's been coordinating the Outlander Division's terrorist plots all along."

She broke off, crying, but before Willy could process the information enough to formulate a reply, she began rambling.

"I've been terribly deceived. I believed His Majesty's promises, his claims of working for peace. Maybe some of it was true, I don't know. But now he's actually declared war on Desmoden. This was part of his strategy—a cold, calculated attempt to weaken Moden's forces before battle."

Willy was still stunned speechless. Truthfully, he'd expected it to be a coincidence. He'd expected Cherisse to say something like, "No, the turkeys were fine, but the public health officials found salmonella in some lettuce." Could Damour really have done something this horrific, something so wholly self-serving?

"I'm sorry I got you into this." She was still rambling. "I'm no longer working for Damour. A lot of us left the island when we learned about this, this—well, I can't think of a word to describe such a shocking, cruel move." She sniffled. "I suppose you could rationalize the adults from the standpoint of a military campaign, but children? I ask you, what sort of monster poisons children?"

"I don't know," Willy answered forlornly. He'd been in the downtown shelter just a few days ago and had taken a few minutes to play Twister with the kids. Now a picture of those children barfing into trashcans plagued him.

Part of him didn't believe this explanation. Yet he couldn't find any grounds to question it. He didn't know Damour personally, so he couldn't say the stunt would be uncharacteristic for him. Actually, it might be totally possible—you don't become the richest man in the world unless you've got a ruthless streak hidden away somewhere. And rulers throughout history had taken all kinds of grisly measures to retain power.

Besides, Willy did know Cherisse, and she'd always been reliable. What's more, she'd worked in Damour's government and knew him personally. If she believed this of him, who was Willy to doubt her word? She could have nothing to gain from propagating such information, and she believed it so strongly that she'd chosen to leave her home rather than to look the other way.

No, it must be true. All of it.

But Willy felt as though he'd been sucker-punched. The man he was working for—volunteering for, no less—had played him for a fool. What's more, he'd been played by his own cousins, too.

His gaze fixed on the sofa where Andy had sat just a few days before. He'd admitted that he was running the Outlander Division and consulting with General Lanáj about its operations. That meant his own cousin had been part of this plan to use him—to trick him—into participating in an unscrupulous monarch's cold-hearted scheme. He felt like a fool. He felt betrayed.

And yet ... he also felt relieved. Vindicated. He'd been right to believe that his relatives could be involved in terrorism. He'd been right to help Cherisse and Ms. Menod. And he'd been right to resist Andy's pressure to trust Doug Damour. He'd been used, yes—and that made him mad. But it would have been worse if he'd been duped into knowingly helping with such an atrocity as Andy had.

Cherisse exhaled a woeful sigh, bringing him back to the conversation. "I'm in New York now with my brothers. You may continue to call me through your transmitter, if you like, but I won't be affiliated with Damour. I simply can't work for him any longer."

"And what will happen to the RAB organization?"

"Oh, my—I hadn't even considered that. General Lanáj and Dr. Moden have always cooperated in managing the RABs and New-RABs, but I don't suppose that will continue—I'm already sensing rancor between them. Yet neither could manage the combined system on his own. I suppose they'll have to split them."

"Which one would take the New-RABs?"

"I don't know, but I could find out for you. Shall I—Oh! Here's my brother; he'll know. Hold on a moment, won't you?"

"Sure."

Willy heard her say, "Garrick, do you know …" He couldn't hear the rest, but Cherisse came back on the phone a few moments later.

"Apparently this has already been decided. The traditional RABs will remain under General Lanáj's purview. President Moden will head the New-RABs. Therefore, if you wish to remain within His Majesty's system, you'll need to resign your post and transfer your membership to the RABs."

Willy frowned at the thought of staying on Doug Damour's side after this stunt. But he'd certainly lose General Lanáj's priceless recommendation to Harvard Law if he didn't remain loyal to the general's side. And a recommendation from someone of that caliber wasn't something to brush off lightly, regardless of his political affiliations.

"On the other hand, you could stay where you are," Cherisse continued. "You need do nothing in that case, and you will see no changes whatever. Your administrative work, your New-RAB membership—all will remain the same."

"Except that I'd lose General Lanáj's recommendation."

"Yes, but your work has already drawn Dr. Moden's attention. I'm sure you'll gain his recommendation before long. He's also an alumnus of Harvard Law and an even more generous donor to their program."

"That's good to hear." Willy stroked his barbiche thoughtfully. "But then there's the contract. I'll still owe Damour for the restitution payment."

"Actually, if you consult your contract, you'll see that your debt is not to any individual, but to the New-RAB corporation. However, if you'd rather switch your membership to the RABs, my brother is telling me that, considering the circumstances, they would be willing to transfer your contract to the RAB corporation."

Wow! See, this was why Willy liked the New-RABs. They were so accommodating, all about respecting a person's freedom. Here are your choices; you decide; no hard feelings. Still, he shouldn't make this kind of decision without thinking it through thoroughly.

"Thank you, Cherisse. That's very generous. I'll sleep on it and let you know what I decide."

"That would be fine," Cherisse said in full voice, but then dropped to a whisper to add, "Hold on a moment."

She soon returned to the line. "I apologize for that, but there's one more point you may wish to consider, and I didn't want to mention it in front of my brother."

"Oh? What's that?" Was there intrigue in the Moden camp too?

"Willy, you've been very conscientious, taking full responsibility for the car accident and its fallout."

The knot in Willy's stomach tightened painfully at this turn of the conversation.

"It's been refreshing for me to see a young person behaving in such a mature manner. That's why I've been happy to handle everything regarding that unfortunate event with utmost discretion. I know how important that is to you."

It certainly is! "What are you trying to tell me?"

"To assure complete confidentiality, I've kept your file in the back of a locked drawer at home. Similarly, the electronic counterpart is kept on a separate thumb drive at home. I don't keep anything concerning you at the office."

"I appreciate that." *Where's this going?*

"The thing is, I can't say what another agent might do. I brought your files with me to New York, but if I have to transfer them to someone still at the RAB corporation, I cannot honestly guarantee that the matter would be handled with the same care."

A vision came to Willy of his mom getting a phone call from some blathering legal assistant trying to fill in the blanks on her follow-up form. Cold sweat beaded on his upper lip as he imagined Mom learning that her seventeen-year-old son, high on pot, had run into a five-year-old girl in a crosswalk, that the little girl had nearly died, had required three surgeries so far, and would probably never walk normally again. It still amazed him that Cherisse had been able to keep the scandalous story out of the news and get the legal record sealed. He was eternally indebted to her for that. Yet none of it would matter one whit if his family found out. He'd never outlive the shame.

Swallowing hard, he realized that he really didn't need to consider this decision further. He'd rather stay with the New-RAB anyway; he'd already gained a certain reputation and status within that organization. And he preferred to distance himself from Damour after the turkey business. The only benefit of switching to the RABs was that recommendation from General Lanáj. But, important though it was, it didn't even come close to overriding his need for absolute confidentiality. That trumped every other consideration.

"I—" he began, and then stopped to clear the frog from his throat. "I think I'll just stay with the New-RABs, Cherisse," he said as casually as he could manage. "I like it where I am."

CHAPTER 18

DENOUNCED

*"In return for my love they denounced me,
though I have done nothing wrong."*
Psalm 109:4, REB.

C hris turned up the TV as the newswoman said, *"Today in New York City, thousands more were hospitalized with the new disease known as Turkey Terror, which has already grown to catastrophic proportions in cities around the globe. Medical facilities are inundated with afflicted patients. The strange disease causes ulcerations throughout the patient's intestinal track, causing vomiting, diarrhea, excruciating pain, and malabsorption, meaning the person is unable to absorb the nutrients from food."*

"Doug save us all," Bethany breathed.

"Experts have identified the cause of this disease as a new and particularly virulent virus in the herpes family that is resistant to antiviral medications. As scientists scramble to find a cure, hospitals overflow with patients who require intravenous fluids and nutrition to keep them alive."

Turning to Chris, Bethany murmured, "How can the health system possibly accommodate a continued influx of such sick patients?"

Chris shook his head sadly before confirming what she already knew. "It can't."

The camera moved to Stan, standing beside the newswoman, as she continued, "But the search for a cure has now received a tremendous, and most unexpected, boost. Dr. Stanley Moden, president of the Allied States of Desmoden, has come forward with information implicating his son."

"I knew he'd put this on me," Sheridan grumbled.

"My wife and I are extremely embarrassed by this, Jeri," Stan said, and he truly looked like a burdened father. *"I assure you, we will do all we can to assist in finding a cure for this ghastly illness."*

"Is your son really involved?" the reporter asked.

"Unfortunately, yes. This isn't an appropriate forum to air our family's dirty laundry, but I will say that Sheridan became jealous of his older brother, Saxon, whom I've named as my successor."

"Me, jealous of *him*?" Sheridan exploded.

"Shh!" Sadira urged.

"Sheridan recently disappeared," Stan continued. *"But we know from analyzing his hard drive that he's been acting as an agent of Mr. Damour. He set these attacks in motion before he left."* He paused, dropping his head. *"He meant to hurt me—and in that, he succeeded handily."*

"Bah!" Sheridan exclaimed. He started to flip a rude gesture at the TV, but caught himself and flicked a guilty glance at Chris instead.

"*But if this is true, General Moden should be turned over to the U.S. authorities for prosecution,*" *the reporter said.*

"*As my son, he had diplomatic immunity under international law, although, naturally, I would have worked with U.S. authorities in such a situation. Nevertheless, he's now been adopted by Mr. Damour and is, therefore, still entitled to diplomatic immunity as his son. So the U.S. authorities cannot prosecute him, although they could expel him from the country if they could find him. We've been unsuccessful in that.*

"*However,*" *Stan continued,* "*the more urgent concern is the care of the unfortunate victims of this disease, and we do at least have enough information from Sheridan's computer to assist in that. My own researchers are working around the clock in search of a cure, and I've made the information available to your country's scientists as well.*"

"*You mentioned Doug Damour,*" *Jeri said.* "*How is he involved?*"

"*Mr. Damour and I have a long and complicated history. Essentially, this attack was directed against me. If you map the cases, you'll see they're clustered around the territories belonging to the Allied States of Desmoden. It was probably an attempt to weaken my troops before our nations go to war.*"

"*War! But your capital is in the middle of Manhattan. Does he intend to attack the United States?*"

"*That was his original intent, but I've negotiated other terms to spare our good friends in the USA the inconveniences of war. We will fight in one of my other states, a virtually uninhabited area of the Kalahari. We're in the process of relocating the few Bushmen that still live there. No innocent bystanders will be endangered.*"

"*That's very good of you, President Moden. I know I speak for all U.S. citizens when I say we appreciate your concern for our safety.*"

Bethany turned the TV down as the segment ended. "He's very believable, isn't he?"

"Oh, yeah," Sheridan said. "Very believable. Took me twenty-eight years to figure out what a liar he is."

"Only took me twenty-two," Sadira said under her breath before asking, "You didn't actually help develop BW-683, did you?"

Sheridan dropped into a recliner. "No. I worked on the system for disseminating it, but I know very little about the virus itself."

Standing behind the sofa, Stanley said, "So he planted information in your hard drive to implicate you. What else would he have planted for the authorities to find?"

"He wouldn't have to plant much. My actual records will make Doug look like a fiend if they believe I was acting as his agent."

Sadira exhaled a chuff. "You should have destroyed your hard drive."

Sheridan bristled, and Chris cringed. Doug still had a lot of work to do with the two siblings. Sheridan clearly harbored a deep resentment toward his sister because of Stan's open preference for her. But she knew how to stand up for herself. Their mutual antagonism was growing tiresome.

"I tried, sister *dear*," Sheridan said darkly. "The first thing I did after my correction was sneak back into my office to get it. It was already gone."

She rolled her eyes. "You can't sneak onto the top floor. Not with all that security."

"Oh, no?" he shot back. "Who do you think designed the new system? I know its limitations better than anyone."

Chris rubbed his temples. "Come on, guys. We're all on the same side, remember?"

"Sorry," Sheridan and Sadira both mumbled.

Drawing them back to the problem, Bethany said, "In a way, I can see why people follow Stan. He has a certain something—charisma, I guess."

"Sheridan has much the same effect on people," Sadira said.

Sheridan lifted an eyebrow. "Was there a jab in there that I missed? That sounded dangerously like a compliment."

"It was neither an affront nor a compliment, just an observation. Father's often made similar remarks. He had you monitored after your falling out, right?"

"Sure. He figured I'd try to kill him."

She shook her head. "It wasn't just that. He always warned me to monitor you. He said that, with your charisma, you could easily turn the troops against us."

A slow grin formed on Chris's face. "Is that so?"

Curious eyes turned to him, and Stanley asked, "What are you thinking, Dad?"

"I'm thinking that I really hate hearing Stan smear Doug's name. But here in this room sit most of his children, who can testify to who Stan Moden really is. That would be pretty convincing testimony, don't you think—especially if one of those children has his charisma?"

"He's right," Sadira said with growing excitement. "We can publish it on the Internet. I'll rig it so they can't track our location."

"Great idea," Sheridan said, bounding up. "We'll send it to the news agencies. It'll be on the news tonight."

"No." Chris frowned at the TV.

"Why not?" Bethany asked. "It sounds like a great idea to me."

Chris pointed to the TV. "It would be more effective if the same reporter interviews you, that Jeri Roberts. If there's some give and take, the world can see you have no qualms about answering questions and challenges. It's more honest, more open."

"Yes, but it also increases the risk," Bethany said. "Someone at the news station could notify Stan that they're there."

"We can take precautions—armed guard, look-outs," Stanley said.

"Okay," Sheridan said. "Let's quit jabbering and get moving."

Holding up his hands, Chris said, "Whoa, troops."

"What?" Stanley said. "This was your idea."

"Yes, it was—*my* idea."

"Ah, good point," Stanley said, nodding.

"I didn't hear a point at all," Sheridan said.

" 'Many are the plans in a man's heart, but it is *Doug's* purpose that prevails,' " quoted Bethany.

" 'Unless *Doug* watches over the city, the watchmen stand guard in vain,' " quoted Stanley.

"Oh, I get it," Sheridan said. "Runners' rule number one: Don't go anywhere without Doug."

"You're doing great, son." Chris slapped him on the back. "Just great."

✲ ✲ ✲ ✲ ✲

Doug's helicopter delivered the three Moden children and Chris, whom Doug had asked to go along for moral support, to a small private island off the coast of New England. Jeri Roberts' television crew settled the siblings in front of the fireplace while Chris perched behind the wet bar to watch.

When all was ready, Jeri looked into the camera and began. "I'm pleased to bring you an exclusive interview with three of President Stanley Moden's four children. They say they fear for their lives after leaving their father, so we are conducting the interview in an undisclosed, remote location that is heavily guarded by Doug Damour's troops.

"I'll begin by introducing my guests." The camera showed close-ups as Jeri presented them. "First is Major General Stanley Strider Lanáj, age thirty-four, who fled from his father at age ten. He holds a PhD in military studies and is the commander of the Outlander Division of the Paradisian Army. Next to him is Dr. Sadira Lanáj, twenty-two, who left her parents a month ago. She holds PhDs in chemistry and sociology and was the president of Moden Industries at the time of her departure. And finally, we have General Sheridan Lanáj, twenty-eight, who left two weeks after his sister. Also holding a PhD in military studies, he was in command of Desmoden's army until his departure."

Sitting back, she exclaimed, "Whew! I don't know when I've seen such a gifted family. Is this typical of Doug Damour's supporters? Does his valuation of people depend on their accomplishments?"

"Doug?" Stanley said. "Oh, no."

Sheridan chortled. "But Stan Moden's sure does."

Stanley and Sadira nodded appreciatively, and Jeri said, "I notice that all three of you have dropped your father's name and taken another. Why is that?"

Stanley answered. "In our parents' homeland, Paradise Island, families choose their surnames to represent their life motto. When we left our parents, we took their original name, Lanáj, which means 'to serve.' "

Turning to Sheridan, Jeri said, "Getting to the reason for this interview, you said you were outraged when your father slurred Doug Damour's name during my interview yesterday. But considering the foul things your father's exposed about you, Sheridan, one has to wonder if it isn't to clear your own reputation."

Sheridan smiled, and Chris realized that, whereas Stanley and Sadira looked composed in front of the camera, Sheridan seemed entirely at ease. He had already formed a bond with his audience. In particular, the female members of the film crew perked right up at his magnetic smile. "Actually, Jeri," he said, "most of his accusations against me are true."

"Really?" the newswoman was clearly taken aback by his honesty.

"Yes. The only lies were that I was working with Doug Damour—I had no ties to Doug then—and that I was involved in engineering the virus that causes Turkey Terror. I developed the system for disseminating it, but I have only the most general knowledge of the virus itself. It was developed at my father's request in his virology lab."

"At his request? Why? The attacks center around his own states."

"Yes. But his people were unaffected by it."

Jeri frowned. "How can that be?"

"The virus is transmitted through the ingestion of infected meat. My father ordered his people to become ovo-lacto vegetarians before he released it. And in answer to your other question, his purpose for the virus was exactly what he's managed to do—to incite public sentiment against His Majesty by claiming that Doug released it."

"But what of the other accusations that have surfaced against you from the examination of your hard drive?"

Sheridan sighed. "They are largely true."

The journalist's carefully sculpted expression faltered. Although she had asked the question, she apparently hadn't believed that one with Sheridan's suave, polished manner could truly be a hit man.

Partially recovering, she asked, "So you admit that the reports we're getting about rapes, torture, murder—all carried out under your direct command—are true?"

"Yes, unfortunately, they are. But they were done at my father's behest, not King Doug's. As commander of Desmoden's army, I was fully knowledgeable of the operations. I even carried out many of those atrocities myself." He paused, capturing her eyes before adding softly, "The fact is, Jeri, I am a fiend."

"Was," Chris said, unable to contain himself.

The nearest cameraman gave him a dirty look and put a finger to his lips. Jeri, however, said sweetly, "What was that, Dr. Strider?"

The camera swung around to focus on him and someone shoved a microphone in his face.

"Pardon the interruption, Jeri," Chris said. "But Sheridan's representation of himself is inaccurate. He *was* a fiend. But he's no longer the man who did those things."

"Why don't you join us, Dr. Strider?" Jeri smiled as she motioned to a chair that a crew member placed next to Stanley's.

Chris reluctantly took the seat. "I'm sorry. I didn't mean to interrupt your interview. And I certainly didn't mean to become a part of it. Truth is, I don't much care for cameras, at least not when they're pointed at me."

Jeri smiled again—a warm, friendly smile that she'd probably spent considerable time perfecting. "But your comment is so interesting, Dr. Strider, especially since Sheridan's records indicate that he was the one who murdered your wife. Did you know that?"

Chris nodded, a sudden wave of emotion stealing speech from him. "Yes," he managed to squeeze out. He bowed his head as he tried to regain control. This was exactly the reason he'd declined to join them. He knew his loss was still too raw. Whenever the subject came up, he couldn't trust his voice.

"There's no reason to drag him through those memories again. I've already told you, I did it." Anger flashed in Sheridan's eyes, amplifying the inherent threat of his intimidating bulk. When Jeri visibly drew back, he paused and softened his manner. "And yes, Chris knows it. I made sure he was watching when I pulled the trigger."

Although Jeri skipped a beat while finding her voice, she then continued in that same unnaturally pleasant tone. "And yet he's the very one who's taken you under his wing since you left your father."

"Yes, and he's been more of a father to me in a month than Stan Moden was in a lifetime."

"Hear, hear," Stanley said.

Jeri shifted in her chair to address the older brother. "I understand he's also the one who adopted you after you fled your father at age ten."

"That's right," Stanley said. "He put his own life in danger to do it, as well as the lives of his wife and children. I'm forever grateful to him."

"But surely all this talk of fleeing and fearing is exaggerated," Jeri said. "I've met your father. He's a charming man."

"And don't think he doesn't know it," Sadira said. "Our parents have spent considerable time and energy learning how to manipulate people and situations to their advantage. Their every move in public, every word, is calculated for maximum effect."

"But underneath that charming exterior lies an evil man," Stanley added. Motioning to Chris, he continued, "If you want living proof of what he's capable of, just look at Dad's face."

Chris grinned. "You don't have to be insulting."

Stanley laughed. "Let me clarify. The scars you see on Dad's face came from an incident in which my biological father had him tortured." He shook his head slowly. "I'll remember that sight until my dying day. He was unrecognizable, his face and torso black and blue, covered with blood and gashes. That's what my biological father calls an 'interview.' "

"You must hate Stan Moden very much," Jeri said to Chris.

"No, Jeri, I don't," Chris said. "I prefer concentrating my emotional energy on loving my family and helping people understand who Doug Damour really is. He's not at all the arbitrary, cruel man that Stan Moden portrays. Quite the contrary. He's the kindest, most generous person I've ever known."

"Then how do you explain the war he's declared on Dr. Moden? If he had his way, it would have occurred in the most populous city in the United States."

"No, that's another of my father's lies," Sheridan said. "But, first of all, you should know that the reason Doug declared war was because my father purposely violated the terms of the truce they had ratified. He deliberately targeted a Paradisian citizen under Doug's protection—specifically, Chris's wife. That's the reason I was to murder her, to accomplish my father's purpose of ending the truce."

"You're saying he *asked* for war?" Jeri said skeptically.

"Precisely."

Jeri hesitated, seeming a bit thrown by that information. "Well, even if that's true, why would Mr. Damour wish to fight that war in New York, involving so many disinterested bystanders?"

"He didn't. Doug's Declaration of Battle called for it to occur in a section of the Kalahari that is almost entirely deserted. And Doug's troops—not my father's—have been clearing the remaining Bushmen from the area."

Jeri lifted one perfectly arched eyebrow. "These are all major deviations from President Moden's story. Do you have any proof of your version?"

"As a matter of fact, yes." Sheridan pulled a light blue envelope from his jacket pocket. Chris noticed Doug's presidential seal on the envelope. Sheridan removed the pages of parchment and handed them to Jeri.

Sadira gasped. "How'd you get that?"

"Is this the original Declaration of Battle?" Jeri asked, clearly excited to be in possession of such exclusive evidence.

"Yes, it is, with the inciting event defined and the original terms specified." Addressing Sadira, Sheridan answered, "Father gave it to me after he read it, don't you remember?"

"I remember." Stanley said, and explained to Jeri, "I was the one who delivered the declaration to Desmon Tower."

"Yes, I remember it too," Sadira said. "But how did you get it out of the building?"

"I had been reviewing the terms and happened to have it in my pocket when Father ran me off the property," Sheridan said. "He was so angry that he altered my hard drive, had me tailed, bugged my phones, the whole shebang." He grinned. "But he forgot to search the clothes I had on my back."

Sadira burst into laughter. "If I'd have made such a sophomoric mistake, I'd be washing Desmon Tower's windows for a month."

Sheridan snorted. "Only because you were his favorite. My usual punishments involved something from Mother's collection of antique torture implements. Father particularly likes whips."

"Surely you're exaggerating!" Jeri exclaimed.

"Am I?" Sheridan eyed her as if weighing a decision of particular import. Chris glanced at Sadira and Stanley for clues but learned nothing. Were they equally in the dark? Or were they all hiding the same truth, one so horrible that they had decided together to keep it secret?

"All right," Sheridan said. "Let me show you something." He stood to remove his tweed jacket, tie, and shirt, which prompted some tittering among the women of the news crew.

Jeri laughed. "Well, if you meant to impress the women with your muscles, it appears you've succeeded."

Sheridan, his torso now bare, smiled ruefully and nodded at Stanley. "You'll notice my brother's equally buff. When you grow up a Moden, strength is necessary for self-defense."

He fell silent, as if still uncertain of his decision, and then, without further comment, simply turned around.

A collective gasp went through the room, and a small shriek escaped Sadira. Deathly silence followed as everyone stared dumbly at the mass of scars crisscrossing the young man's back.

After several moments, Sheridan turned back around. "That's who the great Stan Moden really is."

"Your father did that?" Jeri exclaimed. For the first time in the interview, she seemed to have dropped her scripted responses to react with genuine outrage.

Sheridan nodded. "It started shortly after Stanley left. I was five. It continued until I was strong enough to overpower my father and give him a taste of his own medicine." With a wry smile, he added, "He laughed when I did that."

"Because he'd made you into the tool he needed you to be," Sadira said softly.

Sheridan's brow crinkled. "I guess you're right. After that, he treated me with more respect."

Chris noticed that Sadira's eyes glistened suspiciously, and he wondered if some measure of healing was occurring. Part of the trouble between the two siblings was their mutual belief that they had shared the same experience and should, therefore, have reacted to it in the same "strong" way. Perhaps she, at least, was coming to understand that her basic premise was not as accurate as she'd thought. Whatever means of manipulation their parents had employed on her, she had not suffered routine physical abuse.

Rising, Jeri approached Sheridan. "Do you mind if I touch your back? Those watching may think the scars are make-up."

"Sure." Sheridan obligingly turned his back to the camera.

The cameramen adjusted their shots as Jeri rubbed at one scar after another. "You may not be able to appreciate this at home, but I can literally see scar laid down on top of scar. Some of them, like this one"—she traced one finger along a larger, jagged area—"appear to be areas where large chunks of flesh were torn off."

As Chris watched, he was overwhelmed with the horror of the young Sheridan Moden's life, a life filled with uncertainty and abuse, absent of even the pretense of love. Although he had already completely forgiven Sheridan for Susana's death, he now truly understood it. He could see how someone brought up in that environment of hatred and torment, belittled and degraded by his own father, would grow into a monster himself. In fact, as he looked upon that living record of the unspeakable pain Sheridan had endured, he marveled that he was able to respond to love at all.

Chris was so absorbed in his musings that he didn't notice a camera focusing on him until Jeri addressed him. "Dr. Strider, are you crying?"

Was he? He quickly swiped at the tears on his face. "I'm sorry," he whispered.

When she said no more and the camera remained trained on his face, he explained: "I've always loved kids. That's why I'm a pediatrician. To think of someone doing that to a child—a five-year-old?" He shook his head. "I can see why Sheridan became who he was. It was the only way he could earn some measure of the approval every child craves from his parents. It's truly miraculous that he could be transformed into the tender, compassionate man I've come to know. It's an amazing tribute to the life-changing power of Doug Damour's love."

CHAPTER 19

TORMENT

*"All his days the wicked man suffers torment ... because he shakes
his fist at God and vaunts himself against the Almighty."*
Job 15:20-25, NIV.

30 November 8043 M.E.

Camille and Garrick were both in Stan's office when Madelyn knocked and let herself in. "Pardon the intrusion, Dr. Moden, but you'll want to see what's on the evening news. You all will."

Bustling to Stan's computer, she logged on to the network where Jeri Roberts was interviewing Stanley, Sheridan, and Sadira. As Madelyn left, Camille caught the look in her eye and registered in passing that it was not one of anxiety, as the alarming turn of events demanded, but of satisfaction. However, Camille was too preoccupied with contemplating the repercussions of the newscast to consider the implications of Madelyn's odd reaction to it.

Sitting forward on his seat, Garrick watched the newscast intently for several minutes before muttering, "An island off New England." He pulled out his phone and ordered some planes to the area.

When the interview ended, Stan demanded, "Why weren't we informed of this, Garrick?"

"I don't know. Our informant at that network is usually reliable. I'll check into it."

"Then get to it. Let me know what you learn."

Heading for the door, Garrick asked, "Are we sticking to the current plan?"

Stan frowned at his desk in concentration, and Camille could almost hear his thoughts. Their overall strategy leading into the Final Battle entailed a complex system of events—economic, sociological, and political dominos. Each must be triggered at precisely the right time to topple the next. Delay meant readjusting many interrelated events. Yet attempting the next step now would be simply futile. Sheridan had done exactly what Garrick predicted—he had launched a counterattack that inflicted maximum damage. In fact, this might destroy the effectiveness of the succeeding dominos entirely. Unless they could regain control of public opinion, the final recruitment efforts that were so essential would fizzle like a corroded firecracker.

Looking up, Stan said, "Honestly, I don't see how we can."

Nodding, Garrick left the office, and Camille turned a silent glare on her brother.

"Don't you start," he growled. "I did what I had to with that boy. Don't try to pretend you didn't know about it."

"You could have used less visible methods."

"A little late for that advice now, don't you think? Neither of us ever suspected outlanders would find out about it."

"How will we explain this to the media?"

Stan shrugged. "The Spartans used severe methods of training their offspring, and theirs was a great society. We're Paradisians, not Americans. We can spin it as acceptable in Paradisian society."

She simply scowled at him.

"All right, I'll think up something better." He rose and reseated himself on the desk in front of her chair. "Or maybe my 'better' half will," he added in a tone that was equal parts sarcasm and challenge.

Camille abruptly rose and strode to the door.

"*Kamíl?*"

She spun to face him, hand on hip.

"Deserting me now would be a very foolish mistake." He moved toward her as he continued, "We've always been stronger *together*. We've always accomplished the impossible *together*. Allow Damour to separate us, and you hand him the victory." His tone was stern, but his emphasis on "together" was a not-so-subtle reminder of their business pact. He was asking if she would honor its solidarity.

She knew what her answer must be. However angry she might be with him, her future, her very life, depended on keeping the Allied States of Desmoden as strong as possible.

"You have always had my loyal support, Stan."

"But do I have it now?" he pressed.

Garrick entered, interrupting them, and Stan demanded, "You have news?"

"The island's now deserted. We missed them."

"I expected as much," Stan grumbled with uncharacteristic calm. "Damour's too smart to make a mistake like that. But it was a good try."

Garrick obviously hadn't expected such a tame response either. When he frowned, Stan frowned back. "What's wrong?"

"That's what I was wondering. What's with the Mr. Nice Guy routine?"

Stan grunted and strode to a window. Garrick shot Camille a questioning look, and she shrugged. She could only sense uncertainty—concerning in itself. Stan Moden was nothing if not self-confident.

Still facing the window, Stan said, "Garrick, you're smart. And you've always had the support of the troops. They'd follow you anywhere, as would many others in this organization. Why haven't you tried to overthrow me before this?"

Garrick's eyes widened, and he mouthed to Camille, "Before *this*? This what?"

Sighing softly, she shook her head. Since Stan hadn't brought it up again, she had never warned Garrick of her brother's concern that they were plotting against him.

"And don't give me any nonsense about friendship, either," Stan continued. "We both know how friendships come and go."

Garrick crossed the large office in a slow, measured stride. "You want the truth, Stan? I'll tell you why. Because you couldn't pay me enough to deal with the PR headaches you have to juggle—like that one." He nodded toward the computer screen. "No one could handle them half as well as you do. I suppose it's the edge you have from the link that makes you so much more effective than the rest of us *polini*. But then I really don't care what the reason is, as long as you do the job right."

He took a step closer and dropped his voice. "But why don't you say what's really bothering you? What you really want to know is if you can count on me during the mess ahead, isn't it?"

Stan spun to him, eyes flashing. "You want honest, *Lok Sondem*?"

And with that, Camille understood. Most of the exiled Paradisians had taken different surnames after the rebellion, but Garrick had changed his name in an unusual way. He retained his full preexilic surname, *Lok*, "to stand beside," as his middle name while adding a new surname that meant "ally." However, rather than the more common *miláj*, he chose a rarely used synonym, *sondem*. The significance of this was obvious only if the two names were used in tandem, *Lok Sondem*—a combination that sounded suspiciously like *laksondem,* "enemy."

Camille had always understood the implicit threat, and she was certain Stan had too. The same man who had "stood beside" Damour for two thousand years before becoming his "enemy" would also cease to "stand beside" them as their "ally" and become their "enemy" if his interests were crossed. Furthermore, the two partners knew the majority of soldiers would likely back him in such a course, for he was a charismatic and well-liked commander.

But Garrick had always remained staunchly loyal to them. As a result, he had gradually amassed more and more power. At some point it occurred to the siblings that they might have entrusted him with too much power. But, if they had, they could do nothing to remedy the situation now.

But these misgivings were old suspicions. They'd undoubtedly plagued Stan for centuries. What troubled Camille most was that such shadowy doubts were becoming large monsters in his closet *now*. It told her that the strain of this climactic period was wearing on him.

Garrick hesitated briefly at Stan's hostility. "Yes, old friend," he said softly. "I want honest."

Grinding out his response between clenched teeth, Stan said, "What I really want to know, *old friend*, is when you're going to knife me in the back."

Garrick studied Stan for a moment and then very deliberately took a step backward, snapped his fist to his chest, and bowed deeply. "President Moden, I was one of your first supporters, and I have always been straight with you. I have had one overriding goal since our exile: getting back to the *Viv Zabé*. It so happens that you are by far the best leader we have, no question. If anyone can get us back there, it's you. Furthermore, I hate Damour as much as you do. Even if I could look into the future and *know* we were going to lose this war, I would fight to the end, just for the satisfaction of making him suffer. *Knife* you in the back? I will *have* your back to the end, just as I always have. All I ask is that you watch mine too."

Stan eyed his general closely before extending his hand. "Deal."

Taking Stan's hand, Garrick continued, "Since we're getting this all out in the open, I'm going to say something else. The way I figure it, our chance of succeeding at this little endeavor, now that they have Sheridan, is pretty slim. The only chance we have is if the three of us stick together—you, me, and Camille."

He extended a hand to Camille, and she joined them at the window as he continued. "We each have our own following in this organization. We each have our strengths. As long as we're straight with each other, we'll be strong. But if any of us breaks from the others, it will be like sawing one leg off a three-legged stool. We need each other. I know it. You know it. Camille knows it. Let's just be sure we all remember it through the days ahead. Because these are *not* going to be fun days, even for me."

And with that—Camille hoped—Stan's suspicions were put to rest.

CHAPTER 20
SPEAKING

*"Do not worry about what to say or how to say it. At that time you will
be given what to say, for it will not be you speaking, but the Spirit of
your Father speaking through you."*
Matthew 10:19, NIV.

When Chris and the three siblings returned to their Alaskan hideaway, Melanie and Cherie joyfully met them at the door and led them by the hand to the living room. A partially eaten tray of homemade cookies awaited. "They had a little trouble waiting," Bethany explained with a grin.

Once they'd settled around the fire, Bethany handed Chris a sheet of paper. "Doug forwarded this and asked me to pass it on to you, *Onó.*"

Chris managed to avoid groaning as he read the communiqué, but his face must have shown his discomfort. Sitting cross-legged on the floor beside his easy chair, Sheridan asked, "What's wrong, Chris?"

He silently handed him the message. A moment later, Sheridan let out a whoop. "Yeah! Take that, Father!"

"What is it?" Sadira asked.

"The Bob and Barb radio show," Sheridan said. "They want to interview Chris and me tomorrow. And if one nationally-syndicated show wants us, their competitors will too. It will mushroom from there. By the end of the week, everyone in every large city throughout the world will know what a liar Father is."

"What a great opportunity," Sadira exclaimed.

Chris forced a smile while trying to calm the butterflies in his stomach. Being interviewed by Jeri Roberts was bad enough, but at least his participation had been an impromptu event, so he hadn't had time to get nervous. This, on the other hand—well, he sure wouldn't get much sleep tonight.

"Has Doug approved it?" Stanley asked.

"Yes," Chris said. "He added a note saying he'd like us to do it. There's also a notation from Lanse; a contingent of Royal Guards will accompany us." He released a small sigh. "A jet will pick us up in the morning."

"Are you okay, *Onó?*" Bethany asked softly.

Chris managed another fake smile. There was no sense in burdening his daughter with his irrational fear of unseen audiences. The funny thing was, he had no trouble with live audiences, where he could see people's level of comprehension and adjust his presentation accordingly. But the idea of talking to people blind …

He heaved another sigh. "Just tired, sweet pea. I think I'll head to bed."

Just then, Melanie climbed onto Sheridan's lap with the look of a mission in her eye, and Chris stopped to watch. When she whispered something in her uncle's ear, he asked, "Why?" She whispered something else, and he said, "You won't cry?" With a serious expression, she deliberately shook her head from side to side.

Sheridan chuckled. "All right, then." He shucked the blue polo shirt he was wearing, and Melanie walked around behind him. She stared at his back, her little brown eyes filling with tears, and then began methodically kissing each of his scars. Slowly the room quieted as the others noticed what was happening.

"What are you doing?" Sheridan asked.

"I make 'em better like *Mami*," Melanie explained.

When Sheridan cast a puzzled frown at Chris, the older runner explained, "It's something people do with children. The parent kisses little wounds to 'make it better.' "

"Oh," Sheridan said. "Well, I doubt it has any healing virtue, but it feels nice."

Melanie kissed each of Sheridan's scars, although it took a while. Then she returned to his lap and buried her face against his chest.

"Hey, what's this?" he asked. "You said you wouldn't cry."

"I not cry, Unc' Sher'dan," she answered. "I rain."

Chris chuckled as he bid everyone goodnight. When he got to his room, he activated his transmitter, and Doug said, "I was hopin' you'd call, pardner. What do you think of your assignment?"

"It's a great opportunity, Doug."

"But?"

"But my stomach's flopping around like a fish out of water," he admitted.

"You don't have to do it."

"If it will help, I want to do it. I'm just nervous. What if I get all tongue-tied?"

"Don't you worry 'bout that. The words will come as you need them. You don't need to do anything but stay in touch with me."

✻ ✻ ✻ ✻ ✻

Sheridan was gazing out the window of Doug's private jet, basking in Doug's peace and marveling at the mercy that could grant it to someone like him. Gratitude and joy washed over him as he realized—again—how incredibly fortunate he was to be here, to be forgiven, and to be working for Doug, a man he'd already come to love as both friend and father.

The last few weeks had been difficult. So much to learn. And unlearn. So many memories to haunt him: innocent victims pleading for their lives; terrorized faces of men, women, and children; the sound of his own laughter echoing over it all. It was his guilt, more than anything else, that threatened to separate him from his new *adu*. But whenever he focused on Doug, he was again overcome, as he was now, with gratitude.

His mind wandered over the developments of the last week. He and Chris had been inundated with requests for interviews after the Bob and Barb show. Doug had directed them in which to accept, and they had been flying around the country since. Chris didn't enjoy the public attention, but he never complained. When Sheridan asked about it, Chris had said he was happy to do whatever Doug asked of him, and, after all, what was a little nervousness compared to all that Doug had done for him?

Sheridan had a different reason to be nervous: Father was chasing them relentlessly. They'd already had two narrow escapes. But Chris insisted that he let Doug do the worrying about that. His advice wasn't blithe platitudes spoken in ignorance, either; Chris had been "interviewed" by Garrick himself, the world's foremost expert in torture.

Sheridan shook his head in wonder. What faith his mentor had! Would he someday learn to trust Doug the same way?

He looked over at Chris, asleep on his right side with his left arm hugging a pillow, and a wave of guilt washed through him. Stanley had told him that Chris had trouble sleeping because he was so used to sleeping with his arm around Susana that he didn't know what to do with his arm in her absence. So seeing him like that always reminded Sheridan of the woman who should be lying in the place of that pillow.

Sitting forward, he shook his head resolutely. He couldn't let himself go there again. Those journeys down memory lane were not only fruitless, but harmful. He had been forgiven! Yet how easily he forgot.

Chris had taught him to focus on the *Manual's* promises when his guilt resurfaced, so he resolutely disciplined his mind into that channel. " 'Though your sins are like scarlet, they shall be as white as snow,' " he recited. " 'If we confess our sins, he is faithful and just and will forgive us our sins and purify us from all unrighteousness.' "

" 'His righteousness comes through faith to *all* who believe,' " Chris said, sitting up. " 'There is no difference, for all have sinned and fall short of his glory and are justified freely by his grace.' "

With a smile, Sheridan looked up from his focus on the carpet. "Thank you."

When Gabriel reported that they'd land in Chicago in a quarter hour, Sheridan excused himself to wash up in the bathroom. Today they were to appear on *Marci,* the most popular television talk show in the United States and broadcast in many other nations as well. Doug had said this would be their last show and that he had a special message for Sheridan to share with the world on it. But when he asked what the message was, His Majesty just said, "You'll know when the time comes." Doug sure had more confidence in him than he had in himself.

Marci was an energetic brunette with an engaging personality that immediately put them at ease. She asked the usual questions about Sheridan's past and Chris's forgiveness, and then she asked if Sheridan would show her audience his back. Sheridan complied. He'd come to feel some measure of gratitude for those scars; morbidly fascinating though they were, they had opened many doors to warn people about Stan and point them toward Doug.

After the usual reactions erupted from the audience, Marci asked something no other interviewer had asked: "I have to wonder about that transmitter you have, Sheridan. I've heard that everyone who wears one is a potential target for your father. Is that true?"

"Yes." Sheridan's firm answer triggered a flurry of panicked whispers around the audience.

"Everyone who's wearing this kind," Chris corrected, holding his own up. "However, those people also know that Doug is an ever-present refuge and strength."

"What other kind of transmitter is there?" Marci asked.

"There's another device distributed at the New-RABs," Chris said. "The members are told there's no difference between the RABs and New-RABs, that Doug established them both."

"That isn't true?" Marci asked.

"No. They're two completely separate institutions. The RABs were established by Doug and are managed by his son, Joshua Damour. The New-RABs were established by Stan Moden, and he still runs them, although he encourages the false impression that they're aligned with Doug's institution."

Sheridan shrugged into his shirt and resumed his seat beside Chris. "Actually, as supporters become more involved in the New-RABs, the story changes. Most members are Level 1 supporters, as they're called. They're told that both RABs and New-RABs are Doug's institutions. But supporters who become more involved are taken into increasing levels of confidence. Level 2 supporters are told that they're both Doug's institutions, but that Stan helps manage them both. The story continues to change by stages as a person becomes more deeply involved. Only supporters at the highest level know the truth—that the New-RABs are a counterfeit organization that my father uses to deceive people into joining his camp."

"This is extraordinary information," Marci said. "Can you prove any of it?"

"I'm an eyewitness who spent twenty-eight years in Father's organization." With a wry smile, Sheridan shrugged. "But then, I understand if my word doesn't count for much. I am an admitted liar. So I have another idea. I think I can give you a peek behind the wizard's curtain. Give me just a moment, won't you?"

When she agreed, he descended the platform steps to greet a young woman on the front row whose low-cut blouse clearly revealed her New-RAB transmitter. With a slight bow, he extended his hand to her and said, using the smoothness he'd learned from his father, "What's your name, lovely lady?"

Her cheeks flushed a deep pink color. "June Smythe."

"June, would you be willing to join us on stage?"

"O-Okay," she said uncertainly. She glanced at the friend beside her and giggled nervously as Sheridan tucked her hand into the crook of his arm and escorted her up the stairs.

"It looks like Sheridan's found an example of the fake transmitters to show you," Chris said.

"But it isn't fake," the young woman countered. "Look—you can talk to my agent on Paradise Island yourself." She activated the transmitter and greeted the respondent, who did answer in the British accent used by Paradisians.

Recognizing the agent's voice, Sheridan interjected, "Hi, Tony. How's housekeeping?"

"Oh, same as—" Tony broke off. "Sh-Sheridan? Is that you?"

"In the flesh." Sheridan winked reassuringly at the young woman, who was frowning in confusion at the sudden loss of Tony's British accent.

"But you're—" Tony sputtered. "I can't talk to *you*!"

"Why not?" Sheridan asked innocently.

"You know very well why not, you traitor! Your father will have my hide!"

"Because he's your boss?"

"What is this, Sheridan? You know Stan Moden's my boss!"

When a collective gasp went through the audience, Tony groaned, obviously understanding that this wasn't the private conversation he'd believed it to be.

Sheridan chuckled. "Thank you, Tony. You've been most helpful."

Tony cut the call off, and Sheridan turned to June. "How long has Tony been your agent?"

"Ever since I joined the New-RAB. Five years or so."

"His name is real—his full name is Anthony Fiden. But he's been in Manhattan, working for Stan Moden, for longer than you've been alive. King Doug exiled Tony for treason along with my parents. He's had no association with Doug Damour since."

June removed her transmitter and gazed at it sorrowfully. "So Tony's been lying to me all this time? I've never been part of Doug's organization at all?"

"I'm afraid not," Sheridan affirmed.

An angry glint came into her eye and she threw the transmitter down. Her friend did the same, and then more and more New-RAB transmitters joined it where it fell. Soon there was a little pile of the devices in the aisle.

Looking up to Sheridan, June asked, "How can I join the real RABs?"

He pulled a business card from his pocket. "Here's Doug's number." Lifting his voice he announced, "Doug always talks to his supporters personally. He will give you a coach and connect you to others who can help you, but he will never stop talking to you himself."

As the young woman returned to her seat, Marci said, "I did a program about the New-RABs some twenty years ago. At that time, I interviewed General Gabriel Lanáj, Doug Damour's right hand man, about them. So Damour must have been in charge of the New-RABs then."

"It wasn't Gabriel you interviewed," Sheridan said bluntly.

"I beg your pardon!" Marci exclaimed.

"Oh, I'm sure you believed you were interviewing my uncle Gabriel, but the truth is, he's never had anything to do with the New-RABs. You see, he and my father are identical twins, so Father poses as Gabriel to strengthen the impression that the New-RABs are under Doug's supervision."

"I find that very hard to believe," Marci objected.

"That's exactly what Father counts on. Yet I've watched him tape those programs for the New-RABs myself. But you don't have to believe me. My uncle came with us today—you can ask him yourself." Spying Lanse in the wings, Sheridan called, "General Meshon, where's Uncle Gabriel?"

"On the roof, Sheridan," Lanse answered. "I just asked him down for you."

Gabriel soon appeared, dressed in the casual uniform of the Royal Guard. He walked onto stage and greeted Marci. "I do beg your pardon for my informal attire, ma'am. I didn't expect to be on stage."

"That's not a problem," Marci said. "You were on the roof? So you haven't heard our discussion?"

"I'm sorry, ma'am, but no, I've not heard."

"So much the better. Do you remember when I last interviewed you?"

Gabriel glanced at Chris and Sheridan, obviously bewildered. "I'm afraid there's been a misunderstanding. I'm quite certain we've never met. Oh"—his face cleared—"perhaps you've met my twin brother, Stan Moden."

"The interview was regarding the New-RABs," Marci said.

Frowning darkly, Gabriel leaned back in his chair. "Then it was most certainly my brother you met. I've nothing to do with that fraudulent organization and never have. Stan uses my name to lend credibility to his shameless lies."

Marci paused, touching her earpiece. "My producer wants to run a clip from that interview."

A short clip began, but Chris interrupted with "Freeze it!" when Stan turned his head. The bright studio lights had brought the scar on his cheek into unmistakable focus in that position.

Pointing it out on the screen, Chris motioned to Gabriel. "You'll see that Gabriel has no scar here, so it's the easiest way to tell the twins apart. But there's an even safer way. *The Runner's Manual* tells us that 'If they do not speak according to this word, they have no light.' It also says, 'By their fruit you will recognize them.' "

"Well," Marci said, "if we're talking safety, it seems to me that the safest place is in the neutral zone, wearing no transmitter at all."

The audience applauded their agreement.

"There's no such thing as a neutral zone." As the words leapt from Sheridan's lips, the conviction seized him that this was the message Doug wanted him to deliver to the world. Rising, he walked down to the audience to ensure that the urgency of the message came through.

"My father loves tricking people into thinking there is a neutral zone. He gets a hearty laugh out of it. But the truth is, there are only two sides, as *The Runner's Manual* says: 'He who is not with me is against me.' The unvarnished truth is this: If you use a transmitter like mine, you're on Doug's side." Bending down to pick up one of the discarded transmitters, he held it up. "If you have one of these or none at all, you're on Stan Moden's side."

His gaze swept the spellbound audience before he added soberly, "My father would have you believe that the Final Battle will only affect the Kalahari. It won't."

Cries of alarm and murmurs of disbelief rippled through the audience. Marci had to raise her voice to ask, "You mean Doug Damour plans to attack the United States and other countries?"

"No, not Doug. My father." Sheridan waited for another wave of murmurs to die down. "Please understand: I was the commander of his army. I helped develop his battle plans. I know what I'm talking about. My father has identified key cities around the world that he plans to attack using planes disguised as Doug's. Actually, these were the plans before I left—the details will have changed now that my intel is on the other side. But the objective will not change. My father knows he can't defeat Doug on his own. He needs global support, and he will do whatever it takes to make that happen. Believe me or not, that's your choice. But each person on this planet will, by February 12, have to choose either Doug

Damour's side or Stan Moden's side. Even the pretense of a neutral zone will soon vanish."

"Then you don't believe this war can be averted?" Marci asked.

"No," Sheridan replied. "This war is inevitable. My father won't stop now, not after preparing for over six thousand years—"

"What!" she exclaimed.

When Sheridan's brow furrowed slightly, Chris explained, "You let Stan's age slip."

"Ah," Sheridan said, "I'm sorry—I forgot that not everyone knows about that."

"Are you seriously implying that Stan Moden is 6,000 years old?" Marci asked incredulously.

"No," Sheridan said, and a mollified-sounding murmur rippled through the audience. "He was 8,043 years old in October."

Exclamations of disbelief erupted throughout the audience, and Marci cried over them, "See here, Sheridan—I won't have you turning this forum into a mockery!"

"He's not," Chris assured her. "Paradisian physiology is different from ours for reasons that I won't go into just now. But they actually have lived thousands of years. That's how long Stan has been planning and preparing for this war, how long he's been manipulating world politics to his advantage. He's absolutely determined to overthrow Doug Damour. His life depends on it. He won't stop now."

"Oh, I'm definitely going to need some proof for such an outlandish claim!" Marci insisted.

"If you know what you're looking for," Sheridan said, "it's an easy thing to support. Just search through the records of the oldest newspapers. I've personally seen references to Stanley L. Moden in articles from the *Wall Street Journal* in 1889, the *New York Times* from 1851, and the *London Gazette* from 1666."

"You won't find any pictures of him, though," Chris interjected.

"That's right," Sheridan agreed. "He didn't allow his pictures to be published until Doug issued the Declaration of Battle. He didn't want anyone to get wise to his real age—it's easier to manipulate people if they believe you're just like them."

"Then why—" Marci began, but Uncle Gabriel, who had just cocked his head as if listening to his radio, jumped up and cut her off. "Sheridan, Chris, to the helicopter straightaway. Lift off without me."

Sheridan grabbed Chris by the arm and sprinted off stage toward the back stairway. As they ran, he heard his uncle tell the audience, "We need to evacuate the building immediately. We've information that Stan Moden has bombers en route. Please proceed calmly but quickly to the street and continue until you've cleared the block ..."

CHAPTER 21

IMPRISONED

*"The Lord has anointed Me to proclaim liberty to the captives, And
the opening of the prison to those who are bound."*
Isaiah 61:1, NKJV.

As the live broadcast of *Marci* went off the air, Willy leaned forward and
rubbed his face. His cell phone rang, but when he saw it was his mom, he laid
it down on the coffee table without answering it. The house phone rang, and the
caller ID's mechanical voice announced, "Rose Moore." Willy again rubbed his
face but didn't move from the sofa.

His oldest brother called his cell phone; his other brother called the
house phone. Willy still didn't budge. He knew what they all wanted—the same
thing he wanted: some answers. But he didn't have any answers. He didn't even
know who to ask. Who could he trust? Had Cherisse and Ms. Menod really been
lying to him all these years?

He'd been inclined to chalk everything up to his uncle's paranoia until
he heard Sheridan's description of the different levels of New-RAB supporters
who received different information. That really bugged him. It was exactly what
had happened to him.

He sighed. How important were the answers to these questions? Wasn't
the important thing that, as a New-RAB administrator, he was helping people
who genuinely needed help? Did it change the value of his accomplishments if
he'd been under Moden's umbrella all along? Would that un-shelter a child on a
cold night or un-fill her hungry tummy?

Besides, what proof did he have that Moden was such a bad guy? It was
only Sheridan Moden's word that shifted the blame for the turkey fiasco from
Damour to Moden—and Sheridan was a confessed liar and murderer.

Still, look at what Moden had done to his own son. Willy could easily
imagine such a person engineering a nasty plague.

Unless, of course, the scars were some kind of hoax …

"Grrr!" Willy grabbed fistfuls of his hair. "This is all so confusing!" How
could he ever wade through all plausible explanations of the facts when he wasn't
even sure of the facts?

"All right," he said, grabbing a legal pad from the end table. "Let's start
with what we do know." He'd never met either Damour or Moden, but he dutifully listed his Strider uncles' claims about them both. He jotted down Cherisse's
explanations. He reviewed his own experience in the New-RAB administration,
how people were helped without prejudice. He included his level of comfort, for
he'd never felt truly comfortable in a RAB. They were always emphasizing the

importance of "letting Debora change you," of "confession," and "sanctification." The New-RABs, on the other hand, encouraged him to feel good about himself.

He stopped writing and considered that last point. Even if Sheridan's claims were true, would he want to join the RABs? Would he enjoy attending meetings with hard-nosed critics? Uncle Chris suggested assessing people "by their fruit," but what did that reveal? On Doug Damour's side: intolerant reactionaries hedged in by Damour's arbitrary rules. On Stan Moden's side: open-minded collaborators who trusted an individual's judgment and promoted enlightened self-determination.

His gaze shifted thoughtfully to the top of his list. He had written "#1" there, but left it blank. As he considered that dark secret, too shameful to commit to paper, he realized that no amount of maybes or possiblys would ever overbalance it. In fact, very few actual facts could override it. Certainly not the identity of the New-RAB's leader, past or present. Not even the rumored leanings of that leader, no matter how nefarious. The absolute necessity of guarding that secret overrode all else. And the secret was only safe if he remained loyal to the New-RABs, where Cherisse could protect it.

Therefore, his personal duty was clear. Whatever evil Moden may—or may not—have committed, Willy just wanted to help people. He needed to help people. Nothing else could make up for his mistake. And his ability to help people would be jeopardized if the donors and volunteers lost confidence in the organization he worked for. So, in order to continue his work, he needed to protect the New-RAB's image.

Yes, this perspective simplified the problem immensely.

He activated his transmitter. When Cherisse answered, he said, "I just saw *Marci*. How can we spin this? How can I help bolster the public's confidence in the New-RABs?"

* * * * *

Together with Chris, Sheridan sprinted up the several flights from the studio where they'd been filming *Marci*. But something niggled at him the whole way. Twice before his father had almost caught them—but *bombers*? What could he possibly gain from bombing Chicago under his own flag?

As they climbed the last staircase, it occurred to him that this maneuver might not be Stan's doing; it might be Garrick's. And then he understood: It wasn't about revenge, but simple military strategy. Garrick had long wanted to put Gabriel out of commission.

Chris had just pushed open the door to the roof, flooding the stairs with the noise of the waiting helicopter, when Sheridan grabbed his shirt. "No! It's a trick!" he shouted over the din.

Chris turned back. "What do you mean?"

"It's Garrick's 'Behind You' maneuver. He pretended to order bombers here over a frequency he knew we'd monitor, but the information was only meant to drive the targets into the real trap. He's probably set up two traps. One for us"—he nodded toward the helicopter, likely not Doug's at all—"and one for the Guard at the street level exits."

Chris let the door close. "We need to call Doug."

"No time!" Sheridan dashed down the stairs. "I have to warn my uncle," he called back.

Chris yelled after him, "There's always time to call Doug!"

But Sheridan knew better than to waste precious moments. Chris had no idea how quickly Garrick's men could move. Neither did he know how badly Garrick wanted to remove Gabriel's military genius from the equation. So Sheridan flew headlong down the stairs, knowing he could reach his uncle faster in person than going through the appropriate channels by radio.

When Sheridan burst through the stairway door onto the floor where the auditorium was located, close enough to hear the sounds of the evacuation in progress, he stepped right into a contingent of Garrick's men—all aiming rifles at him.

Instantly he realized his mistake. Garrick had used Sheridan's own intel against him. Right now, he was even more of a liability to Stan's cause than Gabriel. He was the one being driven into a trap. Chris, too, if they could get both. Well, at least Chris was safely away. He had been wise enough to call Doug, who would surely see through the plan.

Chuckling, Garrick stepped out from behind his men. "I was hoping your new mentor's assessment of you as a 'tender, compassionate man' was accurate. You should have figured this out, you know—just as you figured out our other two attempts. But you've let love blind you. Your parents tried to teach you about the vulnerability of love. Maybe they were right after all, h'mm?"

The door behind Sheridan burst open, and Chris stopped alongside him. Sheridan's heart dropped into his gut.

"Ah-oh," Chris said. "A double trick, I take it."

"Well, well," Garrick said. "The bonus prize. We were hoping you'd show up. It's been a while, son of Juan Misi, but I assume you remember me?"

"Yes, Garrick, I do." There was no fear in Chris's voice, and Sheridan felt proud of him for it.

"Good. Then let me introduce you to my son." Garrick motioned Conner to his side. "Dr. Christian Strider, General Conner Sondem. I should warn you, Conner's not yet as experienced as his father. He's been known to kill men unintentionally while interviewing them."

This was true. Sheridan could easily remember at least three such cases. What Conner lacked in imagination, he made up for in sheer violence.

"So if I were you," Garrick continued, "I would be more cooperative with him than you were with me." He clapped Conner on the back. "You have your orders, boy."

"Yes, Father." Conner roughly handcuffed Chris's hands behind him.

Sheridan didn't bother resisting as Garrick handcuffed him. If these had been regular soldiers, he could engage them with a reasonable chance of success. But the dozen troops before him were a mixture of Paradisians and Paradisian offspring who knew Sheridan's moves as well as he knew theirs. He could not overcome such a group.

"I'm sorry I got you into this, Chris," he murmured. "I should have figured it out. I was the primary target and you were a secondary target. Gabriel and the Guard weren't even on their list today."

"Very true," Garrick said as he tightened the handcuffs to the point of pain. "But I'll enjoy watching Gabriel try to explain it to the media when no bombers materialize. That, of course, will make his claims about the New-RABs less credible."

Circling around to face him, Garrick's eyes sparked with fire. Sheridan had never seen the old general lose his cool, but even his practiced façade didn't veil his fury now. Drawing back, he landed a solid, bone-rattling punch on Sheridan's jaw before shoving a revolver under his chin.

"If you only knew the times I've defended you to your father, you ingrate—the punishments I've saved you. I treated you like my son. And you repaid me by joining my enemy."

Sheridan could argue none of these points. Garrick had often been the cushion between him and his father, even if the protection was merely to assure Sheridan's ability to work. And Garrick had indeed treated him like his son, although he was no better at fatherhood than Stan was.

"I've got half a mind to blow your brains out right now and be done with it."

When Garrick cocked his gun, Sheridan thought he'd seen his last hour. Yet he felt no fear, only regret for getting Chris into this mess. If Garrick killed him now, it would be a quick, painless death and he would die with his transmitter. What awaited Chris was an excruciating, lingering death at Mother's hands.

Sheridan heard nothing but the whisper of the general's rapid breaths in the stillness that followed. Garrick's wrath was so apparent that even his own men seemed afraid to move. The familiar scent of Garrick's specially formulated gun oil distracted Sheridan briefly. It recalled the many hours he'd spent cleaning those firearms, for the old general maintained his weapons with compulsive attention to detail.

Wouldn't it be funny if I died by one of the very guns I used to clean for him? Sheridan laughed inwardly. *Poetic justice, they'd call it.*

Garrick's discipline kicked in then, compelling him to uncock his gun and replace it in his shoulder holster—if reluctantly. "But your father wants to kill you himself. And I don't care to have him angry at me over the likes of you."

The sigh Sheridan exhaled was not one of relief. It looked like a long and painful death for him too. But then, he deserved it. Unlike Chris.

CHAPTER 22
PLENTY

"In the midst of his plenty, distress will overtake him; the full force of misery will come upon him."
Job 20:22, NIV.

7 December 8043 M.E.

amille stood in the corner of her office, oblivious to the beauty of the sunset. Even looking down on the tiny people in the street below brought her no consolation, no ability to rise above the worry that consumed her. Since Sheridan went public, she had been unable to eat or sleep, she snapped at everyone, and her eyes were perpetually gray.

Sheridan's skill as a speaker, together with the shock factor of his scarred back, had turned the tide of public opinion against them globally. Political connections had distanced themselves. Thousands of their outlander troops had deserted. And now, with his explicit revelations about the New-RABs, many of the outlanders deceived through that avenue would undoubtedly be lost as well.

Yes, things were looking very grim. She and Stan had brainstormed some ways to counteract Sheridan's testimony, but all hinged on eliminating him so he couldn't rebut them. Garrick had worked tirelessly toward that goal but had thus far been unable to trap him.

Stan had become even crankier than usual. He, too, slept poorly. During the bleakest hours of the night, she often found him profiled in the moonlight at the living room window, simply staring out into the blackness. Needing comfort herself, she usually joined him. They said nothing at those times, both sensing the desolation that neither possessed the strength to share aloud. Yet they found some small measure of solace by clinging to the fragile support they found in one another, in being together during this dark, dark time.

They both knew the incontrovertible truth: they would lose this war. Their long lives would end. The predictions recorded in the *Manual* would prove accurate. Both siblings had suspected this outcome at various points, but they could no longer deny it. Despite their own best efforts, despite the combined intelligence of Moden Industries' most brilliant minds, they would fail.

Oh, they would still look for some happy accident they could turn to their advantage. They would continue to fight tenaciously. The same hatred that had set them on this road would drive them relentlessly onward. Still, in the end, they would lose. And that heartrending knowledge filled every moment of every day and night with hopelessness.

One purpose drove them now—one goal toward which they remained irrevocably united: revenge. Doug had stolen everything they cared about—homeland

and family, position and power. They, therefore, would steal as much as they could of that which he most valued: his darling humans. If she and Stan must be destroyed, they would be consoled in knowing they had destroyed as many humans as possible.

A knock startled Camille out of her reverie, and Stan entered. A new bounce energized his stride, and his eyes were sparked with hope. "Did you see Garrick's chopper land a few minutes ago?" he asked with a hint of playfulness.

"Yes, I saw it. Conner's, too, shortly after." This was nothing remarkable. These days, Garrick's and Conner's helicopters frequently came and went from the helipad on the roof.

"Guess who Garrick brought back with him." Stan's eyes fairly twinkled.

"Really?" She grabbed his hand like a little child. "Don't tease me, Stan!"

Chuckling, he assured her, "Really. Sheridan's now our guest downstairs."

"Oh, how wonderful!"

He chucked her under the chin. "This gives us another chance, *zali,* the ray of hope we needed. And I'm taking full advantage of it. I've already released our statement refuting Sheridan's claims. Is Saxon ready for his part?"

"Yes, he's been working tirelessly with acting and voice coaches. Once his hair is permed, he'll do very well indeed. Only those personally acquainted with the original will perceive the deception."

"Excellent. I'll be gone a few days. I've gotten on the *Marci* show for tomorrow, and Madelyn is lining up other radio and TV appearances."

"Stan, I do wish you'd reconsider your plan to renounce Sadira on *Marci.* The more lies you spread about, the more likely that you'll be caught in one of them. And that tale is unnecessary to our purposes."

"It's necessary to my purpose," he snapped. "Besides, if Sheridan went public, she could too."

"You know that's not your motivation. Unlike Sheridan, she's never craved public exposure, nor does she have his charisma. Even if she went public, she wouldn't approach his level of success."

"Any level of success is more than we need," he insisted. "And we must eliminate further complications. We're cutting things far too close as it is. Besides, I'll have no trouble juggling one more lie. Have a little faith in me, *Kamíl.*"

She knew she would not deter him once he was so obviously intent upon revenge. Far better that she relinquish her stand and preserve their relationship. With a smile of surrender, she placed both hands on his chest and met his gaze. "I do have faith in you, *zuulu.* You're the best actor I know and the best strategist. Do as you see fit."

"Hmph," he responded, but she sensed that he was mollified.

"Is there anything I need to do toward advancing our battle plan in your absence?"

"No. After I've repaired the damage to my reputation by discrediting Sheridan and Sadira, Damour and I will declare peace and unite both RAB organizations. I have a Subject primed to aid us in that objective."

His gaze was focused beyond her as he clicked through the items, assuring himself that all was in place. Camille followed his verbal musings closely to make certain that no point was overlooked.

"Once the control frequency goes live," he continued, "our geologists and meteorologists will trigger as many natural disasters as we can get past the Planetary Defenders. We'll blame those occurrences on the interaction between the two types of transmitters. Our physicists have already prepared a statement full of erudite-sounding language describing their 'new discovery.' They should have no difficulty convincing the masses that the wavelengths emitted by the two devices create a resonance that, when magnified by millions of transmitters, causes physical stresses on tectonic plates and alters atmospheric conditions."

"And that will incite the masses to protect their new form of pain relief," Camille added. "Anger against the runners who won't give up their transmitters should carry them forward, but we can heighten the response through the control frequency if necessary."

"Precisely. The groundswell that develops will result in legal measures to restrict the activities and freedom of the loyal runners. After that, Damour will cause the world's economies to collapse, and I will rally the furious countries against him." His brow furrowed briefly, and then he nodded. "Yes, everything's in its proper place now."

"Excellent, Stan. I'm certain you'll succeed."

And, truthfully, she mostly meant it. Her brother had a remarkable ability to use most any occurrence to rally public opinion against Doug. A boon could be used to distract the masses with Moden Industries' philanthropy. A disaster could be attributed to terrorist attacks by Doug's followers. Whatever the occasion, he could usually spin it to keep the balance of public opinion tipped in favor of Moden Industries. Or merely tipped. He was even able to make general restlessness work in their favor.

Iona's voice over the intercom interrupted them: "Dr. Moden, General Conner Sondem has arrived."

"Ah!" Mischief glinted in Stan's eyes. "I have a special gift for you."

Stepping to the door, he motioned Conner in. "General Sondem, your involvement in today's mission was successful?"

"Yes, sir, it was."

"Excellent. Would you please tell Dr. Desmon what your objective was?"

Conner's dark eyes shone with suppressed excitement. With a deep bow, he said, "My assignment, ma'am, was to deliver a certain Dr. Christian Strider to you."

Camille looked from Conner to Stan in astonishment. In the despair of this hour, the last thing she'd expected was that they would catch this elusive man.

"It's true," Stan affirmed. "He's downstairs. I saw him myself on the cameras."

Camille felt she would explode with pleasure. Shaking Conner's hand firmly, she said, "This man has caused us a great deal of trouble, General. You've provided an excellent service to the organization and have done me a personal favor as well. Strider carries a half-million dollar bounty from the company coffers. Since he's also on my List, I shall match that. I'll have your checks cut today."

The sparkle in Conner's eyes brightened. "Thank you, ma'am. That's very generous."

Stan dismissed the boy, and Camille let out a most uncharacteristic squeal of delight as the door closed behind him. "You've seen him? Really?"

"Only on the cameras. I'll welcome him to our little paradise, but then I'll leave him to you."

"I thank you, *zuulu*—so very much!"

He kissed her on the forehead. "You're very welcome, my dear *zali*. It truly is my pleasure."

"And what are your plans for Sheridan?"

"I've decided to take a different course with him. I specifically raised him to withstand physical pain, but if he's learned compassion—and apparently he has, since that's how Garrick trapped him—he'll have minimal defenses against emotional pain." He grinned. So I'm going to let him listen in on your sessions with Strider before I start on him."

"Splendid idea," Camille agreed.

✵ ✵ ✵ ✵ ✵

Chris rotated his hand in the shackle, trying to reduce the tension on the healed but still tender gunshot wound in his left shoulder. With his arms chained over his head, no part of his nearly-naked body was comfortable. The dungeon's chilly air found and augmented even the smallest annoyance. But that shoulder bothered him most, and he couldn't find a position that eased the constant ache.

He heaved a discouraged sigh. He was already so cold and miserable, and the "entertainment," as Garrick had once put it, hadn't even begun.

At the time, following Sheridan had seemed like a good idea. Well, maybe not a good idea exactly, but at least the better of two awful ideas. With Sheridan so new to Doug's ways, how could he leave him to suffer alone? Yet now it seemed that he wouldn't have the chance to encourage him. They'd apparently been separated, put in different facilities altogether. How could he be of any use to the young runner that way?

Again he called hopefully, "Sheridan? Are you here?" He strained to hear any faint reply, but only silence answered him.

What a fool he'd been! He'd deliberately walked into Garrick's trap, hoping he could help Sheridan. He should have guessed that the cunning old general wouldn't give the more experienced runner a chance to encourage the rookie. Yet, hadn't Doug told him that he would be given that chance? Had he misunderstood him? What exactly had he said?

Chris called up the memory of their conversation on the stairway. "Should I go after him?" he had asked.

"You may if you'd like," Doug answered. "But if you do, you'll be captured too."

"And if I don't, he'll have to suffer alone?"

"That's right, pardner."

"Doug, he's new to your ways. And his past still taunts him unmercifully. Wouldn't it help him to have an encourager?"

"Yes, it would. He's responsible for his own actions, but your presence would strengthen him immeasurably in his new faith. Still, I have to warn you, the cost would be high. If you go with him, you will suffer a great deal of pain."

"Are you telling me not to go?"

"No. You have my blessing, whichever course you choose. The decision is yours."

"Would my presence help Sheridan?"

"Yes."

So Chris had gone. And now here he was, apparently isolated from the man he'd come to help.

But he must walk by faith, not by sight—or hearing. If Doug said he could help Sheridan, then it must *be* so, even if it didn't *seem* so. Maybe Sheridan was here but couldn't respond. And if so, Chris had work to do. Enough hanging around—so to speak. He had come for a reason. Standing here shivering wasn't accomplishing it.

Lifting his head, he began singing number 56 from the *Manual's* song-book. Though meant to strengthen Sheridan, it strengthened Chris as well. After a couple of stanzas, even his shoulder seemed less painful.

The sound of boots hitting the cement floor and fists smacking against chests—the guards coming to attention and saluting—interrupted Chris's song and notified him that he would have a visitor. Knowing how much Stan's crew hated the *Manual*, he belted out the next verse while sharp footsteps neared his cell—a heavy but agile man, Chris guessed from their sound. Probably either Stan or Garrick, who both carried some 100-plus pounds more than Chris did.

That thought triggered the memory of when Garrick had tortured him, and a violent shudder shook his frame, stealing his breath away and setting his heart pounding. As keys clattered in the door of his cell, the song's words vanished from his mind. So he simply chanted the Outlander Division's motto—"We can do all things through him who strengthens us!"—improvising a tune as he went.

The door swung open, and Stan's imposing presence filled the doorway. Silently holding Chris's gaze, he very deliberately removed his expensive suit jacket and handed it to the guard. His eyes glinted with anticipation as he like-wise stripped off his tie and shirt. Then he advanced toward the helpless prisoner, balling up his fists so that the massive muscles of his arms and chest contracted menacingly.

Chris was duly impressed. Furthermore, he hadn't forgotten how much a blow backed by those muscles hurt. But he also knew Stan enjoyed such displays for intimidation's sake alone, and he was determined to give him as little satisfaction as possible. So he forced himself to look the goliath square in the eye and, in as lazy a tone as he could muster, he said, "Howdy, Stan. Nice day, isn't it? A day 'that Doug has made. Therefore I will rejoice and be glad in it.' "

A strong backhand caught Chris on the cheek. It certainly smarted, but it was worth it. "Yup," he said, "I think I'll 'rejoice and be exceeding glad: for great is *my* reward' in *your* homeland of Paradise Island."

Stan's eyes narrowed momentarily, and then he flashed a humorless smile. But in that quiet moment, Chris heard a noise that lifted his spirits immeasurably. From somewhere within those gray confines issued a snicker—Sheridan's snicker, Chris was sure of it. So Sheridan *was* within hearing distance! Nothing could have better fortified Chris for whatever lay ahead.

Stan seemed to understand exactly what his prisoner was thinking. "Yes, that's Sheridan. Did you think I'd let him off with an easy death? Quite the oppo-site. I intend to have a particularly good time with him. Do you know why?"

Stan moved a few steps away and then turned to lock Chris's gaze in his cold emerald glare. "Because, Christian Strider, son of Juan Misi, I'm going to be thinking of you all the while. Just as I did with every stripe I laid across his childish back. Just as I did every time I disciplined Stanley and Saxon and especially Sadira. Just as I did when I taught each of them to torture and maim and kill."

Suddenly grabbing Chris's forelock, Stan jerked his head back and glowered directly into his eyes. "Do you know why, Strider? Do you know why I so thoroughly enjoyed molding these children to my will?"

Chris didn't know, and he had the distinct impression that he didn't want to know either.

"No, of course you don't. I didn't honestly expect an outlander to figure out such an elegant scheme. But I want you to know, Strider, so I'm going to tell you."

He released Chris's hair and sat on the cement ledge jutting from one wall. There he eyed Chris, as if relishing a moment he'd been anticipating for some time. Finally he said, "I'm not human, Strider. We Paradisians are made individually, carefully—each one of us. That's why we're so much better than humans. We don't pass on flawed genetic information. In other words, Strider, we don't reproduce. We don't need to. We don't want to."

He cocked his head. "But this apparently isn't news to you. My chatterbox twin probably told you this much. I'll bet he got no further, though. With his mind dwarfed by centuries of submission to Damour, he's probably incapable of conceptualizing my beautiful plan."

Leaning forward, he asked evocatively, "If we don't reproduce, where *do* these children come from, I wonder?"

Chris had no intention of answering him until he realized the conversation wouldn't continue until he did. And, since he was now curious, he at last answered, "Some type of cloning, I assume."

"You assume wrongly, Strider. We use simple in vitro fertilization."

Stan again paused as if awaiting a reply, but Chris couldn't figure out what reply he wanted. Finally he just said, "Okay."

Stan flashed a condescending smirk. "You still don't understand, do you, Strider? If Paradisians have no germ cells, where did I get the germ cells for these children?"

Chris suddenly realized what Stan was driving at, and his eyes widened in revulsion.

Stan chuckled. "You understand at last. Yes, that's right. These children that I've had such fun tormenting are humans, Strider. They were conceived in vitro from germ cells *sold* to me. Willingly. No blackmail. No threats."

He eyed Chris with undisguised hatred. "Would you care to speculate about who provided the ova for the offspring I raised, Strider? Would you like to guess who sold me her children for paltry sums of mere money?"

Chris didn't care to guess. How could anyone be so cold, so cruel, as to sell her children to Stan?

Stan looked at his fingernails and buffed them briefly against his pants. "Tell me, Strider, do Stanley's eyes remind you of anyone? They remind me of someone." He glanced up. "They remind me of his mother."

Rising, he stood directly in front of Chris as he hissed, "Your. Twin. *Sister.*"

Chris sucked in his breath. He wanted to think this was merely another of Stan's lies, but he couldn't bring himself to believe it. How many times had he marveled at how closely Stanley's eyes resembled Rosie's? How many times had he wondered how Rosie and Ivan managed to live so far above their means?

Stan flashed a poisonous sneer. "So you see, Strider, I've had the pleasure of torturing you for three decades in the persons of your nephews ..." He drew closer to add, "... and even your niece."

Stan surveyed Chris's sickened expression, seeming to savor it like a succulent morsel. With a satisfied smile, he said, "And now that you know, my joy is complete."

Stan left without delivering another physical blow, but the pain he had inflicted was sufficient to set Chris's soul reeling. As he hung there, astounded and horrified, he couldn't wipe the sight of Sheridan's mutilated back from his mind. Rosie had sold her eggs to *Stan*? To produce children who would be abused, misguided, and trained to torture and murder? His head bowed under the weight of the horrible discovery. Stan was right; knowing that those children were his very own niece and nephews made everything he had seen and heard of their lives so much worse.

But as this appalling information danced through his brain, gleefully driving daggers deeper and deeper into the raw wounds it had inflicted, another idea began to peek shyly from the corner: Three out of those four children now wore Doug's transmitters! What's more, he had played a part in their rescue.

"Sheridan?" he called.

No response.

"Sheridan, if you can hear me, I want you to know that I love you, son."

Chris chuckled at himself. "Correction: not 'son.' You probably couldn't hear what Stan told me, but he's not your biological father." He paused as he realized, "Maybe that wasn't the best way to deliver such information. Still, I'm guessing you'll welcome the news. Anyway, he also told me something of your true heritage. Sheridan, we're related! So I want you to know that I love you—nephew!"

✷ ✷ ✷ ✷ ✷

Nephew?

Down the hallway in the same dungeon, the genuine delight in Chris's voice sent a wave of warmth through Sheridan's shivering body. He'd spent his life seeking one thing: his family's love. How ironic that in giving up the quest, he had found the love he craved.

He bowed his head and wept for joy.

CHAPTER 23
MIRACLES

"These are demonic spirits with power to work miracles,
sent out to muster all the kings of the world for the battle
on the great day of God."
Revelation 16:14, REB.

8 December 8043 M.E.

"So Gabriel's claim that bombers were en route was completely bogus, Stan?" Marci was sitting forward on her chair, the textbook picture of interested involvement.

Watching the live program in her own living room, Camille also leaned forward. This road was cluttered with landmines, and much was riding on Stan's ability to negotiate that path successfully. Certainly, no one was more capable of the task. Her brother could mold groups like clay. She had watched him turn frightened mobs into excited teams—or vice versa, when he chose. Still, she couldn't shake her anxiety. Had they truly anticipated all potential problems?

Answering in his smooth bass, Stan said, "I don't want to jump to conclusions about my brother's motives. He's a good man. Misguided, in my opinion, and possessing that sort of blind loyalty to Mr. Damour that induces people to do, well, crazy things—but a good man nonetheless. Maybe he did pick up some communication that he interpreted as originating from us. I really can't say, but I've never known Gabriel to flat-out lie. At least not without a good reason."

Camille chuckled. "Well done, Stan." Lifting her voice, she called, "Saxon, you should watch this."

Saxon emerged from the hallway and settled in an overstuffed chair. "Oh good—I was hoping to catch it. I love watching Father work. He's such a master at manipulating audiences."

"So there was no truth to his claim?" Marci asked Stan.

"Marci, why would I bomb you?" Stan asked with seeming sincerity. "You not only do much good with your philanthropic pursuits, but your excellent reporting keeps America informed and sensitized to the world's problems."

Saxon chuckled. "You old charmer, Father."

"Yes, he certainly is," Camille agreed. "His charisma, together with his striking appearance, has served us well through the ages. Humans, silly creatures that they are, tend to immediately like, even trust, attractive people."

"Thank you for your compliments, Stan, but you didn't actually answer my question," Marci persisted.

Stan wiped the smile from his face. "Then let me be clear. I did not order, or even consider ordering, bombers to your building, to Chicago, or to any other city in this grand country. Neither did anyone else in my government."

"Well, you can understand how we would struggle to believe such a claim, after seeing what you did to your own son."

A shadow fell over Stan's face. "I could never do something like that to my son. I was as shocked by those pictures as everyone else."

"You're saying you'd never seen those scars before?"

"No, I hadn't. I suppose it's some form of parental neglect, but I will admit that I don't make a point of examining my grown sons' backs."

Some bits of laughter scattered around the audience.

"So far, so good," Camille said tentatively.

"We do tend to dress more formally at home than Americans do," Stan continued. "I haven't seen Sheridan's bare back for—well, a long time. But it definitely didn't look like that when I last saw it."

"Then what caused his scars?" Marci asked.

Stan started to say something, then choked up and pinched the bridge of his nose.

"Stan?" Marci leaned toward him, brows knitted together. When he looked up, tears moistened his eyes.

"Hurrah, Father!" Saxon applauded. "What a master. I've never been able to manufacture tears on command. And he does such amazing things with his eyes, augmenting whatever emotion he wants to convey. Look at the audience—some are actually weeping with him."

It was true. Stan's piercing emerald-green eyes were a weapon all their own. They could invigorate people when he called them to action or paralyze individuals with whom he was angry. Still, it was interesting that Saxon had noticed this. Turning to observe him, Camille knew a moment of what must be parental pride. Of all the offspring, Saxon—her special charge—was the keenest observer. Of course, she had raised him to become an astute psychologist, but sometimes her own success surprised her.

Laying a sympathetic hand on his knee, Marci offered Stan a tissue. "What is it?"

"Do you have children?" he asked.

"Yes, a boy and a girl."

"Then you know the depth of love we feel for our children and how a parent's world revolves around them. It's not easy to learn that your son has a serious problem. It's even harder to discuss it on national television. That's why I haven't answered these charges sooner—the emotions have just been too raw."

Setting his jaw, he continued. "But Sheridan's accusations have hurt other people, especially my wife." He gazed intently into Marci's face. "I love my wife, Marci. She's a good woman. She doesn't deserve this. I can't just sit by and watch him hurt her like this."

Saxon threw his head back and roared with laughter.

"Yes, I can imagine it's been distressing for your whole family," Marci said sympathetically.

Stan nodded grimly. "But to answer your question, Sheridan was always a … challenging lad—strong-willed, rebellious, a bit of a wild child. But also violent, unpredictable." He paused before adding gravely, "Unstable." Shifting uncomfortably, he continued, "My wife, herself a renowned psychologist, suspected a psychiatric illness.

We took him to different clinicians, but, well, he's also highly intelligent. Frankly, I think he fooled them all."

He looked down, twisting his diamond-encrusted wedding band. "A few years back, Sheridan started experimenting with different cults. We didn't approve, but"—he shrugged helplessly—"well, he's a grown man with the right to do as he chooses. At one point, he was involved with a cult that practices self-flagellation. We didn't know, never even suspected, he'd gone that far into it." He gave his ring another twist. "I guess we were wrong."

Camille and Saxon both applauded. "Bravo, Stan!" Camille exclaimed as Saxon called, "Good job, Father!"

"So he did that to himself?" Marci asked with a touch of incredulity.

"That's the only thing my wife and I can think of to explain such—" He wagged his head. "—such brutality."

After a brief pause, Marci asked, "Stan, this may sound harsh, but why should America believe your version over his?"

Stan looked up with a surprised expression. "Well, I suppose that's a reasonable question. Let's see … you could start with our respective histories. Sheridan has admitted to committing a variety of truly atrocious crimes including—" He hesitated, looking down before continuing reluctantly, "Including rape and murder." He shook his head slightly and exhaled a weary sigh. "Anyway, I have no such history."

Marci turned to her audience. "I can vouch for that statement. Other than a couple of parking tickets, Stan Moden's record is completely clean."

"Actually, those parking tickets were my chauffeur's fault," Stan said with a little grin, and the audience laughed.

Marci held a document up for the camera. "I also have here a rather impressive list of his contributions to charity—tens of millions of dollars from Moden Industries for this year alone, and even more from Stan Moden and his wife, Camille Desmon. This list includes shelters for abused women, children's hospitals, schools in Africa—the list goes on and on."

"Frank's work?" Saxon asked, referring to their vice president of finance.

"Yes," Camille answered. "He's excellent with creative financial statements."

"Apparently I don't pay my accountant enough," Stan said with a disgusted expression.

"I won't reveal my source," Marci said. "But I will say that it wasn't your accountant. And I apologize if I've embarrassed you, but this is important information that speaks to your generous, humanitarian nature."

"Mmm."

"But I need to ask you about something else." Marci nodded to the screen behind them as the clip of Stan posing as Gabriel played. When it froze on the frame that revealed Stan's scar, Marci turned back to him. "Is that you?"

Stan grinned sheepishly. "Yes, Marci, it is. You caught me."

"So you posed as your twin brother?"

"I did."

"Why?"

"He asked me to."

"He what?" Marci exclaimed.

Stan chuckled. "You may have noticed that we vaguely resemble one another. I suppose most twins think it's entertaining to switch places as youngsters. I know we played our share of such games. As we grew older, we sometimes covered for one another. I, for instance, have always had trouble with time. It just gets away from me. Gabriel watched out for me, meeting appointments on my behalf when he couldn't find me. He, on the other hand, is uncomfortable in front of an audience, whereas it doesn't bother me. So when he approached me with the idea of collaborating on the New-RABs, he asked that I make the public appearances in his place, using scripts he provided." Stan shrugged. "So I did."

"So those were done in collaboration with Doug Damour?"

"Initially, yes. Whatever the differences between the Damours and myself, we've always shared the common goal of making the world a better place. The New-RABs, with their emphasis on improving health and well-being, were something I could support wholeheartedly. When the project mushroomed beyond my brother's capability, he simply turned it over to me. Unfortunately, we later had a falling out, and Gabriel's been, well, vengeful since then." He looked down. "Vengeful enough, I'm afraid, to involve his own daughter in these accusations against me."

"What do you mean?"

"The young lady claiming to be my daughter, Sadira Lanáj. She's Gabriel's daughter."

A murmur of either surprise or disbelief went through the audience—Camille couldn't tell which—and it revived all her qualms about this tale. "Please be careful, Stan," she murmured under her breath.

"Oh, she interned with my company for a prolonged period," he continued, *"and I probably introduced her as my daughter on occasion. That old habit's a product of my native tongue. You see, Paradisian families are very close. We don't even possess words for 'niece' or 'nephew,' but simply call them 'daughter' and 'son.' That's how we think of them. Nevertheless, Sadira is actually my niece."*

"But I'm told DNA testing confirmed the three to be siblings," Marci said.

"Yes, I heard that too and asked my geneticists about it. Apparently it's impossible for DNA to differentiate siblings from first cousins when identical twin brothers marry identical twin sisters. But my wife and I have only three sons, although we would have loved to have a daughter as well."

"Ha-ha!" Saxon exclaimed. "No wonder I'm so smart! I get it from both sides!"

"Yes, though not a fool-proof lie," Camille said. "If Gabriel comes forward with the truth, I'll have to play the part of my twin sister, Gabriel's wife, who is reluctant to defy her husband, but who can no longer bear the lies he's been devising against his brother." She shook her head. "Such shameful goings-on."

Saxon laughed. "That's not likely, is it?"

"Paradisians have never gone public, so we believe it to be a safe risk. Otherwise we'd not have bothered with the story and the forged documents to back it up."

"Why did you? What does it actually accomplish?"

Not a thing! she thought, but answered him as if fully convinced of her response. "It's one more stone to pile on the grave of Gabriel's credibility. The more doubts we provide, the more likely that public opinion will turn against him. It will also discredit Sadira, should she decide to publicly denounce us."

Recalling their attention to the TV, Marci said, "Sheridan made another interesting claim concerning your age. And our research supports it—insofar as it can be supported. But, of course, there are no written records that go back 8,000 years. So tell us, are you really 8043 years old?"

Stan looked her in the eye and said, "Yes, Marci, I am."

A hush fell over the audience.

"How is that possible?" she asked dubiously.

"Perhaps you've heard a certain myth about a Tree of Life?"

Camille chuckled. "A 'myth' because we turned it into one."

"Are you saying it's real?" Marci asked.

"Very much so. In my native tongue, we call it the Viv Zabé, 'Life-Tree.' I ate its fruit for some two thousand years before being exiled. Its effects are starting to wear off only now."

"So this tree is on Paradise Island?"

"It is."

"And your having eaten its fruit is the only reason you've lived so long?"

"That's right."

"Then why doesn't King Doug share it with the rest of the world?"

Stan threw his hands up in the air. "That's exactly what I've been saying! He's sitting on an amazing resource, Marci. But he won't share it. He threw my group off the island because we insisted that he distribute it around the world. But he won't. He says the rest of the human race is too corrupt and doesn't 'deserve' to live longer."

Distinctly outraged exclamations erupted from the audience.

"Good," Camille murmured. "Very good."

"In one sense, Sheridan is right," Stan continued. "The war is inevitable. But only because Damour is so fearful of giving up his advantage. And I intend to keep pestering him until my dying day. That tree may be on his island, but it's a global resource—or should be."

"Truly excellent work, Stan," Camille said. To Saxon she explained, "Since Sheridan exposed our plan to bomb strategic cities under the Paradisian flag, we needed another method of rallying the world against Damour. This will begin to turn public opinion against him."

"Pure genius," Saxon said. "I was wondering how you would turn around the mess Sheridan made, but this is beautiful."

"And speaking of resources," Stan said, "let me say something about the pile of New-RAB transmitters I saw here in the aisle yesterday." He rose and walked into the audience to plead, "Ladies and gentlemen, if you've discarded your New-RAB transmitter, let me encourage you to reconsider. For years, we've been working on a new technology that can provide relief to the millions suffering with various forms of pain. I won't bore you with the physics involved, but we've discovered that emitting a certain pattern of sound waves over the transmitters triggers the release of endorphins."

"Aren't those the body's natural painkillers?" Marci asked.

"They are indeed," Stan said. "So any disease that causes pain, from everyday headaches and backaches to fibromyalgia, even pain associated with cancer, will improve or abate altogether. The volunteers testing this therapy over the last year have experienced amazing relief. Just last night I received word that we'll be ready to broadcast it system-wide beginning at midnight tonight. For those interested, the details are available on the New-RAB website now."

As the audience buzzed with eagerness, Saxon asked, "That's the control frequency we've been working on?"

"Yes. Analgesia turns out to be a most useful side effect," Camille answered. "It wasn't quite ready, but we hurried things along so he could announce it here."

"This is an amazing medical breakthrough!" Marci exclaimed.

Returning to his seat, Stan said, "Yes, we're very excited about it. Since you brought up our contributions," he nodded to the paper at her side, "you'll notice that a key priority for my wife and I is to relieve suffering. Being able to accomplish something of this magnitude gives us a great deal of pleasure. But frankly, Marci, we'd like to do much more."

"What do you mean?"

"Each one of the exiled Paradisians is several thousand years old. We've done a lot of research and observation in those years. We can provide the rest of the human race with much information and new technology if you're willing to accept it. Up until now, we've had to hide our age, because people tend to fear what they don't understand. We've been called everything from lunatics to witches. I'm hoping this time will be different. I hope that the human race has progressed and is now open-minded enough to investigate the answers we have to offer—answers to big questions, like establishing world peace, solving world hunger, and curing heretofore incurable diseases."

"If you have such solutions available, why haven't you leaked them to the public?"

"We have done so on occasion, when we were certain that the innovation could not be turned to harm. But we humans have ever been plagued by dangerous extremists. In recent years, the members of Mr. Damour's Outlander Division have particularly concerned us. As long as individuals with such intolerant attitudes are allowed free rein, we must be very careful of the information we make available. Information truly is power, but that power can often be used for evil as well as for good. We feel that we have a duty to prevent its use for evil insofar as is humanly possible."

As a favorable-sounding buzz went through the audience, Saxon murmured, "Well, look at that. They're buying it."

"Indeed they are." Camille relaxed back into the cushions of the sofa as she said, "Excellent job, Stan. Very well done."

CHAPTER 24

FORSAKEN

"Though my father and my mother forsake me,
the Lord will take me into his care."
Psalm 27:10, REB.

Sadira's mind raced as she watched her father on *Marci*. Why was he going public now? He undoubtedly had a reason, just as he must have had a reason for his week-long silence. Did he know that yesterday's show was to be Sheridan and Chris's last? And where were those two, anyway? Shouldn't they have returned by now?

"A few years back," Father was saying now, *"Sheridan started experimenting with different cults. We didn't approve, but, well, he's a grown man with the right to do as he chooses. At one point, he was involved with a cult that practices self-flagellation. We didn't know, never even suspected, he'd gone that far into it."*

Deep within Sadira something uncoiled, as if a spring that had been wound too tightly relaxed. She desperately wanted to believe her father, at least on this score. She didn't want to believe he was the pitiless fiend unmasked by Sheridan's back.

Perhaps this wasn't entirely logical. She wasn't blind, and she wasn't stupid. After all, she'd left him because she could no longer bear his ruthless scrabbling for power. Yet he was still her father, and she wanted to believe there was a limit to his villainy. Truly, nothing in her own experience would suggest he could beat his own child so viciously. To her, he had always been the attentive, if strict, father.

As the interview progressed, she easily identified the work of the company's vice president of finance in the list of donations Marci produced. And she had seen Father tape those programs for the New-RABs—although she had then believed that Gabriel was merely Father's invention, a role he played for a particular purpose, and certainly not in collaboration with Doúg.

But then came the truly shocking part, and she wondered if her ears were failing her.

"Unfortunately," Stan said, *"we later had a falling out and Gabriel's been, well, vengeful since then. Vengeful enough, I'm afraid, to involve his own daughter in these accusations against me."*

Sadira frowned in puzzlement. What on earth was he referring to? Gabriel had no children.

"What do you mean?" Marci asked.

"The young lady claiming to be my daughter, Sadira Lanáj. She's Gabriel's daughter."

Sadira suddenly had difficulty drawing a breath. She felt as though a giant wrecking ball had hit her squarely in the chest. But she refused to commit the inexcusable sin of telegraphing her discomfort. Bethany, Stanley, and several guards were also watching the program in the cabin's large living room.

As Father continued, Sadira kept her eyes on the television and concentrated on appearing unfazed. *Just breathe in ... out ... in ... out.*

"... Sadira is, in fact, my niece."

Father looked into the camera, directly at her, and Sadira's heart stopped. She read in his eyes that this part of his performance was for her and her alone. She had betrayed him by defecting to Doúg; he was retaliating by denying her. The daughter who had been the child of his heart was now worth less to him than his traitorous sons.

Only her strict training allowed her to finish watching that show and smoothly escape the room, along with its prying eyes, without revealing the frantic state of her emotions. Once she reached the safety of her room, she sought the solace of the only person who had never abandoned her: the girl in the mirror, her one lifelong friend.

She had been a lonely child, since fear of her parents tended to scare off potential friends. Yet she had always found comfort in knowing that she was special to her father. He had even told her so during the occasional tender moment, and his behavior testified to his regard. She alone had been granted the privilege of traveling with him on business trips. He quickly lashed out at anyone, sometimes even Mother, who dared belittle her in his presence. His attentions were so marked that his absence always left a giant, lonely hole in her life whenever he was away, especially since her brothers' jealousy turned vicious then.

Yet now, as Father's devastating words replayed themselves over and over in her mind, she knew that he had purposely surpassed any necessary measures. He had not just defended himself against her words, but had actually disowned her. Thoroughly disclaimed her. Until that moment, she hadn't realized how important her heritage was to her. Even after separating herself from Father, her identity was intimately tied to him. If she wasn't Stan Moden's daughter, she didn't know who she was—or if she was anyone at all.

The world seemed to crumble around her at the thought. Staring into the desolation of her own blue-green eyes, she watched moisture well up in them. She stubbornly blinked to clear it, determined to prove, at least to herself, that she *was* a Moden.

The thought recalled an argument she'd once had with Saxon, Mother's favorite child. Being only four or five years old then, she didn't recollect why they quarreled. But she did remember receiving a mean slap from Mother, who had called her "a troublesome little whelp." That led to Sheridan chasing her around the apartment as he sang, "Father's little darling's a troublesome little whelp!"

This ended only when Father came home, which seemed like an eternity later although it couldn't have been more than a half hour. Sheridan's chant stopped abruptly when he barreled around the corner to see Father, arms akimbo, glaring down at him. As she remembered it, Sheridan simply disappeared, as if vaporized by Father's glare.

Lifting her into his strong arms, Father carried her to his study—usually off-limits to the children. He sat her on his lap and let her relate the whole story.

He agreed that Mother was very unfair, that Saxon was a "pampered brat," and that Sheridan was an "annoying idiot."

Then he lifted her chin until she met his eyes. "The world is an unfair place full of pampered brats and annoying idiots, but I'll teach you how to deal with them. In fact, we'll begin your lessons in self-defense tonight. For you can always count on me, *Diri,* even when the rest of the world fails you."

That nickname became his exclusive endearment for her. She had nodded solemnly at his tone, feeling very privileged indeed to have her own special nickname and to be the recipient of his exclusive attention—in his special haven, no less.

He smiled then, and his smile always warmed her to her toes. "You, *Diri,* are a Moden. Never forget that, and the world will be yours for the taking."

She must have whispered this last part to herself as she stood at the mirror, for a voice behind her answered, "Is that truly what you wish?"

Sadira spun around to see that Debora had silently entered the room.

"What would you do with the world were it granted you? You already know that it can be a very lonely place when one is all alone in it."

Sadira didn't answer. The accuracy with which Debora had hit the most vulnerable point of her musings left her fearing that, if she spoke at all, she may start blubbering. And that would be a most un-Moden thing to do.

"Come," Debora said, and tucked Sadira's hand into the crook of her arm. "I'd like you to see something that is about to happen."

Sadira gave her a bemused sidelong glance, but followed her without resisting. Debora led her down the hallway to the balustrade that overlooked the living room below. She heard the squabble between Cherie and Melanie before she could see it. Apparently both wanted to play with a set of bongos that their father had found. The argument was escalating when Stanley strode into the room. "Hey, what's this?" he said. "Are my two favorite daughters actually fighting?"

Both girls tried to justify their side of the argument, complaining that the other wasn't taking turns. Stanley listened carefully, as if their little disagreement was as important as any of the grownup wartime problems he was facing at that moment.

"Yes, yes, I see the problem," he said at last. "But I think we can find a better solution than tearing the bongos apart." He moved to the piano and opened the keyboard, which sent both girls hopping up and down excitedly. He held up a finger, and they quieted expectantly. "I'd like to hear how the piano and the bongos sound together. What do you think?"

The girls quickly agreed, decided between themselves who would play which, and started pounding away on their respective instruments. Stanley listened intently and then applauded. "Oh, yes—that's beautiful. See how much better things are when we work together?"

He left, and the two girls continued, quite happily, to play their music as Debora led Sadira back to her room. "You may not remember what that argument with Saxon was about, but it was over a guitar."

Sadira gasped. "That's right—I remember."

"Yes. And now you have seen the same argument handled in a very different manner."

Sadira frowned as she realized how true that was.

"Stanley used his children's disagreement to illustrate the value of combining their efforts to work together. How did your parents utilize that quarrel between you and Saxon?"

Sadira sat down on the edge of the bed as she replied thoughtfully, "Mother used it to drive a wedge between my brothers and myself."

"Yes, even tolerating Sheridan's noisy chant to further that aim. But she also called your father home, and with a very specific purpose. What was his contribution?"

Sadira stared at Debora, finding it difficult to speak around the painful lump lodged in her throat. She had never considered that the incident might have been staged. Yet her training immediately allowed her to evaluate it from this perspective, once asked to do so, even if she didn't like the results.

"Father," she whispered, "employed it to create a special bond between myself and him, to foster my dependence upon him." She swallowed hard. "He was manipulating me."

Debora's eyes welled with the tears that Sadira denied herself. "Yes, child, just so. For though he never laid a stripe upon your back, he manipulated you as deliberately and as relentlessly as he manipulated Sheridan. He was so practiced in exploiting your loneliness that he knew how to wound you—oh, so mercilessly—even now, from afar."

She sat beside Sadira and gathered her hands into her own. "But you are no longer under his power, dear one. And you need no longer be alone. You have a new family—a new *adu*, a new *ami,* and a whole world of new siblings. Stan's strikes need no longer harm you, for I can give you the power to rise above them."

When the tears pricking at Sadira's eyes welled over, she no longer felt obliged to repress them, for her new *ami* wept with her. And on her shoulder, Sadira gained new strength.

Once comforted by Debora's tender counsel, Sadira accompanied her downstairs to discover that Gabriel had just arrived. He was still stamping new-fallen snow off his boots when Sadira, now able even to joke about the situation, joined him in the entry. "Why, Father, welcome back," she called cheerily.

His forehead knit together in obvious confusion. "I'm sorry to disappoint, child," he said wearily. "But I'm Gabriel."

"Yes—haven't you heard? Stan Moden has just informed the world that Sadira Lanáj is your daughter, not his."

Gabriel's mouth literally dropped open. "He what?"

"He did, indeed," Debora seconded. "On today's *Marci* show."

Merriment danced into Gabriel's bright green eyes, and a chuckle began deep in his chest that culminated in a belly laugh. Drawing Sadira into his arms, he gave her a great hug and then sobered to kiss her ceremoniously on the forehead. "Then I have gained a very great treasure indeed. Perhaps today has not been so wholly terrible after all."

So wholly terrible? Sadira suddenly perceived the weariness in his manner. Drawing away, she glanced around and immediately registered the problem. "Where are Sheridan and Chris?"

✻ ✻ ✻ ✻ ✻

As Stanley and Gabriel strategized, Sadira paced the study, trying not to think of the horrors that her brother and her coach were experiencing that very minute. Now she understood why her father had confidently proclaimed his innocence on national television; Sheridan was in no condition to argue.

"It's not a viable plan, Stanley," Gabriel said, vetoing the umpteenth strategy for a rescue attempt. "We know that the dungeon was relocated entirely after your defection. As far as we can tell, it's not even under the same city block as it was then."

"But Sadira—"

"It will undoubtedly have been relocated again after she and Sheridan defected." Gabriel heaved a sigh and ran a hand through his hair. "For that matter, we can't even be sure they were taken to that facility. They could be in Africa—Antarctica!—for all we know." Carefully, he added, "They may not even be alive. How can we conscientiously risk the lives of other troops with so many unknowns on the table?"

"Oh, they're alive," Sadira said confidently. "My parents have spent too long seeking Chris to dispose of him quickly."

"That's right," Stanley agreed. "They chose not to kill him when they killed Mom because they want him alive to torture him. The same will go for Sheridan."

"Similarly, they must also be in New York," Sadira added. "Mother and Father will want to torture them personally. They couldn't do that if the prisoners were anywhere else."

"She's right, Uncle Gabriel," Stanley said. "They're alive, and they're in that facility."

"Very well," Gabriel conceded. "But we still have no idea where in New York that dungeon is. It's a rather large city, you know."

The three went back to their respective modes of concentration: Stanley and Sadira pacing at opposite ends of the room, and Gabriel leaning back in the desk chair, staring at the ceiling.

"Wait a minute," Sadira exclaimed. "They couldn't have relocated the entire facility this quickly."

"You think they'd still be in the dungeon you're familiar with?" Stanley asked.

"Yes, they'd have to be." The thought filled her with momentary hope, but then she deflated. "Oh—but they will have sealed that entry into the facility and opened a new one. And they're extremely good at hiding those entrances. I've never been able to locate one without knowing where to look." She shook her head in discouragement.

The three again fell silent until Stanley abruptly swiveled to his sister. "On the other hand, digging another tunnel would also take too long. So the new entrance would have to come off the existing tunnel."

"That's true," Sadira said. "Which means we could narrow the search. Still, the entrances are very well camouflaged. We'd need someone who's extraordinarily observant, who can detect the tiniest of variations between stones—"

"You mean like a really good tracker?" Stanley's eyes twinkled.

Sadira immediately caught his meaning. "Exactly—like the one the Moden camp calls The Phantom."

Stanley turned to Gabriel, and they broke into matching grins. Together they exclaimed, "Jorge!"

CHAPTER 25
FELLOWSHIP?

"Shall the throne of iniquity, which devises evil by law, have fellowship with You?"
Psalm 94:20, NKJV.

The next day a Paradisian army jet bore several of the cabin's occupants away from their rustic hideaway. Sadira was bound for New York; Doug had asked her to assist in freeing Chris and Sheridan—if such a feat was possible. Stanley and Bethany were heading to the Kalahari to establish the battle station. Gabriel was returning to Paradise Island to oversee the final war preparations. However, he also wanted to survey some natural disasters that had literally occurred overnight.

This latter objective made their course a roundabout one. They swung over Southern California, where multiple wildfires burned out of control. They passed over Mexico City, where a violent earthquake had leveled buildings and buried entire families. They flew low over Cuba and the southeastern coast of the United States, where Hurricane Hercules's destruction eclipsed that of any previous storm. And these were but a smattering of the world's ills. A tsunami had flooded Tokyo. In China, catastrophic mudslides had buried thousands. In Greece, a dormant volcano erupted unexpectedly, entombing hundreds in liquid fire.

Flying over the wreckage in Florida, Sadira asked, "What's happening, uncle?"

"All of creation is groaning, *ve nela,* laboring under a tremendous weight of decay and corruption—of *kanuf.*"

She fell silent. His intense expression told her this was no sightseeing tour. Father wore that expression when he was evaluating a situation to draft a sweeping plan. She didn't understand the nature of that plan until Gabriel murmured, "This area will need the greater proportion of troops."

"Troops?" she asked, confused.

"Mmm," he responded in a distracted tone, but then caught himself. "I beg your pardon, child. That makes no sense to you, does it?"

She smiled apologetically. "No, I'm afraid not."

"Only part of our army is military in focus," he said. "Before Stan's rebellion, we concentrated entirely on public works. The word '*ekanu,*' which came to mean 'army,' actually comes from the verb *ekalát,* which means—"

"To serve the group," Sadira finished with sudden comprehension.

He nodded, a nostalgic smile lifting his lips. "Then it was an army of builders and architects, of landscapers and engineers, of—" He sighed. "In any case, I also oversee the redistribution of troops for disaster relief."

"Oh, I see."

He turned to her suddenly. "But why aren't you resting, *ve nela*? Did you sleep at all last night?"

"Very little. When I close my eyes, I see—" She jolted to a halt, not wanting to make her imaginings more real by verbalizing them.

Again he sighed, but not in disapproval. "'Tis difficult for me to respond in these situations. My perspective of such pain is so different from your own."

"Please explain your perspective, uncle. To me it seems as though Doúg has—" She bit her lip rather than voice seemingly disloyal thoughts.

"As though Doúg has abandoned them?" he suggested gently. Perceiving no censure in his expression, she nodded hesitantly.

"You're not the first to believe so," he said kindly. "'Tis another of the rebels' deceptions. In reality, the opposite is true. In such extreme conditions, the faithful runner experiences Doúg's comfort as others never do. With a clearer sense of the power available to them, they know the joy of greater triumph through his grace. They learn firsthand the truth of the promise, 'As thy days, so shall thy strength be.' Often they even come to feel gratitude—although others rarely understand it—when they recognize that persecution means they are following in Joshua's footsteps."

"You're right—that is hard to understand."

He smiled sympathetically. "Consider this: Have you ever heard Chris complain about being tortured?"

"No. He doesn't speak of it resentfully, or even regretfully."

"Quite true. He was a strong, dedicated runner before his 'interview' with Garrick. But he grew even stronger, closer to Doúg, afterward."

An assistant interrupted to call Gabriel to the conference room, and Sadira joined Stanley, who was watching a news program while Bethany slept on the facing bench. Shortly thereafter, the show cut to a live interview of Father at the door of a New-RAB in Los Angeles.

"We're very pleased that so many have been helped by the transmitters," he told the reporter. *"Reports are streaming into our headquarters by the thousands. We're even seeing actual cures."*

"What of the rumors of an inhibitory effect from the old-RAB transmitters?" the reporter asked.

"Sadly, they're true," Father said sorrowfully. *"Imagine dropping a pebble into a quiet pool. The soothing ripples created represent the wavelengths of the healing frequency. Now visualize hurling a large rock into that same pool. Just so, the wavelengths produced by the older devices obliterate the healing patterns of the improved models. The problem surprised everyone involved, but I've been consulting with Mr. Damour to see—"*

"Consulting?" she exclaimed. *"I thought you two were gearing up for war."*

"Yes," Stan said carefully. *"After the outpouring of global support for my position regarding the Viv Zabé, the UN brought its influence to bear upon Mr. Damour. He is, well, reconsidering his longtime stance on that topic."*

"Sure," Stanley scoffed.

"The war's been called off?"

"There's much to resolve, but we are working toward a peaceful solution," Father replied. *"Meanwhile, innocent people shouldn't suffer because our*

communication devices clash. We haven't yet found a solution, but—" He craned his head around the reporter. "Here comes Mr. Damour's son, Prince Joshua. He might have some newer information."

"What?" Stanley cried. "Stan and Josh appearing together on the same show?"

"I always assumed the galaxy would collapse if they got together," Sadira agreed.

Turning to the approaching man, the reporter asked, "Do you have any information regarding the problem between the two transmitters, Prince Joshua?"

"Yes, I do." Offering his hand to Stan, Josh said, "Hello, Stan. Thank you for your patience as we worked through this matter."

"Not at all, my friend. Not at all."

"My friend?" Sadira exclaimed. "When did that happen?"

"If you'd permit me, Stan," Josh said. "I do have an important announcement from my father."

"By all means," Stan said magnanimously. "Please go ahead."

Joshua addressed the camera, his expression somber. "To those runners who have already switched to the New-RAB transmitters, let me assure you that you have our blessing. Your generous spirit and willingness to bridge the chasm between the two organizations embodies the heart of what it means to be a runner."

Sadira and Stanley met one another's astonished gaze.

Smiling ruefully into the camera, Joshua said, "Now to the rest of you—we must make a rather awkward request. The original transmitters have functioned well for a long time but are now outdated. The New-RAB device performs all of the same functions, plus some beyond the capacity of the earlier model."

"But it doesn't connect you to Doug," Sadira whined, feeling wholly disoriented. She loved her newfound capacity to speak directly with her sponsor. She hadn't removed her transmitter since first placing it around her neck.

"Furthermore, we have found unequivocal proof that transmissions over the original devices interfere with the healing function of the new ones. Worse yet, the combination of the overlapping wavelengths creates a resonance—"

He smiled. "I'm sorry. There's no need to bore your viewers with the physics involved. Just know that using the two communication systems in close proximity threatens the planet itself, predisposing it to cataclysmic events."

"The natural disasters that have occurred since the healing frequency went live last night—they're related?" the reporter asked.

Josh nodded. "A direct result of this interaction. Therefore, my parents and I are urging everyone to discard the old equipment in favor of the updated model. And we urge you to do it today."

"But that means—" Sadira began, only to be hushed by her brother.

"Runners," Josh said, "let me assure you that, although we have some details to iron out, the ill will previously existing between the Damour and Moden families is now concluded. We are working together to improve the efficiency of all programs sponsored by both organizations, and we invite the cooperation of all runners. United, we can solve the problems confronting our planet. This is no time to construct barricades from petty differences. Instead, let us, each one, be part of the solution."

"Does this mean the war between your countries has been called off, Prince Joshua?" the reporter asked.

"It does. I'm happy to be reunited with my old friends in Desmoden and expect a long and fruitful relationship with them."

The story ended with a smiling Josh clapping an arm around Stan's shoulder.

Muting the program, Stanley asked, "What on earth did we just see?"

Sadira shook her head. "I have no idea. Is there any precedent for it? Have Father and Josh ever cooperated like this before?"

"Never—not since the rebellion." He paused, considering. "In fact, the *Manual* says, 'For what do righteousness and wickedness have in common? Or what fellowship can light have with darkness?' "

"So what *did* we see?" Sadira repeated.

While the two genius siblings sat staring at one another, a drowsy voice came from Bethany, still lying on the opposite bench with her eyes closed. "An imposter, obviously."

"She must be right," Stanley said. "However much he looks, sounds, and acts like Josh, he doesn't say the things Josh would say."

"Like asking runners to give up their transmitters?" Sadira asked.

"Right. The *Manual* says, 'this is eternal life, that they may know You, the only true God.' And how can you know someone if you can't talk to him?"

"That's why Father and Mother are always plotting ways to separate runners from their transmitters," Sadira added.

Stanley pointed to the screen. "The imposter also urged the RABs and New-RABs to unite for the sake of global welfare. Yet the *Manual* clearly states, 'Those who serve Doug can have *no* agreement with those who don't.' It even urges, 'Leave those people and make yourselves pure.' "

The siblings continued comparing statements from the interview with passages from the *Manual*. Stan implied that Doug's mind had been changed by world opinion; the *Manual* said Doug does not change his mind. Josh said he was expecting a long relationship with his "friends" at Moden Industries; the *Manual* predicted they would be ashes under his feet.

Now fully convinced, Sadira said, "How did Bethany catch on to the deception so easily?"

"It took a lot of complicated reasoning." Bethany sat up to rub the sleep from her eyes and added with a teasing grin, "The *Manual* predicts it."

The brilliant scholars laughed. Rising to kiss his wife on the head, Stanley said, "You have such a way of boiling things down to a pithy essence while I'm still lost among the facts, *mi corazón.*"

Meanwhile Sadira studied the replaying loop of Josh making his statement. "He does look like Josh, doesn't he?"

"And sounds like him," Stanley agreed. "Any idea who it is?"

"Moden Industries has many good impersonators. But most of the parent generation look too old to play Josh so convincingly. And those Josh's height are generally too muscular, too bulky. I think it must be one of the males from the offspring generation."

"But they're generally less convincing actors," Stanley observed.

"True, but Saxon could pull it off."

"Saxon?" Stanley repeated dubiously.

"I don't understand why you and Sheridan belittle him," she retorted.

"Probably because he's less imposing physically," Bethany said. With a shrug she added, "It's a guy thing."

"Well, he does have other talents," Sadira informed her brother. "He's an excellent actor, for one. He's also the right height, and his physique and coloring are similar to Josh's. They could square off his chin with a prosthesis and de-emphasize his cheekbones with make-up. The hair's probably a wig, or maybe a perm."

Gabriel's assistant interrupted to ask them to join their uncle in the conference room. Upon entering, they saw a frame from the same interview frozen on the large screen.

"Your brother's become quite the accomplished actor," Gabriel said as they joined him at the conference table. Sadira tossed a victorious glance at Stanley.

"But this announcement of a peaceful accord with Doúg has us stymied," Gabriel continued. "Both men refer to it, yet it seems counterproductive to their goal of rallying the world against Doúg. Have you any theories to account for such a deception?"

Sadira exchanged a sheepish grin with her brother, who admitted, "Actually, we hadn't gotten that far. We've just convinced ourselves that this Josh wasn't real."

"I see," Gabriel said with a hint of amusement. "Well, perhaps you would consider the question now?"

"Sheridan would know," Sadira said softly, another wave of sadness flooding over her.

"Yes," Stanley agreed somberly. "He'd not only grasp their objective but predict their next several moves."

Gently, Bethany suggested, "Then let's consider what he's told us of Stan's intentions."

"Yes," Stanley said. "He did mention a gap that Stan would have to fill, an alternative method of uniting the world against Doug after their plan to bomb cities under Doug's flag was exposed."

"Wasn't that his intention when he told the world about the Viv Zabé?" Bethany asked.

"That would tip popular opinion in Father's favor," Sadira said. "But probably not to the point of rallying armies so quickly."

"Unless you combine it with more immediate concerns," Stanley said thoughtfully. "Sheridan also mentioned an economic collapse."

"I think you're on to something," Sadira said. "The world has just heard 'Joshua' declare his father's intentions to live peaceably with Desmoden. What if, as a part of that peaceful resolution, 'Doug' purchased some of the loans owned by Father's bank?"

"It wouldn't even raise an eyebrow on Wall Street," Stanley agreed. "Banks are always buying and selling loans. And Father could easily set up an authentic-appearing account for processing those fake transactions."

"And when this fickle version of 'Doug' becomes angry over some supposed insult and severs all financial ties with Father—"

"Then Stan calls in all his loans at once, leaving a falsified paper trail to implicate Doúg," Gabriel finished, nodding. "National economies would crumble overnight, and the devastation would affect all, from prince to pauper."

"And they would all believe Doúg to be responsible," Sadira concluded.

"Nothing like a good global economic collapse to stir up some anger," Stanley said.

"Yes," Gabriel agreed gravely. "And rally armies."

CHAPTER 26

DARKNESS

"My God turns my darkness into light."
Psalm 18:28, NIV.

Sadira tried not to be overly optimistic about the possibility of rescuing Sheridan and Chris. She knew the dungeon was so secure that no prisoner had ever been rescued from its chilly depths. But her hopes rose anyway, buoyed by the knowledge that this operation would be different from all preceding attempts in two key regards: first, she possessed detailed knowledge of the facility that Doug's side had never before had access to; second, no one of The Phantom's talents had attempted to penetrate its defenses. Surely the combination was cause for hope. Besides, Doug wouldn't assign them an impossible task … would he?

Her optimism grew when she met The Phantom. Of course, she'd heard of his talents from the stories (usually mixed with cursing) Father's men told. Still, war stories were often exaggerated. But within fifteen minutes of meeting him, she decided exaggeration was probably unnecessary in this case.

Captain Jorge Strider met the group at a private airfield in New York. He was a small man, perhaps 5'6" in stature, with a petite frame. This rare advantage would allow him to squeeze into or through spaces that most men could never negotiate. Likewise, although his arms were sinewy, his strength was not of a bulky sort; rather it seemed targeted to the tasks of supporting and balancing his body in difficult positions.

His powers of observation were also unusually keen. As he shook hands with Stanley, he brushed a tiny piece of lettuce from his brother's cuff and joked that he always managed to find the jet serving tacos. After bending to examine a bit of ash on the lowered stair, he asked Gabriel what he thought of his pass over California's wildfires. And, pointing to one of a chest-full of medals on the uniform of Gabriel's assistant, he congratulated the officer on his new commendation.

Sadira was duly impressed.

After bidding the rest of the group *bon voyage*, Jorge drove Sadira to the army headquarters housed within New York's Paradisian Embassy. His conversation gave her another reason to value his insight.

"I've noticed something odd about the New-RAB transmitters," he said. "What do you know of this new analgesic effect?"

"The effect is real enough," she said. "But it's actually a side effect of a different function."

"Oh? What's that?"

"Garrick was working on a method of Subject control using inaudible sound waves. He discovered a particular pattern that enhances suggestibility. The analgesic effect was merely a secondary result."

"So Subjects receiving the analgesic benefits would also be receiving some kind of orders?"

"Not necessarily. He decided to make the analgesic effect available system-wide to induce more people to activate the function. Those individuals are controllable, though not necessarily controlled."

"I see. Does this treatment really have all the research behind it that they claim?"

"No. It's brand new. They were still tweaking it in the lab when I left. This general release is actually the clinical trial, except they're doing it en masse. The Subjects don't know they're guinea pigs."

"Had there been problems with aggression, separate from any suggestions made to the Subjects?"

"Not that I know of." Sadira frowned. "Why? What have you seen?"

"Two similar occurrences. The only common factor I noticed was that both individuals wore New-RAB transmitters. In the first incident, a man pulled up to put air in his tires at a gas station where an inexperienced teenager was trying to use the air hose. The older man couldn't have been waiting more than thirty seconds before he just exploded at the boy. He got in his face, called him names, and finally chased him off."

"Did the boy have one of the original transmitters?"

"No."

"So no obvious reason for an agent to initiate an attack," she said thoughtfully. "And the other incident?"

"Two women in line at the grocery store. The first was using coupons, so it took her longer to check out. An older woman with a New-RAB transmitter became very agitated and demanded that she hurry up. Ultimately, she even hit her with her cane."

"You're joking!"

"I'm afraid not. I didn't see an original device in that case either."

Sadira reviewed what she knew of the neurophysiology involved in the control frequency. "We had observed that the same pattern that made the person suggestible also caused the release of endorphins, which is what eases pain. Maybe it also triggers a change in the neurochemicals in the brain's anger center."

"That sounds dangerous," Jorge said.

When they arrived at the headquarters, she and Jorge went straight to work. She briefed him on the conclusions she and Stanley had come to, diagrammed the location of the dungeon on a comprehensive map of Manhattan, and drew detailed illustrations of everything she could remember of the main tunnel.

Jorge studied her information minutely. "This is excellent information," he said approvingly. "But what kind of scale are we talking here? How long is the tunnel?"

"Um ..." She stroked her chin in concentration. "A mile? Mile and a quarter, maybe?"

His eyebrows shot up. "A mile? That's a lot of rock to examine." He tapped a pencil into his palm. "How many guards patrol it and what's their schedule?"

"Only one, but guarding the tunnel is his sole duty. He patrols constantly in an arbitrary pattern."

"I'll have to disable him then."

"Um …" Sadira suddenly realized that she hadn't thought this through very well.

"Yes?"

"Well, the guard has to report in every fifteen minutes. His voice is confirmed by voice recognition software, and they ask him random questions so a simple recording of his voice can't be used. If he doesn't check in, a squad of soldiers is immediately dispatched to each end of the tunnel."

Jorge looked up with a dubious expression. "So if I don't knock him out, I have no freedom to examine the walls; but if I do knock him out, I'll only have fifteen minutes to examine a mile of rock, locate the passage, extract the prisoners, and get out again?"

She rubbed her forehead as her false optimism began to slip. "I'm afraid so."

He sighed softly and returned his attention to the drawings. "Is there anything else—cameras, maybe?"

Sadira dropped her face into her hands. "I forgot about those."

Jorge momentarily squeezed his eyes closed. "Where are they?"

"At every turn." She drew Xs at intervals along the tunnel and counted them silently. "Eight—yes, that's all of them. They make the entire tunnel constantly visible to the guard in the dungeon's Observation Room."

Jorge studied the drawings for some time, occasionally asking her to clarify some marking. Finally he looked up at her. "Sadira, this is—well, I don't like using the word 'impossible,' but I can certainly see why it's never been breached."

All the fatigue of Sadira's sleepless night crashed down upon her, opening the door to the visions of Chris and Sheridan's torture that she'd repressed. She slumped in the chair and stared forlornly at the diagrams. She should never have allowed her optimism to rise. This mission was simply hopeless. The dungeon was exactly what it was designed to be: impenetrable.

Looking into Jorge's deep brown eyes, she whispered, "I'm so sorry, Jorge. I guess—I just wanted so badly for it to work."

"I know. I did too."

CHAPTER 27
SURRENDER

"Some will forsake the faith and surrender their minds to subversive
spirits and demon-inspired doctrines."
1 Timothy 4:1, REB.

Two brawny soldiers in smart uniforms of green and black eyed Willy as he approached the Four Season's Presidential Suite East. Clearing his throat, Willy said. "Hello. I'm—"

"We know who you are," one soldier said curtly. Picking up a wall phone, he said, "Assistant Regional Overseer Wilson Moore to see Dr. Moden."

A formally attired butler opened the door and ushered Willy into a large living room. "Please make yourself comfortable, sir. Would you care for something to drink?"

Willy again cleared his bone-dry throat. "Um, some water would be great."

"Very good, sir." The butler bowed slightly and left the room. Willy had barely settled on the sofa before he returned, carrying a crystal glass and a refrigerated bottle of expensive-looking French-labeled water on a silver tray. Placing the tray on the coffee table, he poured Willy a glass. "Will there be anything else, sir?"

"No. Thank you."

"Certainly, sir. I'll inform Dr. Moden of your arrival. Please feel free to enjoy the view while you wait." He motioned to the balcony.

Hoping the fresh air would calm his nerves, Willy drifted outside to take in the sixteenth-floor perspective of the Hollywood Hills and LA skyline. A smooth bass soon startled him. "Enjoying the view?"

Willy spun around to see perhaps the best specimen of manhood he'd ever laid eyes on. Not that he liked guys, but he did appreciate perfection. And this man was perfect in every way. A tall fellow, probably 6'3", he had a pleasing athletic build and facial features that were exquisite in their symmetry. Of course, he'd seen him on television, but the camera didn't capture his striking elegance. His emerald eyes glowed with almost hypnotic energy. The sun even played off the red highlights in his flawlessly groomed chestnut brown hair to suggest a subtle halo.

"Wilson Moore?" Dr. Moden extended his hand, his eyes betraying amusement. Maybe he was used to people being dumbstruck by his looks.

"Yes." It came out as a croak, and Willy cleared his throat to try again. "Yes, sir, Dr. Moden."

"A pleasure to meet you. I hope you brought your appetite." He motioned to a dining table, where the butler was arranging three place settings.

"My other guest is running late, but we can begin without him." Stepping inside to the table, Dr. Moden removed his jacket and hung it on the back of his chair. This allowed Willy to note that he was beyond athletic—he was really, *really* buff, with muscles bulging out every which way under his closely tailored shirt.

They sat down to salads and breadsticks, conversing easily as they ate. His host was smart, eloquent, and knowledgeable in every subject that Willy brought into the conversation. Nevertheless, he talked to him as an equal. He even bounced a couple of ideas for the New-RABs off him as though his opinion mattered. Soon Willy felt quite comfortable, which he hadn't expected at all. Willy had long suspected that his family members' warnings about Dr. Moden were skewed and exaggerated. Still, he'd half expected to meet an ogre today. Instead, the world-renowned magnate seemed like a genuinely nice guy.

"Well, you've been very forbearing," Dr. Moden said at last. "But you're probably wondering why I asked to meet you."

"You mean you don't have lunch with every insignificant member of the New-RAB?"

Dr. Moden chuckled. "You grossly underestimate yourself, Mr. Moore. I've had my eye on you for some time. In fact, I recommended you for the position of Assistant Regional Overseer."

Willy nearly choked on his iced tea. He'd assumed that was his pacesetter's doing. No wonder Cherisse jumped right on it when he tried to decline the post. Finally he managed, "I'm … shocked."

"I'm not. I knew you'd do well. You're intelligent, sensible, have an impressive talent for both management and problem-solving, and your social interaction is quite polished, particularly for someone your age."

So that's what all the easy conversation was about—he'd been checking out Willy's people skills.

"Although you've only been in that position for a couple of months," Dr. Moden continued, "I think you're ready to move up. I'd like you to join my personal staff. I realize that completing your education is a priority just now—as it should be. But you needn't relocate, and we can adjust the hours to accommodate your schooling. Be assured, Wilson Moore, son of Juan Misi—"

When Willy started, Dr. Moden sidetracked. "Yes, I know your ancestry—a proud heritage, if I may say so. I do my homework, Mr. Moore. I don't take a personal interest in just anyone. I don't fast-track just anyone. When I do, I want to know that I'm dealing with quality stock, so to speak."

"I see," Willy said uncertainly.

"As I was saying, there will always be a position for you in my organization. Since finding excellent attorneys is a particular challenge, I will also happily support your educational goals in any way I can."

"Thank you for the offer, sir." Willy's throat had gone dry again, so he took a quick sip of tea before suggesting tentatively, "A good recommendation would help."

"Recommendation?" A glint of wry humor lit Dr. Moden's eyes. "Mr. Moore, I can be of considerably more help to you than that. I can guarantee your acceptance at several excellent law schools, including Harvard, Yale, and

Princeton. Furthermore, I'm prepared to finance the remainder of your education."

Willy's fork fell from his hand, clattering noisily onto the china plate. Yet he hardly noticed. His vision took on a dream-like quality, and he felt like he might start floating. He wondered if all lottery winners felt the same way. "Are—are you—serious?"

"Very much so." Sitting back, Dr. Moden explained, "You're young. You have no idea how difficult it is to find competent individuals who are well-trained, hardworking, and creative. Organizations like mine require many such individuals. So yes, my offer is very serious—and, I will admit, very self-serving. You're an exceptional young man, Mr. Moore."

Willy took a sip of iced tea while he tried to process such generosity.

"So does my proposition interest you?"

"Yes," Willy said immediately. "Definitely."

"Excellent." Taking his cell phone from his shirt pocket, Dr. Moden added, "Excuse me one moment." He hit a speed-dial number and someone answered immediately.

"Madelyn," he said, "Mr. Wilson Moore is now under my sponsorship. Pay off his car, his school bill, and any other outstanding debts … That's right … Excellent."

As he returned the phone to his pocket, Willy stammered, "B-but—you didn't have to do that!"

"Nonsense. I'm happy to help."

"We haven't even signed a contract!"

"My executive secretary, Madelyn, will send you one. If you don't like what you see, you're free to change your mind. Either way, please keep what you've received as a token of my best wishes for your future success."

Willy was still trying to grasp such liberality, and only beginning to realize he didn't know what joining Dr. Moden's "personal staff" meant, when the butler approached. "Excuse me, President Moden, but His Highness is on the way up."

"Ah, good." Dr. Moden turned to Willy. "You're about to meet the Paradisian crown prince. Are you familiar with the etiquette involved in receiving royalty?"

"Um, I'm going to go with no?" Willy said.

Dr. Moden chuckled. "Well, it can vary from culture to culture, but here's the Cliffs Notes version for Paradisian royalty. First, don't use me as a guide; he and I are friends, so my behavior is governed by a different code. But for you—stand when he enters a room. Stand whenever he stands. In fact, just stand, period, unless he invites you to sit. Make a full bow when he enters and again when you're introduced. Address him as 'Your Highness.' Never initiate contact—you'll alarm his bodyguards—but you may accept his hand if he offers it." He paused, considering. "You'll need further instruction in the future, but that should get you through today."

In the future? Was little Willy Moore going to be routinely hobnobbing with royalty? His brothers would never believe this!

Two beefy men in blue military uniforms entered and proceeded to opposite ends of the suite, presumably clearing it for their prince's entry. When they returned, they took up positions alongside the other soldiers outside the open door. A few moments later, a tall but otherwise ordinary-looking guy in a nice suit walked through the door, flanked by two more guards.

Dr. Moden jumped to his feet. "Joshua!" Joe-SHOO-ah, he pronounced it. "How good to see you. I'm glad you could come."

"Stan!" The prince smiled broadly and clapped him on the shoulders. They exchanged a few phrases in a language Willy assumed to be Paradisian and kissed on the cheek.

Then, leading the prince to the table, Dr. Moden said, "Your Highness, please allow me to introduce Mr. Wilson Moore of Ventura, California. Mr. Moore, His Highness, Crown Prince Joshua Deón Damoúr of Paradise Island."

Willy made a full bow and the prince inclined his head before motioning to a bodyguard to remove his jacket. Then he sat down to apply himself eagerly to his salad. As instructed, Willy continued standing beside his chair when the two men sat. After a moment, the prince looked up with an expression of approval. "I appreciate your deference, Mr. Moore." Motioning to Willy's chair, he added amiably, "But please join us, won't you?"

Willy took his seat, and the conversation continued with a friendly air. Surrounded by bodyguards and opulence, Willy could not easily forget his companions' exalted stations, yet the interaction seemed natural and pleasant.

When the dessert dishes had been cleared away, the prince sat back and said, "I like him, Stan."

"I'm glad to hear it," Dr. Moden replied. "I expect him to be an excellent asset— he's a very talented young man."

"You've always had an eye for promising talent," the prince returned. "I just have one misgiving." His gaze transferred to Willy. "May I presume to speak freely, Mr. Moore?"

"Of course, Your Highness," Willy said, though feeling a bit confused. It seemed they had returned to the topic of his new job, but why would that require the prince's endorsement?

"I once placed a good deal of confidence in another talented young man— your uncle, Dr. Christian Strider. I coached him, I paid his way through medical school, and I helped him in a number of other ways. But he had trouble giving up certain pet notions. For many years now, he's been doing things in my name that I want no part of. Just when this world needs men who reach across chasms and build bridges, he's been calling for separation." He leaned forward, resting his arms on the table. "He's disappointed me, Mr. Moore. Will you turn out to be a disappointment too?"

Willy's mouth had gone dry during this little speech. Uncle Chris always spoke of Josh Damour as someone he remained close to—his best friend, he said. He claimed that his hard-nosed ideas came straight from the prince. But the prince was denying all that and seemed concerned Willy would follow in his uncle's radical footsteps.

Reaching for his water glass, Willy took a swig and tried to clear his throat.

"I realize I'm putting you on the spot," the prince said sympathetically. "Just answer this for me: Do you agree with your uncle's view that the traditional RABs have no business collaborating with the New-RABs?"

Willy licked his lips. "Sir, my uncle is a good man—well-meaning and generous. He's certainly been kind and openhanded with me. However, I don't agree with him on certain matters, including his warnings about collaboration.

I'm a proud member of the New-RABs myself. I consider his conspiracy theories as a bit, well, eccentric. I'm afraid they may even be dangerous. Furthermore, I strongly agree with what you said this morning—that we *must* cooperate and pull together if we're to solve the problems the world's currently facing."

Prince Joshua held Willy's eyes for a long moment. Then he nodded and turned to Dr. Moden. "I'm satisfied, Stan. I believe he'll do nicely."

Willy's forehead crinkled at this. Do what nicely?

"I see you're confused," Dr. Moden said. "That's because I didn't want to bring this up until Prince Joshua had a chance to meet you."

"Bring what up?" Willy asked.

The prince again leaned his arms onto the table. "Your uncle and the Outlander Division are fomenting a divisive spirit just when unity between the RABs and New-RABs is critical. Dr. Moden and I want to make the stance of our respective governments clear by unifying the two organizations and completely eradicating the original RABs. We're looking for someone to help us do that."

"You're an active member of the New-RAB," Dr. Moden added, "as well as a close relative of some influential members of the RABs. Since you also have the requisite skills, this makes you an ideal candidate for the position."

"I'm still not sure I understand what the job would entail," Willy admitted.

"You would be, in essence, a liaison—a diplomat," Prince Joshua said. "You would help us smooth out the wrinkles as the two organizations unite by keeping the focus on the goal of mutual welfare."

Willy nodded, but his mind was spinning. "This is an amazing opportunity," he said. "But I don't think I could do it justice on a part-time basis."

"That's very true," Dr. Moden said. "However, you will be working closely with two experienced statesmen—Prince Joshua and myself—and learning a good deal of political science in the process. So I've spoken to your academic dean about granting you credit for independent study under my tutelage. He finds the prospect of having one of his students fill such an important global position to be very appealing."

"And if you decide that you enjoy the work," Prince Joshua added, "you may choose to remain in the position. Alternatively, it would be excellent experience if you're interested in a future career in diplomacy."

"Actually, I'm very much interested in that field," Willy admitted.

They continued the conversation, discussing the details of the problems each man was experiencing, or anticipated experiencing, as they united the two organizations. The more they talked, the more excited Willy became at the opportunity to resolve the conflicts. By the time they parted, he had accepted the position.

As he drove home, his cell phone rang. He answered to hear Mom scold, "Wilson Moore, are you avoiding my calls? I've been trying to get hold of you all afternoon."

"I'm sorry, Mom. I just got your messages. I was having lunch with President Stanley Moden and Crown Prince Joshua Damour."

"Oh!" she said, clearly overawed. "Well … oh, my. I guess you're forgiven then."

CHAPTER 28

SUFFERINGS

"Do not be surprised at the painful trial you are suffering, as though something strange were happening to you. But rejoice that you participate in the sufferings of Christ."
1 Peter 4:12, 13, NIV.

With ankles and wrists clamped in shackles, Sheridan hung half-standing, half-suspended from the ceiling of his damp cement cell. Somewhere between eighty-four and ninety-six hours before, Moden employees had stripped him down to his boxers and abandoned him in the place they euphemistically called "downstairs." Since then, he'd exchanged one torturous position for another. First he stood upright, his 290 pounds of body weight crushing bruised ankles and painfully swollen feet against their iron restraints. When his strength deserted him, he slumped from the manacles, the same mass straining against equally battered wrists and hands. The cycle was ruthlessly unending.

His uncle's scream again echoed through the dungeon, and Sheridan's body convulsed with a violent tremor. The frigid temperatures, his horror at Chris's predicament, his own guilt and powerlessness to help—all conspired against him. Father was obviously beginning Sheridan's course with the psychological torment of listening as Mother tortured Chris to death. He would undoubtedly get around to physical abuse as well, but no bodily suffering could be worse than this. Sheridan's experience as an "interviewer" transformed the sounds from down the hallway into a mercilessly detailed mental picture of Chris's torment. He could tell which class of implements was being used, how acutely Chris felt the pain, and even when he, too weak to sustain an upright position, had been switched to a supine position on the cement ledge.

Having "interviewed" plenty of subjects himself, Sheridan knew the protocols intimately. That's how he could gauge the passage of time. A guard had let slip that he and Chris were "Class 1 guests," meaning their lives were to be extended to maximize the time available for interrogation. Consequently, his chains were slackened every twelve hours, allowing him to sit on the cement ledge jutting from the wall and sleep for short intervals. After the rest, a guard rammed a large-bore needle into his thigh to infuse a liter of fluid, thus preventing death from dehydration. Sheridan had received seven such liters, so he'd been here between eighty-four and ninety-six hours.

Another scream pierced the air, and Sheridan's mind again reproached him for dragging Chris into this nightmare. Why hadn't he gotten on that helicopter?

He hadn't tried to communicate with his newfound uncle. The facility's procedures encouraged the guards to curb conversation by shocking guests—the speaker, the listener, or both—through the shackles. Chris's persistence amazed him, for he continued talking and singing despite the shocks he must be receiving. Surely his wrists were horribly burned by now. However, Sheridan wouldn't give the guards a reason for inflicting more pain upon his mentor. He'd caused Chris enough misery already.

When his uncle's screams turned to moans, a signal that he had grown too weak to respond maximally to pain, Sheridan knew the session would be ending. Mother would allow her Subject to rest until he was stronger and his pain receptors had regained sensitivity. Still, the sessions were getting shorter; Chris's strength was failing.

Camille's heels clicked back toward the dungeon's secret passageway. She passed Sheridan's cell each time she visited Chris, but she hadn't even acknowledged his presence. When the door closed behind her, the dungeon again fell silent, with only the guards' indistinct exchanges murmuring through the cement walls of the multi-chambered facility. In the quiet, Sheridan's thoughts turned to self-recrimination.

A fine runner you turned out to be. A real runner would have called Doug before turning back. Instead, you got both yourself and Chris captured. Yes indeed, a fine runner.

Father certainly knew what he was doing. This was the worst punishment imaginable, listening to Chris's screams and his own condemning reflections hour after agonizing hour. If only he could do something to derail himself from this train of thought!

What have you ever done for Doug? Said a few pretty words on TV and radio? Was that even for Doug, or because you enjoyed the limelight? Or maybe it was to get back at Stan. What was your real motive for exposing his evil to the world—to warn them, or to satisfy your desire for vengeance? Doug doesn't approve of taking revenge, you know. Chalk up another one on the wrong side of the ledger there, buddy!

A crippling shudder tore through Sheridan's body, as though this subterranean hole had suddenly grown even colder. His body slumped, and his lacerated wrists shrieked at having to accept his full weight again. His past simply overwhelmed him. He had committed such heinous *kanuf* before defecting to Doug's side—and he had done little right since then. He certainly didn't deserve Doug's mercy. He didn't even deserve the honor of being imprisoned in this dungeon. For, as an "interviewer," Sheridan had felt that the guests of this dungeon had been awarded a kind of distinction. After all, it was their faithfulness to Doug that earned them such special attention from Moden Industries. And he was appallingly unworthy of being counted with such heroes.

His head dropped onto his chest in despair, and tears splashed onto the cement floor. *What would Father say if he saw you now, you big crybaby? How miserably you've failed absolutely everybody in your life! You're a wimp instead of the stoic soldier Father trained you to be. You never became the strong runner Doug deserved. You even led the only man who really cared about you into a trap. You're a great big nothing. Transmitter or not, Father's right: Doug would never allow you onto Paradise Island. You merit the full measure of his coming wrath if anyone ever has.*

Sheridan suddenly realized the source of that refrain, with its emphasis on merit, tallying ledgers, and just deserts. It was his faithful though unwelcome companion—guilt. Once he named it, he also recognized the solution. Chris had taught him how to master that adversary, and most of the passages he'd memorized had been selected to combat it. Now he set about recalling them.

" 'Though your sins are like scarlet, they shall be as white as snow,' " he whispered, not wanting to be overheard and "discouraged." The passage quieted his guilt, and he repeated it a few more times. Soon he realized he not only felt better emotionally but physically as well.

But for how long? Do you really think a few words will get you through this ordeal, through torment that an expert has finely crafted over centuries to break even the hardiest, most experienced runner? And you are not *a strong runner, now are you?*

No, he wasn't. He knew that. But Josh was. And if he'd learned anything from Chris, it was to rely on Josh's strength to take one day, even one moment, at a time. His uncle had insisted that Doug would give him the strength he needed *when* he needed it, not before. So if he tried to shoulder the burden of the whole ordeal at one time or in his own strength, he would fail. But if he took it in pieces, one moment at a time, using the strength Doug gave him in that moment—well, then he had a chance.

And that's what repeating the passage had done for him: given him strength for that moment. So he called up another—another passage for another moment.

PART II

DELAY NO LONGER

"[He] swore by Him who lives forever and ever ...
that there should be delay no longer."
Revelation 10:6, NKJV.

When the change occurred, Gabriel was at his desk, speaking with Lanse on the phone. He happened to be gazing toward the timer above the door when its red digits, which had been stuck at 23:59:15, returned to life.

Sitting bolt upright, he interrupted Lanse. "The clock!"

Lanse sucked in a breath. "That there should be delay no longer."

"Just so," Gabriel agreed.

"I'll relieve the Planetary Defenders of their duties then, shall I?"

"Yes," Gabriel said reluctantly. "We must." The visions of Stan's recent catastrophes revisited him, and he shook his head, knowing that what lay ahead would be even worse.

He ended the call and sprinted to the War Room. Halting just inside the door, he gazed intently into the adjoining courtroom through the one-way mirror on the opposite wall. When the colonel he'd left in charge looked up from a console, his eyebrows lifted in query, Gabriel simply pointed directly above himself to the clock. The colonel's eyes widened and then he too rose and turned around. One by one, the other officers did the same until each one was on his feet and staring fixedly into the courtroom.

Prince Joshua, seated at the judge's bench, placed his mark beside the last name in the last volume of the Book of Life. Opening a small lancet, he stabbed himself in the finger, allowed some blood to drop beside the mark, and pressed his signet ring into it. Then he solemnly closed the large, heavy tome.

Passing into the courtroom, Gabriel breathed, "What more can we do before probation closes, *Modén*?"

The prince shook his head sadly. "Nothing, my friend. You have labored faithfully. Those who have chosen life have been sealed, but we can do no more for the others. They have made their final decisions."

Picking up his gavel, he raised his voice in a clarion call: "It is done! He who is unjust, let him be unjust still; he who is filthy, let him be filthy still; he who is righteous, let him be righteous still; he who is holy, let him be holy still."

The gavel fell with a thud that rattled Gabriel's vital organs. Indeed, the sound should have been heard throughout the universe, for it was the sound of probation ending for an entire planet. The fate of Earth's inhabitants, so long held captive to *kanuf,* was decided. Yet those very inhabitants were oblivious to it, unmindful that their future was now irrevocably sealed.

A smile formed on the prince's face. "I'm coming quickly. And my reward is with me."

This reminder of the coming victory—of the end of all struggling, fighting, and misery—brought a smile to Gabriel's lips. A momentous sense of triumph washed over him. Passing with His Highness into the War Room, he led his men in a deep bow before their beloved prince. Then they lifted their voices in song, filling the room with joyous exultation.

Only then did Gabriel realize that Prince Joshua had not removed his judicial robe when he moved to the War Room, and he immediately grasped the sober implication. Always before, the prince had directed his army while dressed in blue and red, the colors of Mercy's Advocate. But today the commander-in-chief of the universe's most powerful army wore solemn black and royal purple—the vestments of Earth's Supreme Judge.

CHAPTER 29

ENDURING

The testing of your faith produces endurance. But endurance must do its complete work, so that you may be mature and complete, lacking nothing.
James 1:3, 4, HCSB.

C hris's own moaning recalled him to consciousness. He lay on the cold cement ledge in his gray cell—stark naked and all alone.

And he hurt. He hurt so badly that it all blended together into one overwhelming groan. Yet his physical pain was dwarfed by another: the agony of loneliness. Though he'd experienced something like it since Susana's death, this was infinitely worse. He wished he could talk to Sheridan, but he'd heard nothing from him since that one snicker. Was he still there? Still conscious? Still alive?

In any case, Sheridan couldn't fill this void; no mortal could.

Chris had been tortured before—"questioned" by Garrick. At that time, Doug had sent him bits of encouragement through the transmitter, even sparks of energy. That's what had carried him through the experience. But, even though Chris had purposely left his transmitter activated after talking to Doug on the stairway, his faithful mentor now remained silent. No answers to Chris's pleas. No glimmers of encouragement. No boosts of energy.

Nothing.

Only rarely had Chris been in a situation where he'd been unable to hear Doug's voice, usually because of some unbelieving or rebellious spirit within himself. Was that the problem now? Had he somehow offended Doug? Had the final reckoning been completed and found him wanting? Worse yet, had he misrepresented Doug and prevented others from turning to him? Is that why his beloved twin sister, his inseparable childhood buddy, resisted running the race? Had she recognized his faults and decided that Doug wasn't powerful enough to change his life? Had his failures distorted Doug's image and dissuaded her from becoming a runner? The idea terrified him.

"Doug?" he breathed, too weak to speak. "Doug, please respond. You've always been there for me. Thank you for that. And thank you that your mercy has never depended on me or whether I deserve it. I really need it now, *Adu*. I need you. Please forgive me for—" He frowned, having difficulty remembering anything specific to fill in the blank he'd created. "Please forgive me."

Silence.

He felt for his trophy, but one of the guards had taken the wedding band that also served as his trophy from the race. Chris particularly missed it because recounting the stories represented by its gems had really strengthened him during the incident with Garrick. Still, the stories had become old friends. Even in his weakened state, he could recite them. So, visualizing the gems, he called the accounts to memory. He especially dwelt on the time Josh rescued him from Stan's gym. He couldn't hear Doug there either, but his merciful sponsor had heard him and sent help. And Doug had promised that he could always hear him, no matter the situation.

Chris seized that thought like a thirsty man clutches a canteen. Doug *was* faithful—he always had been; he always would be. The danger was not that Doug would abandon him, but that he would forsake Doug—that doubt and despair would engulf him because he failed to remember how Doug had sustained him in past difficulties.

He would *not* permit that to happen! He was a longtime runner, trained to endure. He would choose endurance now. He would not give up but meditate on the passages that had always sustained him.

" 'My flesh and my heart may fail,' " he breathed raggedly, " 'but Doug is the strength of my heart and my portion forever.' "

He paused, letting that truth wash over him and through him like a healing tide. Doug had promised him strength, and Doug always fulfilled his promises.

"Doug is my portion forever," he repeated. That's all he needed.

❈ ❈ ❈ ❈ ❈

" 'If we confess our sins,' " Sheridan murmured, " 'he is faithful and just and will forgive us our sins and purify us from all unrighteousness.' "

An inner voice that sounded suspiciously like Stan's piped up. *Does that really apply to you? Have you truly confessed* all *of your many, many sins? What if you've forgotten even one?*

Another violent shiver ripped through him. He had confessed so many vile acts to Doug over the last six weeks. So very many. But what if he hadn't remembered them all? He couldn't get to his transmitter to activate it, so he couldn't confess anything else before he died. What if he had forgotten something? Having come to love Doug, it horrified him to think of never meeting his new *adu* face to face, of never being able to personally express his deep gratitude for his forgiveness. He especially wanted to thank him—oh, so fervently—for the peace he'd known.

So Sheridan wracked his brain, wanting to be sure he'd thoroughly repented—that he'd accomplished the one thing Doug had asked of him. But as he combed through his memories, he found them censored, like a top-secret document with the important information blacked out. He knew he'd done awful things. He'd done awful things in this very place. But he simply couldn't remember any of them.

A familiar melody reached through the fetid air to soothe Sheridan's tortured mind. Chris was humming again. It had become a regular occurrence following his sessions with Mother. After recovering some, he would hum, sing, and quote passages from the *Manual*. Sheridan couldn't make out all the words, but his doubts and gloom lessened. It probably did the same for Chris. And if it was important and useful enough for his mentor to spend his waning strength on it, he should start preparing to do it for himself when Chris—

He stopped himself, refusing to admit the inevitable. Still, he knew what a guest sounded like when getting close to death.

Just then, two guards passed his cell, and Sheridan caught one phrase in particular: "They're both on Class 1R Protocol ..."

Sheridan bolted up straighter. Class 1R Protocol? Well, of course—he should have caught on sooner!

"R" stood for "Restricted Access," meaning that only his parents could torture them. The guards had to keep their hands off—and that meant no shocking for conversation. Using his own knowledge against him, they had tricked him into silence. But the truth was, he could sing, talk—even preach if he wanted to!

Throwing his head back, Sheridan roared with laughter. "Thank you, Salty!" he called after the informer.

The guard in the Observation Room appeared at the window above the main dungeon, and his gravelly voice came over the speaker. "Salty, report to Observation."

Salty groaned, and Sheridan called, "Oh, I'm sorry, Salty. Did I get you in trouble?" He laughed again and then yelled, "Chris! No—*Uncle* Chris!"

"Sheridan—good to hear—your voice. How're you—doing?"

Chris's concern for him, even though the halting nature of his speech itself spoke of his feebleness, touched Sheridan deeply. "I'm—"

He stopped. The guards wouldn't prevent their conversation, but they would still listen and report the vulnerabilities they gleaned to his parents. He needed a language the guards wouldn't comprehend. Yet they, like every other employee of Moden Industries, knew many more languages than any outlander. To communicate privately, he and Chris would need to use an obscure tongue that only they understood.

With a chuckle, he murmured, "Of course. Why else would Doug give me the chance to learn it?" Lifting his voice, he called in the language he had only recently learned, "Can we speak in Rarámuri? I don't want the guards to understand us."

"Sure," Chris answered in the same tongue.

"May I call you *kurichi*?" Sheridan asked, using the only term for "uncle" that he'd heard.

"*Kurichi* is specifically your—mother's older brother. I'm your—mother's younger brother—*raté.*"

Sheridan let that sink in. If Chris was his mother's younger brother, that meant his mother was Rose Strider Moore. "So I'm a son of Juan Misi?"

The awe Sheridan felt must have come through his voice, for his uncle chuckled softly. "Yes—your great-great-grandfather. Just another reason—for Stan to hate you."

That offhand statement hit Sheridan like a flash of lightening. His parents hadn't disliked him because of anything he'd done. They'd hated him before he was born. They'd hated him because they knew he was a descendant of the despised Juan Misi. He never could have won his father's love. But that meant his siblings were also descended from Juan Misi and that Stan hated them too. Even Sadira.

Suddenly, he saw the preferential treatment Sadira had received in an entirely new light. Father had lavished attention on her, not because she was better than Sheridan, not even because he liked her, but to provoke jealousy and antagonism in the brothers. All this time, Sheridan had resented her because of her special privileges, but she had been just as isolated and lonely as he was.

He sighed softly. "I'm sorry for getting you into this, *raté*. I should have seen the trap. I'm really sorry."

"No, no—not your fault." Chris's voice sounded no less earnest for his declining condition. "Doug gave me the choice—to follow you. He warned me— what would happen."

Sheridan frowned. If he could have scratched his head, he would have. "Then why did you come?"

"I couldn't let you—go through this alone. I knew—you didn't have enough—of the *Manual*—memorized. It strengthens you. That's the—the only way to get through this."

Sheridan bowed his head. "I don't deserve your kindness."

"None of us deserve—Doug's kindness."

"Your singing and quoting the *Manual* have really encouraged me. I keep thinking how I've messed everything up, how I've failed Doug, and you, and—and everybody."

"The only way—to fight discouragement, guilt—is with the *Manual*. Shall I—teach you some?"

"Yes, please."

Chris began to sing another song, one Sheridan recognized from the *Manual's* songbook. His uncle had to pause frequently, and often his voice was too soft for Sheridan to catch the words, but after he sang it through twice, Sheridan had learned enough to join in. When they finished it, Sheridan felt that, although nothing had changed in the cold, dark cell, the air seemed a little clearer, the icy temperature a little warmer, and his heart very much lighter.

" 'I can do everything—through him who gives me strength,' " came Chris's halting voice.

" 'I can do everything through him who gives me strength,' " Sheridan repeated, loud and firm. "'I can do *every*thing through him who gives me strength.' 'I can do everything through *him* who gives me strength.' 'I *can* do everything through him who gives me strength.' " With each repetition, he felt a little stronger.

"That's it—you're doing great," Chris said. He continued to teach Sheridan encouraging portions of the *Manual* and its songbook over the next several hours. When Chris intermittently slipped into silence, too weak to continue, Sheridan recited the passages of hope and victory that he'd learned to strengthen Chris.

During this time, one of the guards came in and gave Sheridan his eighth liter of fluid: ninety-six hours. Four days of emotional torture and of progressive weakening by starvation.

He shouldn't have made it this far, he realized suddenly. Probably the only reason he had was because of the living reminder Chris had provided in looking to Doug for strength. This sudden, intense awareness of Doug's love and of belonging brought tears to Sheridan's eyes.

"*Raté*," he called. "Thank you for all you've done for me. Thank you so much. I—" He hesitated. He'd never said this to anyone, and his upbringing made him recoil at the thought of saying it now. But if he didn't, he might never have the chance. Chris might not survive another session with Mother.

"*Nihé nimí garé*," he finally managed. (Rarámuri: I love you)

There was a smile in Chris's voice as he said, "*Nihé nimí garé*, Sheridan."

"Aw, isn't that sweet?" Mother mocked in Rarámuri. Her heels clicked sharply down the cement floor on her way to Chris's cell. But, for the first time, she stopped at Sheridan's.

"Oh, look—the big, bad Sheridan Lakwadín is crying." Opening the cell door, she added, "A few weeks on the enemy's side and he's already reduced you to a pathetic, weepy excuse for a man. Oh, but I forgot—you're not even a man anymore, are you?" She laughed wickedly as she turned to leave.

Sheridan, newly sensitized to the power of the *Manual's* words, repeated a passage he'd just learned from Chris: " 'He said to me, "My grace is sufficient for you, for my power is made perfect in weakness." That is why, for his sake, I delight in weaknesses, in insults, in hardships, in persecutions, in difficulties. For when I am weak, then I am strong.' "

She whirled around, slapped him hard, and sprayed coffee-smelling spittle into his face. But there was a strange look in her eyes. Defeat. Maybe even fear.

Suddenly it hit Sheridan: "You *know* you're going to lose this war, don't you?"

She flinched—a slight twitch in her left eye that most people wouldn't even notice.

"You do know. In fact, you've known for a long while, probably since John first wrote 'The Revealing.' You certainly knew it before we were born. We weren't even brought into this world to help you win, were we? We were merely instruments to help you exact some measure of revenge on Doug."

The look in her eye told him he'd hit the truth dead center. She spun on her heel and stormed out of the dungeon, no doubt to fetch some toy from her collection to use on him.

But before she returned, a commotion broke out. Sheridan could see little of what was happening, but he did spy a blue uniform flash past his cell door—Doug's color.

His pulse quickened with hope, but he reminded himself that Stan's men sometimes donned the uniforms of Doug's army to trick their enemy. Besides, this dungeon was impenetrable; no one had ever been rescued from it. Even he could conceive of no way to breach it. Whatever was going on out there, it couldn't possibly be a rescue operation.

When the face of Kyle Sharp, the sergeant who had helped Sheridan escape his hotel room, appeared at his cell door, Sheridan seriously wondered if he was hallucinating.

"I've got Sheridan!" Kyle shouted. About the same time, someone farther down the hall yelled, "I found my dad!"

Sadira appeared at the door, and keys jangled at the lock. Then she rushed in, threw her arms around him, and hugged him tightly. "Oh, Sheridan, I'm so glad you're alive."

He'd never seen his sister express such emotion. But then, he'd never before felt the brotherly affection sweeping through him. How he wanted to give her that hug Chris had once teased them about.

"Sadira, I need the keys!" someone yelled from down the hallway. This time Sheridan recognized the voice as that of Captain Jorge Strider.

"Oh, I'm sorry—your irons." Sadira unlocked the shackles holding Sheridan's ankles and wrists with the ring of keys that belonged in the Observation Room—keys that only a handful of people knew how to find.

That "small" detail reminded him of all the other obstacles they'd had to overcome to effect this unprecedented rescue, and he exclaimed, "I can't believe you figured out how to breach this place!"

"Oh, we didn't—we pronounced it impossible." Fiddling with the lock on his ankle irons, she glanced up with a grin. "But then Jorge called Doug again. Did you know that nothing is impossible for Doug?"

Sheridan returned her smile. "I'm learning that more every day."

Once released from his restraints, Sheridan was unable to support his full weight, and Kyle grabbed onto him. As soon as he was steady, he wrapped one arm around his sister. "Thanks, sis," he murmured and kissed her clumsily on the head. "I'll never tease you again."

"Sadira!" Jorge's call was becoming impatient.

"Let's get Chris," Sheridan said, releasing her. Energized somewhat from excitement, he leaned on Kyle to hobble down the hall to Chris's cell. He saw Jorge grab the keys from Sadira and disappear into the cell. But Sheridan wouldn't have recognized him. Not only was he dressed head-to-toe in a hooded body suit patterned to blend into the stones of the outside tunnel, but his face was also obscured by camouflage.

Sheridan entered Chris's cell wholly unprepared for the sight that met him, even though he'd seen many torture victims. His uncle's face was bruised and bloodied beyond recognition. His torso, front and back, and the most tender aspects of his arms and legs were covered with various types of wounds. Jorge had tied a jacket around his naked hips, but it undoubtedly hid more injuries.

"Oh, raté—" he began. But the sight was enough to make even the seasoned soldier light-headed, and he swayed.

"Stretchers!" Kyle called.

"I'm okay," Sheridan said.

"No, you're not," the sergeant replied in a tone that brooked no argument.

The stretchers materialized, and Sheridan complied without protest with Kyle's order to lie down. Chris was soon strapped to another stretcher. Sheridan reached over to carefully grasp his uncle's hand, bloodied from having fingernails ripped away.

"Thank you, raté," he said earnestly. "Honestly, I would have been a wreck without your encouragement."

Chris replied in a frail voice, "Thank Doug, son." He started to flash a feeble smile, but his eyes closed and his hand went limp.

"No!" Sheridan cried, desperately searching for a pulse. "No!"

CHAPTER 30
ANGRY

"People ruin their lives by their own foolishness and then are angry at the Lord."
Proverbs 19:3, NLT.

12 December 8043 M.E.

Patric's voice came over the intercom, breaking the tense silence in Stan's office. "He's here, sirs. Camera L-12."

Seated at Stan's computer, Garrick keyed in a command and brought up the feed from a security camera in the lobby. Camille peered over his shoulder to watch Stan storm through the lobby, barking orders at random browbeaten employees. She groaned.

"Well, what did you expect?" Garrick grumbled.

"I know, but I'd hoped—"

"What?" he snapped. "That he'd be understanding? Forgiving?"

She sighed. He had a point.

They had left the door to Stan's office open to hear his approach, and they had no difficulty there. His British accent boomed throughout the floor as soon as he exited the elevator. "Where are they!"

"They're both waiting in your office, sir," Madelyn answered warily. "As you directed."

Garrick quickly logged off Stan's computer and scurried to the other side of the desk so the boss wouldn't catch him in his chair. Stan charged into the office and slammed the door behind him. His rage hit Camille like a wall of fire.

"So you two are in here alone, are you? Too busy conspiring to watch two pathetic guests?"

Garrick glanced at Camille with an unspoken request that she take the lead; her link-sense supposedly helped her manage Stan's anger. However, even that advantage meant little when he was this furious. Nevertheless, she could discern that his accusation wasn't genuine. He was simply lashing out in anger.

Camille approached him cautiously, aware that anything she did could be taken the wrong way. Stan's ire required a scapegoat, and she would do as well as any other. "Come sit down, *zuulu*." She aimed for a soothing, though not condescending, tone. "Let us show you the footage."

Stan's glare transferred from her to Garrick, where it lingered, his eyes flashing like swords glinting in the sunlight. "We've never had an escape from downstairs. The first one happens on *your* watch, Sondem. With *those* prisoners." Brushing roughly past Camille, he dropped into his chair. "Well, show me your negligence, then."

Garrick went through the footage from all the cameras involved in the escape. Finally he summarized, "So you see, Stan, none of these recordings represents a simple loop. We've trained the men to look for that. Instead, the enemy hacked into the system and substituted entire hours of coordinated activity on all eight cameras. Even now that I've figured out how they did it, I don't know how to instruct the guards to watch for it in the future. The strategy is too complex to identify except in retrospect."

"But how did they manage it?" Stan demanded.

"It required an expert," Garrick answered. "Not only in computers, but in our computers. Someone who knew how to evade our security measures, someone who knew which specific computers could be breached and used to access—"

"It had to be Sadira," Camille interrupted. "That's what Garrick's trying to say. It was your daughter, Stan."

Stan's eyes narrowed at Camille before turning to Garrick, who deflected the attention to the computer. "Here's the actual footage from the camera outside the new entrance—not what the guard saw then, but what we retrieved when we figured out how she rerouted it."

Even though Camille had already seen this record, she was again amazed as she watched the invader's work. The small-framed, nimble man inspected minute variations in light and shadows, probed between stones, and quietly drummed with his knuckles to discover the door that was invisible even to Camille—and she knew its location. Furthermore, he managed all this while balancing on pipes and even poising *between* beams in the ceiling to evade the guard. Dressed in a camouflaged bodysuit, he remained undetected for hours, although the guard repeatedly passed below him. To Camille's great embarrassment, even she had failed to perceive him. In fact, it was her own entrance into the dungeon that helped the intruder narrow his field of search.

Stan grunted. "Incredible work. The Phantom?"

When Garrick glanced warily at Camille, Stan snapped, "I asked you a question, Sondem."

"Yes," Garrick said carefully. "The troops used to call this man The Phantom."

"Used to?"

"We now know his identity."

"Well?" Stan demanded.

Garrick again glanced at Camille before answering, "Captain Jorge Strider."

Stan's eyebrow twitched.

"Remember how Damour delayed placing hands-off orders on Strider's family after Stanley's defection?" Camille said. "We were at a loss to explain the delay? This is the child they adopted during that time."

Stan silently returned his attention to the screen.

"After seeing this," Garrick said quietly, "I no longer scoff at the men's accounts of The Phantom. He's got remarkable natural talent, and it was probably honed from childhood; Strider's an excellent tracker himself."

"Once he found the doorway, he disabled the guard and signaled the rest of his contingent," Camille narrated as the tape continued. "Damour's troops swooped in, extracted Sheridan and Strider on stretchers, and exited undetected. I returned minutes later to find only the drugged and restrained guards."

Stan continued to watch as Doug's troops left the facility with Sadira standing guard until the others were safely away. Then she very deliberately looked into the camera and mouthed, "I'm sorry, Father." She hesitated momentarily. "I love you."

With a roar, Stan grabbed the screen and threw it to the floor, smashing it to bits. Then he turned to the window where he stood, arms crossed, staring down on the street below. Camille carefully remained motionless and silent. Garrick likewise seemed unwilling to break the oppressive silence that settled over the room. Minutes ticked by before the general finally cleared his throat. "I do have one piece of good news."

Stan grunted, and Garrick looked to Camille for an interpretation. With a nod, she mouthed, "Tell him."

"The Planetary Defenders have abandoned their posts," Garrick said.

Stan turned from the window, an eyebrow lifted in query.

"Yes, all of them," Camille said.

Under different circumstances, Stan would have been thrilled with this news. Today his gaze merely shifted to Garrick. "What do you want, a medal? You know what to do. Quit standing around."

"Yes, sir," Garrick said, and moved toward the door. Camille followed, but before she could slip out behind him, Stan issued a single word command that pinned her to her place: "*Kamíl*!"

She grimaced before facing him. "Yes, sir?"

"Don't ever betray me. Not you."

His tone was threatening, but Camille sensed the yearning under the façade and inferred his true motivation: his fear of dying alone. She shared his fear, and it drove her response. "Never, *zuulu*. We're in this *together*, you and I, to the very end." She hesitated before continuing softly, "We'll go down, I think. But we'll go down fighting side by side."

It was what Stan needed to hear, and she sensed his relief at her words. But Camille needed more. She needed to feel his protection—to feel her brother's arms enclose her in his strength. Yet when she took a step toward him, he turned abruptly back to the window. "Show yourself out."

CHAPTER 31

ASSIGNMENTS

"The Lord has assigned to each his task."
1 Corinthians 3:5, NIV.

The first thing Chris became aware of was pain. Throbbing, burning, *every*where pain. Gradually, a gentle whirring noise worked its way into his consciousness. It sounded familiar. So did those voices.

The speakers broke into eager chatter, and Chris struggled through the fog of semiconsciousness toward them. The voices became clearer until he recognized Jorge, Sadira, and Sheridan. And was that …?

"Josh." He was looking directly into his best friend's face when he opened his eyes.

"'Bout time you woke up," Josh said with a grin.

Chris chuckled and held up his bandaged right hand. "It's so good to see you." His voice came out raspy.

"And you, *boní.*" Josh took Chris's hand gently in both of his. He was the same Josh that Chris had known so long, yet he was also different. Regal. Solemn. Dressed all in black: an elegant three-piece suit, shirt, and long robe-like overcoat. Only the black tie varied slightly, taking on a purple sheen in the light.

Chris glanced around to see that he lay in a hospital room, a sheet tented over his swollen body. The machine powering the airbed whirred quietly on his left. Jorge and Sheridan leaned against the rails, beaming as if Chris's awakening were some great feat. Maybe it was.

"Welcome back, Uncle Chris," Sheridan said.

Chris focused on his fellow prisoner. "Hey, you look great." He had honestly looked terrible when Chris last saw him: pale, weak, about ready to vomit.

"Wish I could say the same for you," Sheridan returned with a chortle, and Chris chuckled.

"How do you feel, Dad?" Jorge asked.

Chris held up his bandaged left hand to his son. With a weak grin he repeated an old family joke. *"Me duele todo mi hermoso cuerpo, mi hijo."* (Spanish: All of my beautiful body hurts, son.)

Jorge burst into laughter and finished the joke: *"Entonces no te duele nada!"* (Then nothing hurts!)

Chris chuckled again. "How long have I been out?"

"Three days," Jorge answered. "Stanley, Beth, Andy, and Riana all wanted to be here, but Doug needed them to stay at their posts."

"Good," Chris said. "And Sadira? I thought I heard her voice."

"I sent her on a little errand," Josh said. "She'll be back shortly."

"Did you come all this way just to catch me loafing?" Chris asked him.

Josh sobered, a look of great sadness coming over him. "Dad wants you to know how sorry he is for what you went through, *boní*." He paused, his eyes glistening. "We all are. But it was very brave of you, and Dad wants to grant you a special gift."

"Oh? What gift?"

"What would you like?"

Chris hesitated. "Well, there *is* something I want."

"Name it."

"I want—" Chris swallowed a sudden lump in his throat. "I want to be at Susana's grave to greet her at the Awakening."

Josh nodded. "Good choice. The only problem is, the Awakening will happen before you can heal, and you certainly can't fly cross-country in your condition."

"Oh." Chris tried to hide his disappointment. "Well, I'll catch up with her later."

"If only I had something to speed your healing," Josh said with mock pensiveness. Then his mouth twitched and he reached down to pick up a cooler.

His eyes widening, Chris guessed, "Leaves of the *Viv Zabe?*"

"Yup," Josh said with a grin.

"*Bachí*," Chris said, "I've said it before, but I mean it more every time I say it: You're amazing." (Rarámuri: elder brother)

"So are you, *raté*," Sheridan said soberly.

Chris shook his head. "No. I'm nothing like Josh."

"Oh, but you're wrong," Josh said. "You've become more and more like me since the day you surrendered Juan Misi's necklace. As you've come to know my parents and me better, you've come to reflect more and more of our *lashani*. That's what people see and are amazed by.

"But enough chatter. We have work to do." Josh opened the cooler and, taking several leaves in one fist, poised it above Chris's mouth. "Open wide. This is for your kidneys. You've been in renal failure."

Chris opened his mouth, and Josh squeezed the leaves, causing drops of green juice to fall on Chris's tongue. "Mmm. Kind of tastes like jasmine smells. And—Oh! Wow!"

"What, Dad?" Jorge asked anxiously.

"It's—well, a sort of warmth radiating out from my stomach."

"Good. Then it's time to move on to phase two. Jorge, Sheridan, you can help. Just tear the leaves like this and coat each wound with the cream it produces." As he spoke, he tore a leaf and gently spread some of the white cream on a wound on Chris's face.

Following Josh's example, Jorge treated a burn on Chris's left arm. "Does it hurt, Dad?"

"No. It feels good—cool, kind of numbing."

"This is unbelievable." Sheridan stood, transfixed, watching the gash he'd just treated on Chris's leg knit itself together.

"Yes, but don't waste too much time gawking," Josh said. "The leaves wither quickly once exposed to this atmosphere."

The three men worked for some time in a silence punctuated only by the occasional "Wow" or "Fascinating." At last, Josh announced that they'd finished the front of Chris's body. He called a temporary halt to allow time for the leaf-cream to finish healing those wounds, and then they helped Chris turn over so they could treat the ones on his back. By the time they'd finished, he felt as new and fresh as spring's first daffodil.

The healing complete, Josh sent him into the restroom to shower and dress. Afterward, as he stood at the mirror combing his hair, he caught sight of his bare left hand in the reflection and stopped.

"Something wrong?" Josh asked.

Chris flushed. After all he'd been through, it seemed almost petty to mention it. But his wedding band had served not only to remind him of the happy years he'd had with Susana, but also to recall the victories Doug had helped him win. He would really miss it.

"I'm sorry, Josh. It's just that they took my ring."

"It's on its way," Josh said cryptically.

A few minutes later, Sadira burst into the room, carrying a box. "Did I miss it?" Spying Chris, she added, "Well, I guess I did, but I'm glad you're better."

"Actually, your timing couldn't be better, dear one." Josh took the box from her and rummaged through it. "Here we go." He held up Chris's ring.

Chris burst into laughter as he accepted it. "Have I mentioned how amazing you are, Josh? Where on earth did you find this?"

"That would be Sadira's doing." Josh held the box out for him to see. As Chris poked through thousands of wedding rings, he saw that many were, like his, wide gold bands inset with different jewels—trophy-rings from the race.

"Actually, I just fetched it," Sadira said. "Sheridan's the one who knew about it and knew where Salty kept it."

"Salty?" Chris asked. "Wasn't he one of the guards in that place?"

"Yes," Sheridan said. "He's been collecting prisoners' wedding rings ever since outlanders started using them. He liked collecting them because every wedding ring meant that at least one other person, and usually several children as well, was suffering for the loss of that person."

"I'm glad you thought of rescuing the box," Josh said. "Every one of these trophy-rings was as important to its owner as Chris's is to him. It will give me great pleasure to return each one to its rightful owner after the Awakening."

"And that will be soon, then?" Chris asked.

"Oh, yes, *boní*. Very, very soon."

"So what do we do now?" Chris couldn't remember when he'd felt so full of energy.

"Yeah," Sheridan said, catching his uncle's enthusiasm. "Do you want us to go back on the road to debunk those lies Stan and Saxon have been spreading?"

"What have they been up to now?" Chris asked.

"Well, first—" Sheridan stopped with a frown. "Actually, it'll take a while. I'll fill you in later. What about it, Josh?"

Josh shook his head. "Thank you, but no. Those who want to believe the truth about us have all the evidence they need. Those who want to doubt will never have enough. What it boils down to—what it has always boiled down to—is that those who know and trust us will choose to believe the truth. Nevertheless, we could use your expertise in the Kalahari, Sheridan. If you're willing, you can come with me."

"I'm yours to command," Sheridan said.

"Chris," Josh said, "you're also to leave with me, but I'll drop you off in Ventura. My mom will deliver your granddaughters for you to watch while Stanley and Bethany are at the front. We have a safe place waiting for you—as safe as any place can be just now, that is."

He glanced around the circle with a grim smile. "There's still plenty of trouble ahead, my friends, but soon all will be made right. Very soon indeed."

CHAPTER 32

RAVAGES

> " 'I shall heap on them one disaster after another, and expend
> my arrows on them: pangs of hunger, ravages of plague,
> and bitter pestilence.' "
> Deuteronomy 32:23, 24, REB.

Just discharged from the hospital, a drowsy Chris paid little attention as Sadira, Sheridan, and Jorge discussed where to fill up the car. As long as they made it to the private airfield where Josh awaited them, who cared where they bought the gas?

Yielding to a jaw-cracking yawn, he rested his head against the headrest and dropped off to sleep. When he roused, his three companions were again discussing fuel, this time with a filling station owner. While they jabbered, he headed for a convenience store, having awakened with a brutal thirst. He stole a backward glance when the station owner told Jorge, "A lot of people are filling up to leave the city, Captain. So send in all your vehicles today. I won't be able to get any more."

Chris puzzled over that. Was the country rationing gasoline? And why the exodus from the city?

At the convenience store, he grabbed a bottle of water and guzzled half of it on his way to the checkout counter. Pulling a bill from his wallet, he laid it down.

The man looked at it as though it were a snake. "Are you from Mars or something?"

Chris glanced at the bill and joked, "You don't take American dollars in New York?"

The man wasn't amused. Picking up a nearby bat, he snapped, "Don't get smart with me, buddy."

"Whoa!" Chris backed away. "I'm sorry. I didn't mean to be a smart aleck. I've been—well, I've actually been in a coma. I'm a little out of touch with things."

The man didn't look fully convinced, but he did lower the bat. "You don't know about the new laws?"

"Um, I guess not. What laws?"

Flicking his chin at Chris's neck, the clerk said, "You gotta show me the transmitter on that chain before I can sell you anything."

"Oh. Okay." Chris had no idea why politicians would enact such a crazy law, but, hey—they were politicians. He was reaching into his shirt for his transmitter when Jorge yanked open the door.

"Come quick, Dad! Hurry!"

Chris had rarely seen his youngest son so overwrought. Forgetting all else, he left the water and currency on the counter and sprinted after him. He'd barely jumped into the car's backseat before Jorge peeled out.

"What is it? What's wrong?" Chris demanded.

"Did you show him your transmitter?" the others all asked at once.

"No—I was just about to. Why? Why is everyone suddenly fixated on transmitters?"

In the backseat beside Chris, Sheridan rubbed a hand over his face with a relieved sigh. "It's my fault this happened. I should have at least partially answered your question about what Stan's been doing. But who knew you could sneak off like that?"

"Yes," Sadira agreed from the passenger seat. "We're glad Doug knew where to find you."

"I'm sorry if I worried you guys," Chris said. "But frankly, I'm feeling a little lost here. What's going on?"

Sadira explained about the "healing" frequency that allowed Stan's crew to influence people's actions. "But it's also created some anger management issues. People are responding way out of proportion to the offense, whether real or perceived. And seeing one of Doug's transmitters is enough to enrage them."

"But why?" Chris asked.

"They believe the original devices interfere with the pain-relieving effect of the newer transmitters, and that the interference causes natural disasters—and there have been many of those."

Chris suddenly understood the danger he'd escaped. "How could this happen so fast?"

"Saxon's been posing as Josh," Sheridan answered. "He's claiming Stan and the Damours are allies. He's very convincing."

"And Willy hasn't helped any," Jorge added.

"Willy?" Chris asked. "How's he figure in to this?"

"He's a huge bigwig now—Special Liaison for a United RAB—essentially Stan's tool for eradicating Doug's RABs."

"Our Willy?" Chris shook his head sadly. "But why am I surprised? He's a talented kid, he's always wanted to 'be somebody,' and Stan loves using Juan Misi's descendants for his own purposes."

"Don't we know it," Sadira muttered.

Looking to Sheridan, Chris asked, "She knows?"

"That I'm the daughter of Rose Moore, a daughter of Juan Misi, and, most impressively"—she flashed a grin—"a niece of Dr. Christian Strider? Yes, I know. Isn't it amazing that, when I thought I was leaving my family, Doug was actually reuniting me with my real family?"

"His ways are beyond our understanding," Chris agreed with a smile. "But finish the transmitter news."

"Well, Saxon, posing as Josh, ordered runners to replace Doug's transmitters with the New-RAB devices," she explained.

"No!" Chris exclaimed. "They couldn't talk to Doug!"

"Or be raised in the Awakening," Sheridan agreed. "Many runners are either believing him or agreeing to the change to avoid punishment."

"Punishment? Are you saying it's illegal to wear Doug's transmitter?"

"That's right. The natural disasters triggered a huge movement to outlaw them."

Sadira added, "And the fake Josh has ordered the original RABs to merge with the New-RABs to encourage compliance with the transmitter ban."

Chris rubbed his forehead. "Wait a minute. How can a fake Josh dissolve Doug's RABs?"

"Well, he can't, obviously," Sheridan said. "But that's only obvious to people who know that he's not really Josh."

"Right. So the end result is …" Chris again rubbed his head, having trouble keeping track of all the real whatsits and fake whosits.

"The end result is exactly what Sheridan predicted on *Marci*," Jorge said. "There are now only two groups of people. First, faithful runners who see through Saxon's disguise, who won't give up their transmitters, and who know that only Doug's RABs are the real deal. Everyone else supports the combined Stan-'Josh' agenda. To them, the loyal runners are callously worsening problems by continuing to use their transmitters."

"And why, exactly, do people believe the transmitters cause disasters?"

"Because Stan has centuries of practice in making science appear to support his claims," Sadira said. "His physicists have manufactured experimental evidence showing that the frequencies emitted by the two transmitters enhance one another, creating a resonance that grows exponentially as more and more transmitters are added to the system."

"I'm not big on physics," Chris admitted. "But I think I get the picture. These abnormal vibrations supposedly affect the environment?"

"That's it," Sheridan said. "News stations play clips of the Tacoma Narrows Bridge collapsing. It's not the same phenomenon, but it's close enough for the average person, and the shocking pictures generate an emotional reaction."

"And because the New-RAB devices purportedly facilitate healing, the old devices are the ones that were banned," Chris concluded, nodding. "What's the penalty for possessing a real transmitter?"

"A hefty fine for the first offense," Sheridan answered. "After that, imprisonment. And agents are fanning the hostility among outlanders. Since only the wearer can remove the real transmitters, people are calling for remote prison camps for 'willful refusal to consider the welfare of the community.' Some even propose extermination."

"Seriously?"

"Yup. And it's working. Many runners are exchanging their devices for Stan's substitute. The public outcry is so pronounced they've even banned things associated with the original transmitters. It's now illegal to hold an assembly on the Rest Day. And, although it's not illegal to run, you'd better not let anyone see you doing it."

"But this is the United States, a country founded to ensure personal freedom." When Sheridan and Sadira both laughed, Chris added indignantly, "I don't think it's funny."

"Sorry, *raté*." Sheridan slapped him on the shoulder. "But you don't appreciate the extent of Stan's power. Plus he's got 'research' on his side. Don't you see?"

Chris sighed. Yes, he did see. It was completely logical. Though founded on lies and reinforced by more lies, it did, within that world of hyperbole and partial truth, make sense.

"I don't even recognize the world you're describing." Motioning outside his window, he noted, "Or what I'm seeing. There have been several tussles right here on the street. Come to think of it, I don't see any women."

"Women, children, and the elderly generally stay indoors," Sadira said. "The streets aren't safe. Especially for anyone caught with a real transmitter."

"Our people are fleeing the cities to live off the land," Jorge explained. "Some vendors, like the owner of that filling station, have stayed behind to supply runners with necessities. But if anyone finds them out, they'll be the next headline."

Chris turned to the window, his mind numb, his chest constricted with grief. *Kanuf* was running amok—wholly unchecked by reason, rule, or compassion.

* * * * *

Josh flew Chris to Ventura and saw him to the harbor where Debora and his granddaughters waited with a boat. He explained that Chris was to join his brothers' families on San Miguel Island. The westernmost of the Channel Islands was unprotected from the open ocean and prone to severe weather. Further, submerged rocks made the coastline difficult to navigate. With no ranger (thanks to budget shortages) and few people caring to brave its elements, its very harshness made it a perfect hideaway.

"You said my brothers are out there," Chris said as Josh parked the car. "What about Rosie?"

Josh sadly shook his head. "I'm sorry, *boní.* She's chosen the other side."

Chris's heart juddered to a halt. He had often tried to talk his sister into running the race, but she had always been waiting for some better time. Could this really be the end—no more chances?

"Josh, let me see her before we leave. Please? If I talk to her, just once more, maybe she'll change her mind."

Josh sadly shook his head. "No. She won't. Instead, she'll report you for having a transmitter."

"No!" Chris objected. It must be true if Josh said so, but the thought of his beloved sister betraying him was beyond his comprehension. A great inner ripping sensation overwhelmed him, as though someone were tearing his heart from his body. As painful as it was to lose Susana, this was worse. Rosie was lost to him forever.

There was only one word he knew to describe his agony: *d'amoúr,* "I ache for you"—the name Josh and his parents had chosen after Stan's rebellion. Looking into Josh's eyes, he saw his own grief reflected there. "Is this how it feels, *bachí*?" he asked weakly. "Is this how you and your parents feel every time someone dies without a transmitter?"

"Yes. Yes, it is."

"How do you stand it?"

"Consider those dear ones you've played a part in rescuing, *boní.* It doesn't eliminate the pain, but it does make it easier to bear."

Chris did as Josh advised, calling to mind his children, his brothers, Lorenzo and Monica Wells, and so many others. Together, they would all enjoy life in Paradise forever. While that didn't erase the pain of losing Rosie, it helped to know he'd never feel such pain for them.

As Chris got out of the car, Cherie and Melanie ran toward him. *"Aparochi!"*

He caught the two precious girls in his arms, and the gripping pain faded somewhat amid their exuberant love. "I'm so glad to see you, pumpkins," he murmured as he hugged them tightly. When he noticed the wooden box that housed Juan Misi's trophy necklace cradled in Cherie's arms, he said, "Oh, thank you. I'm glad you brought this."

"Ami Debora helped me remember," she said.

"Keep it with you constantly from here on," Josh said. "The time to return it to Juan Misi is very soon, but you'll never know the exact moment."

Chris frowned. How would he manage that? The box was much too big to fit in a pocket.

As if reading his thoughts, Josh reached for the box and removed the necklace. "You've changed a great deal from the arrogant, impetuous youngster who once wore this. Then, your pride would dissolve the *nushaz* of the band, but that's no longer a problem since you've given up your pride. You'll now be able to handle the necklace without fear of either harming it or being corrupted by it." (Paradisian: humility)

As his coach solemnly fastened the trophy around Chris's neck, the runner honestly felt none of the pride or self-sufficiency he had once felt when wearing it. He felt only gratitude.

CHAPTER 33

PANIC

"On that day a great panic sent by the Lord will fall on them, with everyone laying hands on his neighbor and attacking him."
Zechariah 14:13, REB.

Two days after "the big one," an exhausted Willy dragged himself home from work for the first time since the disaster struck. Fortunately, no real estate had dropped into the ocean. Still, forty-eight seconds of an 8.2 earthquake centered in Los Angeles proper was enough to scare even the hardiest Californians.

And with good reason. Hundreds were confirmed dead. Thousands were missing. Millions were scrambling for food and water. The city itself was one chaotic mess: collapsed buildings ... blazing fires ... ruined highways ... spotty telecommunications ... no power ... little food ... less drinkable water. And, with the rest of the country dealing with their own disasters—hurricanes, tornados, floods, blizzards, fires—no one was volunteering any help.

Merry Christmas, California, he thought.

At least Uncle Chris's house had weathered it well. And Aunt Susana had devotedly kept her home stocked with emergency supplies. So Willy was set for a while—at least until someone figured it out and broke in.

He was just finishing a cold dinner of granola bars and canned fruit when his satellite phone rang. Dread washed over him at the urgency in his oldest brother's voice. His eight-year-old niece, Nancy, had come down with a high fever and nasty sores all over her body yesterday.

"What's wrong, Tommy?" he demanded. "Is she worse?"

"Yeah. She's in the hospital. It's an infection caused by a new strain of the Turkey Terror virus—a mutation caused by the interplay between the two types of transmitters."

Willy gritted his teeth as his dread transformed into mingled fear and anger. Turkey Terror was bad enough. Although the doctors had devised some treatments, one in five of its victims still died. If it had mutated and become more resistant, it could only make the prognosis worse.

As Willy headed out the door, the phone rang again—his other brother, Evan.

"Mom's just been taken to the hospital by ambulance," Evan said. "She was attacked by some neighbors fleecing her garden. She was beaten unconscious."

"Oh, no," Willy groaned, although he wasn't surprised. People stealing food from neighbors' yards had become commonplace, and Mom had always maintained a flourishing garden.

The drive home was usually a ninety-minute undertaking without traffic. Tonight, it took some four hours, being riddled with detours because of earthquake damage. That gave Willy plenty of time to think, and what he thought about was the injustice of it all. His sweet little niece lay in critical condition from a bad virus gone wild. His sixty-year-old mom had been beaten senseless by her own neighbors—good people driven to desperate measures by hunger and pain.

And behind it all? Those fanatics who wouldn't surrender their defective transmitters.

By the time Willy arrived at the hospital, he was seething. Up until now, he'd resisted the movement to sequester recalcitrant runners away in rural facilities. He truly believed in protecting personal liberties. But why should their freedom be guarded when they were causing innocent people such pain?

✻ ✻ ✻ ✻ ✻

Mom was still in serious condition on the Sunday after Christmas—the day they buried little Nancy. Needless to say, it had been a rotten Christmas. As Willy followed the hearse that bore Nancy's casket, Dr. Moden phoned.

"Mr. Moore," he said, "I'm very sorry for interrupting you on this most solemn day. However, I need your assistance, and I'm afraid it can't wait."

"Of course, Dr. Moden. After all you've done for me and my family, I'm happy to help however I can."

And he heartily meant it. Stan Moden's generosity had been epic. He had immediately spoken with the physicians involved, placing his resources at their disposal. He'd sent a specialist in pediatric infectious diseases up from Children's to consult on Nancy. And one of his own medical team, acclaimed neurosurgeon Dr. Austin Pim, had flown from New York to operate on Mom. Unfortunately, it had been too late to help Nancy, but Dr. Pim's intervention saved Mom's life. At least she was no longer comatose.

"Thank you for your willingness," Dr. Moden said graciously. "However, what I must ask you to do will be difficult."

Willy lifted his chin in determination.

"I don't have to tell you that the world is suffering, Mr. Moore. You've had your share of that pain. And you know that both Prince Joshua and myself are doing everything possible to alleviate the anguish. But there's something that only you can do."

"I'm happy to help. What do you need?"

"Prince Joshua and I have decided that the Outlander Division, the key support for obstinate runners, must be crippled if we're to get rid of those accursed devices."

Willy suddenly guessed where this conversation was going and fell silent.

"And the best way to destabilize that faction is to cut off its head," Dr. Moden continued matter-of-factly.

Andy. Andy was leading the Outlander Division. He and Riana had come to the funeral.

"You can help us, Mr. Moore. Just give me a time and place where we can find him alone. That's all. I'll take care of the rest."

Willy's mouth had gone dry. Sending nameless offenders to rural camps was one thing, but giving up his cousin? Yes, he'd collected Jorge's trash, but this was more personal, and the consequences were more severe. Did Dr. Moden realize what he was asking? He'd been so sympathetic about Mom and Nancy. Surely he didn't expect Willy to betray his own flesh and blood.

"Andy—" Willy began hoarsely and stopped to clear his throat. "He's my cousin, Dr. Moden."

There was a momentary silence, but it felt like a displeased silence.

"I'm sending you a picture, Mr. Moore," Dr. Moden said quietly. "Think about what's at stake. Think about what you owe me." He paused before adding in a rather menacing tone, "Think about what I know."

Willy parked behind the hearse in the cemetery and checked his phone for the promised picture: an open paper file labeled with Willy's name and sitting on Dr. Moden's desk. Snapshots from that awful accident and a copy of the police report were clearly visible.

Suddenly feeling very cold inside, Willy buried his face in his hands. What choice did he have? He couldn't have everyone knowing about that accident—especially not now, when people all around the world were learning his name. Not only would Mom and Dad be disappointed in him, but they'd suffer horrible embarrassment from neighbors and friends.

Besides, he'd really only be turning in a criminal, someone who was injuring other people. Didn't moral responsibility require him to cooperate?

Quickly deleting the image from his phone, Willy murmured, "It's not my fault." He'd tried to warn Andy that the Outlander Division was dangerous. He should have listened. He'd brought this on himself.

Willy helped carry his niece's small casket to her grave. Then he sat beside Andy and whispered, "Can you come to Tommy's place after this? I need help unloading some stuff before everyone arrives for the reception."

"Sure," Andy whispered back.

Turning away, Willy expelled a soft, ragged breath. Then he texted the time and address to Dr. Moden.

Chapter 34
TRAPPED

"The men at peace with you shall deceive you and prevail against you. Those who eat your bread shall lay a trap for you."
Obadiah 1:7, NKJV.

Willy pulled into Tommy's driveway and, opening his trunk, grabbed a box. "Everything comes in," he called.

"You got it!" Andy called out the window as he parked beside Willy's car. Collecting some packages, he followed his cousin. Riana grinned when he winked at her as he rounded the corner of the garage. He was feeling better, now that his cousin had asked them to help. Willy's recent coolness had troubled him, although Riana had pointed out that it was understandable with Nancy and Aunt Rosie so ill. Willy had had a lot on his mind, and he didn't have Doug's peace to comfort him.

She was still gathering up some bags when her implanted military radio pinged. "Run!" came Andy's voice, low but urgent. "It's a trap!"

Riana's initial reaction was disbelief. He must be joking around; certainly Willy hadn't turned them in!

But Andy was unerringly strict about using the military radio for military communications only. She must accept this message, not as a joke, or even as a suggestion from her husband, but as an order from her commanding officer.

She immediately jumped into their car, pulled out of the driveway, and headed up the street, passing in front of Tommy's house as she did. When she stole a glance toward the doorway, her heart plopped heavily into her stomach. Andy was handcuffed and flanked by two police officers. Two more aimed service revolvers at him.

Willy *had* betrayed them. Oh, how horrifying for Andy, to know that his own cousin and friend had sold him into enemy hands!

As her car passed, Andy glanced over his shoulder toward her. "Love you, angel," he whispered through the radio.

"I love you," she returned, choking back a sob. "Be strong."

She drove up the street as fast as she dared. But when she rounded a corner, she saw police cars barricading the entrance into the track of homes. Throwing the car into reverse, she detoured onto a side street that led to another entrance. But as that one came into view, she hit her brakes. It was also barricaded.

Searching her mental map for other escape routes, she came up blank. She would have to hoof it. Jumping out of the car, she ran toward a thick hedge several yards away. Before she reached it, a police car squealed to a stop behind her car.

"Stop right there, Lieutenant Strider! Put your hands up!" The two officers crouched behind their doors with guns trained on her. They were too close to miss.

She stopped and lifted her hands. Softly, she said, "Doug, I've been apprehended."

"I know, little dove. I'm sorry you have to go through this, but go quietly. Remember, I am with you always. *D'alasház.*"

"D'alasház, Ada." (Paradisian: I love you with lashani love, Dad.)

Policemen surrounded her. One handcuffed her, pulled a black hood over her head (*When did the police start using black hoods?* she wondered), and put her in the backseat of a car. Then he drove. For a long, long time.

* * * * *

Riana restlessly paced her small cell. Sweat rolled down her back and beaded on her face, stinging the cuts and gashes now adorning it. Her first three days in this facility had been filled with "questioning," and that's all she cared to remember. That and the fact that they'd gotten nothing from her.

For the last day and a half they'd left her alone. Ever the optimist, she hoped that meant they'd given up on extracting information from her. Still, she was no idiot—she knew they'd probably try again after she'd been weakened by hunger, boredom, and loneliness.

In some respects, solitary confinement was worse than interrogation. With nothing and no one to distract her, her mind focused inward, examining and reexamining every moment of her life—accusing, condemning. And she didn't have her solid, level-headed husband to help her put things in perspective.

Poor Andy. She could only imagine what terrible agonies he was suffering. As the acting head of the Outlander Division, he wouldn't get off as easily as she had.

And so the hours dragged by, her busy mind chasing from one awful scenario to another. Her windowless cell offered little in the way of diversion. The dim lighting never changed, but the climate alternated between stifling and very cold, so she figured that was day and night, respectively. Based on that wide variation in temperature and the long hours that the officer had driven, she guessed she was somewhere in the desert. That conformed to the rumors of runners being imprisoned in the Mohave to keep their transmitters from "interfering" with the New-RAB devices in populous regions.

At least they had informed her frankly of her precarious position. She was a terrorist in a military state. She had no rights. She would receive no favors. On the other hand, if she gave up her transmitter, she could go home. Failing that, if she cooperated by providing some information, she'd be moved out of solitary confinement and allowed to work in the facility, thereby earning the right to eat. Otherwise, she'd be lucky to get water.

Well, she did get water, at least. Twice a day, the small metal window at the bottom of the metal door slid open and a bottle of water rolled through it. But that was all. No food. No communication.

Dropping onto her cot, she buried her face in her hands. She felt totally abandoned. Her overactive imagination kept suggesting that Doug had forgotten her. Maybe she'd done something to offend him. Or maybe she hadn't done something—

"No! Stop it!" she said aloud, beginning a litany that was growing familiar. "I am *not* abandoned. He promised to be with me always, even to the end. And I *will* trust his word rather than my feelings. What were Doug's last words to me? *D'alasház.* He *does* love me. I *am* his daughter. No circumstance can change that. 'For I am convinced that neither death, nor life, nor principalities, nor powers, not anything in the present or future, not height, nor depth, nor anything else, can separate me from Doug's love.' So there," she added with an emphatic nod.

Nevertheless her mind, jumbled with unanswered questions and confused emotions, wouldn't rest. What she really wanted—needed—was to talk to her *adu*. But they had a jamming system in this facility, as in the police car. She hadn't been able to reach Doug on either her transmitter or military radio since her arrest.

Just to be sure, she activated her transmitter again now, only to immediately turn it off when a high-pitched screeching came through it. Her implanted radio produced the same ear-piercing noise, making her ear ring for several minutes. That made her dizzy, so she lay down on the bunk until the sensation passed.

Well, if she couldn't hear Doug through her transmitter, she would settle for hearing him through his word. So she began quoting passages from the *Manual* aloud. As she did, she remembered that Debora had once assured her that Doug could always hear her on the transmitter, even if she couldn't hear him.

With a spark of hope, she once again activated the device. Plugging her ears against the awful screeching, she rattled off, "*Adu*, I really need help. I miss you so much. I'm so lonely. And they're not feeding me at all. I don't mean to complain, but I really am starving. Please help me."

She received no reply, but then she hadn't expected to. Still, Doug had promised to hear her. He had promised to meet her needs. And he had promised to bring good out of any situation. She would trust him to keep his word. He always had.

Keys rattled at her door, and then a bright light shone directly into her eyes. After days of dimness, the light was painful, and she lifted her arm against it as she stood.

"You ready to get outta here, sweetums?" said a rough female voice. Riana couldn't see the speaker, only the vague image of a hefty individual behind the blinding light.

"Not if it means giving up my transmitter or giving you information," Riana said with as much spirit as she could muster.

"I have something you might want to see. A message from your husband." A hand held out an electronic tablet.

Riana wanted to be excited—oh, how she missed Andy! But another impulse quickly swallowed her eagerness. If these people were offering it, it couldn't be good news.

She hesitantly accepted the tablet and studied the frozen frame. Andy looked awful. His kind face was bruised and bloodied, his dark hair matted with blood. One eye was completely swollen shut; the other was bloodshot. But what really caught her attention rested on his bare chest: a New-RAB transmitter.

Tears pricked at her eyes. What had they done to him? Had he really given up?

When she pressed Play, his raspy voice said, "Riana, Josh came to visit me. He explained what's happening. We've been deceived, babe. We're wrong. It's time we admit it before more people are affected. You need to give them the transmitter, babe. It's hurting people."

When it ended, she pushed Replay, but the guard grabbed the device from her hands and backhanded her. Riana, weak from hunger, sprawled to the cement floor.

"Well, what will it be?" the guard demanded.

Riana's head swam. "I—I need to—to think—"

You will be handed over for punishment and execution; all nations will hate you for your allegiance to me. At that time many will fall from their faith. Be strong and of good courage; do not be afraid, nor be dismayed, for the Lord your God is with you.

No, she did not need to think about it! Whatever Andy had been coerced into saying, or even believing, she would not abandon the man who had never abandoned her. She would never give up her *adu*, not even—

She faltered at the thought, yet knew in her innermost soul that it was the right decision. *Not even for Andy.*

She shook her now-aching head—carefully, but emphatically. "No. I will not give up my transmitter. Never."

The guard slammed the door shut, and the sharp sound echoed painfully through her head. The guard told someone, "No more water for this one."

Riana slumped to the floor, overcome by tears. She was dizzy from the blow, and her head pounded. But mostly she was confused by Andy's defection. He was the strongest person she knew. Whereas people often backed off when their beliefs were questioned, Colonel Andrew Strider only dug in more deeply. He knew what he believed; he knew why he believed it; and he didn't care who disagreed with him. Some called him hard-nosed, opinionated, and stubborn. In truth, he was all of these things, and Riana loved him for it. In a world where men were swayed by every new philosophy, Andy stood firm, even if he stood against a thousand foes.

So how could he surrender his transmitter? How could he give up Doug? She could only envision him doing such a thing if he'd truly been convinced they were wrong. And Andy was so balanced, so rational. If *he'd* been convinced …

Could they really have been wrong all along? Somebody had to be wrong in this debate. Was she being arrogant to believe that her version of truth must be the right one?

I am the way, the truth.

Until heaven and earth disappear, not the smallest letter, not the least stroke of a pen, will by any means disappear from the Law.

I am the Lord, I change not.

It is impossible for Doug to lie.

No, they hadn't been wrong to trust Doug. She could be wrong, but not Doug. He *was* truth, he couldn't lie, and he didn't change. She must not, whatever they did to her—or Andy—give up on her *adu*.

"Oh, Andy!" she cried, overwhelmed with disappointment and sorrow. "How could you? How could you give him up?"

She wept until she had no more tears to shed. When the pain of the hard cement against her hip bone insisted that she shift positions, she pulled herself up and sank down onto the bunk, feeling frail, defeated, despairing.

That thought roused her, for she knew the treatment for low spirits. And now, when her spirits were lower than they'd ever been in her twenty-four years of life, was no time to stop doing it.

Steeling herself against the coming screech, she activated her transmitter. "Doug," she said, her feeble voice scarcely more than a whisper. "I love you. I want to be your loyal daughter. Please keep me faithful. They're taking away my water now. If dying in this cell can further your work somehow, then that's okay. But please—please!—strengthen Andy. Please don't let him give up. Help him. Please."

Curled up on the mattress, she began repeating promises from the *Manual* until she became sleepy. Just as slumber was overtaking her, Andy's words from the video came back to her: *We've been deceived, babe … Give them the transmitter, babe.*

Her eyes flew open. *Babe?* He never called her that.

And suddenly she knew: the tape had been doctored. Maybe it was a real image of him (*Oh, her poor, battered Andy!*), but they had probably dubbed it, splicing words and sounds together to manufacture the message they wanted him to convey—the message he had refused to say himself. Yes, that was her obstinate Andy!   Similarly, they could have covered his real transmitter with the larger New-RAB device to make it look as though he'd surrendered it.

Although she couldn't verify these conclusions, the alternatives were too horrible to dwell upon. So she seized the hope they offered and drew comfort from them, eventually drifting off to sleep.

When she awoke, two slices of cellophane-wrapped bread lay at her nose.

CHAPTER 35

RAVEN

"I have commanded the ravens to feed you there."
1 Kings 17:4, NKJV.

S itting up, Riana tore open a packet of bread, but then made herself eat it slowly, savoring each bite. Never had a simple piece of bread tasted so good.

She had nearly finished the first slice before the question of where the food had come from entered her mind. Someone must have brought it into her cell, but how could she have slept through the door's loud clanging? And why would they feed her if they intended to withhold water?

About that time a pointy little nose poked under the metal door.

"Oh!" she squealed, jerking her feet up onto the bunk.

Two dark eyes seemed to twinkle with laughter, and something like a chuckle came from the creature's throat. She approached it cautiously. At first she'd assumed it was a mouse or a rat, but now she saw a dark band across its eyes, like a raccoon.

"Hello," she said curiously. "Who are you?"

The animal pulled itself along with its front feet to slide through the slit under the door, which couldn't be much more than an inch high. She watched in fascination as the creature reconfigured from the wide, flat shape that scooted under the door into a weasel-like figure as it came out. She never would have guessed that the resulting fourteen-inch animal could have squeezed through such a small space.

"Well, aren't you the little contortionist," she said, and the animal again made that chuckling noise. It was as infectious as human laughter, and she giggled in return.

When the creature flattened itself to go back through the slit, she crouched down to plead, "Oh, no, please don't go." It seemed friendly and harmless, and she'd much rather have the company of a furry friend than none at all.

Ignoring her, the animal continued pulling itself through the slit until it was about halfway through. Then it backed up to return into the room. That's when it registered—the little beast was smuggling something into her cell.

"What have you got there?"

The animal pulled backward, tugging and shaking its head to maneuver a silver bag through the slit. It pulled and pulled, the bag coming gradually under the door until, with one final tug, the object came through all at once. This sent the animal sprawling, and it chuckled some more before bouncing up to retrieve the silver pouch and drag it to Riana's feet.

"For me?" She sat down on the floor to look it over. "Why, it's water!" She looked again at the little creature. "Did you bring the bread, too?"

As if in answer, the animal again slid halfway under the door, retrieved another article, and dragged it into the cell to reveal another cellophane-wrapped slice of bread. Still hauling its gift, it pulled itself up onto the bed and deposited the bread by the other slice before jumping down to return to Riana.

"An acrobat too," Riana exclaimed. "Why, you're an absolute marvel!"

The animal seemed truly pleased by her assessment. Leaping sideways several times, it chuckled heartily until it bumped into the bedpost and tripped over itself, whereupon it rolled over on the ground, still chuckling. This display of unmistakable joy sent Riana into a fit of laughter. "Oh, you are fun, aren't you? And so kind to bring me food and water."

More chuckling.

"But I'm being a very bad hostess. I should share this feast with you, shouldn't I? You must be thirsty after all that work." She poked the straw into the pouch of water and carefully deposited some on the cement floor.

Her new friend lapped it up and looked at her expectantly.

"You want more?"

She put some more on the floor and drank some herself. Then she retrieved the slices of bread and tried to share those too, but her new friend had no interest in bread.

Observing her companion as she ate, she decided, "You're definitely not a mouse or a rat. You look more like a weasel. But I don't think they're very nice, and you seem awfully good-natured. You do look familiar, though, like I've seen a picture of you somewhere." She chewed a bite of bread thoughtfully. "Maybe a prairie dog? No—they're bigger and colored differently. A chinchilla? No—you're too long and don't have their big ears. What else could you ...?"

"Ah!" she said suddenly. "A ferret!"

Surely the animal didn't actually understand her, but it apparently enjoyed her excitement, for it did its little sideways-hopping dance again. Then it grabbed the now-empty water pouch in its teeth and backed away. The gesture reminded her of a dog wanting to play tug-of-war, so she grabbed the other end and pulled. The ferret tugged back, chuckling some more.

She played with her new friend until it laid its little head down on the floor as if tired. "Have I worn you out?" she asked. "Would you sleep here with me? It would be so nice if you would. I'm really lonely."

She hadn't tried to handle the ferret until now, but when she carefully slipped her hand under it, it didn't object. Lifting it up, she set it on the cot, where it turned around in circles and scratched at the bare mattress. However, it didn't seem content until she curled around it. The animal did have a fairly strong musky odor, but she didn't mind. After several days without a shower, she probably smelled pretty musky herself. And it was so comforting to have a companion. So incredibly comforting.

As she drifted into the arms of Morpheus, she remembered that Doug had once fed his prophet using ravens. Gratitude filled her. Doug had sent this little ferret—perhaps the only intelligent creature that could maneuver its way into the cell—to provide for her, just as he'd sent the ravens to provide for Elijah.

"Raven," she whispered to the sleeping animal. "I'll call you Raven."

✳ ✳ ✳ ✳ ✳

Raven faithfully supplied Riana with bread and water at least twice each day. Sometimes she brought a treat—a pouch of milk, a bag of trail mix, even a melting popsicle on one particularly hot day. Sometimes she accepted token bits of her deliveries. Mostly she merely seemed delighted to have her work appreciated.

However, she wasn't a constant companion; she came and went at her own whim. Sometimes, usually when Riana was feeling blue, the little sweetheart spent prolonged periods with her. Other times she appeared only to deliver meals. Riana didn't mind this inconsistency since she suspected the ferret was assisting other prisoners, too. But when Raven was there, Riana gave the animal her undivided attention, eating with her, playing with her, talking to her. It was a great diversion and probably did much toward guarding her sanity.

When Raven wasn't there, Riana did calisthenics and ran in place to promote her physical conditioning. She made a discipline of reviewing passages from the *Manual,* thankful that she'd memorized portions throughout her life. She also talked to Doug, plugging her ears against the screeching noise, at least once a day. Even though she couldn't hear him, it strengthened her to verbalize her gratitude and faith and to renew her commitment to him. She often thanked him for the strength he provided through the *Manual's* passages, and for the comfort he sent through Raven. And she never ceased to plead his fortification for Andy. Wherever he was.

She'd had no further word about her husband (or anything else). But she thought of him constantly, sometimes wondering if he was still alive. As battered as he'd been in the video, death seemed a likely possibility.

She was thinking of Andy one day when she looked up to see him standing in her cell, even though the door hadn't opened.   She   would   have chalked it up to a dream if she'd been lying down. But she was exercising, so she had no ready explanation for his presence. Nevertheless, there he was, his arms extended in invitation.

Flashing his irrepressible grin, he said, "Hi, angel."

She gasped, tears flooding her vision. Then she stepped into his arms … and through his body.

With another gasp, she spun around. "What—?"

His smile melted into disappointment. "I'm sorry. I haven't gotten used to being a spirit yet."

Little fingers of ice worked their way down her spine, and her arms tingled with goose bumps. "A—a spirit?"

"Yeah. I—well, I'm dead, angel. It's not that bad. It's not what I expected, but that's how it goes." He shrugged. "We were wrong about a lot of things."

Stepping toward her, he lifted his hand to stroke her cheek. Her face tingled as if stroked by an icicle. "You're so beautiful," he said wistfully. "I loved you the moment I first saw you. I'm sorry to leave you. I would give anything to hold our child myself. You'll take good care of him for me, won't you? He's the only legacy I'll have."

She stared at him dumbly. *Child?*

All in a jumble it dawned on her that she had no idea when her last period was. In the frenzy of the last few months, she'd forgotten to keep track. She'd also forgotten several of her pills. Which meant she really could be pregnant. But how would Andy know that?

"I hate seeing you like this," he continued. "I wish you'd cooperate with them. You should take better care of yourself, if only for the baby's sake." He shook his head sadly. "If only you knew what's going on outside, you'd understand. The old transmitters are really messing things up. Untreatable sores, unrelenting heat, undrinkable water—people are dying in droves."

Riana's perplexity deepened. Was this really her iron-willed husband saying such things?

"You're so kind and gentle," he continued. "I know you don't mean to hurt anyone. But that is what's happening. We were wrong, that's all. Just accept it, and give up your transmitter. Then you and our son can live in freedom."

The last word jolted her out of the incredulous, creeped-out daze she'd fallen into. "Freedom? True freedom isn't coerced. And it isn't based on lies. True freedom doesn't have one version of truth for the common people and another for the elite. I can't trust anything rooted in Stan's philosophies. Nothing about his administration, however he may disguise it, is freedom." She became increasingly animated, increasingly convinced, as she spoke.

"So guarding your freedom—your particular definition of freedom—is more important than the health, even the lives, of billions of others? Isn't that kind of selfish? And isn't selfishness the opposite of the *lashani* that's supposed to motivate a runner's life?"

These words, expressed by the one who knew her better than any, cut her deeply, laying her soul painfully bare.

Andy took a step closer as he pleaded, "Maybe that's why we ended up here, why Damour didn't rescue us. Maybe we didn't measure up to his strict definition of holiness. Maybe we're just not good enough to live with him on Paradise Island."

This echoed the doubts that had plagued her, the uncertainties that had chased her around her dim cell during these long, lonely days. But precisely because it so closely echoed her own thoughts, her mind, long accustomed to seeking comfort in Doug's counsel, turned to the *Manual's* witness almost automatically.

"I've never been 'good enough,' " she said. "But Josh is. And his work on my behalf gives him the right to clear me. He said, 'I've taken all your guilt from you, and I will clothe you with pure garments.' "

"Then why does he allow you to suffer like this? Doesn't he care about you? Or maybe he's not powerful enough to rescue you. Either way, the Damours have deceived you."

She suddenly realized that he was avoiding Doug's first name. This cemented the suspicion that had been growing—the truth she knew to be incontrovertible despite the deep ache within her heart. Only her yearning to see Andy had kept her from admitting it sooner. Yet she knew in her core that if her husband were dead, he wouldn't be able to appear to her like this. Even now, multiple evidences from the *Manual* reverberated through the hallways of her mind, driving home the point.

Doug alone is immortal.

For the living know that they shall die: but the dead know not anything.

There shall not be found among you anyone who calls up the dead. For all who do these things are an abomination to the Lord.

They are spirits of demons, performing signs.

If she were to rely on the evidence of her senses, she'd have to believe that this was Andy. It looked just like him. It talked and gestured like him. It used his vocabulary and intonation. Yet she knew that Stan's agents could disguise themselves very convincingly as dead relatives.

The conviction that an enemy was impersonating Andy outraged her and caused her to feel very contrary. Deliberately using the Paradisian pronunciation that the apparition had avoided, she exclaimed, "It is impossible for Doúg to lie!"

He flashed a condescending smile that was not at all like Andy, and the incongruent expression made her even more impatient with the deception. "And that's all you guys do is lie! You're lying right now! I know you're not really my husband!"

The apparition looked away with the expression of one dealing with a particularly stupid child. When his gaze returned to her, his cold expression looked nothing like Andy.

"Why are you still alive, Riana?" he demanded. "Where do you get water?"

"Doúg provides for his own," she said.

The image frowned in annoyance and faded away.

She turned toward the door when she heard the quiet swish of the peep-hole sliding shut. The apparition must have been some kind of projection, she decided. Immensely relieved at having an explanation, she leaned against the door and slid down to sit cross-legged on the floor.

Yet she couldn't shrug the incident off. The more she considered it, the more she thought she really might be pregnant. She hadn't had any outright morning sickness, and she tended not to notice minor changes in her body. But she'd had some queasiness lately. She got dizzy easier than she should. Her top fit tighter through the bust than it used to, even though the looseness of her pants testified to weight loss.

And if the apparition had been right about a pregnancy—something nobody knew, including herself—could it be right about the rest? Was she sure the dead couldn't visit her? Was she sure that wasn't Andy? Could her narrow-mindedness really be causing injury to other people?

Something cold clenched at her heart, and tears streamed down her face. Try as she might, she couldn't pull her mind from the confused pit of guilt and despair into which it had fallen. And her muddled brain couldn't call up even one of Doug's promises to steady her.

While she sat there, flailing in a bog of uncertainty, Raven slid under the door and, putting her front paws on Riana's knee, stretched up to peer into her face.

With a sniff, Riana half-heartedly stroked the little head. "Hi, sweetie."

Climbing onto her lap, Raven scaled her shoulder, curled herself around her neck, and nuzzled her ear. The gesture was comforting, but it also tickled and made Riana giggle softly.

"Are you trying to remind me that your very presence testifies to Doug's care?" She stroked the ferret's neck. "That is true, isn't it? And he's able to send you as his messenger because he created you—and everything else, for that matter. And as creator, he's the final authority on truth. So I can trust his word because he both knows what the absolute truth is and he never lies. Therefore, insofar as Doug has revealed truth in the *Manual*, I *can* be absolutely sure of it."

She paused as she reviewed her line of reasoning. "Stan's agents want me to doubt that one foundational principle because if they can get me to doubt Doug, they can get me to believe most anything. But if I rely on Doug—his truth and his grace—I don't have to be taken in by their tricks. I'm safe from their attacks as long as I trust him."

Plucking Raven from her shoulder, she held the little ferret up to look her in the eye. "You're pretty smart, you know that?"

Raven chuckled in agreement.

CHAPTER 36
BUCKING THE PLAN

*"I alone am God! ... Only I can tell you the future before
it even happens. Everything I plan will come to pass."*
Isaiah 46:9, 10, NLT.

4 January 8044 M.E.

Camille entered the Cabinet Room to find Stan already seated. He glanced up with a smile as she took her seat on his right. His mood had improved steadily since he'd reworked world opinion. Perhaps he had good reason. With the upswing in public opinion, their ranks had swollen as never before. Yet she could not be so optimistic. An unrelenting sense of hopelessness still plagued her, an increasing certainty that they would fail.

As she scanned the faces of the cabinet members, she reminded herself that they alone were reason for confidence. Creative, intelligent, and ruthless, these individuals were admired and feared by their underlings. Each was a recognized global expert in his or her field. Some were *polini*. They had helped Stan rally the exiles against Doúg, and they had helped him lead their intrepid band throughout history. If any group could overthrow Paradise Island's dictator, this was it.

Looking up from his agenda, Stan's sharp gaze swept the room. No other call to order was required. "Ladies and gentlemen," he said, "I want to thank you. For centuries you have partnered with us in this campaign against the Damours. You have proven to be worthy allies in a long and difficult fight. Dr. Desmon and I will not forget your loyalty. You will each be rewarded with exalted positions in our new government."

Enthusiastic murmurs embellished the room's already positive atmosphere.

Stan strode regally down one side of the conference table. "This august assembly has remained strong and unrelenting in the fight against tyranny. That fight is now coming to its conclusion." Stopping at the lectern, he faced his cabinet. "We have spent six millennia preparing for this day, my friends. And *we! will! win!*"

Applause interrupted him.

Extending his arms wide, he continued, "Moden Industries has been most useful in financing our cause. But it's time we free ourselves of the weighty duties associated with its administration. We won't need to finance a war effort after the Final Battle, and closing it will allow us to dedicate ourselves fully to the war. So we are selling off our business ventures before we trigger an economic collapse that will make liquidation impossible."

Camille laughed to herself. Translation: They needed to apply every available penny to the battle preparations. If they won the war, they could always establish another conglomerate. If they lost, neither the money nor the organization would be of any use to them. Yet her shrewd brother could rephrase any fact, even one with such stark implications, to his advantage. And the cabinet, responding exactly as he intended, accepted the news as another step toward victory.

"Now, as to the battle preparations," Stan continued. "You've probably heard that my speech at the United Nations was well received. They took precisely the actions we intended. Virtually every country is enacting laws to limit runners' activities. Most also committed troops to support global stabilization, and I was placed in command of the combined force. I will have no difficulty redirecting their focus once we've created the illusion that Damour has caused the world's economies to collapse."

The group broke into cheers, and rightly so. Camille had been present for Stan's speech at the UN—a truly spectacular performance. A naturally talented speaker with centuries of experience in the art of persuasion, he held the group so completely in his hand that not one pair of eyes wandered. Little wonder that the group did exactly as he desired.

"Thank you," Stan said, nodding. "Now I'd like to publically thank a couple of individuals whose work deserves special mention. Motioning to Adlai Menod, now the chair of the joint scientific staff, he said, "Dr. Menod, I'm very pleased with what you've accomplished in the short time since you assumed leadership of your division. That earthquake you engineered in Los Angeles is an excellent example. You scared the general populace right into our hands and then neatly redirected their fear into anger against Damour's followers. That is precisely our goal at this phase."

"Thank you, sir," Adlai replied with a satisfied smile.

Turning to Garrick, their minister of defense, Stan continued. "Dr. Sondem, I must congratulate you as well. The army's discipline and training continue at unprecedented levels despite its exponential growth."

"Thank you, sir," Garrick said.

"Tell me, are you still concerned about Conner's ability to head a rapidly expanding organization?"

In the manner that was uniquely his own, Garrick paused, thoughtfully leaned forward to rest his arms on the table, and answered in a low voice. "Conner is not as talented as"— he checked himself—"as his predecessor. It certainly requires more effort to oversee his work. However, he does relate to the other offspring and to the outlanders more effectively than any Paradisian could. Therefore, I believe we should hold our current course."

"Very well. Then let's consider some problems," Stan said. "Dr. Menod, I need you to watch those meteorologists closely. Destruction is fine, particularly if we can blame it on Damour. And I don't mind losing the old, very young, and infirm to the storms they engineer. But we need to preserve, alive and functional, as many outlanders of fighting age as possible."

"I understand, sir," Adlai said. "I'll keep a tight rein on them."

"And while I'm all for experimentation, that water business doesn't further any of our goals. So abandon those projects. No more red tide along the entire Pacific Rim. No more red sludge along the length of the Nile. Remember, our troops need water, too. So just leave it alone."

Adlai cleared his throat. "Begging your pardon, sir," he said carefully, "but those incidents weren't our doing."

An unnatural silence fell over the room, and Stan's gaze sharpened into a glare. "What did you say?"

Adlai had been Stan's favorite research assistant for centuries. He was highly educated and intelligent, motivated and conscientious; furthermore, his work ethic was unsurpassed. He even wore Stan's signet ring, proof positive that Stan trusted him. Nevertheless, Stan didn't appreciate being contradicted in public.

Submissively bowing his head and lowering his gaze, Adlai reiterated softly but firmly, "My sincerest apologies for not apprising you of this development beforehand, sir. I was only able to confirm my suspicions a few minutes before this meeting. However, I've reviewed all of our projects carefully, and I'm now certain that we did not trigger those outcomes, either purposely or inadvertently."

"Have you taken into account the loss of the Planetary Defenders' interference?"

"Yes, sir. But we still cannot explain those events by any natural law."

Stan glanced at Camille before voicing the question that silenced all others. "Then what, pray tell, caused them?" Everyone seemed to lean toward Adlai to catch his reply.

The imminent scientist dared to do what few others would in that situation: he spoke the truth. "I don't know, sir."

In the tense stillness that followed, a nameplate lit up—a request to enter the conversation.

"Yes, Marvin?" Stan said impatiently.

Their chair of interpretation, a small division that decoded Doúg's predictions, was one of the few cabinet members who had been selected because of his knowledge rather than for his leadership potential. He was, in fact, quite a timid man. Nevertheless, he said bravely, though not without a quaver, "Sir, I believe I can answer your question."

"Then, please," Stan said with exaggerated cordiality, "won't you enlighten us?"

Marvin wasn't stupid. He knew Stan was mocking him. He also knew that his appointment to the cabinet had only been at Camille's insistence, for Stan disliked Marvin and disparaged the contributions of his entire division. Perhaps it was understandable, given the scornful history between them, that Marvin should feel a tad nervous. But what he did next made everyone nervous: He reached into his jacket with his right hand.

The room burst into action. Garrick leapt to his feet and pulled his revolver from his shoulder holster. Others pushed away from the table. Some dove under it. Shouts of "Grab him!" or "Look out!" erupted. The two men sitting on either side of Marvin seized his arms. Stan lunged across the table to grab his right hand and yank it from his jacket.

When the group saw that the offending appendage held nothing but a white handkerchief, a collective sigh went through it. Twice before, this committee had watched someone reach into his coat to produce a pistol. The first occasion had been an attempt on Stan's life. The second time, one of their number who had become rather unstable had shot randomly at everyone in sight.

"Apologies!" Marvin exclaimed. He shakily lifted his other hand in an attitude of surrender. "Just after my handkerchief," he squeaked.

Garrick motioned with his gun, and Marvin opened his suit jacket to reveal no weaponry. With a grunt, Garrick holstered his gun and sat down. This nonverbal "All Clear" prompted the others to resume their positions at the table, though not without numerous dirty looks directed at Marvin.

When order had been restored, Marvin began again, his breaths coming in short huffs. "Sir, the last chapter of *The Runner's Manual* mentions several plagues to be rained upon the world in judgment."

"We're familiar with the reference," Camille said. "Remind us—of what do these plagues consist?"

"The first is an outbreak of painful sores," Marvin answered.

"*We* engineered the Turkey Terror epidemic," Stan growled.

"However," Adlai interjected, "we didn't engineer the variety that's spreading now. In fact, it's stumped our virologists. It's not a mutation you'd expect to occur naturally."

Stan grunted. After a moment's consideration, he asked Marvin, "What else?"

"In the second plague, the sea 'becomes as the blood of a dead man,' and the sea life dies. In the third, the rivers and springs of water turn to blood. These two could refer to the 'water business' you mentioned, sir."

Stan grunted, and Marvin looked to Camille for an interpretation. "Continue," she said.

"Yes, ma'am," Marvin said. "Then, in the fourth, the sun 'scorches men with great heat'—like the unprecedented heat wave now afflicting the southern hemisphere—'and they blaspheme the name of Doú—' " Marvin coughed before continuing, " 'the name of *him* who has power over these plagues—' "

At this mention of Doúg's power, Stan cut him off with a string of epithets that several other members seconded.

Marvin's small eyes darted around the table until they landed on Camille. "Should I continue?" he asked weakly.

"Yes," Camille said tightly.

"The fifth," he said hoarsely, "is darkness on the throne of the beast and his kingdom." He bit his lower lip. "I think that's you, sir."

"Of course it's me, you idiot!" Stan roared. "Enough!" He stalked back to his seat and fell into it. A tense silence filled the room.

Sometimes it was difficult for Camille to separate her own feelings from those of her linkmate. Such was the case with the present dejection that overtook her. She and Stan had believed that the forecasted plagues represented the disasters they themselves would release upon the world. To learn that Joshua was also precipitating disasters was most disheartening, for they would have to finish their preparations while dodging these extra challenges. And they could ill afford more complications.

Stan broke his sulk long enough to growl, "Marvin, you're to work with Dr. Menod. Help his team take Joshua's plans into account in forming their strategies."

Marvin sat up a little straighter. "Yes, sir, Dr. Moden."

Stan lifted an eyebrow at his new air of importance, but didn't raise any further objection. Instead, he resumed his brooding. With Stan abdicating his duty as the committee's chair, Camille searched her mind for some way of lifting the group's morose mood. However, she found herself too affected by it to receive any inspiration.

Thankfully, Garrick came to the rescue. Like Stan, he was a huge, muscular man who not only held godlike control over the military but commanded both respect and fear from these leaders as well. Rising to his feet, he immediately drew the room's attention.

"Friends, let's not be overly concerned about this," he said in his quiet baritone. "Damour's been throwing wrenches in our works for millennia. Little surprise that he should do it now. Yet we've always overcome these obstacles."

A few members voiced their agreement.

"And look at our current position," he continued. "We've recruited a force that dwarfs his in number. Our troops are outfitted with the very best equipment. Our weaponry is unsurpassed. Our stores are massive. We've maximized our strategic position, and we have the entire world behind us. Once we give the word, every outlander soldier on this planet will join ranks against him. Why, Damour's even handed us a page from his battle plan—now that we know how to rightly interpret those elusive prophecies."

Several nods and more concurring remarks emanated from various quarters.

"I won't deceive you, my friends," he continued. "This path is not guaranteed. It's possible that we will fail. But we will certainly fail if we allow Damour's posturing to discourage us. After centuries of tireless combat, will this heroic group now choose resignation?"

His dark gaze slowly circled the table, meeting each pair of eyes with his challenge. By now, almost every member was responding to his rallying call.

"My fellow countrymen, I vow to you today: *I* will not submit—not ever! If I die, it will only be after causing that dictator as much grief and ruin as I can! Who of you will join me in this pledge?"

Each member, to the person, stood and brought his fist to his chest in salute. Camille and Stan joined them.

"Moden Industries is stronger than any other organization on earth when we work *together*." As the old general invoked Stan and Camille's slogan, the siblings obligingly raised their clasped hands in a gesture of victory. "Damour will not bring us to our knees! Unlike our deluded compatriots on the island, we will never yield! We will only fight harder!"

With the group's zeal renewed, Garrick announced, "Today I have the privilege of offering you an example of Desmoden's superiority."

As the executives retook their seats, a soldier in desert fatigues appeared on screen. "Good day, Lieutenant," Garrick said. "Are you ready?"

"Yes, sir," the officer answered with a salute. He stepped back from the camera to signal some other soldiers. They led a bare-chested prisoner on screen and forced him into a kneeling position. The captive was a tall man with a strong build. The small oval transmitter on his chest identified him as one of Doúg's runners. However, because of the wounds disfiguring his face, Camille didn't immediately recognize him. When she did, she smiled at her brother, who winked back. He was rapidly regaining his former optimism.

"My friends," Stan said, "Please allow me to introduce Colonel Andrew Strider, son of Juan Misi and second-in-command of Damour's Outlander Division."

A round of spirited exclamations circulated through the Cabinet Room.

"Colonel Strider," Stan continued, "it is your honor to address my cabinet."

"I hope you'll forgive me if I don't share your enthusiasm," the prisoner said dryly, a swollen lip interfering somewhat with his speech.

"I can't say I'm surprised," Stan said. "You've been rather uncooperative throughout your stay."

"No reflection on your generous hospitality, I'm sure."

"Well, I am sorry that I can't be there to entertain you myself, Colonel. But I can see that my men have not been remiss in their duties toward you. That means we can bring this interview to a rapid conclusion. I merely need you to answer one question for me: Will you surrender that eyesore around your neck?"

"I will not betray my king," Strider said firmly, "nor surrender my method of communicating with him."

Stan rose to level a glare at him. "That's too bad. I always feel that children are best raised by two parents."

Strider's brow crinkled in confusion.

"You don't know?" Stan continued. "Why, you're to be a father, Colonel."

Strider's eyes widened. Camille had no idea whether the announcement was factual, but it had obviously hit a vulnerable spot. She chuckled to herself. Those Striders were so predictable.

"Yes, so let me offer my congratulations," Stan said. "Your wife is about eight weeks along, and the baby has a nice, strong heartbeat on ultrasound."

Strider said nothing. However, he clearly accepted the information as plausible.

"She's done the sensible thing," Stan continued. "She surrendered her transmitter and left that facility a few days ago."

Strider's eyes narrowed. "I don't believe you."

"That won't change the facts. But I thought you should know. The world has become quite dangerous for women and children. They aren't likely to do well on their own. So how much do you love your wife, Colonel? Will you leave her to fend for herself and a newborn, all alone?"

Strider's protective instincts were toying with his convictions, and the battle shone clearly in his battered features. But then he lifted his chin—a gesture Camille had seen often among the stubborn sons of Juan Misi. Firmly, he repeated, "I will not betray my king. I will not surrender my method of communicating with him."

"Very well," Stan said. "Lieutenant?" When the prison's ranking officer came back on camera, Stan said, "Take off his head. Right here. Right now." He leaned forward and broke into a grin. "With a saw." The cabinet members cheered and clapped one another on the back.

"Yes, sir," the lieutenant replied.

While the soldiers prepared for the beheading, Camille watched Strider. She loved that moment when a prisoner realized his life was about to end. That look of unalloyed terror thrilled her as nothing else could. But she was disappointed on this occasion. Strider appeared wary at the word "saw," but otherwise she perceived only serenity.

A soldier forced Strider's cheek down against a wooden block, and the lieutenant began to saw. At the first stroke, the screeching sound of metal on metal met Camille's ears. The lieutenant stopped, lifted the tool to check the blade, and began again. This time he ignored the unpleasant noise and continued sawing. After a minute or so, there was still no sign of blood on the prisoner's neck, although there was an increasingly broad smile on his impudent face.

The lieutenant again inspected the saw and, eyes widening, glanced at Stan. When he wordlessly held the blade up to the camera, a hush fell over the cabinet. The blade had been reduced to a series of blunted serrations, as though sawing something much harder than itself.

Camille's neck and shoulders prickled as if crawling with a thousand tiny spiders. It had been some time since she had seen such a clear demonstration of Deón power, and she did not care for it.

"Use an axe," Stan growled.

The soldiers obeyed. But when the lieutenant swung the axe, the tool clanged against some unseen barrier and rebounded so forcefully that it flew out of the executioner's grasp. The whirling handle whacked another soldier in the head, knocking him unconscious.

"Use a knife!" Stan ordered.

The lieutenant obeyed, but his hands were now visibly trembling as he drew a long blade from his boot. Furthermore, the other troops were giving the helpless prisoner an increasingly wide berth even though they were seasoned Paradisian soldiers who had proven their bravery in innumerable situations. Even Camille's hair stood on end, although she wasn't even on site.

The lieutenant drew the knife across Strider's neck, producing only a nasty scraping sound. He drew it across Strider's throat to the same effect. Finally he made a brutal jab directly at the prisoner's carotid artery, only to have the sturdy blade break.

Stan was beginning another string of curses when they suddenly lost the connection and the room went dark. Camille instinctively turned toward the windows, but, although it was merely ten o'clock in the morning, the blackness outside the building was as dense as that within. The eerie blue screens of cell phones began glowing, but the darkness devoured their feeble light as hungrily as a voracious beast.

Shocked by the dense, palpable blackness, Camille remained frozen in her chair for at least a full minute. In the murky gloom, her skin actually felt numb. She found herself biting her own tongue, just to elicit some sensation— some assurance of life. In vain she searched her mind for a scientific explanation. A power outage could not account for the simultaneous loss of natural light, and no eclipse would produce such complete, suffocating darkness. No, this blackout could not be explained by any natural law. And, as the faint susurration of her colleagues' whispered conversations worked its way into her consciousness, it became clear that they had arrived at the same conclusion. One word became increasingly decipherable among their quiet speculations: plague.

She groped frantically for Stan's hand and clung to him as if to driftwood in a stormy sea. "What is it?" she whispered, hoping desperately that her elder brother would have another answer.

Stan didn't respond. His silent acceptance of their companions' dreadful conclusion scared her further. Through the years, they had conjured up numerous scientific theories to explain the Deón's so-called miracles. There was something comforting in this pursuit, a kind of implicit promise that someday they would share those abilities when they understood the science behind them—an expectation that they, too, would someday become Deón.

But something deep within her screamed that the events their enemy had orchestrated on this day were simply inexplicable—that they were, in every definition of the word, supernatural. And that was an utterly terrifying thought.

CHAPTER 37

HAIL

*"Have you … seen the arsenal where hail is stored, which I have kept
ready for the day of calamity, for war and for the hour of battle?"*
Job 38:22, 23, REB.

The colony of fugitives on San Miguel Island had swollen to over a hundred runners. The desolate island—unfriendly to visitors, prone to harsh weather, and abandoned by the rangers—provided them with a safe retreat. However, it was less obliging when it came to other essentials like food and water. The daily challenge of meeting these needs kept the campers busy with tasks like catching fish and collecting edible cactus. Chris wasn't overly fond of either foodstuff, but it supplied their needs. Obtaining drinkable water was another issue altogether, since the island had no source of potable water. Consequently, the runners had assembled a makeshift desalinization plant. It was time-consuming and labor-intensive, and the awful tasting water ranged from hot to lukewarm; still, it kept them alive.

The whole community worked together to supply these basic needs, so everyone got a day off occasionally. Today was Chris's day off, and he had promised Cherie and Melanie that they would spend it at the beach. As they strolled toward Cuyler Harbor, the girls skipped along beside him, chattering excitedly about getting their *aparochi* all to themselves for the whole day.

They passed a relaxing morning swimming, building sandcastles, and lolling under the palm trees at the far end of the harbor. They were at the lolling stage when they noticed a boat approaching the island. This didn't alarm Chris; he figured it was bringing more runners to the island. When Cherie asked for the binoculars to watch it, he handed them over without a second thought. Lying back, he said, "Let me know when they start boarding the little boats to come ashore. We'll meet them and show them the way to the campground."

"Okay," Cherie said. Then, possessing a chatterbox tendency, she began a running report of every little thing she saw interspersed with her hopes that the new campers would have children to play with and that they had brought some peanut butter. Jam would be good too, but she was especially hungry for peanut butter.

Chris wasn't really paying attention to this commentary until he heard one word: soldiers.

Sitting up, he asked, "Did you say there are soldiers on board?"

"Ayeni abi, aparochi," she said cheerfully and started in about the peanut butter again. (Rarámuri: Yes, Grandfather)

"Pumpkin, give me the binoculars, please. I need to see what's happening."

After quickly scanning the horizon to assure that there was only one boat, he focused on the cutter anchored offshore. Cherie was right—there were soldiers aboard. And they wore the casual uniform of Stan's army. Willy stood at the bow.

Chris's mind raced. Was his nephew truly leading the enemy here in pursuit of his family? His mind balked at such an unthinkable conclusion. Yet even as he groped for a less sinister explanation, he remembered the *Manual's* prediction that family members would turn against one another.

The fugitives had heard about Willy's exploits on their radio. He'd become quite the people's hero—and quite the pal of the false Josh. The common people were increasingly turning to him, along with "Josh" and Stan, imploring them to impose some level of control on a world gone mad. Driven by growing fear, people were enacting new laws to concede more and more power to the trio. Even in staunchly democratic countries concern for safety had reduced personal liberty to a privilege earned by the few rather than a right for all.

Chris processed all this in an instant, and, just as quickly, he released any last hope that this new group's intention was peaceable. Furthermore, they were already boarding inflatable boats to transfer to shore, and they were boarding them fully armed.

He glanced around him. He must do something—but what? How could he protect the girls on this exposed beach? And what about all the other runners—over a hundred lives! The trail leading to camp tracked right along the beach in full view of the approaching soldiers. If Chris were alone, he might be able to sprint there fast enough to warn them; but even then, they could do little more than scatter on this shelter-less island. Besides, he wasn't alone. So, instead of reaching the campground in time to warn the others, he would just lead the soldiers straight to them.

The girls had picked up on Chris's concern, and both now stared at him wide-eyed. "What's wrong, *aparochi*? Cherie asked.

"It's Stan's men, pumpkin," he answered as calmly as he could. "We need to talk to Doug."

Activating his transmitter, he quickly apprised Doug of the situation and asked, "What should we do?"

"I'm on it," Doug said. In a lighter tone for the girls, he added, "Don't y'all be afraid now, pumpkins. Just sit still and watch me save you!"

✳ ✳ ✳ ✳ ✳

On the bow of Prince Joshua's Sentinel-class cutter, Willy scanned the shore with his binoculars. When he spotted some figures under the palm trees, he pointed them out. "Look—there's Uncle Chris and his granddaughters."

The prince aimed his binoculars in that direction. "Sure enough." Clapping him on the back, he added, "Good work, Willy."

Willy and Prince Joshua had really hit it off, almost as if they had an innate personal connection. Consequently, they spent a good deal of time together whenever the prince was in town. Yesterday they were having lunch in the prince's hotel suite when they learned that the fishing boat Willy's four uncles had purchased jointly was missing. As they pondered the significance, Willy remembered that his uncles often visited the Channel Islands, especially

San Miguel. The words were scarcely out of his mouth before Prince Joshua had arranged a look-see.

The trip had been eerie and unsettling—to say nothing of smelly—for they had passed innumerable belly-up fish. A very strange HAB, or harmful algal bloom, had spread around the Pacific Rim, killing fish and poisoning shellfish. Growing up in a beach town, Willy had seen red tides, but he had never even heard of one like this. It extended for miles into the ocean and had lasted for weeks with no sign of abating. It was just another demonstration of how badly the stubborn runners' transmitters were affecting global ecosystems. And that it should occur now, when hungry people critically needed the ocean's food supplies, was a particular tragedy.

Willy no longer had any qualms about giving up family members. He hadn't even felt guilty about betraying Andy, although he'd expected to. Instead, he'd felt satisfied—avenged. An implacable resolve had taken root within him as he watched his niece die; it grew into an all-consuming passion as he encouraged his mom in her struggle to recover from her injuries. In the end, his anger had been transformed into a radical, even militant, lust for peace.

Now he saw that his purpose in life was to rid society of these terrorists. His family was hurting. His nation was going berserk. His world was destroying itself. If a few people had to be imprisoned—or even sacrificed—to restore order for the many, it was a reasonable trade-off. And if those few fanatics happened to be members of his family, it only made them easier to find.

Willy, Prince Joshua, and the detachment of soldiers began transferring to smaller inflatable boats to navigate the shallow waters of Cuyler Harbor. As Willy stepped into a boat, he noticed something bizarre. "Hey, there's no red tide here."

Still on the cutter, Prince Joshua peered overboard. "You're right." He took the binoculars back to the stern and scoured the channel. When he returned, he reported, "There's a distinct line—no algal bloom in this harbor, but everywhere beyond is affected."

"Strange," Willy said. "I understood that it extended well beyond the Channel Islands."

"It does. I saw the demarcation from my plane as I flew into LA."

"Strange," Willy repeated. "But we'd better get moving. The wind's coming up. It looks pretty stormy all of sudden."

As the prince and his soldiers finished loading into the boats, something hit Willy on the arm. He picked up the object and handed it to the prince. "Look—hail! It never hails here!"

The storm intensified rapidly, the hailstones growing bigger than Willy's head. They'd hardly covered a few yards toward shore before two men had been knocked unconscious and another killed. As one of the sturdy inflatable boats burst under the downpour, Willy cried, "This is impossible!"

As impossible as that heat wave that killed thousands in the southern hemisphere last week? As impossible as that blackout along the entire eastern seaboard? The whole planet's out of balance!

"Retreat!" Prince Joshua ordered as he helped soldiers from the sinking craft onto theirs. The remaining vessels made for the cutter. When the last man stepped off the inflatable boats, the hail quit, just as suddenly as it had begun.

The prince scanned the horizon and frowned. "That was peculiar. But it seems to have abated now. Even the clouds are clearing. Let's move while we can."

But the group had no sooner boarded the inflatable boats than they were attacked by more hail. After losing two more boats and several troops, they returned to the cutter a second time. The storm let up once they had all embarked.

Sweeping the shoreline with his binoculars, Willy grew increasingly bewildered. Huge hailstones now floated all around them in the water. But the shore, and the water near shore, was as clear as it had been when he'd first spotted Uncle Chris.

"What's wrong?" Prince Joshua asked.

"Take a look, Your Highness," Willy said. "Do you see any hailstones on shore?"

Joshua scrutinized the scene, turned around to re-examine the very distinct line where the algal bloom ended, and then once again scanned the shore. When he put his binoculars down, his face had gone pale.

"Captain!" he yelled. "Get us out of here! Now!" He speed-dialed Dr. Moden, but Willy couldn't hear the conversation. The prince closeted himself in a cabin below deck for the entire journey back to Ventura Harbor.

❈ ❈ ❈ ❈ ❈

Cherie and Melanie broke into cheers as the cutter turned around and sped away from the island, and Chris's chest swelled with an expansive sense of gratitude.

"I will rejoice in you, Doug!" he exclaimed. "I will delight in your deliverance!"

The girls danced joyfully around the beach. "Thank you, Doug! *Gracias! Natérarabá!*"

Yet Chris's joy was tempered by concern for his beloved nephew, now so deeply involved in Stan's work. And if Willy had come all this way to lock his uncles away, what had he done about Andy and Riana, who lived right under his nose? Had he already betrayed them into Stan's hands? Yet Doug had just proven that he was capable of caring for his own. Chris would have to trust him to take care of them too.

"*Aparochi,* look!" Melanie tugged on his pant leg.

He bent down to accept a fist-sized piece of ice from her. "Where did you find this?"

"The water threw it," she said, and pointed toward their sandcastle. As he watched, the surf deposited more hailstones up and down the beach.

When Willy's landing party had broken into a confused frenzy, Chris had recognized that their assailant was hail—and that didn't particularly surprise him. Not that he'd ever seen hail out here, but he had seen Doug arrange some pretty spectacular rescues. However, as he now looked over the spent missiles, he *was* surprised—he hadn't realized how large the hailstones were. They were so big, in fact, that he had trouble hefting the larger ones.

For the first time, it occurred to him what those huge stones could have done to the campers. The windswept island offered no protection from the elements—it didn't even have shade trees. If this hail had fallen on the encampment, it would have caused untold injuries and deaths. So Doug's hailstorm had been a double miracle—its severity had scared off their attackers; its restricted distribution had protected the runners.

A smile spread over his face. Unbuttoning his shirt, he laid it on the sand and called, "Pumpkins, help me fill this up with ice. We have a wonderful new story about Doug's protection to tell the others."

With no electricity on the island, ice water—especially from fresh, non-desalinized water—would be a rare treat. More important, these stones were tangible evidence that Doug had not forgotten them. Cloistered away in this stark, lonely place, hunted and misunderstood by the rest of the world, living on little more than fish, sometimes the weary group had trouble keeping up their spirits. But, oh, how this account of Doug's loving intervention, complete with visual effects, would strengthen them!

CHAPTER 38

FAMINE

*"I will send a famine on the land, not a famine of bread, nor a thirst
for water, But of hearing the words of the Lord."*
Amos 8:11, NKJV.

Once the excitement died down, Willy realized he'd sustained several inju-ries during the hailstorm. Maybe the physical stress of these wounds taxed his body, or maybe it was the emotional stress of the whole frustrating affair. Whatever the cause, he awoke that night in intense pain. By morning, blistering sores had erupted around his injuries—lesions that Willy immediately recognized. He'd contracted what the lay people called Turkey Terror II.

He first called Dr. Moden, who grunted with obvious displeasure. "My scientists are working on an antiviral agent for that. I'll have one of my physicians fly out and begin your treatment. I need you back to full speed ASAP."

"If they're just developing the medicine, is it safe to use?" Willy asked.

"Safe?" Dr. Moden's tone smacked of amusement. "It's safer than not treating the illness."

Right. Because the mortality rate approached 100 percent.

"I guess that was a stupid question, wasn't it?"

"Yes," Dr. Moden said curtly. "Now, if you'll excuse me, I have a meeting."

Willy hung up feeling worse. He'd hoped for a little pity when he felt so rotten. Instead, the boss he'd worked with so closely just seemed annoyed. But then, commiseration wouldn't cure him; the antiviral might. And only Dr. Moden could provide that.

A few hours later, Dr. Maurice Pim, world-famous infectious disease specialist, the Modens' personal physician, and father of the surgeon who had helped Mom, arrived by private jet. By that time, Willy's fever had spiked to 104 degrees and the blisters had spread all over his body. Dr. Pim hospitalized him and began a series of shots with the experimental antiviral agent. Between the pain medicines and delirium, Willy remembered almost nothing from the next few days. But he survived, so Dr. Pim's magic potion must have worked.

When he returned to his right mind, Willy discovered that the news agen-cies had been following his case on an almost hourly basis. He'd become the face of the disease, the hero injured while battling the foe, and the brave research subject who gave hope to Turkey Terror patients everywhere. When he left the hospital, crowds swarmed the street outside the hospital. Paparazzi camped out on Uncle Chris's lawn. Campaigns for interning runners gained new momentum by adding "For Willy!" to their slogans. The popularity was wonderful—all he'd ever dreamed of. His life had become amazing.

Except for one small thing. Dr. Pim called it PHN—post-herpetic neural-gia. Willy called it RBP—really bad pain. The severe burning sensation affected the upper right portion of his face so that every little jostle, including walking, hurt like crazy. Every blink drove knife-like pain into his eye.

Dr. Pim put a patch on the eye and gave him medicine to blunt nerve pain. These measures helped some, but Willy still couldn't sleep without narcotic pain relievers. When he asked Dr. Pim how long the condition would last, he shrugged. "Oh, a few months—maybe years."

Willy returned to Uncle Chris's house with a whole collection of medicines. Yet they did little toward controlling his suffering. The constant pain destroyed his concentration and robbed him of useful ideas, thwarting his attempts to work. It interrupted his sleep, which came only in short bursts when medicated exhaustion overrode the pain. Dr. Moden got cranky about Willy's decreased output. Prince Joshua told him to buck up and be a man. The unrelenting agony, frustration, and exhaustion led Willy to despair. How could he possibly live with this pain, let alone be productive, if it lasted as long as Dr. Pim predicted?

Finally Willy cracked. About three o'clock one morning, he was lying awake, his tormented mind roiling. Although they'd managed to capture and imprison runners in droves, things were still deteriorating—even more natural disasters, even stranger calamities. Why were things getting worse when fewer of the old transmitters were around to cause problems? And why hadn't King Doug helped? Prince Joshua had promised his aid once the world's population demonstrated its allegiance by restraining their defiant countrymen.

Could they—just maybe—be operating under the wrong set of assump-tions? Might the stubborn runners be right after all? Andy had said Doug blessed those who lived by *The Runner's Manual.* If Willy checked off the right boxes on the right to-do list, would Doug alleviate this awful pain?

It was just the sort of nonsense that desperation gave birth to. Yet Willy *was* desperate, and this idea offered a flicker of hope. Throwing on the lights, he padded downstairs to the study and rifled through the bookshelves. There must be a copy of the *Manual* here somewhere. When his search proved fruitless, he methodically went through the other rooms. Still he found none.

What—do they take the silly things with them wherever they go?

Remembering that Uncle Chris sometimes listened to an online version, he booted up his uncle's computer and searched through the bookmarked web-sites. He easily found what he sought but merely got a message that the site was down. He tried a number of others; they were all down. And then he remem-bered—the runners who maintained those sites were probably in prison.

He muttered a curse and sat back to stare at the disobliging machine. Now what? The New-RABs had an edited version of the *Manual,* but Andy had said it didn't contain truth. Not that Willy cared about the truth, per se. He just wanted to relieve this agonizing pain. To accomplish that, he was prepared even to make the ridiculous changes Uncle Chris espoused. But those petty details were the parts edited out of the New-RAB version.

By now, morning had dawned, so Willy dressed and, grabbing Uncle Chris's keys to Andy's apartment and Stanley's house, made his way to his cous-ins' homes. He explored the looted residences thoroughly but found no copies of the book.

Next he tried the Paradisian embassy, but it lay wholly abandoned. A sign announced that its occupants had returned to their homeland. He couldn't even raise anyone in the Outlander Division's wing. "I'm too good at my job," he grumbled. "I must have wiped out the entire division."

His next stop: the public library. The librarian timidly reminded him that the volume he requested was banned and, therefore, had been removed from all libraries. But, she added quickly, she was certain Willy Moore had a good reason to consult one. So she searched every back room for a stray copy ... and came up empty.

As a last resort, Willy visited the RAB that Uncle Chris had attended. It lay deserted, vandalized, and looted. Willy climbed through a broken window and diligently searched every office and meeting room. He found nothing. Not one lousy copy.

Wholly defeated, he shambled out to the parking lot and slumped into his car. How ironic—he used to get sick of Uncle Chris's preaching from that book, yet now he couldn't find one volume in the whole city.

With a sigh, he rested his forehead gingerly on his palm. If he couldn't find a printed copy, how about a runner who could recite the pertinent points? But that was no good either. All of the city's runners were either in hiding or detention facilities. And, since he was the one who had imprisoned them, they weren't likely to help him.

With one possible exception: Andy. It was about a six-hour drive to that facility, and visitors weren't allowed, but Special Liaison Wilson Moore could probably get in. And his favorite cousin just might have mercy on him.

As Willy considered that option, a limousine pulled into the otherwise empty lot and parked beside him. The chauffeur came to Willy's window and informed him that Dr. Moden would like a word with him. Willy hadn't even known his boss was in town. As he climbed into the limo, his mind raced. How would he explain being here?

Dr. Moden was sipping some mineral water. He didn't offer Willy any. "Good day, Mr. Moore," he said somberly.

"Good day, sir."

"With so much yet to do, I expected you'd be at work. Failing to find you there, I assumed you'd be in a hospital. Or perhaps a grave. Imagine my surprise to learn that you've been touring the city. An outlawed RAB, a public library, the Paradisian Embassy, your cousins' homes. Prior to that, numerous attempts to access some illegal websites on your home computer."

Willy's skin crawled as his boss ticked off his private activities.

"What's the next stop on this tour, I wonder?" Dr. Moden continued. "A trip to see your cousin? Let me save you the trouble—both Colonel Strider and Lieutenant Strider are dead."

Willy caught his breath. But he'd have to process that news later. Dr. Moden continued as if it were of little consequence. "If I didn't know better, I'd say you've been searching for a certain outlawed tome."

Willy swallowed on a dry throat. "I wanted to ensure that all copies of *The Runner's Manual* had been removed from circulation, and that all websites where it might be accessed were unavailable."

He thought it was a decent fib, but Dr. Moden didn't believe him—he could see it in his eyes. Still, he didn't attack the assertion directly. "And this mission was so important that you couldn't delegate it to someone whose time is less valuable than your own?" Dr. Moden glanced pointedly at his expensive watch.

Willy consulted his own watch: almost five o'clock. He'd spent all day on his fruitless—and illegal—search. "Perhaps it wasn't a wise use of my time," he admitted.

"Perhaps not." Dr. Moden took a long drink from the heavy crystal glass, which had the effect of reminding Willy how little he'd had to drink today and how very thirsty he was. Still, he didn't dare request any.

"What did you find?" Dr. Moden asked.

Distracted by the water, Willy had momentarily lost track of the conversation. "Excuse me?"

"Your search, Mr. Moore. Did you satisfy yourself that the terrified populace is adequately protected from the dangers hidden in *The Runner's Manual*?"

Was he making fun of his fib? Willy wasn't sure, but he decided to accept the question at face value. "Yes," he answered seriously. "If there are any copies left, I can't find them."

Dr. Moden turned his head to pinion Willy's gaze with bright green eyes that were nonetheless dark and cold and threatening. "I want you to know that I would consider it a great personal loss if our estimable special liaison succumbed to the dreaded Turkey Terror II, Mr. Moore. We know so little about that virus— you should be careful that you don't suffer a—" His sinewy forearm tightened momentarily, and the heavy crystal shattered in his hand like a fragile piece of blown glass. "—a relapse."

An icicle seemed to slither down Willy's back.

"But perhaps there will be no need to overtax yourself with such 'missions' in the future."

"No, sir," Willy said breathlessly. "I'm sure there won't be."

Dr. Moden's eyes roamed over Willy's face, as if measuring his worth and comparing it to the inconvenience he'd caused. At last, he said, "Very well. You may go."

Willy quickly scrambled out of the limo and into his own car. But when he tried to start it, his hands were shaking so badly that he couldn't insert the key into the ignition. He had to sit there for some time after the limo left before he regained enough composure to drive home.

Then he took lots of pain medicine, collapsed into bed, and pretended the whole day had been a nightmare. Thus ended his foray into insanity.

CHAPTER 39

LOYALTY

"Your loyalty to me is like the morning mist,
like dew that vanishes early."
Hosea 6:4, REB.

27 January 8044 M.E.

Garrick's hushed tone, by itself, would not have soured Camille's stomach. Likewise, his secretive huddle with Conner would not generally have set her teeth on edge. These were common enough mannerisms for their cautious minister of defense. However, when the conversation abruptly stopped as she rounded the corner, and when guilt shadowed Conner's eyes, even as he flashed a friendly smile in her direction, the hairs on her neck prickled ominously. She'd developed a rather finely tuned radar for treachery. And "Treachery!" was precisely the cry her instincts raised now.

Garrick's equanimity never wavered. Gallantly sketching a respectful bow, he said smoothly, "Camille, we were just talking about you. Conner was trying to claim the organization's record in sharpshooting, but I set him straight."

Since Garrick was supremely practiced in deception, his ease did nothing to smooth Camille's hackles. And a misunderstanding about a centuries-old record certainly didn't explain Conner's awkward glance. Yet she responded with equal ease, "Yes, I've heard you're an excellent sniper, Conner. But what has raised the subject—some contest, perhaps? If so, I should like the opportunity to defend my title."

Conner's eyes slipped to his father, who responded, "I'm glad to hear it. No contest would be complete without you. We'll let you know when we get the details squared away."

Camille smiled as she stepped away from the pair, but the impression remained that she was being plotted against—and by the general she trusted as well as she trusted anyone. The encounter so disturbed her that she had difficulty returning to the work on her desk. After several unsuccessful attempts to finish the tasks awaiting her, she decided to distract herself by checking on Stan.

As she left her office, she passed the newly returned Saxon. "Welcome home," she greeted him.

Saxon bussed Camille's hand. "Thank you, Mom. It's good to be home—and to be myself again."

"I'm sure it is. Nevertheless, you did a remarkable job of playing Joshua. Yesterday's performance was particularly skillful. You did an excellent job of conveying Joshua's nonverbal indignation at his father's reaction to the supposed misunderstanding while simultaneously giving lip service as the good son upholding his father's mandate. Very well done indeed."

"I thank you, Mom. I hope the performance netted us the desired effect."

"When last I checked, everything was progressing well. I am just on my way down there again."

She proceeded down the hallway to the VIP elevator and selected the 42nd floor, home to their brokerage firm. Then, on impulse, she also hit the 43rd floor, where MD Bank was headquartered. When the elevator door opened there, a gush of noise flooded over her and she smiled in satisfaction. That was all she wanted to hear. If chaos reigned on that floor, then at least half of Stan's strategy had succeeded. The world, believing that Doug had called in all his loans, was searching for money from MD Bank. They wouldn't find it, of course, for the whole point was to destabilize governments. Nevertheless, the pandemonium testified to worldwide desperation.

When the doors opened on the 42nd floor, she smiled again, this time at the uncanny stillness. She passed into the large open area that, mere days before, had been cubicles bustling with traders. Now the only obstacles to her progress were bits of trash and stray pieces of broken furniture. Still, she stepped carefully, for such unoccupied areas were unlighted. The generators required for continuing business in the persistent darkness guzzled gasoline—and much-needed funds.

Only one of the offices on this floor remained lit, and it was to that office that she proceeded. She found Stan, their vice president of finance, and the president of the brokerage firm monitoring live feeds from every major stock exchange in the world. Camille inspected the screens and chuckled. In every single locale, the market had crashed.

She turned to her brother, whose face beamed with victory although he hadn't slept for two nights. Personally overseeing the most important economic maneuver in history was an arduous business, but the thrill of the contest energized him in its own mystical way during such challenges.

Grasping his hands, she kissed him on the cheek. "Congratulations, *zuulu*. I'm so very proud of you." She congratulated the other two executives as well. The trio was rightly pleased with their accomplishment. She even indulged their wish to regale her with the high points of how they had flooded the markets by selling all stocks in every portfolio managed by the agency while calling in every loan transferred to the counterfeit accounts established in Doúg's name. The result was a world of collapsing economies—whose citizens believed that Doúg had caused the fiasco. Not surprisingly, countless nations were joining with Desmoden in denouncing King Doúg. Most were also committing militarily to the "reinstated" war against Paradise Island.

"Perfect," Camille said as the president of the brokerage firm finished her account.

Stan's cell phone buzzed, and, when he glanced at it, Camille sensed a pang of anxiety. "I have to go," he said. With a troubled glance at Camille, he added, "Military strategy meeting."

She returned to the top floor with him, but he spoke little en route. When they parted outside the VIP elevator, she said, "Congratulations again, Stan. You have every right to be proud of your work."

He flashed only a half-hearted smile, as though the joy of his momentous success had already lost its luster.

✽ ✽ ✽ ✽ ✽

Camille stood at the corner window in her office, gazing at the place where the sun would be setting if the infernal darkness hadn't cheated her of that simple pleasure. For the first time in centuries, her desk was clear. Her work here was finished. Most of Desmon Tower was already deserted, its furniture liquidated, its occupants gone. Tomorrow she and Stan would join them in the Kalahari.

She found it irrationally difficult to leave this place. It would be her last view from the lofty perch of the award-winning building she had designed. If the unlikely happened and they won the Final Battle, she would stand at Stan's side as he ruled the world from Paradise Island—from Doúg's own throne. If they didn't … well, she wouldn't be viewing much of anything, would she?

Despite this morning's very great victory, that persistent sense of foreboding had settled over her again in the afternoon. And she could find no reprieve. For over sixty centuries they had prepared for this moment in history—but was it enough?

She sighed and moved to the nearby loveseat. As she settled into its cushions, her mind replayed her life. Those 8043 years seemed to have flown by, leaving so many things undone. She had always intended to run the Iditarod, to spend a year living underwater and exploring the ocean's depths, to live on the Space Station for a month …

So many things she had wanted to do "someday."

Yet it was not the unreached goals that troubled her. Nor the unrelenting premonition that their mission would fail and her life would end. No, all these were eclipsed by that one moment in the corridor this morning. With that single unguarded expression on Conner's face, all her fears of being alone had returned. That was the one thing she did *not* want to be; yet it was the one thing that all of her money, power, and status could not ensure against. What's more, being alone was so tiring. She was so very weary of being constantly watchful, of being unable to trust anyone.

No. No, that wasn't so. She could trust her brother. True, he had betrayed her once to save his own life. But that was thirty-five years ago, and he had even apologized for it since—the only time Stan Moden had apologized for anything. Furthermore, he had been a loyal and concerned, sometimes even doting, elder brother since then.

A gentle smile played at her lips. Yes, she could trust Stan. And that meant something, because Stan was the reason she'd left Paradise Island in the first place.

As though summoned by her thoughts, the latch of her office door released, and Stan made his way through the dim room to ease onto the loveseat beside her. "All ready?"

She hesitated. "My work here is done, but … no."

He laid an arm across her shoulders, drew her close, and kissed her temple. "It'll work out, *zali.* It'll all be fine."

She turned to study him. "Will it, *zuulu?*"

He searched her face—for what, she didn't know. "I suppose that depends on your definition of 'fine,' doesn't it?"

She nodded dully.

"I can't promise you a good outcome this time," he said, almost gently. "And you're too smart to believe me if I did. But I can promise that, if we go down, we'll go down *together*, fighting side by side."

She laid her head on his shoulder. "Perhaps that's all I've ever really wanted." It was certainly the best she could hope for now.

Sitting with him in the silence brought a vague comfort to Camille's troubled soul. For several minutes she was content to enjoy the brief respite. Then she realized that, absorbed as she'd been in her own reflections, she'd not bothered to tune in to Stan's mood. When she did, she learned that his apparent serenity was a façade. In truth, he was also quite unsettled.

Sitting up, she asked, "What brings you here, Stan?"

He stubbornly stared out the window rather than meeting her gaze. "The Sondems are waiting for you in my office."

A great, gaping, empty sensation opened in her chest as a suspicion—no, more than a suspicion, a grim certainty—settled upon her: Her brother had betrayed her. Again.

She had once promised herself that she would never give him the opportunity to wound her that way again; she would never renew her faith in him. But she had relaxed her guard and allowed herself to trust him anyway. And now she was vulnerable to the one anguish that had neither equal nor remedy.

When it became clear that he didn't intend to explain his statement further, she pressed him. "Stan, the military council takes its orders from you. Why would they be waiting for me?"

Still the stubborn refusal to meet her gaze. "I want you to know—this wasn't my idea."

She found it suddenly difficult to swallow. "What wasn't your idea?" she whispered.

"We tried all afternoon to find another option."

She didn't respond.

He glanced at her. "NT-213. You're our best marksman."

She leaned back into the sofa, her ancient bones heavy with a weariness that no rest could cure. "I see." She hesitated before asking softly, "And if I refuse?"

His sharp gaze found hers. In his trademark menacing tone, he said simply, "Don't."

CHAPTER 40

SHOOTER

*"The wicked bend their bows; they set their arrows against the
strings to shoot from the shadows at the upright in heart."
Psalm 11:2, NIV.*

"That's an excellent—" Stanley broke off when he spotted his youngest brother coming toward the tent that served as their command center. The ranking officers craned their necks in the direction that held Stanley's attention. When they caught sight of Jorge, they broke into excited chatter.

"Jorge!" Stanley exclaimed, even before his brother crossed the threshold. "Welcome to the Kalahari!"

"Thank you," Jorge said, and Stanley read the answer to all his questions in his brother's dejected expression. "I'm sorry to disappoint everyone," Jorge answered the others. "We couldn't retrieve them. Andy, Riana, and the rest are still imprisoned in that facility. But they're all alive."

Murmurs of mixed relief and disappointment went through the group.

Hiding his own disappointment, Stanley said, "If The Phantom couldn't pull it off, I dare say it can't be done." Motioning to Jorge's empty place at the table, he added, "Take a load off, *hermanito*. You can brief me on the details later."

Bringing them back to the question at hand, he said, "We were discussing the possibility of needing to repulse an early attack. With the chaotic political climates around the world, our troops are having difficulty getting here. So, whereas a large portion of Stan's massive army is already on site, less than half of our division has arrived. If the enemy launches an early attack, it could be catastrophic for us. Sheridan, what's your opinion—is a preemptive strike likely?"

Although he had no official position in Doug's army, Sheridan's place at the table was uncontested. He'd quickly earned the respect of officers and enlisted soldiers alike, having proven himself both knowledgeable and hard-working. He'd been of incalculable help in fine-tuning their battle plans, but he was just as willing to dig trenches.

Sheridan unhurriedly sat forward to lean his elbows onto the conference table. The gesture mimicked Garrick Sondem precisely, but Stanley had refrained from making the comparison. Any hangers-on from his earlier training might discourage the new runner. Besides, the quirk was quite effective, focusing the group's attention as if Viv fruit itself might issue from the speaker's lips.

"I think," he said without raising his voice, "it's unlikely they'll launch a preemptive strike as long as Stan's in charge. Highly unlikely."

"Why?" Jorge asked. "It seems like exactly the sort of thing he'd do."

"Ordinarily, yes. But there's a curious clause in the Declaration that's made him wary—"

"The one Josh calls the Cavalry clause," Stanley said to Jorge. "As in, 'Here comes the cavalry!' "

"That's it," Sheridan agreed with a laugh. "Essentially it says that if they attack before February twelfth, they release Prince Joshua from any restrictions in his use of weaponry."

"Wouldn't they expect that anyway?" Jorge persisted.

"They're not sure what to expect," Sheridan said. "The terms of battle are very specific, yet so broad that they don't restrict Stan at all. Chemical, biological, even nuclear weapons are allowed."

Jorge frowned. "What's left?"

A grim smile twisted Sheridan's lips. "That, my dear sir, is the million-dollar question. The fact that the 'limitations' don't limit Stan makes him wonder if the restriction is on Joshua's part."

"In other words," Stanley said, "he thinks Josh has some kind of devastating weapon he doesn't know about."

"Precisely," Sheridan said. "Camille's opinion—and Garrick agrees with her—is that Doug only included that clause to make them think he has something else up his sleeve. But Stan isn't so sure. And since his is the final word, their decision on preemptive strikes was a very firm 'no' when I left. However, they were considering other types of lesser assaults—raiding food or munitions, setting up minefields, maybe even some sniper attacks."

"So we should prepare for those," Stanley said. "But wouldn't your defection alter their strategy? After all, it's a huge liability to work against."

"Yes, but is it big enough to make Stan willing to risk facing a weapon of unknown type and capability? I doubt it. He considers Joshua's threat a very serious one. I can't say why, exactly—I'm guessing that he saw something, probably before the rebellion, that he doesn't want to divulge. Whatever it was, it has him spooked."

"Creation," came a firm bass from the doorway.

The group turned to see Gabriel, who had come for Jorge's debriefing. After the appropriate greetings, Sheridan questioned, "Creation?"

Gabriel's nod spoke absolute certainty. "Prince Joshua once invited Stan and me to tag along while he created a new world. It was—" He shook his head. "Well, words fail me. It was far beyond unimaginable. The raw power in Joshua's voice alone! The idea of opposing that awesome force would definitely have Stan 'spooked,' as you say."

Sheridan frowned. "He says the secret of creation, even of life itself, is merely a scientific discovery that needs to be unlocked. He says the Deón have unlocked it but keep it a secret to maintain their superior position."

"Yes," Gabriel said. "I know what he says. And it's possible he's talked himself into believing it. But, even if he has, he's still left with the unpleasant reality that the Deón have discovered this 'secret' and he hasn't. Whatever Stan may have become, he is certainly *not* daft. He well knows that if Joshua were to unleash that force in an offensive strike nothing could stand before him. You're right, Sheridan—my elder brother would have to be in a very tough spot indeed to risk seeing that power turned against him."

Before dismissing the group, Stanley appointed a subcommittee to develop contingencies for the unlikely event of an illegal attack. Then he directed, "This committee will reconvene at 0800 tomorrow. First thing on the agenda will be finding a secure location for a command center."

"What's wrong with this spot?" Jorge asked. "Don't the terms provide for the guaranteed safety of command centers and medical tents for both sides?"

"Yes," Stanley said. "But there's no 'cavalry clause' to discourage violation. So, while we won't fire on their command center, they'll consider ours a prime target—a chance to eradicate several leaders in one shot."

After dismissing the officers, Stanley stayed to answer some individual questions and to set up a meeting with Gabriel and Jorge. He noticed Sheridan hanging back, but he didn't approach him until the others left. Then Sheridan asked quietly, "General, are you aware of the danger to the medical tent?"

Stanley's gut knotted up. "Yes, I am." Another reminder of his foolishness in showing his parents that card.

"I see," Sheridan said. "Then you haven't figured out how to protect it and don't wish to worry your men."

"Can't hide a medical tent in some inaccessible spot in the cliffs," Stanley summarized as he gathered his notes. "Do you have any suggestions?"

"No. That's going to be a tough problem to solve." As they moved toward the tent door, Sheridan added, "If you're heading to dinner, I'll join you. Maybe we can brainstorm some ideas."

"Thanks, but I'm meeting Bethany. Tonight's our date night."

The brothers parted, and Stanley let his link-sense guide him out of camp and into the mountains at its eastern edge. Following a trail that wound up the cliffs, he came to a flat spot staked out with a blanket and picnic basket. He didn't see Bethany, but he sensed her near presence.

Although the aromas issuing from the basket coaxed a rumble from his empty stomach, what really grabbed his attention was the panoramic view. Their campground lay directly below, nestled close against the peaks. On his left, the rocky mountain range continued south another two miles before ending in a westward curve. Desmoden's army had settled in the shelter of that curve. A buffer zone—a large basin dotted by scattered bits of scrub and the occasional shepherd's tree—separated the two encampments. Sentinels under protective tarps stood guard at regular intervals along its borders. Beyond this, the red desert sand extended to the western horizon, providing a seemingly limitless battlefield for the coming warfare.

"A spectacular view," he mused aloud. His mind naturally returned to the problem of relocating their command center and then rejected this location as a possibility. The great vantage point would be of little value in an area so easily visible from the enemy's position.

Looking around for his wife, he called, "Mmm, lots of good food here. Looks like I get it all to myself, too."

Bethany's laughter seemingly came from within a cliff. She emerged from a naturally hidden passageway, wrapped her arms around his waist, and plied him with a kiss. "Will you share it with me if I promise not to eat too much?"

"With a little more of that kind of pressure, I might be convinced to share," he conceded. "But where'd you come from?"

"Oh, there's a great spot back here—sort of a cave with a view." She led him through a short passageway that ended at a large cave. An opening on the other side offered a comprehensive outlook of the area below, though shielded from view by overhanging rock. Stanley looked around in amazement as his mind methodically checked off every prerequisite. With a laugh, he said, "Well, now, I think you've stumbled on to the perfect spot for our command center."

When they returned to their picnic, they found Sheridan munching on a piece of corn. Stanley planted a fist on his hip, but grinned as he bellowed, "You haven't changed a bit since you were five! You're still getting into my stuff. And why are you following me?"

With an unrepentant grin, the thief said, "I was scouting the area for that command center we need and just happened upon a feast. And, of course, you should never bypass sources of food in the wilderness."

Bethany good-naturedly invited Sheridan to join them and, as they settled down to eat, he said, "I was thinking about that other problem."

"I'd rather not talk about it now." Stanley saw no reason to worry his wife with an unsolvable problem.

"But if my idea's to work, she'll need to be in on it," Sheridan insisted.

"In on what?" Bethany asked.

When Sheridan glanced at him, Stanley emphatically shook his head, but his impudent brother proceeded anyway: "The medical tent will be in danger because of you."

"Me?" Bethany asked. "Why?"

"Stan and Camille know you two are linked," Sheridan said. "So they know that eliminating you would affect Stanley's ability to think and strategize effectively."

Bethany's eyes widened. "But the wounded! The terms—"

"Are useless in this case," Sheridan said. "They'll do whatever they believe will give them the best advantage, and once the fighting begins, they can easily claim they hit the medical tent accidently."

Bethany reached for Stanley's hand, but not for reassurance. Instead, the sympathy in her eyes communicated that her concern was for him. "That's what you've been trying to hide from me, isn't it?"

"Apparently not doing a very good job of it," he noted with a snort. Looking down at their entwined fingers, he said, "It was a stupid mistake, letting our link slip when I delivered the Declaration."

"Stan and Camille are linked," Sheridan explained. "But they hide some of their link-related abilities and even pretend antagonism toward each other—at least, sometimes it's pretense. I didn't understand why until I ran across a reference in Garrick's files. When Camille was kidnapped centuries ago, the possibility of losing her drove Stan nearly mad—according to Garrick's account, at least. He felt that only his intervention kept Stan sane, Camille alive, and the organization intact. Since that incident, they hide their real feelings to discourage more kidnappings."

"Oh, those poor people," Bethany said sincerely.

Sheridan burst into laughter. "I'm telling you your life is in danger, and you feel sorry for them?"

"Well, I can imagine how difficult it would be."

"Yes, but more to the point, they can imagine how difficult it would be for Stanley. And they *will* use it against him if given the opportunity."

Stanley grumbled, "Well, now that you've so thoroughly spilled the beans—thank you very much—"

"Sure, no problem," Sheridan interjected.

"—what's your idea?" Stanley finished with a scowl.

"They won't make that strike unless they know the target's there," Sheridan said. "They could only reasonably claim an 'accidental' strike once."

"All right," Stanley conceded, "but how does that help? How do we conceal the only pregnant woman in camp? She's kind of hard to hide."

"Exactly. So we don't hide her. We keep her in plain sight, but as a short, bald guy with a potbelly."

Bethany giggled, but Stanley turned to critically examine her appearance. "It could work," he agreed. "How good are you at disguises?"

"Not bad," Sheridan said. "And Sadira's better. Between the two of us, we can make her into a convincing man, especially from a distance."

"They would note her disappearance, though," Stanley observed.

"Yes, they would," Sheridan agreed. "That's why you'll make a show of seeing her off tomorrow after the arrival of this new Dr. X. They'll think she was here only to set things up. They'll curse their missed opportunity, but they won't target the medical tent. There's no tactical reason to waste ammunition on disabled soldiers."

"What do you think, Beth?" Stanley asked.

"I think we should talk to Doug," she said. "But it sounds like a good plan to me." She turned to Sheridan. "Bald?"

He grinned. "And bearded."

"You're having way too much fun defacing my wife," Stanley said with a chuckle. Stroking her long hair, he added, "Just don't cut her hair, okay?"

"We won't cut it, just shave it," Sheridan said evenly. Stanley hoped he was kidding.

✲ ✲ ✲ ✲ ✲

They moved into their new, naturally concealed command center during the darkest hours of the moonless night. The next afternoon, Stanley was watching the camp below, the continuous tattoo of the enemy's target practice in the background. He was noting key landmarks when he noticed one of his officers fall to the ground. Picking up his radio, he called to the soldier nearest the afflicted man. "Private, Captain Klein just went down near the tanks. No enemies in sight, but approach with caution."

The soldier made his way to the downed officer and called for a medic. The two loaded the captain onto a stretcher and carried him to the medical tent. About a half hour later, Bethany called to report, "Stanley, I have an epidemic down here, but I have no idea what's causing it."

"An epidemic—like an infection?"

"It must be, but I've never seen one like it. The onset's very sudden, with no prodromal symptoms. The patients are paralyzed but don't lose consciousness. By the time I see them, they can't move or speak. Within the hour, they're unable to breathe. I've had to put them all on ventilators." She was describing the three officers, two men and a woman, when Stanley cut her off.

"Wait! Another man just fell outside the mess tent."

A team of medics transported the new victim to the medical tent. While Bethany evaluated him, Stanley called Sheridan to the command center. When he arrived, Stanley handed him a pair of binoculars. "Watch for people dropping."

He proceeded to fill him in on the new outbreak, but Sheridan interrupted with, "There—near the officers' quarters."

Stanley refocused to see a lieutenant grab at her thigh and fall. He radioed help to her and then turned back to Sheridan. But rather than watching the ground, he was searching the mountains on the southern border of Desmoden's camp.

Finally Sheridan lowered his binoculars and faced him with a grave expression. "I think I know what this is. Give me four of your stealthiest snipers, and we can stop the attack. In the meantime, I respectfully suggest that you order your officers to remain indoors."

Stanley motioned for his assistant to radio the orders. "So it's not an infection? What is it?"

"NT-213—the combined genius of Stan and Garrick. It's a neurotoxin that blocks the electrical impulses that signal muscle contraction."

"Causing paralysis," Stanley said with a nod. "Which muscles are involved?"

Sheridan rubbed the back of his neck. "All muscles, eventually. The onset's very rapid. It will affect respiration within the hour. The last thing affected is the heart."

"That fits Bethany's description. What about treatment?"

Sheridan sighed heavily. "There's no antidote. You can try buying time with ventilator support and a pacemaker. The body might eventually metabolize and clear it."

"Might," Stanley repeated woodenly, his mind clicking through the faces of the officers affected. Good men and women. Some had children. "You're sure there's no antidote?"

"None."

Stanley stared at his hands on the table. "Colonel," he said to his assistant. "Call my wife. Tell her that the patients' hearts will soon be affected. They'll need pacemakers." To Sheridan, he said, "Tell me what you know about it."

"It was still untested when I left." Sheridan spoke thoughtfully, as if trying to solve some puzzle. "It makes sense that they'd target officers and leaders. Their supply is limited, and it's difficult to manufacture." He shook his head. "But it's so unstable, dangerous even to handle. Frankly, I'm shocked that they're using it at all. Especially because there's only one person who could use it effectively from that distance." He paused and then continued with a shrug. "But maybe that's why they brought it out—they expected me to summarily dismiss the possibility that they'd employ it. I almost did, too."

"You're rambling," Stanley said. "You said you knew how to stop it."

"Yes, because I know who the sniper has to be—I found the nest."

"Sniper?" Stanley exclaimed. "But you were surveying the southern mountains—that's over two miles away."

"That's right. What's more, they hadn't been able to create a stable final product. So they have to dose the subject with two components that combine in vivo to form the final compound. In a normal, healthy adult that process occurs rapidly. But that was still the primary limitation to its use—it requires that two doses be delivered into a large, well-vascularized muscle."

"You're telling me they've got a sniper who can consistently deliver two shots back to back to the same location from that distance?"

"That's right—using different rifles, no less."

Stanley whistled. "That's some kind of marksmanship."

"That's how I know who the sniper is, because there's only one individual capable of pulling it off."

"So we take out that sniper, and we effectively destroy their ability to use the weapon. Good plan. Who is he?"

"Not he. She. It's Camille."

"Camille?" Stanley exclaimed. *Camille? I've never known Stan to risk her safety like that!*"

"You're right, he doesn't like placing her in harm's way—but he will do whatever's needed to realize his goal. It tells us something of his level of desperation, especially since just handling this substance to load it into the rifles is hazardous."

"Why would they use an unwieldy, untested agent of this sort? Simple sniper attacks would be more effective and less hazardous."

"Yes, but also more easily identified. What did you believe this to be before I suggested a sharpshooter?"

"Some type of infection."

"Exactly—and why would you suspect anything else? You recognized that it was limited to the officers, but you still would have merely looked for the source of the pathogen in an area frequented by officers."

Stanley nodded his understanding. "I see. They could theoretically immobilize all officers before we even realized it was a military strike, let alone took defensive action."

"That's right. Even I, knowing of the toxin's existence, couldn't convince myself that Stan would use it in its current form until I spied Camille's nest."

"Speaking of that, you seemed to have a specific plan."

Sheridan nodded. "If Stan's been convinced to put Camille out there, he won't rely on the distance alone to protect her. I counted three other snipers guarding her position. There might be one more; I can't fully assess the situation from this vantage point. We can neutralize the threat by approaching from the back of those mountains and getting close enough to take her *and* all guards out simultaneously. Otherwise, one or more will radio in the problem, and we'll have half their army on us before we can clear out."

"A quick, quiet, highly coordinated strike. Five shooters will have to get situated without being seen, take out their respective targets concurrently, and get out again before being detected."

"Exactly."

Stanley sat back in his chair, mulling over the idea. The precarious operation involved sending troops right into enemy territory, but he could see no other way of solving the problem. As it was, his officers couldn't step outside their tents without jeopardizing their lives. Still, he didn't want to take the risk without consulting Doug. Seeking a more private setting, he stepped outside the cave and discussed it with him.

When he returned, he addressed his assistant. "Colonel, get our four stealthiest special ops troops up here, starting with my brother."

CHAPTER 41
FALLEN

"My heart is in anguish within me;
the terrors of death have fallen on me."
Psalm 55:4, NIV.

"Attention all officers: Take cover within the nearest tent until further notice. Repeat: Stay inside. No exceptions."

The announcement awoke Jorge from a nap. Sitting up, he combed his hands through his hair and wondered vaguely what could have precipitated such an order. But between jet lag and lingering fatigue from his mission in Arizona, his brain was stuck on "foggy."

The reminder of that unsuccessful operation filled him with a fresh sense of failure. Gabriel's order to abandon the assignment had only compounded the self-doubt dogging him. How wrong he had been about Sheridan! How arrogant his mistrust! He had no more claim to Doug's grace than Sheridan; yet he had stubbornly clung to his self-righteous stand. Only after Sheridan's imprisonment in Stan's dungeon had Jorge released his pride and admitted that Sheridan "deserved" the title of runner too.

He buried his face in both hands, groaning with the sting of a new revelation: that's why Doug had saddled Riana with Sheridan's rescue. That mission, made especially dangerous by Sheridan's high rank, should have gone to the most experienced operative—to The Phantom. But Doug couldn't trust Jorge with the job. His proud, elitist attitude had made him unfit for it.

Is that why he'd failed to rescue Andy and the others in Arizona? He'd always known that he owed his unusual success to Doug's special help. Had he lost that because of his pride? Had he lost Doug's favor?

"Enough," he admonished himself. "You know the cure for this." Reaching for his *Manual*, he reviewed the passages that had often rescued him from the enemy's poisons. Doubt, shame, fear—Doug's pledges of faithful mercy and unchanging love robbed them all of their virulence.

He was feeling more clear-headed by the time his implanted radio pinged. "Captain Strider, report to the command center. Stay out of sight of the southern cliffs."

Jorge arrived to find Stanley and Sheridan bent over some detailed topographic maps. After three more special ops troops arrived, they briefed the team on the operation. Stanley assigned Jorge to the second most dangerous target, the fourth guard. If he existed, he lurked in an area nearer the enemy camp that would be particularly difficult to access. Sheridan was taking the most challenging target, the one that all of the guards would be focused on—Camille herself. Jorge tried to object to this, pointing out that Sheridan's knowledge of the enemy's strategies made him too valuable an asset to risk on such a dangerous mission, let alone on the most protected target.

Sheridan seemed unusually affected by the objection. When he swallowed hard, apparently at a loss for words, Jorge realized that, although his protest had been expressed as an objective concern, his tone revealed a more emotional component. The truth was, he'd grown to admire, even like, his former enemy. He'd rather risk his life on the most difficult target than see Sheridan in that position.

No one ventured to break the charged silence that fell between the two. At last Sheridan cleared his throat. "Thank you, Jorge. You have no idea how good it feels to have somebody care about me—not the soldier, but me. I've never had that before." He clumsily grabbed him in a bear hug. Because of the difference in their sizes, it felt to Jorge like an actual bear was hugging him.

"I share your concern," Stanley said. "But Sheridan's in the best position to take out Camille, to judge her position within the camouflage. The decision stands.

"There's no room for mistakes in this mission," he continued. "You'll be matching skills with Desmoden's best operatives. You must each act precisely in concert with your teammates. If you either anticipate or delay executing the order by even a second, it will likely trigger an overwhelming counterattack." Looking each soldier in the eye, he said, "If anyone wishes to be relieved, speak up now, and I'll find a replacement."

Not a sound broke the somber stillness that followed.

"Very well," Stanley said. "You each have my gratitude for your willingness. You're dismissed to work out the details. Captain Strider, Doug requested that you lead the team."

Relief filled Jorge at this distinct sign that all of his worst imaginings were indeed false. Doug had specifically asked for him. He had not lost his best friend's favor!

He quickly organized and deployed his team. As they left the cave, Sheridan suddenly turned back. "General, do you have a visual on Stan?"

Stanley aimed his binoculars toward the enemy's command center. "Yes, I do. Why?"

"That link thing—"

"Oh, that's right. Does Stan sense Camille's pain?"

"Yes. You should be able to tell if we get her by his reaction."

❊ ❊ ❊ ❊ ❊

Stanley schooled his features into expressionless lines as he watched the team leave the command center. It required every shred of his self-control not to call them back, for he knew he was sending his best troops, as well as his two remaining brothers, into the lion's very den. Already short of troops and officers—and brothers—he couldn't help but second-guess the decision.

He had once expected to grow accustomed to such responsibilities, for Stan and Garrick had never seemed burdened by them. But he now knew that conclusion was erroneous. Making these life-and-death decisions would never—should never—become routine. Still, the weight of his duties sometimes overwhelmed him. Just now, it threatened to suffocate him. Yet he couldn't indulge such feelings. The team needed a cool head to watch the enemy camp, evaluate any menacing activity, and decide if the mission should be aborted.

He determinedly directed his binoculars at the enemy. They had been involved in target practice all day, probably to cover the sound of Camille's shots. But he saw no other significant activity. After minutely observing the area for what seemed like forever, he glanced at his watch and sighed—only three minutes had passed since the team left. At this rate he'd be a wreck before they even got into position.

He suddenly became aware of Bethany's nearness and turned to see her entering the cave. Despite his glum spirits, the sight of her in her bald-bearded-potbellied disguise coaxed a chuckle from him. And, apart from the humorous disguise, he also felt a measure of relief; he knew without asking that his need had summoned her.

Rising, he handed his binoculars to his assistant, who needed no further instruction to understand his duty. "I'll be monitoring their frequency," Stanley said as he proceeded outside. He followed Bethany to a rocky seat that, though not far from the cave's entrance, was tucked behind prominences that made it invisible from the enemy's vantage point.

"How are the NT-213 patients?" he asked.

"Stable on ventilators. The pacemakers are functioning well. I'm less concerned about them than I am about you."

He rubbed his face. "I just sent Jorge, Sheridan, and three other good people into hell itself."

"And it was the right decision."

"Yes, it was." Despite the heaviness in his heart, he knew it to be true. And Doug had agreed.

She smiled sympathetically and opened the *Manual* she had brought with her. Then she began flipping through it, reading passages from here and there that flowed together into one beautiful, uplifting message that precisely addressed his concerns. Her lifelong love of the *Manual* allowed her to use it with such facility, and the link helped her direct these readings to the exact trouble plaguing him.

Leaning back against the rocks, he closed his eyes and allowed Doug's message to enter his soul. The healing words soothed his troubled spirit and fortified his lagging strength. She had often ministered to him in this way, but he had never found the language to aptly express how effective the unique therapy was. Or how grateful he was for it.

Today, enjoying the encounter in such close proximity to Stan and Camille, he also wondered anew at how much they had given up. Having lived as linkmates for two thousand years in Paradise, they must have known and appreciated this intimacy. Yet security would demand that they forego it after their rebellion, for they couldn't risk being so vulnerable, even with each other. How much *kanuf* had cost them!

By the time the first team member signaled her readiness, Bethany's reading had wonderfully calmed Stanley's turmoil. Leaning forward to kiss her on the head, he said, "Thank you, *mi corazón*. You've been of inestimable help."

Shortly after he resumed his position in the command center, a second team member whispered, "Delta green."

"Echo in position," Sheridan said just before the fourth member whispered, "Charlie green" and Jorge reported, "Affirmative on fourth Tango. Alpha green."

Stanley trained his binoculars on Desmoden's command center, where Stan and Garrick were calmly conversing outside the tent. All five team members were in position; four were ready to fire. Together with the team, Stanley waited in tense silence for Sheridan to set up his shot and Jorge to give the order to proceed.

Neither signal had come when Stan and Garrick suddenly spun toward the southern cliffs, and Garrick signaled a contingent of soldiers up the mountain.

"Execute!" Jorge instructed just as Stanley ordered, "Retreat!"

Clapping a hand to his neck, a visibly agitated Stan directed medics to Camille's position. *We got her,* Stanley deduced. He redirected his binoculars to the mountainside, where enemy forces swarmed up the cliffs. The three visible guards had fallen. Yet Jorge hadn't acknowledged Stanley's order. What's more, Sheridan was not only easily visible, but was sprinting toward the enemy's advancing troops.

"Retreat!" Stanley ordered. "Team leader, respond."

No answer.

"Alpha, respond!" he repeated.

"Unable," came Sheridan's winded response. "Alpha down."

✲ ✲ ✲ ✲ ✲

Jorge was still waiting for Sheridan to deduce Camille's position and work out the trajectory of his shot when he heard the blast of a teammate's rifle. He didn't know who had anticipated the order. He didn't know why. But the early shot would endanger them all.

This left him with two options. Either he could order the attack now, forcing Sheridan to take his best guess at Camille's position, or he could order an immediate retreat.

"Execute!" he ordered.

His teammates' gunshots rang out at the same moment that Jorge also dropped his mark. A split second later, something hit his skull. Lights exploded in his head. He flew forward, but blacked out before he met the ground.

He regained consciousness briefly when something pawed at him. He cracked open an eye to see a dark, hazy world. And what looked like a bear.

The bear lifted him. Clutched him to its chest with crushing force.

Jorge tried to resist. His body wouldn't respond. And then all again went black.

Chapter 42
Injured

" 'This is what the Lord says: "Your wound is incurable, your injury beyond healing." ' "
Jeremiah 30:12, NIV.

31 January 8044 M.E.

"Camille, don't you dare check out! Let me help you!"

Stan? Where is he? He sounds so distant.

"He needs quiet for this." Garrick's voice, even farther away. "Everyone out. Pim, you too."

"But I need to—"

"Out!"

So dark—can't see them. And why is everyone speaking Sumerian?

Camille felt pressure against her left cheek. "Kami, don't leave." Stan's voice, now laced with pleading. She tried to move toward it. Her legs wouldn't budge.

"Focus on your left hand. Let me help you, *zali*. Together, we can get through this."

Through what? And where's my hand? I can't feel it.

"Do you hear me, *Kamíl?*" He broke off to swear vehemently. "Don't you dare bail on me!"

Where does he think I'm going?

"I can help you!" he exclaimed with another curse. "Just take some of my energy!"

Oh—he's trying to transfuse me.

The idea of concentrating for an energy transfer, even one in her favor, sounded simply exhausting. Yet Stan was clearly angry—desperately angry. Or perhaps angrily desperate. Either way, resisting him would require more strength than complying. So, since she still couldn't feel her hand, she addressed her thoughts toward the pressure against her cheek.

She felt none of the tingling that usually went with an energy transfer. Nevertheless, he exclaimed, "Yes! Now keep it up."

She directed all her attention to her cheek. But it was so hard …

✲✲✲✲✲

Some groaning invaded Camille's consciousness.

"Stop!" Garrick shouted and spit out a curse. "What do you think you're doing, Pim? Are you *trying* to kill her?"

"Can't you hear her moaning?" Maurice retorted.

"Look at her blood pressure, you idiot! You can't give morphine to some-one with those numbers."

Who are they talking about?

"I hate to admit it, but he's right, Stan," Maurice said.

"Then let me try." It was Stan's voice, still far away. When she tried to move toward it, fire instantly flared up in her neck.

"Everyone out." Garrick's voice. "Give the man room to work."

Something prickly pressed into her left cheek. "Camille, concentrate on me," Stan said. "I can help with the pain."

She could feel him holding her left hand now, so she focused on that. Her hand began to tingle, and the fire in her neck receded somewhat.

"Excellent. Keep it up."

He sounded closer now, near her left ear. Then, all in a rush, she realized that she was lying on a gurney, that she was the patient they'd been discussing. She struggled toward them until her eyes fluttered open. She lay toward the back of the command center. Garrick stood at the open door, facing a dim sky. Stan sat on her left, his cheek against hers, grasping her hand.

"You need a shave," she whispered.

He sat up, looking truly exhausted. "It's about time you rejoined us." His stern voice didn't convey the immense relief she sensed.

"She's awake?" Garrick approached and clapped Stan on the back. "Good work, old friend. And good to have you back, Camille. I'll get Pim."

As Garrick left, Camille whispered, "What happened?" She didn't seem to have a more substantial voice.

"They shot you twice," Stan said, "shoulder and neck. Your spine's okay, but you bled profusely. I've lost track of how many units Maurice has given you." He nodded toward a bag of blood dripping into her IV.

"Who shot me?"

"Sheridan in company with several others. All of your guards were downed almost simultaneously. We shot two of the invaders, including Sheridan. He carried out someone who we think was fatally wounded."

Suddenly realizing the surprising truth, she cried, "You've been worried!"

Lifting an eyebrow, he said sharply, "If I was, I had good reason." He glanced behind him before continuing in a softer tone, "Maurice said you should have died, *zali*. At one point, he thought you were gone for good."

"Awake?" Maurice exclaimed as he followed Garrick in. "Stan, I really wish you two could bottle that transaction. It's truly miraculous." He came to Camille's side, put his stethoscope to her chest, and checked her bandages. "Truly miraculous," he repeated. "How are you feeling?"

"Neck hurts," she whispered.

He nodded and looked up at her monitors. "I think I can safely give you something for that. And Stan, you need to get some rest. You look almost as bad as she does."

"I'll stay," Stan said. "In case she needs more."

"I'll have a cot brought in," Garrick added quickly and motioned to an aide.

"But his tent's just—" Maurice looked from Garrick to Stan with a puz-zled expression. "Why doesn't somebody tell me what's going on here? Why can't

I simply treat her in the medical tent?"

"I told you why," Garrick said. "It's not my fault you're too stupid to understand that it's easier for you to practice medicine here than for us to run a war from the medical tent."

Maurice snorted. "A lot you know about practicing medicine."

Garrick stepped up to him, his 6'3" frame towering over the 5'8" Maurice. "Have you forgotten that I out-ranked and out-scored you in medical school?"

"Yeah? And how much help was all your so-called medical experience—if you can call torturing people medical experience—when it came to saving Camille's life?"

"As though you brought her back?" Garrick snarled. "It was only Stan's link that saved her."

"That's not fair—"

The increasingly heated exchange culminated with Garrick grabbing a fistful of Maurice's shirt and lifting him off the floor. "I'm warning you, Pim. As far as I'm concerned, you're expendable. And I'm getting tired of your whining."

Stan put a hand on Garrick's shoulder, and Garrick dropped the doctor, who quickly scrambled away from him. "I'm just saying that Stan's health is at least as important as Camille's," Maurice exclaimed. "And he'd sleep better in his own tent."

"I want him here where he's handy," Garrick growled.

Maurice shook his head and muttered, "Whatever." He strode out the door in a huff.

"Thank you, old friend," Stan murmured.

That's when Camille understood the basis of the argument. Ever since her kidnapping centuries before, she and Stan had presented a discrete charade to the world. They acted cordial toward one another (even when they weren't) to convince their employees they were united. On the other hand, they couldn't reveal that they actually needed one another (even when they did) or they might encourage another kidnapping.

The precise steps to this dance could get complicated. In a critical situation, the possibility of a misstep multiplied significantly, but her unconscious state would have elicited an intense protectiveness from her linkmate. Someone unfamiliar with the link might confuse this with love, although it really represented the kind of utilitarian defensiveness that compelled a lioness to protect its kill from vultures. To prevent such misunderstandings, Garrick—the only other person who understood the dance—had invented reasons to keep her here, where he could guarantee the siblings' privacy. Nevertheless, his insistence had further strained his relationship with Maurice, with whom he'd never gotten on well.

In a low voice that was barely above a whisper, Garrick replied, "Get some sleep and get yourself together, Stan. You've been of precious little help since the shooting. I expect better of you today, starting with a strong rallying speech at this morning's meeting. Otherwise, we're going to lose every last outlander in this army and half the offspring besides." Glancing at his watch, he added, "That gives you three hours."

Stan responded with a nod and a dispirited "All right." The tame response to Garrick's rather disrespectful address worried Camille.

The aide set up a cot and Stan collapsed onto it without even taking off his boots. He immediately fell sound asleep.

Coming to Camille's bed, Garrick said, "I'm glad you're back with us. I'll call Madelyn in now. Her experience as a nurse and Patric's as a medic have been very useful. They've been trading off as your private nurse."

"Excellent thinking," she said. After working so closely with the siblings for centuries, Patric and Madelyn already knew many of their secrets. "But Garrick, tell me honestly—how are things going?"

He eyed her for a moment before leaning down to whisper in her ear. "We tried to keep the news of your injuries from the troops, but it got out anyway. A bit of a panic ensued, including a rash of deserters. And Stan's been too—" He glanced down. "He hasn't left your side."

"Garrick, if I was critically injured, Stan could no more leave me than he could abandon an injured part of his own body. I experienced the same thing during the war when he was injured. That's one of the many bothersome aspects of this accursed link."

"Hmpf." Garrick's tone conveyed something between displeasure and disapproval. "I think he also overestimated how much of his own energy he could give you."

"Then I won't accept any more. And I'll talk to him. He'll be fine—you'll see."

* * * * *

When Stan awoke, still looking quite tired, he came to Camille's bed and ordered Madelyn to give them some privacy. This prompted a grumpy, sleep-deprived Garrick to object, "I hope you're not planning any more energy transfers, Stan. You still look pretty bad yourself."

"I wasn't aware that I needed your permission," her brother snapped. Camille found his irritable response encouraging.

"You know I'm right," Garrick pressed.

Stan took a step toward him and Camille reached out to catch Stan's hand. When they were both cranky, it wasn't uncommon for them to carry a disagreement to fisticuffs. "Garrick," Camille whispered, for she still had no voice, "would you give us a minute?"

Garrick yielded to her request, and Stan leaned over her bed. "How are you doing? And remember, I know when you're lying."

"I'm well, Stan. The pain's not too severe with the medication. I slept well and feel much stronger now. I don't need any more transfusions from you. Truly."

He studied her for a long moment and then nodded.

"And how are you?" she asked.

He smiled slightly. "Much better now that you're well enough to scold me."

She squeezed his hand. "*Zuulu,* you once promised that I'd never be sorry if I left the island with you. I want you to know that I'm not. I don't know if we'll win this. But if we do, it will be because of *your* relentless hatred of Damour, *your* untiring drive, and *your* superb leadership. I admire you more than anyone I've ever known. If I could go back and do everything again, I would still follow you through it all."

It was obviously what he needed to hear. "Thank you, Kami." He leaned down to kiss her on the forehead. When he stood up again, the spark had returned to his eyes. "I have a speech to deliver," he said with renewed resolve. "I'll be back as soon as I can."

He turned to go, but then retraced his steps. Pulling a pistol from his boot, he slid it under her pillow with a grunt that, for her, fully explained the action. Though conscious, she was still highly vulnerable; the link simply wouldn't allow him to leave her unprotected. And the firearm wasn't enough to mollify his anxiety. As he exited the tent, he called to the ranking Presidential Guard and added another four guards to the six already surrounding the command center.

Garrick reentered the tent looking flummoxed. "What did you do? You didn't give *him* any energy, did you?"

"No, but I would have if I could. We both know that our fate depends on his ability to motivate this army right now."

"Good point," Garrick said. Turning to follow Stan out, he added, "I'll let you know how he does."

Camille couldn't hear Stan's speech from her bed, but when Garrick followed him into the tent afterwards, he flashed Camille a broad smile and two thumbs up.

What neither Stan nor Garrick could see, however, were the expressions of the two offspring that followed them into the tent. Saxon and Conner both looked quite unhappy. And Camille could think of only one reason why that would be so.

CHAPTER 43
BETRAYED

"Woe to you, betrayer, you who have not been betrayed!
When you stop destroying, you will be destroyed;
when you stop betraying, you will be betrayed."
Isaiah, 33:1, NIV.

31 January 8044 M.E.

J ust as Stan had never made a secret of his preference for Sadira, Camille had made no secret of her preference for Saxon. She had always allowed him liberties denied to the other offspring, including the unique privilege of calling her "Mom." And her preference for keeping him as her trainee probably had much to do with Stan's passing him over for the company's president.

Nevertheless, she didn't love Saxon; she simply preferred his more sedate temperament. She also didn't necessarily trust him; she understood, better than most, how much could be hidden under a calm exterior. And so, as Camille watched the interactions during the strategy meeting, she could do so quite objectively.

What she saw concerned her deeply, and she knew she must warn Stan immediately. She called out to him as soon as the meeting ended, but between her weak voice and the commotion in the tent, her bid for his attention was lost. Absorbed in an animated discussion of the morning's victory, he exited the tent with the two offspring.

Camille quickly considered her options. Should she trust Garrick? Or might he be part of the plot? She wouldn't ordinarily expect him to turn on them, for their current arrangement granted him exactly the position he preferred. Furthermore, his high regard for Stan's abilities was sincere. But he might betray them if he no longer believed Stan was best suited to lead them—an opinion he seemed to be flirting with this morning.

Still, she truly had very few options in her current condition. She would have to trust Garrick … or, at least, trust in her ability to read him.

After first sliding her left hand under the pillow to grasp Stan's pistol, she summoned Garrick. "I'm concerned about a coup d'état," she whispered.

His pupils dilated, and she saw the flash of surprised indignation she had hoped to see. He grabbed a chair, turned it so he could watch the door, and sat down close to her bed. "What have you seen?" he said in a low voice. "Who?"

"Saxon and Conner."

Surprise again sparked in his eyes, though anger swiftly replaced it.

Reassured of her general's loyalty, she removed her hand from under her pillow. "After Stan's pep talk, both of them appeared unhappy, even though you, Stan, and Errol seemed pleased."

"Yes, the troops rallied well, which would not be encouraging to anyone planning a coup."

"As you were consulting, they often exchanged looks and nods—subtle and inappropriate to the discussion—as if they were carrying on their own non-verbal conversation apart from yours. In addition—"

She gasped as a sudden wave of terror pulsed through her. She jerked upright, but immediately became light-headed and collapsed back onto the bed.

"Madelyn!" Garrick bellowed. From their long acquaintance, he knew that little could elicit such a melodramatic response from her. So, as he adjusted her IV, he guessed, "Stan?"

She clutched Garrick's arm as another wave of terror swept through her. "He's in life-threatening danger."

Madelyn ran into the tent, and Garrick paused to enumerate some medical orders before asking Camille, "Where is he?"

"The mountains." Camille nodded to her left, and Garrick rushed out of the tent.

When another wave of urgency shot through her, she instinctively tried to sit up. "I have to go find—" Again she swooned.

"Get Dr. Pim!" Madelyn called to one of the Presidential Guards. Pressing gauze to Camille's neck, she said, "Dr. Desmon, you must remain quiet. Your last blood count was extremely low, and now you're bleeding again. You can't even sit up, ma'am, let alone go anywhere."

Responding to Garrick's shouted orders, two Presidential Guards entered and stood at either side of her bed. One of them was Errol, Garrick's trusted brother and the commander of the Presidential Guard. Garrick returned looking no less troubled, but talking calmly into his radio. He held a finger to his lips when Camille started to speak. "General Conner Sondem," he said into his radio, "report to the command center immediately."

"Commander," came Conner's hesitant reply. "Request permission to delay that order—fifteen to thirty minutes, sir."

Garrick's jaw clenched, but his voice remained calm. "Negative, General. Your input is required urgently."

During the ensuing pause, Garrick's hard stare shifted between Camille and Errol. She knew he was thinking the same thing she was: the planned attack was imminent, probably within the hour.

"Copy that, Commander," came Conner's reply at last. "On my way."

Garrick visibly relaxed and signed off. "They're not quite ready. And Saxon's a smart kid. He won't attack without his military leader."

When Camille nodded in agreement, Maurice groused, "Hold still." He had come in during Garrick's radio call and was working at Camille's neck.

"Apologies, Maurice," Camille said.

He grunted. "What's going on?"

"A coup attempt." Camille watched Maurice's eyes closely as she spoke. Saxon and Conner were indeed intelligent boys. They wouldn't attempt to overthrow a leader as deeply entrenched as Stan without backing among the parent generation. One or more of the exiled Paradisians close to Stan and Camille must be intimately involved in the uprising.

"A coup?" Maurice's hands jerked slightly. "Now? Lousy timing." But the surprise in his voice was not reflected in his eyes, and Camille had her answer. When he followed up by glancing at Madelyn, Camille recalled the secretary's inappropriate gloating when Sheridan had gone public. She also remembered that Stan had once arranged to marry Madelyn and then reneged on his proposal to marry Camille instead. Although this involved no love or jealousy in the usual sense, Madelyn had been extremely displeased at having such a lofty and lucrative position torn from her grasp, especially since she had already boasted of it to her friends. Camille had warned Stan at the time that she might retaliate.

Thankfully, Stan had taken Camille's warning to heart. Madelyn no longer had the free access to confidential information that she'd once had. However, she still possessed a significant amount of sensitive intelligence. In fact, Saxon's luring her to his side might have been the deciding factor for his proposed uprising. Or, perhaps more likely—maybe she had envisioned the coup, flattering herself into Saxon's confidence and manipulating him to carry out her revenge.

Striding into the tent, Conner asked, "Yes, Father?"

"Where's Dr. Moden?" Garrick asked. "Didn't he leave with you?"

"He did, sir, but then he went to the mess tent."

Garrick glanced at Camille, who shook her head and pointed to her left. The mess tent was north of the command center—to her right—rather than in the southern direction of the "tug" that informed her of Stan's location.

When Garrick glanced beyond Conner to Camille, the boy looked over his shoulder at her, following his father's gaze. The old general took advantage of Conner's momentary inattention to coldcock him on the jaw. He followed this with an immediate blow to the gut that left Conner on the ground gasping for air.

Maurice and Madelyn stiffened and exchanged glances before returning their attention to the wound. If Camille had any remaining doubts, they were dispelled when Errol, apparently catching the same signals she had, nonchalantly took a couple of steps back and gradually adjusted his rifle to aim it at them. Likewise Camille, having slipped Stan's pistol under the sheet, trained it on Madelyn, the more dangerous of the two. But with no real evidence with which to confront the pair, she would only defend herself if necessary. Otherwise, she would release them once the medical crisis was over; given their heads, they would likely incriminate themselves.

Meanwhile, Garrick had his heavy boot on Conner's throat. "Where's Dr. Moden?" he growled.

"I told you what I know!" Conner cried.

Garrick pulled the pistol from his shoulder holster and aimed it at the boy.

"Father!" Conner protested. "I don't know what this is about!"

"A more reliable source says you do." Garrick pulled the trigger, shooting the ground beside Conner's head.

"Father!" Conner screeched. "You've got the wrong man!"

"I sincerely doubt that, but apparently I've trained you well."

Garrick called in two more Presidential Guards. "Set this traitor up for an interview." Striding to a section of the tent on Camille's right, he slit a vertical hole in the canvas with his knife. "Exit this way and stay out of sight of the south-ern cliffs."

As the two guards pulled Conner to his feet and marched him out through the slit, Maurice taped a new bandage over Camille's wound. "There, I think that will do unless you try any more acrobatic stunts."

Maurice left the tent, and Camille said solicitously, "Madelyn, haven't you been here all night? Why don't you send for Patric and get some sleep."

"Thank you, ma'am," Madelyn said.

As soon as she left, Camille motioned Garrick to her. "Tail Maurice and Madelyn," she whispered. "I believe they're involved."

"I had the same impression," Errol agreed. "And she seemed awfully eager to be on her way."

Garrick nodded and the two stepped to the door of the tent, where they conferred with some of the Presidential Guard. When they returned, Garrick told Camille, "We're going to relocate you until we've quashed this. One of our scouts knows of a suitable temporary location."

Turning to Errol, he said, "Get her and Patric there as quickly as you can. I'll set up some activity to cover your escape. But be careful with her, *zule*. Her condition is still unstable."

Hesitating, he asked Camille, "How's Stan?"

Camille concentrated, whispering her impressions. "Alive. Not good—unconscious, I think. Or perhaps drugged."

"You can find him, can't you?"

"Yes," she answered confidently.

Turning to Errol, he said, "Take two scouts. Let Camille direct their search. Should they discover Stan's location, don't attempt a rescue. I need you to stay with her and assure her safety. Just send word via messenger. Maintain radio silence."

CHAPTER 44

ALERT

*"But about that day or hour no one knows, not even the angels in
heaven, nor the Son, but only the Father. Be on guard! Be alert!"*
Mark 13:32, 33, NIV.

Jorge's head throbbed. Horribly. As if someone with a jackhammer was inside
his skull trying to get out. He reached up to the offending body part, but someone grabbed his hand.

"It's all right." Bethany's voice—low, calm, reassuring. "I know it hurts,
but I don't want you to touch the dressing. I'll give you more pain medicine right
now."

He struggled to open his eyes and, when he somehow succeeded, she
kissed his cheek. "It's good to have you back, *hermanito*. We missed you."

"M-mission?" he managed hoarsely.

"Your mission was a success, Captain. You disabled Camille, and the
whole team returned alive."

"When?"

"Two days ago."

"Injuries?"

"Two. Yours was the worst. A bullet grazed your head, causing a concus-
sion and a fair amount of blood loss. Sheridan took a bullet in the shoulder as he
carried you out."

"Sheridan?" he asked, and then remembered, "Oh—the bear."

Bethany giggled and turned to someone. "He's asking for the bear—I
think that's you."

Sheridan's laughter rumbled through the medical tent. He approached
Jorge's bed, his left arm in a sling. "Good to see you awake. Stanley was accusing
me of breaking his Phantom."

Jorge smiled weakly. "You saved me—thank you."

Sheridan laid a hand on Jorge's arm. "As your father once told me, thank
Doug."

✳ ✳ ✳ ✳ ✳

Sheridan bounced into the command center. "He's awake!"

Relief washed over Stanley. "Thank Doug! How is he?"

"He seems okay—memory's intact and all."

Stanley's assistant interrupted, "Sir, I think you should see this. Look at
their command center."

Aiming his binoculars at the enemy's camp, Stanley watched a large vertical slit materialize in the command center's side. "What are they up to?"

"What is it?" Sheridan grabbed a pair of binoculars, and they watched Conner emerge from the new opening with his hands secured behind him and two guards holding guns on him.

"Why, Conner, you dog!" Sheridan exclaimed.

"Are you thinking what I'm thinking?" Stanley asked.

"Yup. I have to say, I never trusted him." Sheridan wagged his head before addressing the absent Conner: "But you don't have the imagination to mount an uprising. So who are you working with, I wonder? Has your father finally gotten tired of playing second fiddle to Stan?"

"Is Stan in the tent now, Colonel?" Stanley asked his assistant.

"No, sir. He left about a half-hour ago with Conner and Saxon. Neither he nor Saxon have returned yet."

"So who's sneaking Conner out the side of the tent? Who's in there?" Stanley asked.

"Garrick and Camille, Maurice and Madelyn, Errol and another Presidential Guard," his assistant answered easily. His sole duty today had been to keep track of activity around that tent.

"Then how do we interpret this?" Stanley mused aloud.

Sheridan laid down his binoculars. "I can configure that cast into several plot twists. One: Garrick's rebelling with the Presidential Guard backing him. They're holding Camille as leverage against Stan. Conner got in the way, maybe discovered the plot at an inopportune moment."

"Using Camille as a hostage has been tried before," Stanley pointed out. "It didn't work then. Why would Garrick think it could work for him?"

"Good point. Plus this would be odd timing for him. If he'd wanted to overthrow Stan, he could have done it under more favorable circumstances. Still, it wouldn't be beyond him if something's happened to affect his allegiance."

"Okay, so that's one possibility. Others?"

"Well," Sheridan drawled, "A similar scenario, but Camille's in charge and discovered the coup attempt. She's separating Conner and Garrick, who were working together, to interview them separately."

"Neither scenario explains the odd exit through the side," the colonel interjected.

"Yes, and that suggests some very interesting possibilities," Sheridan said.

"I agree," Stanley said. "Namely that the instigator of the revolt isn't in the tent at all, or even in camp, but in the mountains on their southern flank. We're certainly not the ones they're hiding from by sneaking out this side of the tent."

"Unless, of course, they did that because they wanted us to see it—part of some ruse."

"Right," Stanley grumbled. He lowered his binoculars and ran a hand through his hair. "You know, we could come up with a dozen or more possible explanations. And we'd have to wade through at least as many potential changes to their battle strategy."

"A fun problem to work out under usual circumstances."

Stanley raised his eyebrows. "So that's your idea of fun, is it?"

"Well, it would be if it weren't so urgent that we solve the puzzle quickly and correctly."

"Or if so many lives weren't depending on the answer?" Stanley asked mildly.

"Right," Sheridan said. "That too."

The brothers fell into a pensive silence. At length Stanley's assistant, still observing the tent, asked, "Does it bother anyone but me that Stan still hasn't returned to the command center, and that I can't locate him anywhere in camp?"

The brothers' gazes met, and Stanley knew they were both thinking the same thing. "Has it ever happened?" Sheridan asked.

"Not successfully," Stanley said. "But if Stan's been kidnapped, then all bets are off. There's no predicting how it will affect their battle strategy."

Sheridan squinted at the enemy camp. "Or how rapidly. And with our limited ability to react, we don't have the luxury of waiting to see how things play out. We need more intel."

"Agreed. We need to get someone in there. Quickly."

"Um," Sheridan said, drawing the word out. "That might be a problem."

"I'm well aware of the potential hazards. I've been sneaking spies into their camp for longer than you know."

"I'm sure you have. But this time you're sneaking one into their command center, the highest security area, during a field operation."

"Not a problem—I've got some excellent spies." Stanley turned toward an assistant.

"But do you have an excellent spy who speaks Sumerian?" Sheridan pressed.

"Excuse me?" Stanley's head swiveled abruptly back to his brother. "Did you say—?"

"Sumerian, yes. One of the precautions taken after you left."

"But it's a long-dead language. No one's spoken it for thousands of years."

"Precisely why they figured you'd never learn it. It's now the only language permitted in high security areas during a field operation."

"Do you speak it?"

"Yes, it's required of all ranking military officers. And executives, too, I think. At least Sadira studied it."

"Did she? She's trained in undercover work, too. Is she any good?"

"Frankly, Sadira excels at everything she does. And yes, she's a top-notch spook. But I'm not too bad myself."

"You're injured. And harder to hide. Your physique pegs you as a soldier, and you're too well known to their troops to disguise easily. Sadira could be an orderly, or a cook, or—"

Stanley sat back in his chair, the weight of his position suddenly weighing on him again. He'd already gotten one brother and one sister-in-law imprisoned and two other brothers wounded. His baby sister was about the only sibling he hadn't yet hurt in some way. Was he really going to ask her to risk torture and death too?

✲ ✲ ✲ ✲ ✲

Sadira ran along the backside of the mountains at full speed, taking no measures to disguise her advance. Although she wouldn't ordinarily rely so implicitly on their sentries' assurances, speed was critical.

Yet she was already feeling the physical strain. Her lungs burned, and sweat poured from her, though the sun's position low in the western sky cast her route in shadows. In truth, while she'd improved under Chris's dedicated coaching, she still wasn't an accomplished runner. Even this short route, the approximate equivalent of a 5K, would test the limits of her abilities.

What's more, her mother's voice pursued her, encumbering her steps and dampening her spirit: *Running is for losers. Endurance merely allows the conquered to escape his conqueror. If you would conquer, seek strength.* She had lived by that advice all her life, seeking strength and scorning endurance training.

A sharp pain stabbed her left side. She clutched at it, determined to push through. "Help me, Doug," she breathed. "Please don't let the rest of your runners suffer for my ineptitude."

She felt a distinct tingling under the transmitter, and a sense of renewed strength washed through her. The fire in her lungs dulled, and the pain in her side diminished.

"Slow your pace, child," Doug said.

Sadira followed his instruction without argument, and her pain gradually resolved.

"Y'all can pick up your pace a little now, but don't try to run as fast as you were."

She complied.

"Now watch your breathing—make it regular, like this: in, out, in, out ..."

As she breathed with him, she remembered that Chris had tried to teach her the importance of breathing, too. Again her mind taunted her: If she were a more experienced runner, she wouldn't need all these extra reminders. If she'd switched sides sooner, the right breathing pattern would be second nature by now. If she'd been a better student, her incompetence wouldn't be jeopardizing the lives of the whole camp.

Suddenly one of Chris's most oft-repeated lessons sprang to mind: when tempted to dwell on your own weakness, focus instead on Doug's strength. "I can do all things through Doug, who strengthens me," she breathed. "I will trust and not be afraid. Doug himself is my strength and my shield." As she continued to recite the *Manual's* passages, she fell into a rhythm that helped her maintain both her breathing and her pace.

Finally she reached the farthest end of the hills, where the enemy's firing range was situated. Finding a little cleft, she cooled down, chugging sports drink and downing a small snack, until steady enough to assume her cover. Then she stripped off her running clothes, toweled herself down, and threw on some desert fatigues with Desmoden's insignias. Practiced in the art of disguise, she pulled a makeup bag from her pack and quickly made herself into a bespectacled, bushy-browed boy. Brown contacts and a blond wig completed the transformation.

Last of all, and with great reluctance, she removed her transmitter. Garrick's new jamming system would detect it. Placing it carefully on top of the other paraphernalia in her pack, she stopped to stare at it. Of everything required to pull this off, leaving her transmitter, her precious connection to Doug, was the most difficult. She pressed a kiss to her fingers and touched them to the device before tucking the pack out of sight. Then she strode purposefully around the bend of the mountains. With a rifle slung over her shoulder, she appeared to be a private returning from the firing range.

She left her rifle on the table positioned at the entrance to the firing range, and noted who the supervising officer was. She was turning to leave when he called, "You! Private!"

Sadira's heart jumped into her throat. Discovered already?

She saluted and barked in her best boy-voice, "Yes, sir, Sergeant Fletcher."

He approached and returned her salute. Cocking his head, he said, "New recruit?"

"Yes, sir. Private Maxwell Smith, sir."

"Do you know where the command center is, Smith?"

"Yes, sir."

"Good. Go ask General Sondem how long he needs me to keep the target practice going. Go now—double time!"

In her relief, she almost blew her cover by asking which General Sondem she was to petition. But a new recruit wouldn't know to ask that. Catching herself, she set off at a double march cadence. At least she wouldn't have to invent an excuse to inveigle her way into the command center.

Once beyond the sergeant's view, she slowed to better observe the camp's goings-on. When she arrived at the command center, she saluted the Presidential Guard at its entrance. "Sent from Sergeant Fletcher with a question for General Sondem, sir."

The guard's eyes narrowed distrustfully. "Which General Sondem?"

Sadira feigned surprise. "Begging your pardon, sir, but he didn't say. I'm new to camp—just arrived with the last transport. Is there more than one General Sondem, sir?"

The guard's wary expression relaxed, apparently convinced that the naïve newcomer had no association with the traitorous General Conner Sondem. "What's the question, private?"

"Sergeant Fletcher wants to know how long General Sondem needs him to keep the target practice going."

With a perfunctory nod, the guard held out his hand. "Leave your weapons with me."

Sadira dutifully removed the knife from her boot and the pistol from her holster. She had brought them precisely so she could lose them at the tent's entrance; it would look suspicious if she had none.

The guard took her weapons and motioned her inside. "You're looking for General Garrick Sondem—the tall man at that console."

"Thank you, sir." She removed her helmet and passed into the tent. Pretending timidity, she took her time arriving at Garrick's position and caught bits of several conversations in Sumerian—not enough to understand what was happening, but enough to understand that Garrick was in charge. Had he truly initiated a coup, then?

When she approached him, he was addressing his brother, General Errol Sondem, and Sadira waited quietly. A few paces away, partially concealed behind a folding screen, Camille was being transferred to a stretcher. The generally vigorous woman was slow-moving and quiet, her insipid complexion matching her sheets. Though obviously severely compromised by her injuries, she issued orders as the ultimate authority in camp—which meant Stan was ... where?

When Errol mentioned searching for Saxon's hideout with scouts directed by Mother's link-sense, Sadira understood: Father had been kidnapped—by Saxon.

Garrick turned to Sadira as Errol stepped away. "Yes, soldier?" he said nonchalantly, but in Sumerian.

She'd expected this test. Garrick didn't expect an outlander recruit to know Sumerian; in fact, he'd be suspicious if she did. But the experienced general trusted no one beyond his family. He vetted everyone he didn't know with his own little test, no matter how many others had vetted them before.

She returned a blank stare. "E-excuse me, sir?"

Switching to English, he said, "What is it, private?"

"I have a question from Sergeant Fletcher, sir. He wants to know how long you need him to continue target practice."

Garrick sucked on his teeth. "Tell Sergeant Fletcher that, if it isn't too inconvenient, he will continue that"—he injected a few expletives, still in the same deceptively calm tone—"target practice until I"—more expletives—"tell him to stop."

"Thank you, sir," she said, but his attention was already elsewhere.

As Sadira started back toward the tent's entrance, a soldier pushed her aside to make way for Camille's stretcher. The upper-level Presidential Guards carrying her, though ordinarily so proud of their elite uniform, were dressed as enlisted men in the regular army. They had also placed a sheet over her as if carrying a corpse. So they were keeping her relocation secret—probably because they didn't yet know how far the rebellion went.

Sadira exited the tent and, reclaiming her weapons, made her way back to the firing range. She omitted parts of Garrick's message since she knew that Sergeant Fletcher's annoyance at Garrick's sarcasm and choice of adjectives would be visited upon her. When he dismissed her with a nod, she picked up another rifle from the table and returned to the firing range. Then she just kept going, slipping around the mountain to recover her pack from the cleft. The first thing she did was activate her transmitter.

Doug responded immediately: "Hide!" he whispered.

Sadira dove into the depths of the fissure, flattening herself against the rocks in its deepest shadows. An instant later, she heard some scrabbling above her. Then two officers from Desmoden's army jumped to the ground near the entrance of her hiding place. She recognized them immediately; Sheridan had once counted these members of the offspring generation as friends. For her part, she'd never liked them—sadistic bullies, the pair of them.

From their exchange, she gathered that they hadn't seen her, just as she hadn't seen them. Rather, they were patrolling the area for deserters. When one of the pair stepped into her cleft—not ten feet from her!—to relieve himself, her heart beat furiously against her ribs.

Her restraint was tested further when some creature chose that moment to jump on her and walk leisurely across the top of her head. She couldn't tell what the animal was, but two possibilities came to mind, and neither were companions with whom she preferred to share a cramped, dark space.

Reaching the other side of her head, the animal picked its way down the right side of her face, tickling her as it progressed. When it stopped on her shoulder, Sadira cautiously swiveled her head to glimpse the beast. At least it wasn't the scorpion she had feared. It was a large, hairy tarantula.

She searched her mental data banks for information on the tarantulas of Southern Africa and found her knowledge severely lacking. Anyway, it was too dark to identify the species with any certainty. Yet one question licked at her brain like a searing tongue of fire: Was its bite dangerously poisonous or just painful?

Sadira managed to remain frozen, although she constantly fought the impulses to recoil from the ugly, monstrous spider, to scratch its still-itching trail on her face, and to gag. The spider was now immobile too, as though it had arrived at its destination and had settled in to stay awhile. On her shoulder.

Almost like a sentry. She bit back a chortle at her perverse sense of humor.

Frederic finished his business, zipped up his pants, and turned … toward her.

Slowly, silently, she raised her hand to release the safety strap on her holster. But she couldn't take the gun in her hand without making a sound that, though small, would alert Frederic to her presence.

And let's not forget our little hitchhiker.

Yes—what would the tarantula do when she made the quick movements involved in pulling her gun?

Let's hope for merely painful on that bite.

Peering into the shadows, Frederic's hand went to his own revolver. He shuffled toward her. One step. Two.

Her hand hovered over the butt of her gun. Was she quicker on the draw than him? She couldn't remember.

Three steps.

Suddenly the tarantula jumped from her shoulder to land squarely on Frederic's face. He screamed and swiped at it frantically. Then, as Sadira struggled to fend off an untimely fit of laughter, he stumbled blindly out of the cleft.

Frederic and his partner mounted a quick battle against the spider, but it scuttled away into the safety of the shadows. They might have sought revenge except that her little sentry had actually bitten Frederic on the nose. Apparently neither officer knew any more than she did about arachnology, for they decided retreating to the medical tent was the most prudent course.

Still frozen in the shadows, Sadira waited until Doug issued an all-clear before venturing out. She noticed the tarantula climbing up the rocks near the entrance and whispered, "Thanks, little guy." Certainly it was her imagination, but she thought she saw it wink.

She kept bursting into songs of praise from the *Manual's* Songbook as she jogged back to camp. Darkness was settling over the desert when she reached the command center. She particularly wanted to tell Sheridan about Frederic's bite on the nose—he would *so* appreciate the humor in the situation—but she never got that far. As soon as she informed them that Saxon had kidnapped Father, her brothers had more important things to consider.

"Saxon wouldn't go through with this unless he had a significant following," Sheridan said gravely.

"Yes," Stanley agreed. "And the loss of manpower will make Camille's actions even more difficult to predict.

"In Stan's absence, I'm afraid it increases the chances of a preemptive attack exponentially."

"And we could do little in that event. We're still minimally staffed."

Sheridan looked out over the camp. "All that beautiful equipment—useless with no one to man it."

Stanley drew in a deep breath and exhaled slowly. "Colonel," he said to his assistant, "put the camp on red alert. Get every able-bodied soldier to battle stations."

CHAPTER 45
LOSSES

"Both of these will overtake you in a moment, on a single day: loss of children and widowhood. They will come upon you in full measure, in spite of your many sorceries."
Isaiah 47:9, NIV.

1 February 8044 M.E.

Camille was transported to the chosen refuge without incident, and Garrick kept her, as acting commander-in-chief, fully informed throughout the night. She would not have relished the new role under any circumstance. But in her current state the weight of the added responsibility was very nearly overwhelming. To complicate matters, the cave was so remote and completely surrounded by rock that she could sense nothing of Stan's condition. This loss of connection, especially at such a crucial time, only magnified her anxiety. She felt as though she truly were balancing the world on her wounded shoulders.

Garrick soon discovered Maurice and Madelyn conspiring to rescue Conner. Although he was unable to obtain any useful information from Conner or Madelyn, the doctor whom Stan had once counted as a friend was more susceptible to Garrick's interview techniques. From Maurice's tortured ramblings, Garrick determined which officers were involved in the revolt and, ultimately, put an end to it. When Saxon's supporters realized that it had been foiled, some tried to flee while others turned their guns on the group faithful to Stan. By the time hostilities subsided, twenty-seven percent of their troops lay dead.

When the messenger related this information, Camille perceived a wave of alarm pass through her guards. Indeed, she shared it. If their chance of defeating Doug had been slim before, what was it after losing a quarter of their army? But as commander-in-chief, she could ill afford to brood over negative news. If she had learned one thing from her brother, it was that troop morale was both fragile and highly sensitive to the commander's reactions. Strangely, this thought brought a new calm, for it led her naturally to the answer she sought. To deal with this catastrophe she merely needed to think like Stan: How would he handle the situation?

So, maintaining an unruffled exterior, she conceded nonchalantly, "That is unfortunate. However, let's not overstate the loss. We still grossly outnumber the enemy's forces."

Her measured reaction had the desired effect. The recovering optimism among her soldiers was palpable.

When the messenger returned again, dawn was casting pink hues around the cave's entrance. He approached her hesitantly. "Dr. Desmon, ma'am." He bowed again. "Ma'am ..."

"Well, what is it, man?" she rasped.

"Um, Commander Sondem directed a detachment to rescue Dr. Moden," he reported reluctantly. "It was a difficult mission, ma'am. Saxon was well situated, with a clear view of invaders and a system of booby traps. But in the end, we exterminated all traitors."

"Excellent. Then why do you look as if the sky has fallen?"

He hesitated.

Errol snapped, "Deliver your message, soldier!"

"Yes, sir," he said. "Well, ma'am, General Sondem—" He cleared his throat. "General Garrick Sondem, that is, isn't answering. We think, well ..."

"Are you saying that he went on the mission himself?" she asked incredulously. Garrick knew better than to jeopardize his own safety in such a way!

"Yes, ma'am."

"He what?" In her anger, she jerked upright—and again nearly fainted.

"Doc, you can't sit up!" Patric scolded. "You just— Oh, no."

Camille felt blood trickling down her neck.

Patric slapped more gauze over the wound and pressed hard. When Camille winced, he said, "Not my fault, doc. You can't jump around like that. General, hold this."

Errol lifted an eyebrow at being addressed in this manner, but he complied. Oblivious to the offense he'd caused, Patric worked on the wound, alternately complaining and apologizing. Then he abruptly went silent. Slowly, he lifted a tiny piece of suture with his forceps and puzzled at it intently until a strange expression came over him.

"What is it?" Camille whispered.

"Doc, I—" He looked again at the suture. "You know I'm only a medic."

"Yes, and a very capable one. What is your concern?"

"It's just that I've never seen a surgeon use such fine suture on bleeders like these. It's too fragile, not intended for this kind of surgery. I can't imagine why Dr. Pim would use it, unless—" He met her eyes.

"Unless he wanted to keep me unstable," she finished.

Patric nodded.

"In light of his defection to Saxon, I wondered why he'd let me live at all."

"Probably at Saxon's orders," Errol said. "Saxon was very attached to you. He probably thought he could convince you to come to his side once Dr. Moden was out of the way."

"Perhaps you're right." Camille said. "So Maurice preserved the illusion of adequate care while hoping I would bleed out."

"It does seem that way," Patric agreed.

"Well, do your best, Patric. We have no other option at the moment." Addressing the messenger, she brought them back to the more crucial question. "And what news have you of Dr. Moden?"

"They—" He nervously cleared his throat. "That is, we're not sure—"

"Speak up, man!" Errol ordered.

The messenger shifted feet. "Well, we've now thoroughly searched their hideout," he said carefully. "It appears that the rebels started a fire at one point. We're not sure whether that was intentional. But we never found Dr. Moden." Another throat clearing. "We did find General Garrick's pack near two charred bodies that look like—" Another foot shuffling. "That is, we believe them to be ... Commander Sondem and—" The messenger gulped audibly. "—Dr. Moden."

A haunted stillness filled the cave. Errol seemed to physically deflate, as if he'd received a forcible punch to the gut. The other soldiers exchanged glances of horrified disbelief and then snatched off their berets to bow their heads in a gesture of respect.

No. Camille's heart fluttered madly in her chest. *No!* Yet the feeling that plagued her, the complete absence of connection with her brother, only supported the unspeakable conclusion.

Regaining his composure, Errol came to attention and saluted her smartly. "I'm yours to command, my liege." The other soldiers, as if coming to themselves, echoed his pledge.

Camille saw them as if watching television—aware of the movements, yet feeling that they were far away, wholly unassociated with her. She didn't feel grief, exactly; it was more like being severely off balance—like a butterfly missing a wing. Stan was the charismatic leader. Stan was the military genius. Stan had begun this rebellion; he knew how to finish it. How could she lead the movement without him? How would she know what to do?

She looked to Errol—more fiery in temperament than his brother, but strong, capable, and dependable. "General Errol Sondem, I place you in command of my combined forces, army and Presidential Guard—"

A heaviness in her chest momentarily robbed her of breath, reminding her of her own fragile condition. What if she should die too? The rebellion—6,000 long years of work—must not die with her!

"If I should become incapacitated through natural causes or the action of anyone other than yourself," she continued, "I place you in full command. You are all witnesses to this decree. The rebellion must go on, with or without me."

"Yes, ma'am," the others chorused.

Errol sprang into action. Within minutes, he accomplished several vital tasks. He sent a contingent back to camp to reestablish discipline and to assure the troops that Camille was in control. He arranged to transfer the command center to the cave. He summoned the remaining senior officers for a military strategy meeting. He sent for Dr. Adlai Menod to reevaluate Camille's medical care.

Still feeling terribly off balance, Camille watched him in amazement. How could he behave so rationally? He'd just lost his elder brother too.

But she'd lost more than a brother—more than an elder brother. She'd lost her linkmate. And then, all at once, her panic, her sense of lopsidedness, her feelings of inadequacy, her loss—all this and more coalesced into one overriding emotion: rage.

Motioning Errol to her bedside, she rasped, "Can you think of any reason why we should delay attacking the Outlander Division? Why we should not launch a preemptive strike while they are still incomplete, unprepared, and without Paradisian reinforcement?" Her tenuous voice was becoming increasingly strident as her emotion rose. "Why we should not mobilize our allies to slaughter every runner in every corner of this pathetic planet while we have the means to do so? Why we should not annihilate our enemy *now*?"

A grin spread over Errol's dark features as her fury found an answering chord within him. "No, ma'am," he answered firmly. "I can think of no such reason."

CHAPTER 46

ANSWER US!

*"You answer us in righteousness, with awe-inspiring works,
God of our salvation."*
Psalm 65:5, HCSB.

Stanley and Sheridan sat side by side in the command center, each with a pair of binoculars stuck to his face like a new appendage. Together, they had watched in bemusement as the Moden camp turned on itself, wiping out a significant minority of its own troops. They'd seen Garrick lead a large contingent into the mountains after the still-missing Saxon. Each brother had turned to the other with the same unspoken question: Was Garrick's confidence in his officers so shaken that he felt he must endanger the commander's safety by leading the expedition himself?

When Garrick's contingent returned to camp, the two brothers particularly noted the absence of two key individuals—Garrick and Stan. While they discussed the likely reasons for and consequences of this deficiency, Errol returned to camp to reorganize the troops. Watching the activity closely, Stanley said idly, "Screens? Odd time for training films."

The enemy gathered around the hastily erected screens, and Sheridan noted gravely, "They've lost a good chunk of their army, maybe as much as a quarter of it. Even so, Desmoden's legions still grossly outnumber us."

Stanley was silent for a moment. The same troubling observation had occurred to him. Finally he said, " 'This is the word of the Lord unto Zerubbabel, saying, Not by might, nor by power, but by my spirit, says the Lord of hosts.' History has repeatedly proven that Doug doesn't require large numbers to gain the victory."

"It's a good thing," Sheridan replied quietly. For once, there was no humor in his tone.

When Camille appeared on screen, the brothers both sucked in a breath. "She looks awful," Stanley breathed.

Dr. Adlai Menod, a highly regarded physician and scientist, stood at Camille's side. When the camera zoomed in on him, the enlarged image allowed Stanley to read his lips. In a manner that was uncharacteristically frank for Moden communications, he made an announcement about Camille's health. She was still in serious condition from her injuries, he conceded, and they would have to listen closely because swelling around her vocal cords had affected her voice. Nevertheless, she was perfectly lucid, wholly in control, and absolutely determined to overthrow the Damours.

"Do you read lips?" Stanley asked, suddenly realizing that his brother might not be able to decipher the announcement.

"Of course," Sheridan said, and then added jokingly, "Why—need me to translate for you?"

"Hmpf," Stanley grunted with a sidelong glance.

With Adlai's introduction completed, the camera returned to Camille. She announced that the attempted coup d'état, led by Saxon and Conner, had been crushed and the treasonous leaders executed. However, Stan and Garrick were both missing in action and presumed dead.

"Whoa!" Sheridan breathed. "I never would have believed it."

"Me neither," Stanley agreed. "Yet it must be true. There'd be no benefit to relaying such devastating news to the troops. It would only destabilize an already fragmented camp."

Sheridan hesitated, as if searching for an alternate conclusion. Finally he said, "That's true. I wonder how she'll turn it to her advantage."

But Camille's unveiled fury seemed to have roused some latent abilities, for she did manage to rally her beleaguered forces. Harnessing the general anger over fallen comrades, she refocused it squarely on Doug. She spoke with a zeal that Stanley had never before seen in her. The generally calm, measured woman almost seemed to be channeling Stan's passion, talent for oratory, and even his charisma.

The words themselves were powerful. Their delivery by an obviously injured speaker in a frail voice would only add to their effect. Stanley could truly say that he had never seen a more effective call to arms, not even from Stan. And the message achieved its desired results, evoking fist pumps, cheers, or focused silence at all the right places.

When the time came to outline specific battle plans, Camille turned the audience over to her new commanding officer, General Errol Sondem. She assured them that she had fully discussed the needed changes with her general, and that they were of one mind. Confessing her need to conserve strength, she then signed off. The troops saluted her with an extended cheer.

Stanley and Sheridan were unable to derive any further information. Errol's image wasn't projected onto the screens, so distance prevented them from reading his lips. However, it didn't take long to understand the gist of the new strategy once the meeting adjourned and the troops scrambled to carry it out.

Sheridan caught on first. Turning to Stanley with sudden intensity, he said, "It's a full, all-out preemptive strike—right now!"

Stanley radioed to warn the camp since those on the ground wouldn't discern the enemy's movements until after the attack had begun. But he received no response. His aides scurried about, trying other methods of communication, but also received no response. Stanley reached for the anti-ballistic missile controls; he could deploy them remotely. But they also did not respond. All radio frequencies were jammed. The implanted military radios buzzed with static. Even Doug's transmitters merely screamed a shrill siren.

A wave of horror shot through him. They were completely cut off! They could transmit no instructions or warnings to camp. They could not remotely deploy the defensive missiles. They could receive no instructions from Paradise Island.

He instinctively sprang up, intending to fly down the mountain and rescue his camp—his wife! Sheridan seemed to anticipate this. Beating him to the cave's entrance, he blocked it with his own bulk. Stanley ran headlong into him, sending them both sprawling in the dirt.

With his good arm, Sheridan clamped hold of his brother. "You can't go! Not you! A commander doesn't have that prerogative!"

"Send me!" was the immediate response of Stanley's two assistants.

"It's a suicide mission," Sheridan warned. "They're deploying missiles immediately—there's little chance that anyone will have time to escape. Even if they do, Errol's poising snipers to pick off any who flee. The only chance of survival will be up here in the hills, although we'll sustain damage from the blasts too."

Still the officers begged for the opportunity to run the message. And Stanley—wishing he could go himself, feeling the weight of his responsibility as never before—gratefully granted their request. The two sprinted for camp, leaving behind a deathly stillness.

Mere seconds later, the enemy released an overwhelming barrage of missiles.

Stanley watched helplessly. How had the enemy jammed his camp's radio frequencies without affecting their own? Another of Garrick's famous inventions? But the answer was moot, for they had clearly managed it.

So there he stood, helpless. He could do nothing to counter the attack. Those on the ground could do nothing to escape it. Oh, they would manually deploy some anti-ballistic missiles, one by one; they might even intercept a few inbound warheads. But it would not change the outcome. The inbound attack truly was overwhelming.

Slumping back into his chair, Stanley breathed, "Doug, help us."

PART III

SILENCE IN HEAVEN

"And when he had opened the seventh seal, there was silence in heaven about the space of half an hour."
Revelation 8:1, KJV.

Gabriel rose from the War Room's command console, his eyes fixed on the clock. The other officers, noticing his focus, also turned to watch the red digits' fateful advance: 23:59:57 ... 23:59:58 ... 23:59:59 ... 24:00:00.

The clock stopped, never to resume.

Absolute silence filled the room, and every eye turned to Gabriel. Awed by the historic nature of this moment, he soberly lifted the microphone that transmitted to every communication device on the island. Carefully, he enunciated the long awaited announcement: *"Ejo risaju ish Mikaél."* (Paradisian: The Commander-in-Chief's *risaju* is departing.)

As he set the microphone down, his comrades' continued silence struck him as inappropriate, and he realized he hadn't conveyed the proclamation's true sentiment. Every citizen on Paradise Island had worked toward this event for thousands of years. Though singularly important, it was also an occasion of unparalleled rejoicing—the day Prince Joshua rescued his faithful people! The day he claimed his bride!

Breaking into a great smile, Gabriel again lifted the microphone. This time his voice vibrated with joy. How great was his privilege of extending this open invitation to his countrymen. *"Ts'aderót: Ejo risaju ish Mikaél!"* (Paradisian: I repeat: The Commander-in-Chief's *risaju* is departing!)

Applause erupted within the War Room. Shouts of exultation filled the building's hallways. When Gabriel exited the building, he heard cheers flowing from every building. On all sides, the beaming faces of happy patriots crowded the walkways. This was the celebration the prince deserved!

Gabriel lifted his hand, and the expectant throng quieted. At his signal, Lanse opened one of the large double glass doors while he threw wide the other. Prince Joshua stepped forth, arrayed in his glorious royal robes, radiant with might and majesty. And with joy—oh, such joy! Not only did it beam from his face, but from his person, causing the light of his gleaming white garments to radiate outward into a shimmering rainbow.

Cries of jubilation met him and carried him forward. A cascade of blossoms flowed down upon him as he strode through the golden streets. And when Gabriel began to sing—*Hallelujah! For our Lord Almighty reigns. Let us rejoice, be glad, and give him glory!*—the assembly joined him, forming a grand symphony:

For the wedding of the Lamb has come, and his bride has made herself ready! Hallelujah!

Soon they reached the *risaju* outside the city gates. Hovering just above the ground, the open aerial vehicle almost seemed to quiver with elation, as though anxious to begin the long-anticipated journey.

When all had boarded, Gabriel returned to close the city's gates. He was struck by the contrast between the festive strain rising from the *risaju* and the silence of the city they were leaving behind. Since all were eager to celebrate with their beloved prince, the normally busy streets lay abandoned. It almost seemed as if the city mourned its inability to join the jubilant throng.

Giving the gate a pat, Gabriel murmured, "Be patient. Your time will come."

CHAPTER 47
AWAKE!

" 'At that time Michael, the great prince who protects your people, will arise ... Multitudes who sleep in the dust of the earth will awake: some to everlasting life, others to shame and everlasting contempt.' "
Daniel 12:1, 2, NIV.

Riana was sleeping, curled around Raven, when something woke her. Listening for the disturbance, she realized it was actually the absence of something. The hallways, usually echoing with the guards' footfalls and complaining, lay eerily silent.

Cradling Raven in her arms, she moved to the door. Still hearing nothing, she called, "Does anyone know what's happening?"

"The guards have deserted the place," someone answered from far away.

"Are you sure?" Riana asked.

"Yes. I heard them say they were leaving."

"Why?" someone else asked.

A brief hesitation. Then the first voice answered in a triumphant tone, "Josh is returning very soon, sisters!"

A round of cheers erupted throughout the cells.

The same questioner pressed, "But did the guards say why they were leaving?"

After another hesitation, the first woman answered more softly, "Yes. They received a general order of execution."

Riana found herself wondering how they'd do it. If they all left the building, were they were going to blow it up? To gas them? To—

"Stop it!" she told herself. "I won't spend my last moments thinking about Stan's plans." Instead, she determinedly lifted her voice and sang #46 from the *Manual's* Songbook. The other prisoners joined her, making the abandoned halls ring with triumphant strains.

* * * * *

"Wake up, *aparochi*!" Melanie exclaimed in a hoarse whisper as she shook Chris's shoulder. "Wake up!"

Chris opened his eyes to peer through the dimness. "Morning, pumpkin," he whispered. "What's up?"

"It's t'morrow, *aparochi*, 'member? We get to ride in the boat. And, and go waaay over the water. And, and get stuff!"

"So, it is, pumpkin," Chris conceded. He was boating to the mainland today to pick up Ted, an old friend he hadn't seen for some time. While there, he would also replenish some supplies from an underground source. When the girls learned of the trip, they begged to go too, and Doug had consented.

Chris yawned and stretched. "I suppose you can't wait to get started, huh?"

"I a'ready waited so long! Almost forever!"

Chris glanced outside the tent opening, where the sun was barely peeking over the horizon. With a chuckle, he said, "Well, it is a long boat ride. We should probably get an early start." He sat up and noticed Cherie's sleeping bag was empty. "Where's your sister?"

"Here, *aparochi*," Cherie called cheerily. She bounced through the tent's entrance with a paper bag.

"Shh," he reminded her. "Uncle Steve and Aunt Jeannie are still sleeping next door."

"Oh," she said, clapping one hand over her mouth. She plopped down beside Chris and opened the sack to reveal three sandwiches crudely wrapped in plastic wrap and smudged with jam. "We made lunch," she whispered.

"Yum. Peanut butter and jelly—my favorite," Chris whispered back. They must have wheedled the coveted foodstuffs out of the latest arrivals. "You two have been busy this morning, haven't you?"

"Yes," Melanie agreed with an emphatic nod. "We ready."

Chris chuckled. "Well, maybe we should get dressed first." The girls still wore the large t-shirts their Uncle Steve had presented to them (with great cere-mony) as "princess nighties."

Chris got up gingerly, gently warming up his left shoulder and right knee, where the aches of age had settled, and set about getting them ready to go. Despite his attempts at maintaining the early morning quietude, the rest of the family was soon awake to see Chris and the girls off.

✵ ✵ ✵ ✵ ✵

Willy awoke well before dawn. He wasn't sure what awakened him. The pain maybe, or maybe the noise of smashing glass—probably looters at a run-ner's vacated house. He flipped on the light and swallowed some pain pills. Then, pulling on his jeans, he went into the living room to illuminate that area as well. The lights warned looters that the house was occupied. If they weren't enough, the recently installed bars on the windows and the semi-automatic pistol he now carried were pretty good deterrents too.

With a yawn, he padded into his mom's kitchen to start the coffee maker. He'd come home for a very special reason. Today he would finally arrest his uncle, a feat that Dr. Moden promised would prevent much bloodshed by quashing the Outlander Division's morale and causing many of those gathered in the Kalahari to desert. And this time, Willy's plan didn't require confronting his uncle on that strangely booby-trapped island. Today Uncle Chris was coming to him.

The boat ride from San Miguel took about four hours, so Willy didn't expect his uncle until around noon. Nevertheless, he immediately readied to leave. Detaining Uncle Chris had become something of an obsession. With his goal so near at hand, he couldn't concentrate on anything else.

As he stepped out the door, he heard more glass shattering. He moved to the sidewalk and scanned the street to see a family running from their home in pajamas. Lately the looters had been organizing into gang-like organizations—armed, dangerous, and increasingly bold. Some were even storming homes and evicting its occupants at gunpoint.

Willy pulled out his cell phone and dialed 911 to report the problem. The police dispatcher probably would have laughed—they were simply overwhelmed with such calls—if he hadn't first identified himself. Once assured that backup was on the way, he walked down the street and approached the gang's apparent leader. Unzipping his jacket to casually expose the pistol tucked in his belt, he said, "Do you know who I am?"

The leader gave him the once-over, his gaze lingering on the pistol, and said, "You're Wilson Moore."

"That's right. That—" he pointed to his home—"is my house. And these—" he indicated the pajama-clad family—"are my neighbors."

The gang leader glanced beyond Willy to a police cruiser pulling up at the curb. "We won't bother you no more," he offered and motioned to his companions. The whole lot ran off, scattering and disappearing from view.

After receiving the family's gratitude and the officers' promise to watch the neighborhood, Willy returned to his car, glad to have helped out. On the way to the marina, he stopped to pick up Ted. The rehabilitated runner had agreed to cooperate with Willy's plan but was having second thoughts. Willy reviewed the plan with him, assuring him that he wouldn't have to actually face Uncle Chris.

"We just need you to be visible on shore," he confirmed. "Once his boat's in the marina, the Coast Guard will block his exit, and you can take off."

✳ ✳ ✳ ✳ ✳

As soon as they left Cuyler Harbor, the results of the extensive red tide became obvious. "Why's the water that icky color?" Cherie asked, while Melanie whined, "Why'd the fishies die?"

Chris explained about the algal overgrowth and how Doug had protected their island so they would have food to eat. Prompted by their questions, he segued into a more extensive explanation of the plagues predicted by the *Manual* and how they had been occurring throughout the earth. The girls listened solemnly as he described the dense darkness covering the eastern US and much of South America, the red sludge contaminating Africa's waters, the scorching heat from Asia to Australia, and the deadly sores afflicting people worldwide.

When he finished, Melanie asked plaintively, "But why, *aporochi*?"

"Because the people are very bad," Cherie answered gravely. "They've been killing the earth. Now the earth is killing them."

Chris blinked in surprise. Had she come up with that all by her little six-year-old self?

He was about to ask when the boat's engine sputtered and died. He frowned at it. He and his brothers kept this motor in tip-top shape. Plus they'd given it a thorough going-over yesterday in preparation for today's trip. Nevertheless, it showed not a spark of life.

While the girls amused themselves with coloring books and puzzles, he worked and tinkered and fiddled with the thing—for hours. He never found a cause for its strange behavior, but, as suddenly and inexplicably as it had died, it finally sprang to life again.

Chris nervously glanced at the setting sun. He was a decent enough skipper during the daytime, but boating at night was a very different matter, one he'd had little experience with. What's more, dark, menacing clouds had filled the sky.

A raindrop plopped onto his nose, as if underscoring the need to get moving, and Chris turned the boat toward Ventura. He didn't really have any other choice. He'd just take it slowly and carefully. If he got in a bind that put the girls' lives in danger, he'd call for help. As a runner, though, he'd be signing his own arrest warrant … and transfer back to Camille's dungeon.

Darkness fell, and the wind whipped up. The rain began in earnest. Chris's visibility, already reduced by the darkness, decreased further. So did his confidence in his ability to navigate the boat safely into Ventura harbor.

"I don't understand any of this, Doug," he murmured. "Wasn't I following your instructions? Why are you allowing this to happen?"

✳ ✳ ✳ ✳ ✳

"I don't think he's coming," Ted said for the umpteenth time. He actually sounded relieved.

Willy glanced again at his watch. It was fully dark now. Uncle Steve regularly took the boat out at night, but Uncle Chris hadn't done much evening boating. Surely he wouldn't purposely do it now, not in this weather.

"You're sure it was this marina?" he asked, also for the umpteenth time.

"I told you—I'm sure!"

Willy shot him an irritated glare. "What's the back-up plan?"

Ted wilted under the glare. "They said that if something goes wrong, they consider the operation rescheduled for the next day at the same rendezvous point."

Willy drew in a slow breath and exhaled it in a loud chuff. "Tomorrow then."

He called off the police and Coast Guard and arranged to rerun the operation on the following day. Then he started home. Ted whined and second-guessed himself all the way. As they pulled into Ted's driveway, he said, "Maybe this was a sign. Maybe I'm not supposed to help you."

Willy jammed the car into park and turned to pinion his gaze. "You *are* helping me tomorrow. Do you understand? Or should I station police around your house tonight?"

Ted seemed to shrink into the seat. Swallowing hard, he squeaked, "No, I understand." He fumbled to open the door and then got out so quickly that he stumbled to the pavement.

Willy watched him enter his home with an odd sense of satisfaction. As he drove away, he decided he was getting good at this business of wielding power. He kind of liked it.

✳ ✳ ✳ ✳ ✳

It was the strangest thing. The boat came out of nowhere. Suddenly the white navigation light of a boat's stern simply appeared in front of Chris. For two hours it guided him toward shore and straight into the marina. As Chris maneuvered his boat into the slip, the other vessel turned around and headed back out to sea. The skipper, dressed in navy slacks and a ruby red polo shirt, waved a greeting as he passed.

Recognizing the informal uniform of the Royal Guard, Chris broke into a wide smile and called, "Thank you!"

"Thank Doug," the guard called back. "Hunker down in the cemetery—it's going to be a rough night."

The boat was gone before Chris could confirm the odd directions. But he'd heard them well enough and decided to simply comply. He found the car that their underground supplier had left for him and, while explaining the plan to the girls, drove the few miles to the Ivy Lawn Cemetery. He'd expected them to think it a bit creepy, but they seemed to consider it an adventure.

He planned to park outside the locked graveyard and sleep in the vehicle. However, the short drive convinced him that would be unwise. Despite the imposed curfew, the streets swarmed with noisy people whose intentions were obviously hostile. Then he recalled the guard's words—"hunker down *in* the cemetery"—and Chris wondered if he'd meant it literally. But how would he manage it? The gates would long since be closed.

Chris arrived at his destination to find that one gate was ajar. With a chuckle, he drove in and parked near Susana's grave. Little Pete, the baby they'd lost so many years ago, was buried beside her; his parents, brother, and grandmother were also buried nearby. Even in the tempestuous weather, the sense of family, of connectedness, that he always felt here comforted him. He wrapped the girls and himself in some blankets left in the trunk, and they dropped off into a sound sleep.

✳ ✳ ✳ ✳ ✳

Willy returned home and relaxed in front of the TV. During a commercial, he wandered into the kitchen for a snack and found his mother arranging several bouquets.

"What's with all the flowers?" he asked.

"Oh, I just thought I'd take some down for the graves tomorrow."

He whirled around to stare at her. Glancing up, she said, "Why does that surprise you? You know I put flowers on the graves every month or so."

"The graves!" he exclaimed. "Why didn't I think of that sooner?"

Calling a quick goodbye, he charged out the door. En route to the cemetery, he arranged for a groundskeeper to open a gate and called for police backup. The officer he spoke to sounded skeptical, but Willy insisted: If Uncle Chris made it to the mainland, he'd surely visit Aunt Susana's grave; and if he'd been warned away from the marina, finding him at the cemetery might be their only opportunity. Besides, Willy knew in his gut that he was right.

✳ ✳ ✳ ✳ ✳

Chris awoke to a blinding light shining directly into his face through the windshield. At first he thought it was morning. But the light was brighter than the sun, and darkness surrounded him in every other direction.

"IT IS DONE!"

The trumpet-like voice thundered from the brilliance and sent shock waves in every direction. The earth quaked. The very heavens shook violently. Screams of pain and shrieks of terror pierced the air. Chris felt frozen to his seat.

"AWAKE! AWAKE, YOU WHO SLEEP IN THE DUST!"

The voice again shook the still-trembling ground. It bucked and heaved, tearing tombstones from their foundations and flinging objects pell-mell through the air.

But Chris saw the tumult only peripherally, for his attention was now fixed elsewhere. Grabbing the girls' hands, he moved as quickly as he could toward Susana's grave, dodging flying debris and struggling to remain upright. By the time he arrived, her casket had popped to the surface, like a giant gopher burrowing through the dirt. The lid sprang open and Susana jumped up, her face radiant.

The girls let out squeals of delight, and Susana exclaimed joyously, "Oh, death, where is your victory?" Chris joined her as she continued, "Oh, grave, where is your sting?"

Embracing her, he swung her around and kissed her. That's when he realized: he didn't hurt anymore. The leftover pain from the gunshot wound—gone. The arthritis in his knee—gone. He felt young and nimble.

He still had his face buried in Susana's luxurious hair—once again black as it had been in their youth—when he felt a tap on his shoulder. "Ahem."

He turned to see a grinning Lanse holding a bundle wrapped in a baby blanket. "Petey!" Chris and Susana exclaimed together. Lanse handed the tiny bundle to Susana, who cried for joy as she repeatedly kissed his little cheeks.

"Who's the baby, *aparochi*?" Cherie asked.

Chris reached down and lifted one girl up in each arm so they could see him. "This is your Uncle Peter."

"Uncle?" Cherie asked as she grasped his tiny hand. "He's too little!"

"Yes." Chris too marveled at his son's minute size, still small enough to fit in his hand, yet wriggling and very much alive. "That's because he died before he was born."

While Chris introduced his granddaughters to their long-lost uncle, Lanse had disappeared. Now he reappeared with a young couple.

"Dad!" Chris exclaimed as he fell into his father's arms, still holding the girls. "Oh, Dad, how I've missed you!"

His father wrapped him in a bear hug. When he pulled back, he said simply, "This is your mom, kid."

Chris turned to the young woman beside Dad, whom he recognized from the pictures hanging in Rosie's hallway. He set the girls down and hugged the woman who had been killed only a year after giving him life. "Mom, I'm so glad to meet you."

"And who are these cuties?" Dad asked, squatting down in front of the girls.

"These are my granddaughters, Melanie and Cherie," Chris said as he patted each on the head. Then, with a big grin, he added, "The daughters of"—he paused for emphasis—"my *daughter*, Bethany Rose, named after you, Mom."

Dad gasped. "I don't believe it! You gave me a granddaughter? Why didn't you get around to doing that before I died?"

Chris laughed. "Because I had to marry Susana first. Remember Susana?" he added, drawing her beside him.

"Of course, I do! Welcome to the family, Susana! And who's this little munchkin?"

"This is our son who died before birth," Chris said. "Peter, named after Susana's father. We'd already named one son Andrew Benjamin after you, Dad."

"Will—will I meet him too, kid?" Dad asked, suddenly serious.

"Yes, Dad. Yes, you will. In fact, you'll meet all our children, four boys and one girl. They're all faithful runners. They're—well, there's so much to tell, I hardly know where to start."

"No need to rush it," Dad said with a smile. "We have forever to catch up."

"May I hold Peter?" Mom asked. When Susana handed him to her, she gazed into his face for a long moment. Her eyes were moist when she looked up. "Do you believe it, Ben? Our baby's baby."

Again Lanse interrupted them, this time holding the hand of a little boy. "Eddie!" Chris exclaimed, and, together with his parents, hugged the brother who had drowned at age ten.

Josh's voice thundered: "BLESSED ARE YOU, FOR YOU HAVE OVERCOME THE WORLD BY MY BLOOD!"

"Hallelujah! Glory to Crown Prince Joshua!" cried Chris with the others.

"YOU HAVE KEPT MY COMMANDMENTS AND GUARDED MY TESTIMONY!"

"All praise to Prince Joshua!"

"I WILL ESTABLISH YOU AS A HOLY PEOPLE TO MYSELF, JUST AS I PROMISED YOU!"

"Hallelujah!"

The voice continued, drawing nearer as it pronounced blessing after blessing on those staring fixedly up, earnestly straining for a glimpse of their prince. A collective gasp went through the group when, at last, he emerged from the radiance in the sky, riding on a platform and surrounded by a huge crowd of runners.

Yet Chris barely saw these. He was too enraptured by Josh, who was himself the source of the brilliant white light that had awakened him. Enveloped in a shimmering rainbow, with a golden crown on his head and a golden scepter in his hand, he was the same Josh that Chris knew so well—and yet he was so very different.

Bedazzling in glory.

Spectacular in majesty.

Breathtaking in power.

Transcending all magnificence.

"How ... amazing," Susana breathed.

"Amazing," Chris agreed.

He was so absorbed in this vision of Prince Joshua, so filled with unutterable joy, that he didn't realize at first that he was moving. Nevertheless he, together with the other runners, was rising, drawing nearer and nearer to the huge platform until they stepped onto it. Prince Joshua received each one personally, honoring them with a kiss on the forehead.

✼ ✼ ✼ ✼ ✼

The day had dragged by without incident, but also without any guards returning. Riana and her fellow prisoners passed the hours singing and calling passages from the *Manual* to one another until they were hoarse.

Because of the delay, Riana guessed that the guards were busy wiring the building with explosives. She was not surprised, therefore, when a low rumble began in the ground below her. However, the rumble did not culminate in an explosion. Instead, it grew into an earthquake.

A trumpet-like voice proclaimed, "IT IS DONE!"

Elated cries went up and down the hallway: "It's Josh! He's coming! He's coming to rescue us!"

"AWAKE! AWAKE, YOU WHO SLEEP IN THE DUST!"

The earthquake intensified. The floor of Riana's cell heaved. The building crumbled around her, the walls collapsing in their places. The ceiling seemed to have been plucked off. Somehow she was not injured in all the commotion.

Still carrying Raven, Riana began working her way through the wreckage, heading for the perimeter of the building. As she progressed, she recognized many of her fellow prisoners who, like herself, had been freed during the earthquake. Through the long days and nights of her imprisonment, she had often petitioned Doug to give them comfort and strength. Now she rejoiced to see that they had remained faithful.

Nevertheless, she was constantly glancing up. A brilliant white light pierced the dark night, but where was *he*? This must be it—the Awakening! But where was her beloved prince?

Suddenly Colonel Jané Lanáj was at her side. Raven let out an excited squeak and jumped from Riana's arms to Colonel Lanáj's shoulder. There she curled around the colonel's neck with obvious contentment.

"Welcome home, dearest," Jané said. "You've done excellent work."

The ferret chuckled in response, and Riana asked, "She's yours?"

"Yes, when she's not ministering to prisoners. She very much enjoys that occupation. But come, I'll help you find him."

"Josh?"

"Oh, no—you shan't need help seeing him when he arrives. I mean Andy. He's in the men's side of the prison."

"He's alive?" she exclaimed.

"Alive and faithful," Jané answered with a tender smile.

Riana followed as Jané adroitly picked her way through the rubble. Then she saw Andy—and he saw her! By the time they fell into each others' arms, Riana's face was swimming with joyful tears.

"They told me you'd died," she cried.

"They told me you'd defected, but I couldn't believe it," he returned. "They also said you were pregnant?"

"I think I may be."

A beloved figure broke through the bright light in the sky, and Riana's heart swelled with sheer ecstasy. "Josh!" she cried. "Look, look! It's Prince Joshua!"

The mass of freed runners—thin, pale, and weak from their long ordeal—seemed instantly transformed, their bodies healthy, their faces gleaming. As one, they lifted their voices in joyful exclamation. They were going home!

CHAPTER 48

THE OTHER SIDE

*"Throughout the night the cloud brought darkness to the one side
and light to the other side."*
Exodus 14:20, NIV.

Willy and the police officers arrived at the cemetery just before midnight. Storm clouds conveniently obscured the moonlight, making the cemetery eerily black. They stole upon Uncle Chris's car to find him sleeping, totally defenseless and unsuspecting. As Willy reached the rear bumper, a shiver of excitement shot through him. *We actually have him! Nothing can go wrong this time!*

Suddenly, the eastern sky seemed to rip open, like someone tearing dark paper off an immense window. An excruciating brilliance shone right in Willy's face. Crying out in pain, he clapped his hands over his eyes.

A trumpet's raucous blast and deafening peals of thunder emanated from the light, driving fear, like ten-penny nails, into Willy's very bones. A massive earthquake rippled outward, and the sky recoiled like the barrel of a monstrous canon. The police officers ran for cover. He followed as quickly as he could navigate the heaving ground.

The trumpet roared again, and the planet shook even more violently, the sky mirroring the tremors. Willy pitched forward, hitting the ground as a tremendous shockwave split the earth. He scrambled frantically away from the yawning maw.

Glancing back, he gaped in horror. The ocean's boundless expanse now flooded the ground where he had stood mere seconds before. Lightning played over the restless water, creating an almost constant sheet of electricity that whipped the water into boiling cauldrons and rocketed stones into the air.

A wave sloshed over his legs, and the cold spray stung his eyes, reviving his survival instincts. He staggered to his feet and ran for shelter, dodging tombstones and hurtling debris.

As he reached a small outbuilding, the earth lurched again, and his face slammed to a violent halt against the wall. The saltiness of his own blood filled his mouth. Dropping to the sidewalk, he covered his head and huddled into a ball, desperately wishing the nightmare would end.

When he heard Aunt Susana's voice, he peeked from beneath his arm to see a jubilant Uncle Chris swinging her around only a few yards away. Protected within a distinct rainbow-bordered bubble, the whole family remained amazingly stable amid the chaos.

"Uncle Chris, please help!" he yelled. "Help me!"

Though he continued to call, they couldn't hear him above the ruckus or see him groveling in the shadows. Only when he fell silent did the glaring impossibility strike him—Aunt Susana was *alive?*

Suddenly he understood: the Awakening was real! Uncle Chris had talked about it often enough. But Willy had persistently filed those tales in the same category as creation—superstitious myth. Yet if Uncle Chris had been right about this, where did that leave Willy, who had tried to silence him? What's more, if the Awakening was real, all that other stuff must be real too —judgment, destruction, eternal death.

A shudder ripped through him, one that had nothing to do with the night's chill or the earth's reeling. His muscles trembled wildly and he curled into a tighter ball, determined to master the terror that had seized him.

When he dared another glance, two others were joining his uncle. He'd never known his grandparents—they'd both died before he was born—but these people looked exactly like the young couple in a wedding photo on Mom's wall. Sorrow washed over him in suffocating waves. How he wanted to be part of that group, to know his grandparents, to be reunited with his family!

But he never would. Though repeatedly invited to accept Doug's rescue, he'd turned down every offer. Oh, he'd had doubts. But, convinced that every individual could determine his own version of truth, he'd systematically suppressed every uncertainty, bargaining for a reward he could earn on his own terms. And now he knew: He'd believed a lie. Personal truth? What a ridiculous notion! Preferences and hopes could never transform a lie into truth, no matter how sincerely held.

Another round of uncontrollable trembling overtook him. The screeching winds seemed to shriek, *You chose the wrong side—and it's too late to change your mind!*

Panic forced an anguished plea from his lips. "Mercy! Mercy, please!"

He honestly wasn't sure what he meant by that plea. He surely didn't mean he'd accept Doug's rescue on Doug's terms rather than his own. Even now, with the planet breaking apart under his feet, he still balked at the idea of baring his soul and admitting everything he'd done. He just wanted some relief from this awful mixture of terror, grief, and hopelessness. He just wanted the nightmare to end.

As if in answer to his cry, the trumpet resounded again. The runners gazed fixedly into the light, unfazed by its intensity. In fact, their faces reflected its radiance. "Hallelujah!" they cried, apparently understanding the noise as language. "Glory to Crown Prince Joshua!"

But while the runners exulted, Willy clearly heard the same trumpet declare, "IF ANYONE TAKES AWAY FROM THE WORDS OF THE MANUAL, I WILL REMOVE HIM FROM THE BOOK OF LIFE."

Willy stared toward the light with a crushing sense of despair. Isn't that what he'd done? Hadn't he removed the full version of *The Runner's Manual* from circulation and replaced it with the revised—no, the corrupted—version?

The voice thundered again, and the runners shouted, "All praise to Prince Joshua!" But while they shouted, apparently oblivious to the declaration Willy could decipher, he heard, "WOE TO THEM WHO FLED FROM

ME! THOUGH I REDEEMED THEM, YET THEY HAVE SPOKEN LIES AGAINST ME!"

Suddenly Willy recognized that voice. He'd heard it since childhood. Through Uncle Chris's stories, it had wooed him. Through Andy's concern, it had warned him. Through Susana's kindness, it had pled with him. But he had argued, rationalized, and fled from it.

"CURSED IS THE ONE WHO ATTACKS HIS NEIGHBOR SECRETLY!"

He squeezed back wretched tears of defeat. How could he argue with one who obviously knew the depths of his heart?

"WOE TO THE SHEPHERDS WHO DESTROY AND SCATTER THE SHEEP OF MY PASTURE!"

How many people had he led astray with false assurances? And why? To make something of himself—to be famous? He'd realized that goal, but at what cost?

"ALL THESE CURSES SHALL OVERTAKE YOU UNTIL YOU ARE DESTROYED, BECAUSE YOU DID NOT OBEY MY VOICE, TO KEEP MY COMMANDMENTS!"

Willy hung his head in hopeless resignation.

"NOTHING IS SECRET THAT WILL NOT BE REVEALED, NOR ANYTHING HIDDEN THAT WILL NOT COME TO LIGHT! YOU SHALL BECOME AN ASTONISHMENT, A PROVERB, AND A BYWORD AMONG ALL NATIONS!"

Willy surrendered to open weeping. It had all been for nothing. In trying to cover up that one terrible night, he had consigned himself to destruction ... and his secret would still be known.

A collective gasp went through the runners, and Willy braved the pain to look directly into the blinding light. A magnificent figure, literally pulsating with power, stared directly at him. Flaming eyes penetrated to his core. Sternness and consuming wrath flashed forth, baring his every secret. The runners' shouts identified the figure as Prince Joshua, but it was not the Prince Joshua Willy knew. Not the one he'd helped to publicize. And certainly not the one whose orders he'd carried out.

He sprang to his feet. Although the planet still writhed, he'd rather die trying to escape than face that single fearsome being. He made it as far as the toppled graveyard wall before one of the police officers caught sight of him. Launching himself at Willy, he battered him with his club. "You! You lied to us! That wasn't Prince Joshua!"

Another tremor separated the two, but it also hurled a massive granite headstone directly at Willy's head. He sank to the ground, knowing he had drawn his last breath—and felt relieved.

When his head plunked to the earth, just before the last spark of life faded from his eyes, he saw Uncle Chris. Rising in the air to meet his prince, his face beamed with joy—a joy Willy had never known. A joy he would never know.

✳ ✳ ✳ ✳ ✳

Camille sat atop a rocky prominence with all the dignity of a queen watching her army march off to certain victory. Her excitement rose with every passing moment. In the desert below, the missiles that would annihilate her ene-my's faithful servants, his favored Outlander Division, were whirring to life. Her victims stood before her like so many pitiful lambs awaiting slaughter. Elsewhere, the prisons housing millions of runners were rigged with explosives. She had already given the order. Any minute, they too would consume their burnt offer-ings and vomit their vile ashes into the sky.

And she would savor every fiery vision, every scream for mercy, every aroma of roasting flesh. Thanks to Adlai's expert ministrations, she had grown strong enough to sit upright and had insisted on being carried to this overlook where she could enjoy her triumph—her revenge. She would admit no disap-pointment, no regret, save one: She could not enjoy this crowning achievement with her brother.

A sigh escaped her, but she refused to dwell on her disillusionment. If Stan was unable to enjoy this moment, she must reap double the pleasure on his behalf. They had both worked too hard to permit any lament to dampen the wondrous victory.

Patric and her guards suddenly bowed and backed away, and she turned to see Stan stomping up to her chair. "What have you done!" he bellowed.

"Stan!" She rose as quickly as she dared and threw herself into his arms. "Stan, you're alive! We can share this magnificent triumph together!" She motioned toward the missiles, even now rising en masse from their launching pads.

Thrusting her away, he repeated, "What have you done?"

Now perceiving his anger, she quailed. Her imprudent exertion caught up with her at the same moment, and she swooned. Stan caught her and set her back on the chair as he scolded, "I said no preemptive strikes! Why did you coun-termand my orders?"

A dazzling light, far brighter than the sun, suddenly beamed from the east. A trumpet rang out and thunder crashed. Terrible thunder. Louder and longer than real thunder, it actually shook the earth.

Slapping her hands over her ears, she glanced anxiously at Stan, who mirrored her concern. They both knew that noise. They couldn't distinguish the Deón's words when they spoke this way, but no Paradisian could mistake the sound.

Too weak for such strange goings-on, Camille carefully stood to draw close to her elder brother, seeking his strength. "He's never spoken to us in that voice before!" She had to yell directly into his ear to be heard over the din.

"It's not speech!" Stan shouted back. "Not entirely! It's the weapon!"

"Weapon?" Camille repeated dumbly. Just then the missiles from which she had expected such great things hit some invisible barrier and simply disinte-grated, like antacid tablets fizzling in a glass of water. She turned from gaping at them to stare at her brother. How did he know what was happening? And if he'd expected this, why hadn't he warned her?

"Run! Every man for himself!" he shouted to the guards. Then, lifting her into his arms, he sprinted for the nearest cleft in the rock. Camille hid her face against his chest, but peeked over his shoulder when the stench of sulfur filled her nostrils. As she watched, a great shaft of lightening struck a mountain, and its top exploded, spewing burning rocks and lava in every direction. A quick glance around told her that other volcanoes were also erupting.

Stan ran mightily, but even he had difficulty negotiating the retching earth. At last they reached the rocky cove. Even tucked within its protection, the thunder grew painfully loud. She gritted her teeth to keep from shrieking in agony.

The earth shook, ever louder and harder. Mountains shifted so violently that boulders flew through the air like tennis balls. Some peaks disappeared, completely flattened. Giant burrows formed within the earth, pushing dead people to the surface. Occasionally tiny twisters materialized into people who had apparently been cremated. Worse, all these people who should be dead jumped to their feet and rejoiced at whatever the voice was saying—triumphant even as the earth crumbled.

When the runners gasped and fell silent, Camille turned eastward to learn what had captured their attention. She squinted into an excruciatingly brilliant *risaju*. Her eyes teared and involuntarily squeezed shut. Even when she forced them open, she struggled to comprehend what her senses told her. Finally the image resolved, and her racing heart turned to ice.

Modén Joshua Deón!

This being could never be confused with the one humans blithely called "Josh." No, there was no cloaking of his true nature in human frailty now. This was *Mikaél*—commander-in-chief of the most powerful army in existence. Crown Prince of the Universe. Creator of all things, seen and unseen.

Deón.

Camille had spent most of her lifetime convincing herself that this being didn't exist. She had gradually rationalized him away, persuading herself that memory had inflated his glory and power. Thus she had imagined him fully explainable, fully knowable—rather like herself.

How very wrong she had been! As her every sense now informed her, Joshua Deón was real. Terrifyingly real. Power emanated from him in visible waves. The brightness that threatened to blind her was but the uncloaking of his true nature. This being did not merely possess all power; he *was* all power. He governed life and death, galaxies and quarks. He literally spoke planets into existence. Worlds fell before him in worshipful awe.

And I'm in rebellion against him!

The thought lifted every hair on her head. How could she have been so exceedingly wrong?

As the hideous truth dawned, she turned to her *beloved* elder brother. He had known about this mysterious—this dreadful!—power. He had expected this response to a preemptive strike. So, even as he had suggested rationalizations to lead her astray, he had known they were lies!

Another jolt of the earth threw her backwards into stone. She did not rise, but lay still, feeling puny and pathetic, desperate and duped. She even wished the great rock that sheltered them would fall on her and snuff out her life, relieving her of this horrible vision of herself—and of Joshua. But alas, although so many other rocks fell, this one stood fast.

She turned a sluggish gaze eastward to watch the runners rising in the air to join Joshua on his *risaju*. She even distinguished Sadira, her face glowing with the reflection of Joshua's radiance as he drew her toward himself.

Yet the same power that drew the runners within its protection killed all others. Desmoden's mighty legions fell without a fight, wholly overwhelmed by Joshua's mere presence. Six thousand years of preparation were swept aside in an instant. Only she and Stan were left to gaze, transfixed, at the catastrophic results.

But no. As the *risaju* glided past, Paradisian exiles gradually crept from their hiding places. Exposure to Prince Joshua's power had killed only the humans. Though obviously overawed, no exiles had died. They only looked as though they wished to.

CHAPTER 49

SAFELY HOME

*"Christ suffered for our sins once for all time. He never sinned,
but he died for sinners to bring you safely home to God."*
1 Peter 3:18, NLT.

C hris's children were already aboard the great airborne platform when he arrived. Now they crowded around to greet him. All were bursting with news—botched beheadings, moldering missiles, food-bearing ferrets, and more. Chris noted each story teaser and determined to get the full scoop later.

But right now, his brain couldn't handle any more wonders, being too busy processing this incredible journey. The vessel—*risaju*, Gabriel called it—was itself a marvel. With more and more outlanders joining them, Chris often thought it had reached maximum capacity. But then it somehow expanded, and they continued to receive even more.

The atmosphere aboard the *risaju* buzzed with joy and anticipation. The Royal Guards constantly moved ahead of the vessel to reunite people, as Lanse had done for Chris's family. The vessel's other occupants kept busy welcoming new arrivals with rounds of renewed celebration.

The *risaju* continued steadily westward, traveling to every corner of the earth. Chris sometimes tried to determine their location but found it difficult. The planet's topography kept changing. He didn't even recognize his own state. California's coastline had shifted to the east by perhaps a hundred miles in some areas. And right after they picked up the refugees on San Miguel, the ocean's raging waters swallowed the entire chain of Channel Islands. He also couldn't tell how long the tour took. Maybe it was moments; maybe it was days. Night and day were alike dispelled by Josh's brightness, and Chris's continual wonderment overrode all sense of time and fatigue.

Finally the *risaju* came to rest on a large island in the South Pacific. Led by their prince, the vast group disembarked and reassembled before some city gates. An expectant hush fell as Josh stood before them. At his side, Gabriel called out an order, and the Outlander Division drew up in military formation before their prince.

Beginning with the Outlander Division, and with Stanley as its commander, Josh proceeded around the entire group, presenting each runner with a golden crown. Some contained many gems and others only a few. Yet from the way each regarded his crown, Chris knew none would trade it for any other, no matter how richly adorned. Nevertheless, after a brief inspection of the gift, every runner, without exception, fell to his knees and placed the crown at the prince's feet.

Once Josh presented Chris with a heavily bejeweled crown of his own, he had no trouble understanding this reaction. As with the trophies from the race, the gems told stories. Together, the jewels of Chris's crown told the story of a wonderfully full life, of victories won, challenges met, and fellow runners rescued. But the large blood red ruby occupying the central place—as it did in every crown—testified that he had earned this crown, not by his own works or goodness, but through the incredible, selfless gift of Crown Prince Joshua, who had given his life for each one.

This reminder of how abundantly Doug had blessed him would have alone drawn grateful praise from Chris's lips. The acknowledgement that all these blessings were won by Josh's amazing sacrifice would have itself driven Chris to his knees. But the crown included yet more. Inside, Chris's new Paradisian name was engraved: *Tsula Pats'ehali*—"He ran it barefoot."

It was a play on the Rarámuri name bestowed by his mother—*towí ke akemi,* "He who runs barefoot." That name, while capturing the essence of Chris's relentless determination, also embodied a mother's dream that he would serve Doug with uncompromising faithfulness. Throughout his life, Chris had tried to fulfill that commission. And now, with the name he'd granted him, his coach was declaring that he'd achieved the goal.

Nothing could have meant more. No gift could have surpassed this evidence of Josh's approval. Nevertheless, the name that meant so much was inscribed directly behind the ruby's position, for Chris had reached his goal only by way of the Damours' empowerment.

Overwhelmed with gratitude, he dropped to the ground and placed the trophy before his regent's feet, tears of joy flowing unchecked down his face. Josh pulled him up and wrapped him in a hug that ended with a kiss on the forehead. Then, with his own hands, Josh settled that amazing crown and that amazing name on Chris's head.

"You have been my faithful friend," he said. "Welcome home."

Once Josh had distributed the crowns, he swung open the gates, which looked like gargantuan pearls. "Come in!" he exulted. "Come in, all you who have been blessed by my father!"

Golden streets led toward buildings on either side of the gates, but Josh led them straight ahead, toward a river. When they reached it, the path opened into a large central garden. They followed the course of the river, and Chris marveled at it the whole way. Jewels of every hue dotted the riverbed, and it teamed with exotic plants and fish. But the water itself particularly drew his attention, being the clearest, cleanest water he'd ever seen. More than that, it was—well, happy. He laughed at the thought, yet the description fit perfectly. The gurgling stream really seemed to be exulting at their arrival.

"Everything's so colorful," Susana breathed. "So … alive!"

"Yeah," Chris agreed. "The trees, flowers, even the grass—such vibrant colors."

"It's soft, too," called Cherie.

Chris looked behind them to see the two girls frolicking barefoot in the grass. Melanie lay prone in it, rolling her face back and forth and giggling. He bent down to run his fingers through blades of velvet softness. Then, kicking off his shoes, he reached for Pete so Susana could enjoy the delightful carpet too.

As they continued walking—and they'd never enjoyed a simple stroll more—a tree in the distance drew their attention. As tall as a giant sequoia, its boughs soared high above the landscape before arching outward and then draping downward in a pattern reminiscent of a weeping willow. It first looked like two trees because separate trunks straddled the river; but as they came nearer, they saw that the trunks joined above the water. Diverse colors dotted the lower portion of its branches, giving the appearance of a Christmas tree decorated only along the bottom. As they approached, they saw that these colors were an assortment of fruits growing within easy reach. Varying widely in size, the fruits came in every color from snow white to eggplant purple, all overlain with accents of gold and silver. The leaves resembled large grape leaves, bluish-green in color. These, too, were flecked with silver and gold so that they sparkled to life as the breeze moved them.

"The *Viv Zabé*," Chris breathed in wonder.

"Then this is Viv fruit," Susana said with equal awe.

"This one's my favorite," Josh said as he popped out from under the tree. He plucked the eggplant-purple fruit and offered it to Chris. "It's called *lelima*."

Chris took the egg-shaped fruit and bit into it. An explosion of tangy orange and sweet coconut delighted his taste buds.

"May I hold your son, Chris?" Josh asked.

"Of course." Chris handed Pete over.

"Hello, little one." Josh stroked Pete's cheeks, and the baby's hands pumped excitedly.

The coach reached up, plucked a leaf from the *Viv Zabé* and chewed it without swallowing. Taking in a deep breath, he placed his mouth over Pete's mouth and nose, as though doing artificial resuscitation, and slowly exhaled into the baby. As he did, Pete's tiny body matured. Although he had awakened vigorous, he otherwise looked exactly like the twenty-one-week premature baby they had buried. Now he grew and developed before their eyes until he looked like a healthy term newborn.

When he'd finished the transformation, Josh wiped the sparkly bluish-green residue from around Pete's nose and mouth. "There now, Petey. You're all caught up." He kissed him on the forehead and handed him back to Chris.

"Thank you," Chris whispered, pulling Josh into a one-armed hug.

"You're welcome, *boní*."

Just then, Sheridan caught up with the group, and Susana peered up at him. "You look familiar," she said thoughtfully. "But I can't remember where I know you from."

"I ..." Sheridan began uncertainly.

"He's a runner I coached while you were resting," Chris said. "His name's Sheridan."

"Oh, that's wonderful!" But her confusion quickly returned. "Wait—then how do I know you?"

"I'm, well, the reason you were resting," Sheridan stammered.

Susana's face cleared. "Oh! You're the general that ..." She trailed off uncertainly and then broke into a smile and threw her arms around him. "Well, I'm so glad you're here!"

Sheridan looked taken aback, but, recovering quickly, he laughed and hugged her back. "Thank you. It's good to be here."

As the two fell into conversation, the group walked on, following the general flow of people up a gentle incline. They topped a low hill to see a grassy valley spread out below them. At the opposite end was the most perfect, most complete, and most vivid rainbow Chris had ever seen. Josh had once told him that, compared with the Paradisian original, the outlander version of things was like an old, faded photograph. That's exactly how he would describe all rainbows he had seen before—faded images of the real thing.

"Other rainbows result from a combination of water and light only," Debora said. "This one results from the merger of justice and mercy."

Chris couldn't say when Debora had joined them, but the whole group now greeted her joyously. Still, he had trouble keeping his eyes off the rainbow. It moved, as though it were alive, and bordered an immense dome of white light.

"The Dome of *Lashani*," Debora explained.

As Chris stared into the dome, more details became apparent. First he perceived the outline of a person who was the source of the radiance—when the person moved, the dome moved, and as the dome moved, its rainbow border moved. They were all connected. Next he distinguished the different colors that made up the white dome, as if seeing it through a prism. Then he actually saw the individual rays of light emanating outward. Still studying the phenomenon, he saw that the rays were composed of little blips, like units of moving energy. Following the paths of these blips, he realized that they were going out from the person in the dome to every other thing. Plants, animals, people—all were continually receiving energy from the person within the dome.

"That," Debora said with a loving smile, "is Doug."

"Wow," Chris breathed. Long ago, he had expressed to Josh his amazement at all that Josh was. His coach's response had been, "Just wait till you meet Dad." Now he understood.

"Doug is the source of all *lashani*-based energy—light and love, truth and beauty, life itself. Even those who reject him still rely on him." She pointed to some red-colored rays that extended far beyond the island. "Those rays of life are sustaining the exiles' lives even now."

"Can he move around—go places?" Chris asked.

"Oh, yes. Wherever he goes, his Dome of *Lashani* goes with him. However, his mercy has prevented him from leaving the island since the rebellion."

"Mercy?" Chris asked. "I don't understand."

"The dome is an extremely concentrated form of *lashani*-based energy. Were it to contact energy corrupted by *kanuf*—hatred, jealousy, and so forth—it would raze it. As the *Manual* says, 'he is a consuming fire.' "

Within the Dome of *Lashani*, Doug sat on a large throne situated on a clear crystal platform. The river originated precisely under Doug's throne and flowed from beneath the platform. The colors of the dome's light reflected in the crystal and in the water as it bubbled forth, providing a magnificent, ever-changing base for the throne. Sometimes it shone calm and clear like a glassy sea; other times it bubbled, vibrant and active like the pool below a waterfall.

Twenty-four smaller thrones also sat on the crystal floor around Doug's throne. Debora said those seated there were elders, special assistants chosen from among humanity. He was about to ask for more information when an athletic man who resembled Mom approached them.

"I see that you have something of mine." Smiling broadly, the man nodded to Chris's neck. "I hope that means we're related."

Debora laughed. "Juan Misi, allow me to introduce your great-grandson, Chris Strider."

"I'm very happy to meet you," Chris exclaimed. "Your stories have meant a great deal to several generations of your descendants." Unfastening the necklace at his throat, Chris handed it back to its owner. "Thank you so much for sharing them with us through your trophy."

Juan smiled fondly at the necklace before fastening it around his own neck. "Thank you for returning it. And maybe you'll introduce me to those descendants you spoke of."

"I'd love to," Chris said. He started by presenting the several family members standing nearby. It seemed their animated conversation had just begun when Doug's voice thundered, "COME!"

Debora broke into a grand smile. "Begging your pardon, but I must leave you," she said, and jogged toward the platform. Josh jogged by right after, along with another Debora … and another … and another …

How many Deboras were there, anyway?

As he watched, Chris saw hundreds—no, thousands, maybe more—of Deboras jogging toward Doug. As the Deboras got close to one another, they converged, and as they merged, her appearance gradually altered. At first the changes were so subtle that Chris barely noticed them, but soon he realized that her hair, usually a rich brown shade, had turned red. Then her torso became more fluid, a transformation that gradually worked its way down into her legs. The color of her body shifted too, taking on hues of red and orange, so that she began to resemble a large flame rather than a person. By the time she reached the platform, there was just one Debora, who was now one large flame. The crystal platform, reflecting her presence, took on the appearance of beautiful fiery stones.

When Josh and Debora reached the steps at either side of the platform, strains of wondrous music spread over the valley. Chris glanced around for the orchestra, but found none. Instead, the rich refrain seemed to emanate from the rainbow. What's more, the entire dome seemed to dance, the units of energy jumping about like exuberant children unable to contain their excitement. As Josh and Debora ascended the steps, lightning flashed from Doug's throne. A grand eight-part chorus, which seemed to emanate from the throne, joined the orchestral music. Then, together, they crescendoed until Chris actually felt their vibration in his core.

Debora and Josh advanced toward Doug. When they reached him, he enclosed one in each arm, and the rainbow burst into a million hues that danced around the sky, exploding, rejoining, and exploding again and again in a magnificent play of light. At the same moment, the symphony burst into glorious, wonderfully complex harmonies. The whole experience—the music, the lights, the resonance vibrating within him—simply defied words.

The light show obscured the trio for several moments. When Chris could again see them, they were one being. The face and body gradually alternated between those of Doug and Josh, and the flame that was Debora blazed within.

But the Dome of *Lashani*—where was it? Chris looked up and, spying the rainbow, traced its arc in the sky to see that it now arched over the entire congregation. He no longer saw the dome because he was in it, sharing an unspeakably joyous sense of love and community.

The twenty-four elders burst into song. Chris, along with the rest of humanity, joined with them in a song of thanksgiving that he had never heard, yet knew instinctively. As the entire valley resounded with joy, his skin broke out in gooseflesh. Every part of his body seemed to vibrate with the music, as if his very atoms were joining in the magnificent chorus.

Had someone once assembled a list of the world's seven greatest wonders? They were wrong. There was only one—and this amazing ecstasy was it.

Joy continued to swell within him, constantly expanding to levels he had never imagined, much less experienced. It occurred to him that if he were to add up every hardship and trial, every pain and discomfort he had ever experienced as a runner, the sum of it—the pain of a lifetime—would easily be worth this one glorious moment in the Deón's presence. And eternity awaited him. What further wonders would he meet?

Tears of gratitude pricked at his eyes. "Thank you, Josh," he whispered as the song ended. "Thank you so very much."

"You're very welcome, *boni.*" Josh seemed to be speaking the words directly into Chris's mind. "I'm so glad you're here to enjoy it with me."

CHAPTER 50
A PLACE FOR YOU

"In My Father's house are many mansions ...
I go to prepare a place for you."
John 14:2, NKJV.

Sheridan sat unmoving in the defendant's chair, desperately wishing to be anywhere else. Stan was an exceptional prosecuting attorney. He had documented, complete with pictures and videos, every one of Sheridan's crimes against Doúg. The combined weight of the offences threatened to crush the forlorn defendant. He could in no wise argue them.

But his defense attorney did argue. Pointing to a picture from the Battle of Grace Hill, Josh calmly said, "The price is paid, Stan. You extracted the punishment from me, remember?"

"Not for him!" Stan bellowed. "Not *him*! You cannot possibly justify forgiving him if you condemn me. He's more surely mine than any human has ever been. I genetically engineered him using my own *mij dinósh*. I personally mentored him from birth, teaching him to hate and kill, to steal and maim, to blaspheme you Deón and flagrantly reject your laws!" (Paradisian: restoring enzyme) Stan was clicking through more slides to prove each point, and Sheridan was feeling much like a wounded fawn being stalked by a voracious lion.

"Yours, is he?" Josh said. "Did you spark life in that embryo?" A picture showed Doug's ray of life touching the embryo under Stan's microscope. Returning to the picture from Grace Hill, Josh asked, "Did you pay the price to redeem him from slavery? Did you teach him to know sorrow for *kanuf* and yearning for holiness?" He ended with a picture of Sheridan weeping on Debora's shoulder, and Stan turned away in disgust.

"Yes, he *was* yours." Josh rounded the bench to sit in the judge's seat. "He fell deeply into *kanuf*, deceived and trained at your hand. But he responded to Doúg's grace. He repented. He accepted my payment of his debt. He allowed Debora to change him. And so I can—and do—forgive him. I find him innocent of all charges." He brought the gavel down hard. "He is no longer your slave. He is my father's son."

Stabbing himself in the finger with a lancet, Josh allowed a drop of blood to fall onto the large book lying open before him and pressed his signet ring into it.

When Stan stormed out of the courtroom, Sheridan stared after him in wonder. He had lost the case! Though correct about every charge, he had lost. Josh had pronounced Sheridan innocent!

Filled with deep relief and overpowering gratitude, Sheridan turned to his judge, frozen in place with his signet ring in the drop of blood. "Thank you, Josh," he murmured.

"You're welcome." The real Josh had slipped into the room unseen. "Computer, end *Trial of Sheridan Lanáj*."

The images dissolved, startling Sheridan back to the present. The holographic footage felt so real, he'd forgotten it was a recording. In actuality, his trial had already occurred. Josh had appeared on his behalf, as well as served as his attorney and judge.

Making his way across the room to stand before him, Josh asked, "Now do you believe me?"

"I don't deserve that verdict," Sheridan answered, lost in wonder.

"What *you* deserve has nothing to do with it."

Sheridan nodded thoughtfully. "I believe you've earned the right to redeem me. And I believe you have the power to transform me into someone who belongs here." Looking into Josh's face, he continued, "Because it has nothing to do with me, and everything to do with you, I accept your verdict and believe it can stand forever."

"Computer," Josh said, "proceed with the final edit for *Trial of Sheridan Lanáj*."

"What's that mean?" Sheridan asked.

"Our kingdom is built on trust," Josh answered. "We want our subjects to feel confident in our decisions. So everyone has the right to review all footage. However, in line with our promise to blot out your *kanuf,* the tape is edited once you accept your verdict."

"So what will other people see?"

"Computer," Josh said, "play *Trial of Sheridan Lanáj*."

Sheridan didn't want to relive that awful experience again, but he dutifully watched as the holographic images retook their places. However, this time he couldn't distinguish any specific crimes. Stan's accusations were dubbed over with a recording of Sheridan's repentance. Stan's pictorial evidence was replaced with pictures of Josh on Grace Hill.

When Sheridan caught on, he roared with laughter. "You can't even prove jay-walking from this!"

"That's the idea," Josh agreed with a grin. "Your life record has been similarly edited."

"That must make all but the last month pretty boring," Sheridan said wryly.

"Maybe not as boring as you think," Josh said. "Computer, play *Life of Sheridan Lanáj*. Begin at noon on Day One."

A new room instantly materialized, and Sheridan saw his newborn self being checked out of Desmon Tower's hospital—not by either of his parents, but by Mrs. Jenkins. Grinning with pride, she took him home, introducing him to every random person she met along the way. Sheridan was touched by her obvious love for him. Although he didn't remember receiving any affection before defecting to Doug's side, this kindly older woman—someone he barely remembered—expressed love even in the way she held him and spoke to him.

When the baby Sheridan grew tired, Mrs. Jenkins carried him into the nursery, took out a pen, and walked around the room with it. The grown Sheridan jerked out of his chair and drew close to inspect the device. With a laugh, he exclaimed, "She's sweeping for bugs!"

Josh nodded. "My father prepared her well. Even your parents were never suspicious of her."

Mrs. Jenkins settled into a rocking chair and, right there in his parents' home, softly told him all about Doug and his rescue. Then she sang a runner's lullaby to him.

She continued rocking the sleeping babe for some time, tears forming in her eyes. "Doug has told me that yours will be a very difficult life, little one. My heart aches for what awaits you. You'll know so little of love or approval. But I want you to know that you are a beautiful child. Already I can tell that you're smart, yet easy-going. You'll be a mischievous creature, you will, and you'll probably tax my patience. But you'll be a true joy as well."

She held him a little longer, gazing adoringly into his sleeping face, before finally laying him in his crib. "I love you, sweet baby Sheridan," she whispered. "I always will."

As the door closed behind her, Sheridan said, "I remember so little of her. She was killed during Stanley's rescue, wasn't she?"

"Yes. But she's here now. Would you like to meet her?"

"I'd love to," Sheridan exclaimed, spinning to him. Then he reconsidered. "But, well, how much will she know about—" He glanced down at the holographic newborn. Surely she would be horribly disappointed by what that baby had become.

"Your life record is already edited. All your *kanuf* has been blotted out. She will know only what you tell her. But you'll find that she—that all faithful runners and Paradisians—will only find more reason to praise my father in whatever you care to divulge."

"If that's the case, I want to tell it all."

❅ ❅ ❅ ❅ ❅

Riana was lounging beside a small lake, enjoying the company of several family members, while awaiting her turn to meet Doug. She was watching Cherie, Melanie, and Eddie feed the ducks when Colonel Jané Lanáj appeared at the top of the nearby knoll with a sturdy blond woman. Stanley immediately sprang up and bee-lined straight for her. After wrapping her in a long hug, he returned with tears in his eyes and introduced her as Anna Jenkins, his long lost childhood nanny.

During the reminiscing that followed, Riana mused that she'd never seen the usually staid man laugh so much or with such abandon. Perhaps he, who had known so much about the enemy's strategies and on whom so much responsibility had rested, had never had the opportunity for such unrestrained joy. Or maybe reuniting with his nanny had brought out the child in him—although Anna insisted he'd been somber even as a boy.

On the other hand, many of the memories they shared wouldn't have been funny when they happened, not while under the threat of Stan's detection. Only now that they were safely beyond danger could they see incidents in a different light—one full of wonder, even amusement. Jané's contributions also added new perspective, for she had been a Royal Guard assigned to both Anna and Susana and related elements that revealed how closely Doug had protected them. Consequently moments of quiet admiration and thankfulness often followed periods of boisterous laughter.

"Auntie Jané," Cherie called during one of the quieter moments. "Sashi's hurting the ducks."

Jané looked over her shoulder and laughed. Her goat, Sashi, was splashing around, intent on catching a duck, but was taking more nips than she was handing out. "Sashi, will you never learn? You shan't win against the whole flock." To Cherie she added, "She won't hurt them, sweetheart. Animals here have no aggressive tendencies. They're merely playing their own version of tag."

At that moment Anna let out a squeal. "Sheridan!" Jumping up, she dashed toward her former charge, who had just topped the knoll with Josh.

"Mrs. Jenkins!" Sheridan caught her and swung her around and around until they both fell down, dizzy.

Laughing, she panted, "You always were the mischievous one. Oh, I'm so happy you're here."

"From what I've seen," he said with sudden sobriety, "you played a big part in that. I was just too young to consciously remember your lessons."

She patted him fondly on the cheek. "I thank Doug if that's so. He honored me greatly by allowing me to minister to you children."

They joined the group, and more reminiscing followed. After a while, Josh turned to Riana. "It's your turn to see your home and to meet *Adu*. Are you ready?"

Riana jumped up. "Am I ever!"

"Prince Joshua?" Jané said excitedly.

He laughed. "Of course you may join us. Felíp, too, if he'd like."

While Jané made a quick call, Josh explained, "Jané's an architect, and Felíp, her brother, is a structural engineer. They worked with me on your home. It provided some unique challenges."

"Is that because it's constructed on sand, by any chance?" Riana asked. She loved the ocean and had once considered becoming a marine biologist. She'd always dreamed of having a home on the beach.

Josh chuckled. "You're not getting any more information out of me. I don't want to spoil the surprise."

Riana's hopes rose when Josh led her away from the city toward a tranquil beach. But when he stepped onto a jetty, those hopes plummeted. The gazebo she saw at the end of it looked beautiful—but awfully small for a house, especially since she and Andy now knew they were expecting a son.

When they reached the gazebo, a man rose from a chair, his face full of anticipation. He introduced himself as Felíp Lanáj. He and Jané eagerly pointed out the many gorgeous details of the room. A hand-woven rug softened the granite flooring that supported a roll-top desk, matching chair, and credenza. On either side, walls of hibiscus bushes provided a wind break. Beyond the flooring, above the sloshing waves, a suite of outdoor sofas circled an in-ground fire pit.

Riana gazed over the restful scene as she took in a long draft of the salt air. "It's beautiful, exactly the study I've always wanted."

Jané and Felíp grinned at one another and congratulated themselves with a high-five.

"Is that the only room you wanted in a—?"

Sashi interrupted Josh's question with a sudden, demanding bleat.

"Oh, Sashi!" Jané exclaimed with a laugh. "Must you spoil Prince Joshua's surprise?"

Sashi answered by repeating her demand. Her insistence drew Riana's attention to the pole she seemed to be petitioning. Situated off the stone flooring among the bushes, it hadn't come to Riana's notice before.

"What is that?" she asked as she moved toward it.

"Push the button and find out," Josh challenged.

Riana did, and somewhere beneath her a motor hummed to life. The granite floor sank to become part of a much larger room beneath the jetty. The study now looked out through a semi-circular glass wall, the waves slapping at its lower edge. She could hardly tear her gaze from the breathtaking view. But when she did turn around, she saw overstuffed chairs, sofas, and bookshelves topping an ivory carpet, and a circular stairway descending to another level.

"Oh, my." Leaning over the railing, she gasped. "Oh, my!" She rushed down the steps to a large kitchen and dining area. The window showcased swaying kelp with fish swimming lazily through its leaves. The stairway led to yet another level.

Descending again, Riana came to a bedroom and nursery where the windows looked out on graceful manta rays and lobsters scuttling along the ocean floor. Andy sat at the window, trailing his finger along the glass in front of a curious porpoise.

"Wow," Riana breathed, wholly overcome. "This is—it's just—"

"It's fantastic, isn't it?" Andy jumped up, grabbed her hand, and pulled her to a different section of the window. "Look at all these anemones over here. Aren't they amazing? And look there—the coral."

The two of them continued to explore the house, their excitement constantly adding to the obvious delight of its designers. Several times Andy assured her that it was real, for she kept wondering if she were dreaming—the home was so far beyond even her wildest imagination.

Finally Josh announced that it was time for her to meet Doug. Together they made their way to Doug's throne, situated in the very center of the park that was at the center of the city. When she had realized that the valley was actually Doug's throne room, she'd been a little confused. She'd never seen a throne room, but she'd heard they were lavishly decorated. It seemed odd for the world's wealthiest king to have his outdoors.

Yet as they approached the throne now, Riana reconsidered. Behind and on either side of the dais grew walls of golden flowers—thornless roses and bougainvillea, poppies and daisies, hibiscus and birds of paradise, plus other varieties she'd never seen. The combination was not only visually stunning, but, as her closer perspective now allowed her to appreciate, imbued the air with an intoxicating perfume. Songbirds flitted among the shrubbery, adding their music to the scene. Above, feathery clouds embellished a sky of cerulean blue. Below, the river's multicolored gems blended with the rainbow's varied hues to paint the crystal canvas of the floor with wondrous colors, creating a portrait that was constantly changing, ever magnificent.

No, she realized—no enclosed throne room could possibly surpass this one. They might very well be more gaudy, but they could never be more glorious.

When Josh formally announced her, Gabriel and Lanse, on either side of the dais, lifted trumpets to their lips to blow a musical welcome. The joyous tune set Riana's heart dancing. When Doug's gaze rested on her, her feet suddenly seemed to have a mind of their own. She found herself dashing up the central stairs to rocket herself into her *adu's* arms.

Doug laughed—a deep, hearty, welcoming laugh—as his loving arms encircled her. "Oh, I've waited a long time for this hug. I'm so glad you're finally here."

He took her by the hand and showed her around some of his favorite parts of the garden as he leisurely answered all her questions—at least, all the ones she could remember to ask. They must have strolled together for hours, and she never felt rushed.

It's like in the song—meeting Doug in the garden, walking and talking with him, having him tell me I am his own.

Stopping to face her, he said, "You are, you know."

"I am what?"

"You are my own, Riana. My own dear daughter—forevermore."

CHAPTER 51
BOUND

*"He laid hold of the dragon, that serpent of old, who is the Devil
and Satan, and bound him for a thousand years."*
Revelation 20:2, NKJV.

4 March 8044 M.E.

Slumped against the opening of the cave that had become her home, Camille half-heartedly fanned her face as she looked out upon the vast emptiness. She had stayed in the African wilderness since Joshua's appearance a month before. Most of the exiles had. They had no reason to move until their scouts finished surveying the planet. Here, at least, they knew where to find food, water, and gasoline for their generators.

However, the scouts' preliminary reports were disappointing. The cities were mere heaps of wreckage, absent any functioning utilities, communications, or conveniences. Eventually, they would plunder the ruins for supplies, but they had no need to do so now. Indeed, they had two excellent reasons to postpone the work: sanitation and stench. Corpses littered the world like hotdog wrappers after a ballgame, as Garrick had so aptly phrased it. Near the cities, the stench was simply unbearable, and it would remain so until the scavengers had finished their work.

She lifted a tangle of hair off her sticky neck and considered the tedium ahead. With no outlanders to deceive, or even to use as slaves, her days had degenerated into an unrelenting round of mind-numbing activities. Fetching and boiling water, locating and extracting food from the debris, protecting her prizes from raiders and caring for the wounds she earned in the process—this was the sum of her life. She was surviving. Period. And she had nothing to look forward to tomorrow except more of the same. For an intellect as advanced as hers, such menial work was excruciatingly boring.

She had never thought she could miss humans. Yet with none to plot against, she had no reason to perform any of the activities that had consumed her for 6,000 years. And neither did anyone else. Furthermore, if the war was indeed over, the future promised nothing but punishment for treason—which did nothing to improve the general mood. They had become a community—

She snorted at the thought. Community? No, not even in the loosest sense. Rather, they had become a mass of angry, marginally connected individuals with no common goals. Furthermore, the attempted coup had reignited all the smoldering personal antagonisms kindled through centuries of infighting, reducing the possibility of cooperation even further. Frayed nerves turned any minor provocation into a major confrontation. Even siblings who had never fallen out were no longer living together. That she and Stan maintained separate living quarters surprised no one—but Garrick and Errol? They had always been inseparable.

She blew out a harsh sigh. Something must be done. Their group included the most brilliant scientists of all time, as well as the most ingenious inventors and builders. They ought not be sitting around in these primitive conditions. They had built this world once; they could do so again—if they would only cooperate.

But Stan had always been the glue that held them together. Or, perhaps, the fire that kept them huddled together. Either way, nothing would happen without his leadership. This meant she must visit him. Talk to him.

"Ugh," she groaned.

She and Stan hadn't spoken since "that day," as they now referred to Joshua's return. She had learned the story of her brother's rescue only from Garrick. She had managed to wheedle it from him in pieces once his mood improved from an overwhelming fury at Stan to a mere brooding annoyance with all living things.

On that fateful day, when Garrick and some of his troops located the drugged and unconscious Stan, Saxon's men started a fire to snare them. The trapped contingent found an escape route, but, in the confusion and low visibility, believed Stan and Garrick had been killed. Meanwhile Garrick, carrying Stan on his back, had discovered another way out, though it required abandoning his gear. With neither light nor radio, he couldn't safely negotiate the mountainous terrain with his burden so he sought shelter and waited through the night. Once Stan regained mobility, the two found their way back to camp.

It comforted Camille that Garrick didn't blame her for the disastrous outcome of the battle. He appropriately laid that blame squarely at Stan's door. Nevertheless, it angered her that Stan had withheld such vital information from her. Garrick believed Joshua would have used the weapon anyway. Still, they could have planned differently if they'd only known …

"If only, if only," she mocked herself. Dwelling on nonexistent possibilities was almost as imbecilic as Stan's withholding the information in the first place. She really ought to use her time more productively.

She grabbed her bucket and descended the mountain toward a pool of water that had formed after the last aftershock. When she detoured to Stan's abode, she found the cave strangely quiet, even though her link-sense insisted he was within.

"Stan?" Receiving no answer, she called more loudly. "I know you're here. You might as well answer."

A low moan preceded a grumpy, "Go away."

"You're still asleep at this hour?"

When she received no answer, she entered and picked her way past the uncharacteristic clutter. She soon encountered a sour, nauseous scent that grew increasingly strong. She didn't immediately recognize the foul odor, primarily because she'd never had reason to associate it with Stan. But by the time she found him, her stomach was threatening to heave, and she'd recognized the distinctive mix of vomitus and alcohol.

Nudging him with her foot, she exclaimed, "Have you actually been drinking?"

He grabbed his head. "Quit yelling."

She lit a nearby lamp and crouched down to examine him. He groaned and turned away, but not before she had stifled her own groan and turned away in disgust. Dried vomit spotted his matted hair and beard while dirt and body odor saturated his expensive clothing. Overcome with revulsion, she bolted from the cave to gulp in clean air. She'd always abhorred the sight of drunken men; the stronger the man, the more repugnant the sight. But she'd never seen her brother in such a state.

In her loathing of such weak displays, she almost left him to his own decay. But she reconsidered. Revolting he might be, but he was still her elder brother, and people's opinion of her would be altered by their opinion of him. She wasn't sure why that still mattered, but she wouldn't have anyone else see him in such a state.

Snatching up both her bucket and Stan's, she marched down the mountain to fill them. When she returned, she gleefully splashed one entire bucket of cold water over him.

He rose up like an angry bear. "What the—! How dare you! I'll—!"

Then his hangover caught up with him. He stumbled, grabbed his head with both hands, and sank back to the ground.

"Behold," she mocked. "The great Stanley L. Moden, D.Sc., J.D., Ph.D.—hung over."

"Quit yelling!"

"I'll yell if I choose. You're in no condition to stop me."

She set the other pail of water near him and squirted shampoo over his head and clothes. "Here's a towel and fresh clothes. Wash yourself, or I'll do it for you. You're disgusting."

"So what?" he challenged, though nonetheless shucking his shirt to comply. "We've lost. No reason to keep a clear head anymore, now is there?"

She picked her way back to the front of the cave where he'd set up a plank as a desk. "So that's your assessment of our situation, is it? Hopeless?"

When his grunt of affirmation reached her, she asked, "Then if the war's over, why are we still alive?"

For several minutes, she heard only grunts and sloshing water. Sitting on the rock that served as a chair, she leaned her elbows on the makeshift desk and waited. Finally Stan joined her, bringing the lamp with him. "Do you really want to know why we're still alive?"

As he spoke, he placed the lamp on the desk, bathing it in light. For the first time, she saw that the book before her was *The Runner's Manual,* opened to the description of the ancient Day of Atonement. Beside the book lay a page of his notes. Camille's eyes widened at the heading: "Azazel."

Memory instantly transported her back some thirty-five centuries to a similar mountainside near Sinai. The Hebrews had dedicated their sanctuary a year before, and Moden interpreters had scrutinized every aspect of the newly instated services. The different sacrifices, the structure's embellishments, the priestly garb—everything had special significance. Yet many questions remained unanswered. Consequently, Moden interpreters had gathered to observe the first *yom kippur,* the completion of the sanctuary's yearly cycle, hoping it would clarify some points. Stan considered it sufficiently important that he trekked out to the desert too. And Camille, her interest piqued by the sense of dread overshadowing her brother, accompanied him.

How many, many times she had since wished that she had not.

That first Day of Atonement differed in several respects from the twice-daily sacrifices that the priests had been offering over the previous year. However, the most compelling variation involved two goats. These were tied near the sanctuary's entrance while Aaron sacrificed a bull and sprinkled its blood within the tent. Then one of the goats was also sacrificed and its blood carried into the tent.

Marvin, their chief interpreter, was confident of the symbolism thus far, for Moses's writings explained it. Aaron, he said, was sprinkling the goat's blood within both inner compartments. Then he would sprinkle it on the altar outside. Since sacrificial blood was used for cleansing, this action purged the sanctuary of all the *kanuf* that had been forgiven and symbolically carried into the tent during the previous year's sacrifices.

Aaron exited the tent and, just as Marvin had predicted, sprinkled blood on the altar. The interpreter grinned and announced triumphantly, "The sanctuary is now purified."

Stan had glanced at her with a frown then. While identifying with Marvin's joy at having a prediction fulfilled, they had discerned something quite alarming, something that had apparently escaped their chief interpreter. They had recognized the physical sanctuary as a representation of Paradise Island's throne room, and Stan had deduced that its ceremonies afforded a glimpse into Damour's plan to rescue humans from *kanuf*. So if the king intended to "purify" his world, he intended to purify it *of them*.

Aaron bent over the second goat, the one that had been selected for "Azazel." "This is the part I can't figure out," Marvin murmured. "The first goat is designated as the goat for the Lord, presumably representing Prince Joshua. So Azazel must also represent a specific person. But whom?"

Aaron laid both hands on the living goat's head and confessed the nation's *kanuf*—an entire year's worth.

"Why is he doing that?" Camille mused aloud. Those evil deeds had already been confessed over a sacrificial lamb; they had been symbolically forgiven through that lamb's blood; they had been moved to the sanctuary. Why were they still an issue?

When the meaning came to her, she caught her breath. Yes, the individual humans had been forgiven for their part in those deeds. But the deeds themselves lived on through the consequences that had resulted, through the egocentric attitudes that had prompted the actions, and—most importantly from Camille's standpoint—in the minds of the exiles who had first conceived the deeds and urged their completion. The *kanuf* had been forgiven, *but it had not been eradicated*.

So this atonement business was about more than forgiving humans for their misdeeds. It was about returning the world to purity—the eternal annihilation of *kanuf* itself. Placing it on the live goat symbolized its removal from Doúg's universe ... and its attachment to the originator of all *kanuf*.

In seeking a better vantage point, Stan had moved closer to Camille, close enough that she could feel him trembling. He had already reached this conclusion—and knew himself to be Azazel.

Camille lifted a hand to brush some hair from her face, only to find that she, too, was trembling. She had no doubt that her fate, and the fate of all the exiles, was bound up with Stan's. Although they hadn't originated *kanuf*, they had, each one, instigated some of the deeds confessed over that goat. If they lost this war, they would bear their portion of that onerous burden—centuries of accumulated *kanuf*.

Aaron handed the animal's halter to another man, who led the goat away and released him in the wilderness. As she watched, Camille searched feverishly for an alternate explanation of this ceremony. Just as she was beginning to hope for a less ominous interpretation, the man who had led the goat away returned empty-handed. However, he was not allowed to reenter the camp until he washed both himself and his clothes.

As though contaminated by his contact with that goat.

Marvin said thoughtfully, "So the live goat isn't sacrificed. Its death isn't required for either forgiveness or purification."

"That goat doesn't have to die?" Stan asked hopefully.

"Oh, no, it's meant to die," Marvin assured him. "But its death isn't required for *this* ceremony. Damour is saying that the live goat has no part in accomplishing his work. Its death is required for justice, not for atonement. And unlike the sacrificial animals, contact with that goat leads not to cleansing, but to pollution—at least from Damour's perspective."

If he had stopped there, the remainder of Marvin's life would have been considerably more comfortable. Like many academics, however, he tended to become over-excited at the mere fact of a discovery—any discovery—and to over-estimate the excitement it would bring to others. So, turning eagerly to Stan, he continued. "It must be you! You're Azazel! You're the one who will bear the ultimate guilt for originating *kanuf*, the one who—"

Marvin stopped short, finally registering the glare on Stan's face. But it was too late. Until then, Stan had neither liked nor disliked Marvin; forever afterward, he loathed him. Yet the hatred was merely reactionary, an emotion begotten by the dread and horror consuming him at that moment.

She and Stan hadn't discussed that ceremony again, and no Moden employee who valued their health mentioned the word "Azazel" in Stan's presence. Indeed, to Camille, its presence on the notes swimming before her sickened gaze fully explained her brother's despair. She now understood his unprecedented need for a period of drunken forgetfulness.

Looking up, she met Stan's eyes, all mockery gone. "I'm not sure I want to know what you've discovered, *zuule*. But I think you should tell me anyway."

He settled on a nearby rock, his head dropping heavily into his hands. "The war is over. And we did lose."

"That's *not* my fault," she snapped.

With a grimace, he hissed, "Quit yelling or get out."

"Apologies. I will try to control my volume. But if you had trusted me with that information, things might have turned out differently."

"Actually," he said with a weary sigh, "I don't think it would have made any difference at all. But that wasn't my point."

Mollified by his tacit acceptance of her accusation, she said, "Very well. Then what is your point?"

"Our fate is decided, but Damour has yet to mete out—" He paused before finishing softly, "—justice."

A chill passed through her, and she whispered, "So why are we still alive?"

"I think he's only finished judging his runners. Now he's judging the others—the dead humans. Although we have no part to play in that, he apparently wants us alive during the whole process, from start to finish."

"Why?"

He shrugged. "So we can watch what he's doing—or not doing—in the outlander world, I suppose. He doesn't want to give us grounds for claiming that he breached the terms of war while we were dead and unable to observe it."

"So ... we're alive to watch him do nothing?"

He rubbed his face. "Yeah. That's one way of putting it."

"Sounds rather dreary."

Quietly he said, "In the last chapter of the *Manual*, John likened this time to us being 'bound.' "

"An apt metaphor. With all the humans dead or on the island, we have nothing productive to do. We're simply surviving, existing." She swallowed before whispering the forbidden words, "Like the goat for Azazel."

He looked up sharply, but resignation quickly replaced his anger, and he nodded. "Wandering in a desolate wilderness until—" She sensed the terror that ripped through him, stealing the words from his mouth: *Until justice demands our punishment.*

She swallowed on a dry lump in her throat. "For how long? The whole …?"

"Millennium," he said with another sigh. "That's right."

A flood of despair washed over her. She had been a workaholic since the rebellion—happily and proudly so, for her work made life worth living. In her entire 8,044 years of life, she had never lacked a goal. She felt hopelessly bored and worthless after only a month of this purposeless existence. What wretchedness did another thousand years of monotony guarantee—never mind the anxiety that would plague her over her certain future?

"Wait a minute!" she exclaimed, and then dropped her voice when Stan winced. "The *lakviv*—we can't survive nearly a millennium." How strange that the possibility of death should bring hope. Yet, filled as she now was with anxiety over her future, she yearned for a respite, just as Stan had needed a period of temporary oblivion.

Stan again rubbed his face. "Sorry—no such luck. There's no longer any trace of *lakviv* in anyone, even Adlai. Apparently Joshua's presence acted like a booster shot of *viv* for us."

Grave silence descended upon them, further deepening the misery that had gripped Camille. But a lifetime of activity was not easily put aside, and her mind eventually returned to its original goal, as if desperately seeking any glimmer of purpose.

Straightening her posture, she said firmly, "Well, if our lives have been extended for a millennium, we should at least organize to better our situation."

Stan cast her a glance that said, *You've got to be kidding.*

"I'm serious," she said adamantly. "If we must remain alive during this time, we might as well be comfortable."

Stan snorted. "Fine. If you can get anyone to cooperate, go for it."

"I?" she shot back, for she knew exactly how to enlist him. If she required a goal to give her life purpose, Stan required a position of power. "You've led us for 6,000 years, Stan. You are our leader still."

* * * * *

The general atmosphere of antagonism, blame, and hopelessness was not conducive to building community spirit, but Camille's challenge had the desired effect upon her brother. Like the great man he had always been, he rose above his depression. He even managed to restore a measure of organization to the dispirited exiles. Where this required physical coercion, the exercise served only to boost his self-confidence and further energize him. Within a week, he had brought most of the group's leaders back within his influence and convened a meeting of his cabinet.

Nevertheless, Garrick remained conspicuously absent. He considered Stan's failure to share key information to be a betrayal of his lifetime of support and friendship, and he would not quickly forget such an injury. Errol took his brother's place at the table, dutifully reporting that the minister of defense had been unavoidably detained on his latest scouting expedition. But this fooled no one. Garrick had always been Stan's closest friend and staunchest supporter. His refusal to attend hung like a pall over the meeting, dooming it from the start. Within an hour, all of the tentatively forged bonds between them had dissolved.

They had degenerated into a noisy mob when Garrick appeared. Quiet and unmoving, he stood a little apart from the quarrelling group until the others gradually noticed him and fell silent. When he had the entire group's attention, he wordlessly set up the laptop he carried and flipped through a series of pictures.

There were many excellent artists among them, including Camille herself. And these had frequently channeled homesickness into splendid paintings depicting their homeland. Garrick, ever the art lover, though not a talented artist, had often photographed these works. His slideshow began with these, reminding them all of the land of unparalleled beauty and bliss that they had left behind. Then he systematically clicked through present-day slides from every continent. He said nothing during the entire presentation. He didn't need to.

Camille watched these latter slides in morbid fascination. The island nations were unrecognizable, many islands having vanished. Similarly, numerous seaports had disappeared, dramatically altering the coastlines of every continent. Entire mountain chains had been flattened, whereas other mountains had been uprooted, leaving cavernous gashes in the landscape. Huge stones littered the highways, rendering them impassable. But perhaps the most striking change was the planet's eerie emptiness. Except for the scavengers that glutted themselves on the abundant corpses, no living creature walked the planet. All that remained of once great cities were immense piles of rubble and pools of blackened blood. No sign of civilization remained in any quarter.

Although Camille had heard the earlier reports, she was not prepared for the comprehensive nature of this destruction. She quickly abandoned any hope of finding an area with functional modern conveniences. But she sensed much greater mourning in her brother. Under his impassive exterior he grieved with the anguished keening of shattered dreams. Those ruins were to have been his glorious kingdom. Those corpses were to have been the legions he would rally against Damour. And what had he realized instead? Enmity. Unending conflict. Absolute devastation.

They had left Paradise Island with such great expectations! Stan had promised them a better life—one without restrictions or limits, a life of unquestioned liberty and unending fulfillment. But after six long millennia of untiring labor, they had reaped only failure and ruin. And Stan, once the most exalted mortal in the universe, had become the scorned ruler of a planet in shambles. Rather than rising higher, they had all sunk lower ... then lower still.

When Garrick's merciless slideshow ended, he closed the laptop and lifted deep black eyes full of rage to Stan. Quietly, he asked, "What happened to your 'better idea,' Stan?"

CHAPTER 52

JUDGMENT

"And I saw thrones, and they sat on them, and judgment was committed to them ... And they lived and reigned with Christ for a thousand years."
Revelation 20:4, NKJV.

"Computer, pause." Jorge rose from his judge's throne and walked around the large semi-circular bench to move into the holographic re-creation of a small chapel. Behind the bench, a subdued silence fell over the other eleven judges.

"I'd always hoped she'd be here," he said as he gazed at the small woman kneeling before a candle. Getting into that position had been awkward, her pregnancy advanced as it was, yet she had refused Debora's help, even to kneel.

"Me too," said Mom, who was one of the other judges. "I never really had the chance to know her when we lived in Santa María, but people said she attended services regularly, so I'd hoped that she'd known Doug."

Gazing into her drawn face, Jorge said, "No. She feared him; she didn't know him, much less love him."

"Debora repeatedly tried to change that," noted Dad, also a judge.

"Yes," Jorge agreed. "In fact, I'm amazed at how relentlessly Doug pursued her. Seen from a larger perspective, she had no outstanding talents or abilities to commend her." Nodding at a couple of the judges, he added, "Some of you tried to show her the truth about Doug."

"She was too proud to accept Josh's pardon as a free gift," replied a runner who had known her well. "She wanted to earn it. She was always doing penance and scraping together little sums of money, hoping to buy Doug's favor."

These weren't conjectures based on speculation. In evaluating her life, the judges were made privy to her most secret contemplations and motivations; the recordings documented thoughts as clearly as conversation.

Jorge glanced at the holographic image of Debora sadly leaving the chapel behind and then at the date stamp. "These are her final hours," he whispered, the words catching in his throat. "She'll die tonight." While delivering the child she carried—him.

Susana said quietly, "She wasn't what you'd call a 'bad person.' She just never appreciated how bad *kanuf* is. She wanted to stand on her own merit, never realizing that no amount of human goodness can undo *kanuf*."

Jorge nodded. "She wanted Doug to change her world, but she consistently resisted Debora's efforts to change *her*. And when she didn't get what she wanted, she had no qualms about going to Doug's enemies, the *brujas* and *curanderos*." (Spanish: witches and shamans)

He returned to his seat with a sigh of resignation. He hadn't honestly expected to find a reason to acquit her. If Josh hadn't found one, nobody else would be able to either. Still, it was difficult to give up his lifelong wish of someday meeting his birth mother.

"Computer, resume," he said, and watched her last day play out. With no deathbed change of heart, she just quietly bled out and died. Forever lost.

The recording ended, and the room lights came up. After a long moment of silence, Jorge found his voice. "Judges, please register your verdict now." Focusing on the bench before him, he soberly hit the button labeled "Guilty."

Since he chaired the panel, the decisions of each judge registered on his screen. He announced the result: "The verdict is unanimous. María Mendoza Corona is guilty of supporting Stan's treason against her creator, King Doúg, and she has chosen to bear the sentence herself." Lifting his eyes to the few spectators, he asked, "Does anyone wish to dispute the verdict?"

The spectators shook their heads and murmured their agreement.

"Then this court finds that María Mendoza Corona is justly excluded from Paradise Island." Lifting the gavel, he brought it down, forever sealing his mother's fate.

They slowly filed from the room, their moods dampened by the sober nature of their work. Coming alongside him, Dad clapped him on the shoulder. "That couldn't have been easy, but you did well."

"Thanks, Dad. It was hard to watch her reject Doug. But it was also inspirational to watch Doug's persistence. He did everything possible to rescue her. So if it was hard for me to see her reject him, I can't imagine how hard it was for him."

"Yes—especially to experience it for billions of people over thousands of years. He certainly earned the name *D'amoúr*." (Paradisian: I moan for you)

Jorge shook his head. "Yet he continued to pursue us, each one. What amazing love."

They passed the kiosk outside the third-floor courtroom, and they stopped to consult the docket. Jorge had no assignments, leaving him free to watch any case that interested him. Most of the hearings involved people he'd never heard of who had lived in earlier centuries. However, when he came to the last entry, he caught his breath and pointed.

"Ah, Sheridan's review," Dad said.

"And in the big auditorium," Jorge added.

"Yeah, I expect plenty of runners will want to be in that audience." Glancing over his shoulder, Dad called, "Suze, you're one of Sheridan's judges. They're waiting for you to start."

"Oh!" she exclaimed with a bright laugh. "I guess I'd better quit gabbing then."

She excused herself from the group she was visiting with, and they headed off to support Sheridan. As they descended the steps to the Hall of Justice's main auditorium, Jorge pondered the system Josh had set up for this important judicial work. Several types of hearings were underway: trials of exiled Paradisians; trials of humans who had not been rescued; and reviews of humans Josh had acquitted. In each case, the prince selected a panel of judges that would be most likely to challenge his verdict. For the trials, he chose judges likely to be biased in favor of the individual, just as Jorge had been appointed to his birth mom's panel. For the reviews, Josh picked judges likely to be biased against the individual, such as Sheridan's twelve judges, all of whom he had murdered.

With all cases held in open court, anyone could join an audience. And any dissenting opinion, whether from judge or spectator, would trigger a reexamination. Although that hadn't happened yet, the provision proved Doug's intention to hold these judgments to the strictest possible standard.

It was standing room only in the main auditorium, so Chris and Jorge joined those standing in the back. The audience quieted expectantly when Susana sat in the last of the judge's thrones. A moment later Josh stood and addressed the crowd.

"We will now review the life of Sheridan Lanáj, previously General Sheridan Moden. I have acquitted him of treason. This assembly will reexamine his life with the purpose of assuring that my verdict was justified. I remind you of the gravity of this responsibility. The eternal security of the universe requires the thorough eradication of *kanuf.* But my parents and I will not carry out that radical cleansing until *all* question of its fairness is settled. I therefore charge each of you, judge and spectator alike, to examine this life with due consideration."

When the audience nodded and murmured its acceptance of the task, Josh motioned to Sheridan. "The defendant has asked to preface this hearing with a few words."

Sheridan moved to the front, and the auditorium stilled. He thoughtfully scanned the group, and then, with a deferential nod toward the judges, he began. "Prince Joshua tells me that this auditorium seats over two thousand people, and I see that it's filled to overflowing. I would have once been gratified by such a turnout, considering it a tribute to my skills as an orator. But as I look into your faces, I'm filled only with remorse."

Stepping into the audience, he continued, "Because, you see, I know you, each one. I know your names. I know where you lived and worked, whom you loved, and who loved you. I knew who would suffer the most for the crimes I perpetrated against you. I know this because each and every person here today suffered at the hands of the arrogant and merciless General Sheridan Moden."

A murmur went through the audience, and Sheridan turned to address the judges. Stopping before the first one, he said, "I was eight years old when I killed you, Mr. Malcolm Holder. Yours was my first murder, although you might have considered it a mercy killing. You were beaten beyond recognition after being my father's 'guest' for three days."

When the man nodded, Sheridan paced around the large semi-circular bench. "Over the subsequent twenty years, I terrorized and killed the rest of you as well. My final murder victim was you, Dr. Susana Strider." He stopped before Mom, on the far right. "Your biggest crime was that you were so greatly loved."

Jorge found himself smiling at the truth of this statement.

Sheridan returned to face the audience. "Besides these judges, I killed 136 more of you in this audience. If I did not kill you, I tortured, maimed, or raped you or someone you loved. In short, my earthly life was a series of one heinous crime after another. Yet—incredibly—you'll see *none* of that on the recordings you're about to consider! All record of my atrocities has been expunged, washed away in the cleansing fountain of Prince Joshua's blood. Consequently, you'll review the twenty-eight years of my mortal life in only a few years; that's how much *kanuf* has been edited out of these recordings."

He paused, apparently overcome with emotion, and then continued in a husky tone. "Prince Joshua has asked you to determine whether my acquittal was justified. I will tell you honestly that *I* do not deserve to stand here. What I deserve is torture and death—a long, lingering, painful death. I am here only because one who does deserve this life took that punishment for me."

Focusing on Josh, he shook his head. "I am awed at the mercy that allows such a transaction to also be accounted justice. My presence here testifies to the remarkable love and power that could transform even Sheridan Moden, hopeless degenerate that he was, into a pure and holy child of King Doúg. And I will bow before you in grateful wonder, *Modén*—you who alone are worthy of the title— for all eternity."

As Sheridan bowed with his face to the marble floor, spectators and judges alike stood and rocked the auditorium with a song of praise to the lamb who had redeemed each one.

PART IV

AS A BRIDE

*"I saw the Holy City, the new Jerusalem, coming down out of heaven
from God, prepared as a bride beautifully dressed for her husband."*
Revelation 21:2, NIV.

Gabriel lifted the ringing phone to his ear with both excitement and fore-boding. Just now, precisely 1,000 years after Prince Joshua had rescued his people, the executive secretary at the Hall of Justice could be calling the War Room for only one reason.

"General, the millennial phase of the judgment is complete," the secretary reported. "All verdicts have been confirmed, and the records are ready for transport. Prince Joshua is ready to proceed to the executive phase."

"Thank you," Gabriel replied. "We'll proceed immediately."

He returned the phone to its receiver and picked up the microphone to address the populace. "Attention all citizens: We are now preparing for transport. I repeat: Prepare for transport."

Replacing the microphone, he met the eager blue eyes of his new co-commander. After 7,000 years, Prince Joshua had finally filled the vacancy created by Stan's expulsion. And, although nobody could replace his own twin, Gabriel was nonetheless thrilled with the prince's choice.

"Why don't you give the order, *nulu,*" Gabriel said.

Sheridan grinned back. "Thank you, uncle. I'd be honored." Flipping a series of switches on the console, he announced, "General Sheridan Lanáj on command. Be advised: We are now initiating transport protocol. All transport stations, please convey your status."

Stations immediately began checking in, and the vast array of engines beneath the city's foundations roared to life.

While Sheridan directed the complex procedure, Gabriel enjoyed the luxury of stepping to a window to observe. Similarly, all around the city his countrymen were emptying the buildings to watch the long anticipated event. Slowly the massive 1,400-mile square city rose into the air and left Paradise Island behind.

Flying an entire city, particularly one so large, was an accomplishment of epic proportions, and Gabriel marveled as he watched it unfold. Yet the emotions warring within him dampened his exhilaration. Shifting his gaze to his compatriots on the streets, he realized he was not alone. He searched for a way to accurately describe the general mood. Excited horror? Eager dread? This moment would be recorded in the chronicles of the universe, and he would be called upon to recount it. Yet the atmosphere that had spread through the citizenry—indeed, the sensation churning within his own chest—was too bizarre to express.

Sin coming to an end—huzzah!

Sinners suffering eternal death—oh, what anguish!

How could any being experience two such divergent emotions at once? Surely the creator had never intended that he should.

When Joshua strode into the room, the officers broke into applause. He made his way through them, clasping hands and murmuring his appreciation for each person's contribution to the success of this grand feat of engineering.

What a generous spirit! The prince could have accomplished the whole move by himself with a word. Yet he had included these others so they could share in the accomplishment.

Joshua joined Gabriel at the window and clapped him on the back. "A job well done, my friend."

"Yes, sir. Very well done indeed," Gabriel said with a chuckle—as if anyone but the prince deserved credit for the triumph.

Joshua sobered as he faced the window. As if to himself, he said, "Yet we still have such a strange work ahead of us, don't we?"

Gabriel nodded gravely. The upcoming task weighed heavily upon his regent's compassionate heart. He had often disciplined errant runners to prod them back onto the right track, but such punishment was ever mitigated with mercy. Administering eternal punishment unmixed with mercy was a difficult prospect indeed for one who personified love and mercy. To ease the prince's burden, Gabriel would willingly lend a hand. But the very idea was smoke in the wind. He had not the ability, much less the authority, to complete the needed work. So he simply replied, "Yes, sir. 'We' indeed have a very strange work ahead of us."

Prince Joshua nodded absently. Then he faced Gabriel and grinned, "Well, clearly no one needs me around here. I might as well go prepare the landing site."

As he moved to the door, Gabriel called, *"Modén?"*

"Yes?" the prince said, turning back.

"We all need you."

CHAPTER 53

RELEASED

"When the thousand years are over, Satan will be released from his prison and will go out to deceive the nations in the four corners of the earth–Gog and Magog–and to gather them for battle."
Revelation 20:7, 8, NIV.

Stan banged through the front door. "Camille!"

"What, now?" she answered from her studio.

"It's happening," he said as he blew into the room. "We need to get airborne—fast."

She focused on the bowl of water on the table to avoid the eye-roll that would enrage him. Swishing her paintbrush in it, she said mildly, "Are we quite certain this time?"

"He's been spotted!" he roared. "This is not another false alarm!"

When she didn't move, he stormed toward his bedroom. "Well, I'm leaving. Stay if you want. Won't be my fault if you're buried in rubble."

"Very well, I'm coming," she called after him. She removed her smock and retrieved her pre-packed suitcase from her bedroom. In truth, even though these little frights had thus far proven groundless, they did provide a reprieve from the chronic boredom. A thousand years, as it turned out, was an exceptionally long time to sit around waiting for something to happen. Once the disgruntled exiles tired of the inconveniences of living as hermits, they'd had some tasks to complete: houses to build, communication systems to repair, modes of transportation to restore. Some groups had even managed to reestablish civil (if not exactly friendly) relations between them. But reinstating these conveniences required less than a decade. And that still left a great deal of leisure time. A very great deal indeed. Even painting no longer held any fascination for Camille; it merely served to wheedle away the time.

The erroneous alerts began a couple of decades ago, shortly after the interpreters announced that Joshua would soon return—and bring the entire capital city of Paradise Island with him. After the devastation wrought by Joshua's last trip, the exiles nervously granted the possibility that he just might be able to accomplish such a feat. Consequently, every unusual cloud formation resulted in someone raising an alarm. Additionally, the interpreters claimed that Joshua would plant the transported city in the area of old Jerusalem. Since this happened to be where Stan's group had resettled, each false alarm put the whole settlement to flight.

After Camille boarded the helicopter, it rose into the air and retreated to a safe distance. Should Joshua actually reconfigure the landscape, they intended to be clear of the destruction. Soon two hostile aircraft—a small *risaju* followed by the enormous city—breached the horizon and proceeded steadily toward Jerusalem. The *risaju* hovered over the Mount of Olives, and Joshua, in that grand trumpeting voice he had used at the Awakening, called, "ARISE, YOU WHO SLEEP!"

"Yes!" Stan shouted. "We were right! Do you realize what this means?"

Camille smiled supportively, though unconvinced. Would Joshua really revive the billions of dead who had not been resurrected at the Awakening? The *Manual* seemed to predict this—rather clearly, actually: "The rest of the dead were not raised until the thousand years were finished." Yet it made no sense. Surely he knew that, if he put an army within their reach, Stan would do what Stan did best—rally them against Doúg.

Or did the Damours think that giving Stan a few centuries to reconsider would weaken his craving for the most powerful position in the universe? If so, the great Deón were quite mistaken. Stan would ever covet the Great White Throne. His obsession with it had merely escalated during this detention.

Yet, wherever she looked, humans were issuing from their graves. They were not regenerated, arising young, healthy, and vibrant as those revivified in the Awakening did. No, these came forth as they'd been laid to rest—aged and weakened by unhealthy habits. Nevertheless, they were alive. Useful!

As their ranks continued to expand into legions upon legions, Camille's spirits soared. She excitedly clasped Stan's arm, and he flashed an answering grin that said "Told you so." She forgave his self-congratulation in light of the far more important implication: They had another chance to overthrow Damour! Thankfully a bored Stan had planned for this possibility. Even now, his lieutenants stood near the burial sites of the world's great leaders. By tomorrow, all would be united under Stan's command.

Joshua set his *risaju* down upon the mount. As soon as his feet touched the ground, it rumbled like a monstrous beast. Then the mountain split, the two halves moving away from him to the north and south. Unlike the geologic changes that occurred at his last return, this was not chaotic and ruinous, but finely controlled. The resulting plain lay clean, smooth, and beautiful in the midst of the broken landscape. The airborne city landed on it, sparkling like a fabulous jewel amidst rubble. The sight incited a keen pang of homesickness within her.

Stan's grin gave way to the wide-eyed stare of astonishment, and she sensed his alarm. But when Joshua merely entered the city and closed its gates, hope sprouted anew in her brother's ambitious heart. He looked again upon the masses of his revived subjects—seas of them covering the planet's rocky surface. An army of unprecedented might. And she knew his thoughts: Even Doúg's throne could not withstand such an onslaught.

✵ ✵ ✵ ✵ ✵

Willy awoke suddenly with a groan, the intense burning pain of his post-herpetic neuralgia complicated by a throbbing headache from his collision with the gravestone.

A hand reached down to him. "Welcome back," its owner said. Clasping Willy's hand, he pulled him up. The planet was still rumbling and shaking, but night had given way to day, and the painful brilliance in the sky had dissipated.

"The quick scoop is this," the tall blond man said. "You've been dead for 1,000 years. President Moden resurrected you and the rest of mankind, and he appointed you and me as his assistants. I'm here to collect you."

While Willy struggled to assimilate this enormous information dump, his change in position sent another wave of pain through his pounding head. He groaned involuntarily as he grabbed it.

"Here." His guide slipped a transmitter over Willy's head. "We perfected the healing frequency. It should relieve all discomfort."

As promised, the pain subsided. Fingering the sleek new transmitter, Willy exclaimed, "I like it!"

"Great." The comment dripped with sarcasm. "I'm sure Dr. Moden will be ever so pleased that *you* approve." Striding toward a helicopter, he called, "Come on—don't waste my time with your dawdling."

Willy ran to catch up and clamored aboard the chopper. "Where are we going?"

"To meet President Moden."

"Where is he?" Willy had to shout since his companion had started the engine.

The man cast him a my-aren't-you-the-chatty-one frown and handed him a headset. "In what you knew as the Middle East—Jerusalem. But you won't recognize it, or any part of the planet. Continental drift accelerated after Joshua's last arrival. Excepting Paradise Island, all land masses are united into one supercontinent."

Willy determined not to bother him with more questions. However, as the chopper rose, he realized, "I don't know your name."

"Dr. Adlai Menod. You may call me Dr. Menod."

"Oh—Ms. Menod's husband. I spoke to you once by phone."

His companion's brow furrowed, as if searching his memory for some remote bit of information. "Taylor Menod?"

"Yes, Ms. Taylor Menod."

"That was a long time ago."

Oh. Oops. Silly of him to assume a couple would be together after a thousand years. This would require a major brain-shift.

✵ ✵ ✵ ✵ ✵

"I raised you all back to life," Dr. Moden proclaimed from the large dais. His voice boomed over the plain and echoed against the hills, carried far beyond Willy's sight by an extensive system of cameras and microphones.

Standing attentively at the left of Dr. Moden's throne while Dr. Menod occupied the corresponding position on the right, Willy gazed out across a veritable sea of people. Their first project, organizing the enormous company into thousands of language subgroups, had been complicated by the smoldering animosities between once warring factions. Willy enjoyed a well-earned sense of accomplishment as he checked the monitor with the aerial view. All stood quietly—and peacefully—listening to their respective translators.

"Now I need your help," Dr. Moden continued. "While you were in your graves, my people have been fighting the worst foe this world has ever encountered. As you can see from the planet's condition, it's been a devastating war. And it's not over. We need your help to vanquish these enemies. If we fail now, the entire human race is doomed. These beings, aliens from another galaxy—"

Exclamations of surprise and disbelief interrupted him, and he waited for them to die down.

"Yes, you heard me correctly," he said. "These enemies are extra-terrestrial life forms from a planet called Paladisi. Their leader is called Deón. Though not human, they have taken human form. The humans within the city were deceived into believing that the aliens came to rescue us from a dying planet. This is a blatant lie. Earth is fine—or it would be if they would leave us in peace to repair the damage they've caused."

Dr. Moden paused as his listeners responded with outraged protests. After a few moments, he cleared his throat, and the grumbling ceased.

"I realize you sensed no passage of time in your graves, and I know this will be shocking for you to discover, but you have all been dead for quite a long time. The date, according to our current dating system, is the year 9044, what most of you would call the 31st century. We've been battling these invaders on and off for 1,000 years. Our weapons and technology have improved markedly during that time, and, now that I've resurrected you, we grossly outnumber them. However, we must attack them quickly, while they are still recharging their weapons and regrouping from the last battle. This is our only hope of victory. Nevertheless, working together, we *will* win this battle! We *will* reclaim our planet!"

This time a round of cheers intruded, and Dr. Moden waited for it to subside before continuing.

"There are some excellent leaders among you. Some commanded legendary armies and possess outstanding military acumen. Others led your peoples as kings or chieftains. We especially need your talents at this critical time. So if you've received an invitation to the special reception, please proceed there immediately following this briefing. If you consider it difficult to subjugate yourselves to the rule of another, understand this—the primary reason we failed to repel these invaders at their first attack was disunity. Territorial squabbles divided our planetary defense. I'm warning you now: I will *not* allow that to happen again."

He stopped, his gaze darting from one king to another. Willy felt certain that he knew exactly where each threat stood. Gradually a tense silence descended over the group.

"Hear me well on this point," Dr. Moden said in what could best be described as a growl. "As the global ruler since this invasion began, I alone have the up-to-date knowledge necessary for victory. I can save you from the cruel tyranny that's been foisted upon the poor humans you see within those gates. But we have no time to waste on power struggles. Therefore, at least until we overcome this enemy, *I! Am! King!* I will tolerate *no* opposition. Remember—I unlocked the science that raised you to life. I can as easily return to dust any who resist my authority."

Willy wasn't sure why this hard-nosed stance succeeded. Maybe it had something to do with the upward angle of the cameras meant to create a larger-than-life impression. Perhaps it was the retinue of tall, brawny bodyguards surrounding Dr. Moden. Or maybe it was the dazzling rainbow of jewels atop the alabaster throne that suggested a grander, even celestial authority. But whatever the reason, the tactic worked. The massive crowd roared its approval and began chanting "Moden! Moden! Moden!"

Dr. Moden gazed out over the immense company, his vibrant green eyes reflecting his satisfaction. For his part, Willy was simply relieved. His job would be much easier if peace reigned.

Dr. Moden rose majestically from the throne and strode off stage, the train of his gold-embroidered white cape flowing behind him. The two assistants followed at a respectful distance, and the trio, surrounded by bodyguards, proceeded to the command center. Kings and generals were starting to assemble, each in their own brand of finery. Dr. Moden's charming wife, Dr. Desmon, was already circulating, putting the great rulers at ease.

Willy had never met Dr. Desmon before, although he had seen pictures of "America's #1 Power Couple" in the media. Yet, just as pictures couldn't capture Dr. Moden's physical perfection, they couldn't capture a fraction of Dr. Desmon's beauty, let alone her elegance or grace.

Trumpeters announced Dr. Moden's entrance into the tent. As he stepped forward, his white robes glittered impressively while draping his body to accentuate the intimidating musculature of his arms and chest. This moment of his presentation to the global leaders had been carefully choreographed and rehearsed. The music, the lights, the positioning of his retinue, his attire—all had been calculated for maximum impact. And when Willy checked the monitors, the breathtaking effect left gooseflesh on his arms. What's more, that assembly of worldly-wise royals actually gasped.

A period of less formal mingling followed, which allowed Drs. Moden and Desmon to reestablish their relationships with history's greats. Although Willy was aware of the bodyguards' sharp eyes, the Modens gave the impression of socializing freely and easily, as if certain that no one would dare question their authority. They seemed to know and be known by each leader. And they spoke to them all in their native languages, smoothly switching from ancient Greek with Alexander the Great to French with Napoleon and Latin with Nero. To facilitate the planning sessions that would follow, the VIPs had all been given portable headsets with computerized translators. But Dr. Moden and his inner circle didn't require them; they actually knew all those thousands of languages.

As they made their way through the large tent, it occurred to Willy that he really should be feeling overwhelmed, or proud, or at least impressed, by the status of the people surrounding him. Jezebel, Cesar Augustus, Hitler—everywhere he turned he met another famous, or infamous, person. But the names registered only long enough to process Dr. Menod's whispered warnings about keeping Brutus out of Julius Cesar's way, Octavia away from Cleopatra, and so forth.

The sheer quantity of information Willy needed to keep straight was staggering. Yet he felt only gratitude for it. It meant temporary escape from the dozens of questions nibbling at his brain. Before dying, he'd come to the conclusion that Dr. Moden had deceived him—that the man he'd introduced as Prince Joshua wasn't the real Prince Joshua, that at least some of what Uncle Chris claimed about him must be true, and that Willy himself had ended up on the wrong side of this war. All this led him to wonder just how much of what he was now being told was true.

On the other hand, did any of it matter? Clearly, there were now two opposing camps—those barricaded in New Jerusalem and those rallied around Dr. Moden. And, since Willy had no way of switching sides—and since he really preferred to stay alive—he needed to support the group in which he found himself. Therefore, figuring out which liars and imposters were in which camp was moot, just as whatever idealistic dreams he might have once entertained were unimportant. Simple pragmatism dictated his actions now.

Once the Modens had adequately stroked the VIPs' egos, they transitioned into a series of strategy meetings that lasted late into the night. Nevertheless, with victory depending on a rapid strike, Willy arose early the next morning to supervise the distribution of weapons to the massive army. Complicating this already colossal task was the stipulation that a weapon be placed in the hands of a soldier who could actually wield it. While the troops themselves liked experimenting with new toys, numerous injuries resulted—such as when some ancient Roman soldiers became a little too curious about guns, or when some modern Americans thought it would be "fun" to try out the swords.

Even with these delays, the combined military forces were drawn up in ranks and ready to attack by the following dawn. As Willy studied the aerial views of the great host, he was simply stunned. Orderly ranks, each headed by acclaimed military leaders, surrounded New Jerusalem and extended throughout the entire supercontinent. Literally the whole world, armed with weapons of daunting power, glared down upon a single city with no obvious means of defense.

Such a plight might have once aroused Willy's sympathy. After all, he had relatives in the doomed city; he'd actually seen Andy standing on the city's ramparts. Yet he could arouse no pity for those he had once loved. Instead he felt only anger—anger that they, by their transformed lives and faithful commitment to Doug's Law, had proven him wrong. Anger at Prince Joshua for pronouncing his efforts to redeem himself insufficient. Anger at Doug for refusing him any credit whatsoever for all the humanitarian work he'd done.

And so, when Dr. Moden at last gave the order to advance upon the city, Willy felt only satisfaction. The Damours and their runners should have been more tolerant. They should have paid him more respect. They should have recognized his potential, appreciated his hard work, and bent those silly, intolerant laws to take his good intentions into account. They deserved their fate.

CHAPTER 54

SURROUNDED

*"They went up on the breadth of the earth and surrounded
the camp of the saints and the beloved city."*
Revelation 20:9, NKJV.

D r. Moden clapped a beefy hand on Willy's shoulder. "Enjoy this moment, son
of Juan Misi. You've helped make it a reality."

And as they watched the overwhelming army march toward the hapless
city, Willy did enjoy it. An expansive sense of pride swelled his chest and spread
a great smile over his face. He'd worked hard. Some had said that organizing the
vast multitude into a coordinated army so quickly was an impossible task. He'd
even overheard Dr. Menod praising his managerial skills, and Dr. Menod didn't
often praise anyone.

But as the massive force rushed the city, surrounding it from every side, a
confused frown replaced Willy's grin. What was that sound within the city? Were
its occupants actually singing a song of victory?

A great light suddenly ignited in the middle of the city and ascended into
the air. At first, Willy thought it must be some weapon. But as his eyes adjusted
to its brilliance, he realized it was a gleaming white throne. It rose above the
plain, above the city, and above the surrounding mass of hostile soldiers. Upon
the throne sat Prince Joshua, encircled by a luminous dome and overarched by
an astounding rainbow.

Dr. Moden's throne, which Willy had considered magnificent before,
now struck him as a gaudy knockoff. Was the similarity intentional? And what
about all the effort the special effects people had put into getting Dr. Moden's
grand entrance just right? Joshua didn't need any special illumination. His natural radiance did it all.

When the throne reached its apex high in the sky, trumpets rang out
a majestic anthem. Someone approached the throne and placed a magnificent
crown on Prince Joshua's head. Then the prince spoke, his voice shaking the very
ground. "YOU STAND ARRAIGNED BEFORE THE SUPREME COURT
OF PARADISE ISLAND."

His clarion voice carried easily to all, no extensive PA system needed. His
piercing gaze bored like a laser into Willy's soul, immediately bursting the great
bubble of self-satisfaction that had sent his spirits soaring only a moment before.

"THE CHARGE AGAINST YOU IS HIGH TREASON AGAINST
HIS MAJESTY, KING DOÚG, RULER OF THE UNIVERSE."

The prince lifted a pair of stone tablets engraved with fiery letters.
Even from this distance, Willy had no difficulty reading or recognizing them

as Doug's Ten Laws—the original Ten Laws, not the abridged version from the edited *Runner's Manual* that he had championed. His heart quivered in his chest. Suddenly he wanted only to run away, to hide from that law, to escape those all-seeing, all-knowing eyes. But terror riveted him to the ground.

"LET THE BOOKS BE OPENED."

A giant circular screen appeared above the throne, and Willy watched his life play out upon it. He relived innumerable rebellious choices, from his first babyish refusals to obey Mom to his obstinate attempts to cover up the accident. Each step along the paths forbidden by Doug's Laws led him into deeper pain, even slavery. And the consequences of each mulish choice extended ever outward, gaining momentum, steamrolling more and more people.

As he witnessed the extent of the pain he'd caused, remorse gave way to shame, and shame to horror. Maybe Doug had been right in rejecting his efforts to redeem himself. How could any amount of good deeds ever atone for, much less undo, such extensive damage?

The pictures on the screen changed. Willy now watched Prince Joshua live through similar events and make different choices. Wonder filled him as he saw him always helping, strengthening, and blessing those around him. Then the Battle of Grace Hill played out in all its grisly detail. He watched an innocent Joshua accept the punishment for Willy's crimes, giving him a chance—his only real chance—to escape the guilt and punishment he deserved.

The pictures returned to Willy's life to review the times when Doug, through his runners, repeatedly offered Willy an opportunity to accept Joshua's payment on his behalf. With new perspective, he watched himself arrogantly reject these offers and insist on fixing his own problems. He marveled at his own stubbornness, his own blindness when, even after admitting his error at Joshua's last coming, he again took the most expedient course and sided with Doug's enemies after being resurrected. No matter how many chances Doug gave him to make the right choice, he always chose the defiant course of rebellious pride.

The pictures ended, and Willy seemed to be standing alone before Prince Joshua's judgment seat. The eyes of the universe were fixed on him. All awaited his defense. But he had not a shred of an excuse to hang about his naked soul. What possible defense could he present in light of this overwhelming evidence of his guilt?

As the prince's holy gaze rested upon him, the weight of the righteous verdict against him grew extreme—unbearable. Self-condemnation filled him with hopelessness beyond any he had ever known. The truth burned within him, demanding release. Dropping to his knees, he cried, "You're right, Prince Joshua. And you are just. I am full of evil, and I have persistently rejected your rescue. Your verdict against me is just."

CHAPTER 55

JUSTICE

"By justice a king gives a country stability."
Proverbs 29:4, NIV.

Camille lost all track of time as she stood arraigned before Prince Joshua's Great White Throne. Perhaps the review of her 9,044 years of life took days, perhaps years. Or perhaps Joshua managed it in moments. She no longer believed anything beyond his ability. Whatever the interval, it recalled every bit of *kanuf* she had ever committed or inspired.

What's more, the wall of callous indifference that she'd constructed to protect herself from pain crumbled under Joshua's keen eye, making *kanuf* as hideous to her as it had first appeared. Thus, she relived the heartrending loneliness of leaving the Deón's presence. She gasped in horror at the first death of a flower. She wept at the betrayal she felt when Stan first inflicted pain upon her. And still the merciless recordings continued.

How she wanted to flee! But she could not. Something within her, something long dormant, had awakened for this moment. Some innate sense of justice demanded that she assess her life honestly, if only this once.

The longer she watched, the more clearly she saw her determined rebellion. How dreadfully she had perverted the course of nature! All creation was designed to give; she had chosen to take. All intelligent creatures were meant to act from love; she was moved by pride. All creation was intended to joyfully worship the creator; she had remained stubbornly devoted to her ambitious brother.

She could summon no justification for her course, for all her excuses now revealed themselves for the lies they were. Nor could she claim ignorance, for the recordings documented Debora's earnest pleas before her expulsion. The simple truth was that her rebellion had been unnatural in the most basic sense. Her *kanuf* had upset myriad complex systems, both scientific and relational. The resulting disorder, compounded over centuries, literally threatened the existence of the entire universe.

Indeed, the exiles' eviction from the island was not only justified, but essential; Doúg needed to protect it from their damaging influence. He was right to limit their sway over humans lest they induce the pathetic creatures to self-destruct. He was even just in annihilating the exiles before they destroyed the planet altogether.

Simply put, she had left the creator no choice but to destroy her.

Without the shield of her emotional wall, her anguish continued to grow as she watched the relentless images from her life. Finally it ballooned beyond her ability to withstand, driving her to her knees. "You were right, holy Deón!"

she cried. "You offered me mercy when I rebelled. And though I rejected that, you still treated me fairly. Your verdict against me is just."

She had long since forgotten about the massive assembly surrounding her. She seemed to stand before the Deón alone—alone and solely responsible for her choices. When she did recall the others, she saw that they were, like her, kneeling. The weight of *kanuf* had forced all to their knees. Truth, that great inquisitor, had extracted a confession of the Deón's justice from each mouth.

Except for one solitary figure who remained standing. Her brother, seemingly paralyzed, was yet absorbed in the images of his life's journey. As she looked again upon the sky-screen, she saw Stan, clothed in the glorious robes of his pre-exilic station, in Doúg's throne room. The king was detailing what his rebellion would cost. She heard of disease and death, of betrayal and grief—of matters she had never imagined before they unfolded after the rebellion.

At last Doúg summarized, "My son, this experiment will not only fail, but it will cost everything you hold dear. Your homeland, your friends, your brothers and sisters. Even your relationship with Camille, the one who is as part of you, will fall prey to *kanuf*."

Tears moistened Doúg's face. Rising from his throne, he placed a hand on Stan's shoulder. "I see these things written in the Book of the Future, but today it is written in pencil and can be erased. Tomorrow it will be written in a hand that cannot be altered. My dearest son, this is your last chance. Please, I beg you, accept my mercy and turn from this course while you still can. To persist in it will hurt you, and Kamíl, more than you are capable of understanding."

Camille stared at her brother in disbelief. He knew the full horror from the beginning? Even as he had promised to love and protect her forever, he had known that his course would bring her sorrow and loss?

Tears of remorse streamed down Stan's face, and those tears assured her that he really had known all along. Yet, knowing the cost, he had pushed the rebellion forward, placing them all in unimaginable jeopardy. And why? Because he was willing to sacrifice their happiness and wellbeing on the altar of his ambition. He was even willing to sacrifice her.

Stan at last collapsed to his knees and admitted the Deón's justice and truth. But as Camille watched him, something kindled within her, energizing her, consuming her—the old, familiar fire of hatred. She now loathed the brother she had promised to stand by to the end. The notion of meeting their fate together no longer comforted her; it sickened her. Everything she had been through in the last 7,000 years was Stan's fault. He could have prevented it all! Stand by him? Never!

Jumping up, she ran at him. "You could have stopped it!" She pummeled him with fists grown hard from centuries of fighting, and kicked with feet grown deadly in aim and power. "Why didn't you turn back when there was still time?"

Stan sprang to his feet to shield himself from her attack, but his eyes grew wide as he looked beyond her, for the whole throng was now rushing him. So he turned and ran. Like a common coward.

"ENOUGH!" Joshua cried. "JUSTICE IS MINE, AND ITS TIME HAS COME."

Camille abruptly stopped, her eyes riveted on the great throne.

Joshua stood, lifting his arms into the air, and the rainbow shimmered with painful brilliance. Then, gradually at first, his Dome of *Lashani* began to expand outward. It first encompassed all those in the city, causing their faces to shine with its luminescence. And in those countenances, Camille saw all that she might have had—indeed, all that she had once had. All that she had ever truly wanted was now theirs—the unadulterated joy, peace, and honor with which Doúg imbued each of his children. A great ache pierced her, a great yearning for the wonderful holiness that she had rejected.

But she had little time to dwell on this loss, for as the dome expanded beyond the city, things began exploding. Abandoned guns, swords, grenades—all burst into flames as they fell under the dome.

She suddenly recalled some failed experiments in which they'd tried to replicate the life-sustaining atmosphere of the island. Then, as now, things kept exploding. Passages from the *Manual* sprang to mind: "Consuming fire runs ahead of him, and round him a great storm rages." "You will make them burn like a fiery furnace when you appear; the Lord will engulf them in His wrath, and fire will devour them." Their experiments hadn't failed because of contaminants, as they had thought. In fact, they hadn't failed at all. Their researchers had simply been ignorant of one key physical law: *lashani* and *kanuf* cannot coexist.

Instantly, she understood Joshua's plan. He would merely expose them to himself. But, as she now understood, his Dome of *Lashani* was for them a dome of destruction. Their weapons would be incinerated. *They* would be incinerated.

Camille turned tail and ran. She no longer cared that fear was weakness—she didn't even know if it was true. She only knew she must escape that dome.

But she couldn't outrun it. Soon she felt a burning pain that, illogically, started deep within her chest and spread outward. She screamed with an intense pain that halted her flight. Simultaneously, the sheer terror of a drowning victim seized her—the sudden and certain knowledge that one is forever cut off from a life-giving element. Her connection to Doúg, that which had maintained her even when she denied her need of him, had been severed.

Still the dome was spreading, spreading, reaching far beyond her. Her people—the ones she had helped to convince and trick and coerce into following Stan—glowed and burst into flame, burning until they became ashes. Another passage came to her: "All the arrogant and every evildoer will be stubble; they will be ashes under the soles of your feet." In that moment, she knew her fate. The great Camille L. Desmon, PhD—"the most powerful woman in the hemisphere," as the media knew her—would be mere ashes.

Screams of pain and anguish filled the air around her. Her own cries were less from pain than from anguish. She had never imagined the depth of despair that filled her now. She could summon not the slightest ray of hope, not the tiniest comfort. She was doomed. Forever. She would never enjoy the peace and joy of her homeland. She would never again experience her family's love. She would never bask in the *lashani* she had once known. What's more, she—with all her celebrated talent, intelligence, and beauty—would eventually be forgotten. A byword at best.

Shame filled her. Self-abhorrence overcame her. Her long life had been pointless. She had wasted her extraordinary potential. Worse than wasted—she had squandered it trying to destroy all true beauty. And, in the end, she had not succeeded even in that depraved goal. If the halls of eternity remembered her at all, it would only be for how absolutely she had failed.

She fell to the ground, writhing and screaming, as truth, in all its unmerciful fullness, forced itself into her consciousness. Hers alone. For she had earned exactly the death that she had always most feared: She would die alone. Completely, hopelessly alone. Without comfort, without triumph, without significance.

The end came quickly for some. But it would not be so for her. The Deón must rid the planet of *kanuf*, so the fire was not fueled by any physical component, including her body. Rather, it was fueled by evil itself. The humans, filled with less *kanuf*, contained less fuel and were consumed more quickly. But those who had embraced more would burn longer. For her, the process would take a long, *long* time.

She did not beg for mercy. The Deón had offered her mercy, and she had refused it. Indeed, were it offered now, she would refuse it still, preferring oblivion to living with such shame.

Besides, the day of mercy was past. This was the day of justice.

CHAPTER 56

A New Earth

*"Then I saw 'a new heaven and a new earth,' for the first heaven
and the first earth had passed away."*
Revelation 21:1, NIV.

The smoke surrounding the city seemed to go up forever, its top being well above the limits of Chris's vision. Yet it was not so thick that it obscured the suffering of those caught in the cleansing fire. Chris watched the spectacle in silent agony, his face awash in tears. He had already mourned the loss of his grandmother and of his beloved twin sister. Both had died rather quickly. But Willy still thrashed about on a nearby overlook. Many within the city had turned away from the awful scene. But Chris couldn't. He would never again see these individuals whom he loved so dearly.

A sudden sensation of consolation preceded a light brush on his arm. He turned to find Debora at his side. She gently wiped the tears from his face with a handkerchief woven in her own loom and imbued with soothing properties that complemented the aura of comfort that surrounded her. The resulting relief—a feeling that all was well in an eternal sense—allowed him to rise above current circumstances.

"Thank you, *Ama.*" Looking back at Willy, he said, "I wish I could do something to help them."

"I know, and I cherish your caring heart. But you can do nothing. *Kanuf* does not die easily. Before submitting to oblivion, it will extract from its host a price for services rendered. It will inflict upon them the pain it once inflicted upon others at their behest."

"He will repay him according to his deeds," Chris quoted from the *Manual.*

Debora nodded sadly. Her gaze was fixed on Stan, who suffered on the same overlook as Willy. Wistfully she said, "He knew he was rebelling against the creator to whom he owed allegiance, but he had no idea what he was unleashing. *Kanuf* is as a living creature that requires nourishment. Its hunger must be satisfied—if not by a hapless victim, then by its host. Stan thought to control it, to use it toward his own end. But it will not be tamed. All through time, it waited, growing ever stronger, biding its time as long as he provided it with more victims. Now it will extract from him the heaviest penalty."

Chris received no gratification from knowing that Stan would get what he deserved. He didn't enjoy watching any of his enemies suffer, even those who had tortured him. In fact, he'd been immeasurably relieved when Doug placed a shield over the city so they no longer heard the screams or smelled the nauseating stench of burning flesh.

"We had to do it," Debora said sorrowfully. "The faithful would never have known peace as long as evil existed."

"I understand," Chris said. "We all do. After reviewing their cases for a thousand years, we know their sentence is justified. If any doubt remained, it was extinguished when they attacked a peaceful city." He swallowed hard as he recalled, "And the resentment, the malignant hatred, I saw on Willy's face when Stan ordered the onslaught—that alone told me he couldn't be redeemed. He wouldn't allow it."

Debora nodded and, leaving the handkerchief with Chris, moved down the wall to comfort another.

Chris stayed at his self-appointed post, as if his presence could somehow grant Willy a measure of relief. Finally, the flames reduced his nephew's body to ashes. The sight reminded him of a lie that Stan had circulated, one that claimed an eternally burning hell. It had deceived many by painting Doug as cruel and unjust. Though he'd never believed the lie, Chris found relief in knowing it was decidedly false. How could he possibly have enjoyed the bliss of Paradise while Rosie was in agony on this plain—while she would *always* be in agony on this plain? He couldn't imagine living with such heartache. But Rosie, Grandma, Willy, and the rest were gone. Their misery was over. Just as the *Manual* had promised.

Josh came up beside Chris and slipped an arm around his shoulders. "How are you doing, *boní*?"

"It's awful."

"Yes. But necessary."

"I know," Chris said. "They left you no choice."

They stood together in silence for a few moments. "I really am glad the burning doesn't last forever," Chris mused aloud.

"That would be neither just not merciful. Not for them. Not for us. It's bad enough that the consequences are eternal."

A picture of Rosie's teasing grin came to mind—a sight Chris would never see again. "Yes. That's bad enough."

Turning to look into Josh's tear-streaked face, he asked, "But how are *you* doing, *bachí*?

Josh was silent for a moment. "We always knew this day would come—must come. Yet it's a strange and alien work we do." He sighed. "Very, very strange."

✲ ✲ ✲ ✲ ✲

Sheridan immersed himself in his work during the Cleansing. In truth, he invented work—anything to keep unwelcome thoughts at bay. Unlike Sheridan Moden, Sheridan Lanáj received no pleasure in watching others suffer. Still, he couldn't escape the reality of what was happening. Little tasks took him to the city wall, and his office window afforded a panoramic view of the ever-rising smoke. Every inadvertent glance reminded him of the fate that should have been his. The idea of losing that fellowship with the Deón that had become so precious to him—both the reason for and the greatest joy of his life—struck horror to the depths of his soul.

"Still burning," he murmured one day as he stood, transfixed by the abhorrent sight below. He hadn't meant to look. He'd only gotten up to retrieve something from his credenza. But as he stood there, the vision triggered the fragment of a memory, and a sudden wave of nausea swept over him. He could no longer recall in detail his deeds of *kanuf*, but he had suddenly remembered burning the flesh off a runner's feet with a blowtorch. His mind—and stomach—recoiled at the mere idea now. How could he ever have considered that "fun"? How had he ever thought that the jokes made by Stan's men about "roast human" were funny?

Still, those atrocities had taught him one thing: death by fire was excruciating in the extreme. What's more, victims of this cleansing fire did not pass out during their ordeal. They were aware and screaming in pain, or trying to, until the very end.

He should be out there, suffering that fate. How close he had come to that end! He might not have burned as long as Stan, Camille, or Garrick, but he sure would have burned longer than Saxon, who still writhed on the fiery plain.

A sudden change in the atmosphere of his office claimed his attention, and he turned to see Debora approaching. Gently dabbing the tears from his cheeks (had he actually been weeping?), she said, "You are—and will ever be—secure, because you know him who is your redeemer."

She pressed a kiss to his forehead and the handkerchief into his hand. And then she was gone. But in her wake, the burdens he had needlessly carried vanished beyond thought or memory, and his heart swelled with unutterable peace and thanksgiving. He *wasn't* out there—thanks to Josh.

✲ ✲ ✲ ✲ ✲

Finally the Cleansing was complete, and the fire burned out. Celebrations erupted on the city walls and spread throughout the city in waves of joyous song. Evil was vanquished, nevermore to raise its ugly head!

The fire had burned everything infected by *kanuf*—animate and inanimate, liquid and solid, flammable and inflammable. Steel, cement, stone, even water—it all eventually liquefied and joined the great molten mass, leaving the city standing like an island in a lake of fire.

Along with those around him, Sheridan was singing a song of victory when his radio pinged. "*Nulu,* come at once," Uncle Gabriel said excitedly. "*Modén* wants us to join him outside the eastern gate."

His uncle's almost giddy exhilaration piqued Sheridan's interest. Dashing out of the army headquarters, he sprinted for the eastern gate. His uncle swung the gate open and murmured, "Covering positions" as Sheridan passed. Sheridan obediently stepped onto the small *risaju* and took up the position on Prince Joshua's left as Uncle Gabriel filled the corresponding position on the right.

Josh turned to Sheridan, his eyes twinkling. "Ready?"

Having no idea what the two were up to, Sheridan nonetheless answered heartily. "Yes, sir."

"Then let's be off."

They flew several hundred miles in every direction, but saw nothing but a monotonous expanse of molten rock. No mountains, no canyons, no oceans. All geologic landmarks had vanished.

Finally Josh turned to him. "Seen enough?"

"Enough for what?" Sheridan asked.

"Enough to want to see something else," Josh said.

"Sure," Sheridan said. "I don't care if I never see lava again."

A thoughtful expression came over his friend's features. "Actually," he said, "you never shall."

Turning back, Josh maneuvered the *risaju* through the clouds and high above them, high enough that Sheridan and Gabriel would have required oxygen if they hadn't been in Joshua's presence. The prince studied the air so intently and for so long that Sheridan finally whispered to Uncle Gabriel, "What's he looking for?"

"He's taking note of the atmospheric distortions caused by *kanuf's* influence. Holes in the ozone layer—that sort of thing. Here"—he handed Sheridan some glasses—"you'll see it better with these."

Sheridan donned the glasses, which, although the lenses were clear, cast the world in various shades of violet while allowing him to perceive structures invisible to the naked eye. Among these were several bands that arched around the planet like a succession of sheer curtains—but old curtains, shredded and holey.

"Together, those layers form the firmament—or atmosphere, if you prefer," his uncle whispered.

"And they're in very poor condition," Josh added. Glancing over his shoulder at Sheridan, he said, "You'll want to take those glasses off now. It'll be too bright for them in a minute."

A glow began to emanate from the prince—slowly at first, but then becoming brighter and more intense. Soon it pulsed in powerful waves of energy. The air grew electric. Sheridan's skin tingled. Discharges of energy zapped and popped all around. Light sparked, like tiny fireworks, in every imaginable color.

As Sheridan experienced the veritable electrical storm that surrounded Josh in his "uncloaked" form, as Gabriel called it, he understood why Stan had considered it a weapon to avoid unleashing at all cost. But, thanks to Doúg's mercy, Sheridan was no longer an enemy, and he felt no fear. Instead, he was filled with eager anticipation. Anything seemed possible.

With his thundering trumpet-voice, Josh said, "LET THE FIRMAMENT BE RESTORED." He pressed his arms forward, palms out, as if pushing something away from his chest. A purple wave rolled away from him and circled the globe. As the wave settled into place, it faded into a colorless glistening, which then faded into invisibility.

The prince directed the aircraft above the firmament's path, inspecting it with the expression of a new mother admiring her baby's features. Finally he nodded. "That's good."

He dimmed his brilliance somewhat and said, "Sheridan, you can take a quick peek with the glasses."

Sheridan replaced the lenses and marveled at the beauty of the newly fashioned curtains—smooth, complete, and full of color, albeit invisible to the human eye. He thought he would be content to study their intricate patterns all day, but the sparks of energy that still zapped around Josh soon became unbearable, and he had to remove the glasses again.

Josh piloted the *risaju* nearer to the planet and, spreading one arm out and away to the right, he said, "LET THERE BE LAND ..." Glistening waves of brown and red rode on the thunder's wake. It hit the fiery liquid like a giant fist, whipping it into a great churning mass that resolved into solid earth.

Spreading his left arm in the other direction, Joshua added, "... AND SEA." Iridescent waves of blue and green followed this proclamation and, upon hitting the lava, churned it into clear, aqua water.

Sheridan watched, speechless. He had witnessed the restored firmament as a final product, but he hadn't observed the restoration process itself. Now, watching the energies do their astounding work, and all initiated by a few words, he was simply dumbfounded.

"*Nulu*," Uncle Gabriel said with a chuckle, "your mouth's hanging open."

Snapping his mouth closed, Sheridan turned to Josh—no, that form of address suddenly seemed far too small, even presumptuous. He turned to His Highness ...

No, not big enough. He turned to Crown Prince Joshua ...

Still not right. He turned to the great, the almighty, the one and only—Deón.

When the prince met his gaze, Sheridan searched for some way to express his admiration. But the best he could come up with was the obvious: "My creator," he breathed.

"Yes, but still your friend," Prince Joshua said. Then, with a wink, he broke into a playful grin. "Did you like green grass, or shall we make it another color this time around?"

"Um, uh," Sheridan stammered. "Green's good."

They descended near enough that Sheridan could smell the fresh, earthy scent of newly turned ground. Sweeping both arms outward, Prince Joshua said, "LET THERE BE GRASS." Sparkling waves of green left a carpet of lush grass in their trail. The creator pointed here and there, generating little twisters of light that resolved into trees or bushes. Gradually, the landscape took on the appearance of an artist's colorful palette.

As they coursed above the completed canvas, Sheridan caught whiffs of ripe peaches, of fragrant pink roses, and of a mouth-watering aroma coming from a vine unfamiliar to him.

The prince seemed satisfied. "Yes, that's good," he said.

He proceeded to recreate animals—sea creatures, birds, and those that walked the land. When they returned to the city, Sheridan discovered they'd been gone for four days. It didn't surprise him. He'd grown accustomed to losing all sense of time in Joshua's presence.

At the prince's command, all city gates were thrown open and its occupants invited to explore the new world. Three days later, when they returned for the weekly Rest Day assembly, everyone buzzed with excitement. Curious explorers swamped the antediluvians with questions about unfamiliar life forms that had disappeared after the flood. Sheridan and Gabriel were repeatedly called upon to describe how the magnificent world was recreated. Everyone was in such a festive mood that the holiday turned into a full week of special celebration.

To cap the gala, the Deón gathered everyone together and united, treating them to the wonderful exhibition of light and sound that accompanied this.

"Now is everything made new," they proclaimed, their intertwined voices creating a joyful symphony all its own. "Henceforth we will no longer be *Damoúr*, for all mourning is past. From this time forward, we shall be, as we once were, only *Deón*."

With tears of joy streaming down his face, Uncle Gabriel, standing at the Deon's right, shouted, "Hallelujah!" and bowed to the ground in worship. Sheridan, on the left, and the entire assembly followed his example, and all lifted their voices in grateful praise. Earth had been polluted, corrupted, and perverted for tens of centuries. Now, at long last, the Deón had put everything right. And it would never go wrong again.

CHAPTER 57
FOREVER

I shall praise you for ever for what you have done."
Psalm 52:9, REB.

Chris readjusted his backpack as he reached the top of the gentle rise. The galazi had all arrived before him, but this was no disgrace. The tall, long-legged species from the planet Galazát was truly built for running.

"This looks like a good place to camp," he said to Petrov, the group's leader. Like so many others, they had come to Earth to sightsee and to hear first-hand the stories of those who had survived The Great Rebellion.

Reaching his side, Susana said, "Oh, yes—we'll have a great view of the stars, too."

"Where are we?" Petrov asked, his curious gaze roaming over the verdant plain.

"This was part of our home state, California," Chris answered. "It was the driest place on the continent."

Petrov did a comical double-take. "Dry?"

"Very dry," Dad affirmed. "It was called Death Valley, a name it certainly earned. Many, many people and animals died of thirst here."

"*Kanuf* changed even the physical aspects of the planet," Chris explained.

Petrov shook his head thoughtfully as he surveyed the lush plain. His young daughter, Lusi, took advantage of the lull in conversation to ask Chris, "Will you tell us the story of how Prince Joshua saved you?"

"Sure," Chris answered enthusiastically. He'd lost count of how many times he'd recounted the tale, but the privilege of extolling his deliverer would never grow old. "But let's set up camp and have dinner first. Then we'll tell as many stories as you like—right, Dad?"

"You betcha," Dad answered with a wink.

While the party dispersed to set up their tents, Susana released a contented sigh. "What an amazing sunset."

"Yes, it is," Chris said. "It's funny—I've seen hundreds, probably thousands, of sunsets now, but I never tire of their beauty."

"Me neither," she agreed. "I wonder how many sunsets we have seen since Earth was restored? How long's it been—3,000 years or so?"

"Three thousand four hundred and nineteen years," Mom said. With a grin, she added, "I just asked Debora last week."

"Wow," the earthlings chorused.

Petrov, still within hearing distance, glanced at them with a puzzled frown, and Chris exchanged a knowing glance with Susana. They had seen that expression often—such discussions always bewildered visitors from other planets. The concept of time was simply incomprehensible to beings who had no experience with death.

"To you, these are meaningless answers to a meaningless question, aren't they?" Susana asked Petrov.

"Yes. I guess they are," he said, obviously still perplexed.

"It can be difficult to appreciate something you've never lacked," she explained. "Time has no meaning for you because you'll always have more of it. But I died after living only sixty years—less than one century. So the idea of having lived thirty-four centuries—"

She broke off, overcome with emotion, so Mom helped her out. "It may never cease to amaze us. I hope that's the case. Remembering how things used to be helps us keep in mind how wonderfully better our lives are because of Josh's rescue."

"That's so true," Chris said. "When I think of all the things I've experienced during these years, it blows me away. I've studied sciences I never knew existed. I've walked in space and on the ocean's floor. I've met people I used to call 'aliens.' "

"And run!" Susana interjected.

He smiled. "Yes—oh, how I've run! Throughout this world and on many, many others besides. While living in a world stunted by *kanuf,* I never imagined running in so many places or with such diverse running partners. But Josh swept away all those limitations at the Cleansing."

They fell silent at the mention of that day. The memory had faded with time, just as the sense of loss had dissipated. It wasn't pain that silenced Chris now, but awe. He knew the Cleansing was the most merciful course for both the rebels and the rescued. Rosie would never have been happy in this pristine world, so untouched by fashion and fancy, so devoid of soap operas and gossip. The things she had enjoyed were incompatible with this new world; the things treasured here would have been boring to her.

Yet he also had a better understanding of how difficult it had been on the Deón's hearts of love to carry out that necessary decontamination. They had chosen the merciful course of ending the suffering of the unrighteous, even though they would never forget them. His memories of Rosie had faded, as had the pain of losing her; but the Deón would never forget her—they *could* never forget her.

And that was exactly why storytelling was so important. For those rescued from The Great Rebellion, it served the same function it had always served among Juan Misi's people: to remember the past in order to better live the future. And for those who had never experienced *kanuf,* or even pain, the stories made its horrible consequences more real. What's more, they proved that the great experiment with *kanuf* had already been run, and that Doug had been proven trustworthy.

Yes, storytelling was important. It guarded the lives, security, and happiness of every person gathered here today.

Suddenly Lusi let out a squeal of delight and raced off, the other children trailing her with whoops and cheers. Chris turned to see the hero of all his stories striding toward them.

Breaking into a great smile, Chris waved and called, *"Bachí,* welcome!"

Josh returned the wave. "Thank you, *boní!"* He bent down to greet the children as they reached him. Returning their kisses and hugs, he answered them all in turn. "Thanks, big fella. Yes, I brought the *risaju.* I missed you, too, buddy. Yes, you can have a ride in the morning ..."

After dinner, some foxes, rabbits, and a mountain lion with her playful cubs gathered to provide entertainment and cuddling. Chris had come to see these creatures as the creator intended them: special gifts of love to his children—living toys, so to speak. Under the winking stars and full moon, the group gathered around a merry campfire, and the children pressed close to Chris's knees. "Tell it now," they begged. "Tell the story."

He pulled a perfectly toasted marshmallow from the fire and, with a grin, handed it to his dad. Then, casting a glance at Josh that he hoped conveyed his undying gratitude, he sat back to begin the story he never tired of telling.

"Once, a very long time ago, I ran a long race ..."

FOREIGN WORDS AND PHRASES

P = Paradisian: Spoken in the fictional country of Paradise Island (More information on the rules and grammar of this invented language is available at DellaLoredo.com)

R = Rarámuri (Tarahumara): Native American language used by the tribe of the same name located in Mexico.

S = Spanish (as spoken in Mexico)

Áchimi tamí bichíima? (R): Will you trust me?

ada *(AH-dah)* **(P):** dad; **adu** *(AH-doo):* daddy

ama *(AH-mah)* **(P):** mom; **ami** *(AH-mee):* mommy

aparochi (R): maternal grandfather

arijíb *(ah-ree-JEEB)* **(P):** I am

ayena abi (R): yes

bachí (R): older brother

boní (R): younger brother

brujas (S): witches

curanderos (S): traditional healers; shamans

d'alasház *(dah-lah-SHAZ)* **(P):** I love you

d'amoúr *(dah-moe-OOR)* **(P):** I moan (yearn, long) for you; **Anglicized:** Damour *(duh-MORE)*

Deón *(day-OWN)* **(P):** eternal one (always capitalized; is both singular and plural)

desmón *(days-MOAN)* **(P):** one who inspires awe; **Anglicized:** Desmon *(DEHZ-men)*

Ekanu Mejad Paladisi *(eh-KAH-noo MAY-zhad pah-lah-DEE-see)* **(P):** Paradisian Royal Army

fidén *(fee-DANE)* **(P):** one of unusual cunning; **Anglicized:** Fiden *(FIE-den)*

fuj *(foozh)* **(P):** faith

hermanito (S): little brother (endearment)

kanuf *(KAH-noof)* **(P):** selfishness, evil, sin

keni raná (R): my child

lakviv *(LOCK-veev)* **(P):** degenerative condition caused by a lack of Viv fruit

lanáj *(lah-NAZH)* **(P):** to help or serve

lashani *(lah-SHAH-nee)* **(P):** selfless love

Lejani Mejad *(lay-ZHAH-nee MAY-zhad)* **(P):** Royal Guard

lok *(loke)* **(P):** to stand ready

mami (S): mommy

menod *(MAY-node)* **(P):** to complete a task to perfection; **Anglicized:** Menod *(Mee-nahd)*

meshon *(MAY-shone)* **(P):** one who shows compassion

mij dinósh *(meezh dee-NOSH)* **(P):** restoring enzyme

mikaél *(mee-kie-EL)* **(P):** commander-in-chief

misi (R): cat

mi tesoro (S): my treasure (endearment)

modén *(moe-DANE)* **(P):** exalted one; his/your highness: **Anglicized:** Moden *(MOE-den)*

Modén Eshí (M.E.) *(moe-DANE eh-SHEE)* **(P):** Moden Years (a dating system instituted by Stan and used within Moden Industries in which the year 0 is the year of Stan's birth.

muchachón (S): big boy (Chris uses as an endearment)

natérarabá (R): thank you

nulu *(NOO-loo)* **(P):** the endearment form of **nulo**, "son" or "nephew"

nushaz *(NOO -shahz)* **(P):** humility

onó (R): father

papi (S): daddy

poli *(POE-lee)* **(P):** a crown-shaped, red birthmark

polín *(poe-LEEN)* **(P):** one possessing a particular type of birthmark; also, a top-level government official; plural: **polini** *(poe-LEE-nee)*

rokab *(ROE-kahb)* **(P):** stallion; **roku:** the endearment form

sondem *(SONE-dame)* **(P):** ally; **Anglicized:** Sondem *(SAHN-dem)*

tío (S): uncle

towí ke akemi (R): lad who runs barefoot

tsuma *(TSOO-mah)* **(P):** praise

ve nela *(vay NAY-lah)* **(P):** my daughter

viv zabé *(veev zah-BAY)* **(P):** life-tree

yushún *(yoo-SHOON)* **(P):** family of siblings; **yushuni** *(yoo-SHOO-nee)*: families

zali *(ZAH-lee)*: the endearment form for **zala**, "sister"

zule *(ZOO-lay)* **(P):** brother

zuule *(zoo-OO-lay)* **(P):** elder brother; **zuulu** *(zoo-OO-loo)*: elder brother (endearment)

We invite you to view the complete
selection of titles we publish at:

www.TEACHServices.com

Scan with your mobile
device to go directly
to our website.

Please write or email us your praises, reactions, or
thoughts about this or any other book we publish at:

TEACH Services, Inc.
P U B L I S H I N G
www.TEACHServices.com ● (800) 367-1844

P.O. Box 954
Ringgold, GA 30736

info@TEACHServices.com

TEACH Services, Inc., titles may be purchased in bulk for
educational, business, fund-raising, or sales promotional use.
For information, please e-mail:

BulkSales@TEACHServices.com

Finally, if you are interested in seeing
your own book in print, please contact us at

publishing@TEACHServices.com

We would be happy to review your manuscript for free.